Urban Governance
in Canada

Urban Governance in Canada

REPRESENTATION, RESOURCES, AND RESTRUCTURING

Katherine A. Graham

Susan D. Phillips

with Allan M. Maslove

Carleton University

School of Public Administration

HARCOURT
BRACE
CANADA

Harcourt Brace & Company, Canada

Toronto Montreal Fort Worth New York Orlando
Philadelphia San Diego London Sydney Tokyo

Requests for permission to make copies of any part of the work should be mailed to: Permissions, College Division, Harcourt Brace & Company, Canada, 55 Horner Avenue, Toronto, Ontario M8Z 4X6.

Every reasonable effort has been made to acquire permission for copyright material used in this text, and to acknowledge all such indebtedness accurately. Any errors and omissions called to the publisher's attention will be corrected in future printings.

Canadian Cataloguing in Publication Data

Graham, Katherine A., 1947–

   Urban governance in Canada : representation, resources, and restructuring

Includes bibliographical references and index.
ISBN 0-7747-3392-6

1. Municipal government — Canada. I. Phillips, Susan D.
II. Maslove, Allan M., 1946– . III. Title.
JS1708.G72 1998   320.8'5'0971   C97–930725–2

Senior Acquisitions Editor: Daniel J. Brooks
Developmental Editor: Megan Mueller
Production Editor: Louisa Schulz
Production Co-ordinator: Sheila Barry

Copy Editor: Karen Kligman
Cover Design: Sonya V. Thursby/Opus House
Interior Design: Steve Eby Production and Design, revised by Opus House
Typesetting and Assembly: Carolyn Hutchings
Printing and Binding: University of Toronto Press

Cover Art: Eleanor Bond, *Departure of the Industrial Workers*, from the Work Station series, (1985). Oil on canvas, 239.5 x 237.5 cm. Image courtesy of the Winnipeg Art Gallery. Reproduced with permission of the artist.

This book was printed in Canada.

1 2 3 4 5   02 01 00 99 98

Dedicated to our parents and loved ones
who have taught and supported us in so many
different ways:

Phyllis and James Hamilton
Doris MacMillan

Mary Phillips Sweet
Ada Little

Helen and Harry Maslove

PREFACE

We started this book in 1993 as the result of a corridor conversation in the School of Public Administration at Carleton University. All three of us had long been interested in urban governance as both teachers and researchers. To us, the time seemed ripe for a book that looked specifically at Canada's big city-regions and the response of urban governments to the major challenges they face. The rapidly changing terrain of public policy and management in our city-regions also struck us as something that would benefit from an interdisciplinary approach. This was at the core of our work as a research team and we have tried to embed an interdisciplinary perspective throughout this volume.

To paraphrase Victor Hugo, nothing can stop an idea whose time has come. In fact, we met with unanimous enthusiasm and support for the project, beginning with Dan Brooks, Senior Acquisitions Editor at Harcourt Brace. He and his colleagues guided us with unfailing support. We owe special thanks to our editor, Megan Mueller. She kept us on track and provided us with timely and very sound comments and suggestions. Her voice at the other end of the telephone line was something we looked forward to, providing us with a sense of where we were in the process and guidance concerning how best to proceed. We would also like to thank Louisa Schulz for handling the production of this book.

In the course of writing, we undertook field trips to each of our selected city-regions. These trips were partly supported by a grant from the Canadian Studies Program of Heritage Canada. We gratefully acknowledge this assistance. We owe particular thanks to local and provincial government officials and academic colleagues in each place. Many people spent time talking to us and provided us with background material, often taking care to keep us up to date after we had departed. Special thanks go to Judy Barbeau, Merv Beckstead, Lynda Black, Noelle Boughton, Celia Chandler, Gerry Couture, Rick Daviss, Ken Dobell, Rob Dolan, John Dunfield, Lionel Feldman, Jeff Fielding, Richard Frost, Edd LeSage, Ken Meech, Allan O'Brien, Dale Poel, Phil Ryan, Rosanna Scotti, John Sewell, Patrick J. Smith, and Valerie Spencer.

Anyone who has written a book like this knows the amount of work behind each word. Research has to be done, facts have to be checked, elusive sources have to be pinpointed, and the final manuscript has to be clean. We were ably helped by a number of people in this regard. Thank you to Carmen Abella, Sandra Bach, Dawn Bradley, Jaqueline Carberry, Elizabeth Casuga, Martha Clark, Kathy Jerome, Hilary Little, Jane MacArthur, Erin O'Gorman, Aileen Pangilinan, and Catherine Parker.

Three reviewers, selected by Harcourt Brace, examined the penultimate draft. Caroline Andrew (University of Ottawa), David Siegel (Brock University), and Peter Woolstencroft (University of Waterloo) were extremely constructive and helpful. We have tried to incorporate as many of their comments into the final version as possible. Of course, final responsibility for this volume and for any errors of commission or omission rests with us.

Finally, we would like to thank our families. They have been unreserved in their support, even when the work impinged on what otherwise would have been family time. Given the opportunity to read the product of our labour, we hope that Andrew and Katherine L.H. Graham, Brian and Benjamin Little, and Marsha, Lisa, and David Maslove will understand our sense of urgency even more.

Katherine A. Graham
Susan D. Phillips
Allan M. Maslove

Instructional Design

Each chapter in this book contains student-friendly features such as detailed notes, annotated suggested readings, and a comprehensive bibliography. The book endmatter includes a superior glossary of terms, a name index, a subject index, and a reader reply card.

A Note from the Publisher

Thank you for selecting *Urban Governance in Canada: Representation, Resources, and Restructuring*, by Katherine A. Graham and Susan D. Phillips with Allan M. Maslove.

We want to hear what you think about *Urban Governance in Canada: Representation, Resources, and Restructuring*. Please take a few minutes to fill out the stamped reader reply card at the back of the book. Your comments and suggestions will be valuable to us as we prepare new editions and other books.

Brief Contents

CONTENTS

CHAPTER ONE

CONTEMPORARY CHALLENGES TO URBAN GOVERNANCE

INTRODUCTION

Urban governments are becoming increasingly important players both internationally and domestically. At the international level, world cities are in direct competition with one another to attract capital investment, highly skilled workers, and mega-events, such as the Olympics and world expositions. On the domestic scene, urban governments are gaining prominence in the overall operation of the federation and the exercise of citizenship as Canada redefines a new social union — a redefinition of the rights, roles, and responsibilities between citizens and governments, among governments of the federation, and between markets and society (Biggs, 1996; Bach and Phillips, 1997). Economic restructuring and **downloading** of responsibilities from federal and provincial governments have a direct impact on urban governments. It is municipal governments that eventually must fill many of these program and financial gaps or bear the social costs of poverty and related displacement in other ways, such as increased demand for police services. In a highly urbanized and culturally diverse country like Canada, urban governments are also critical in promoting social harmony and cohesiveness.

There has been a tendency in Canadian political science and policy analysis, however, to see municipal governments as bit players. They are often viewed as mere purveyors of services rather than as governing institutions to be taken seriously. As a result, Canadian scholarship on **urban governance** has been meagre and the nature of politics and policy making at the urban level poorly understood. The purpose of this book is to fill some of these gaps in scholarship. It is intended primarily as a textbook for students of local government in the broadest sense, including practitioners and citizens keen on influencing local government policies.

Our focus is on the governance of eight Canadian metropolitan areas: Halifax, Montreal, Ottawa-Hull, Toronto, Winnipeg, Calgary, Edmonton, and Vancouver. Collectively, these city-regions constitute 45 percent of the population of Canada, as of the 1991 census, yet their governance, politics, and economics have not received the attention they deserve. In many ways, major cities encounter distinct political and economic challenges. For example, more diverse populations accentuate the role of municipalities in promoting social cohesion; direct competition with international cities is felt more acutely; and larger administrative structures present more complex organizational and human resource management issues. In many other respects, however, the issues discussed in the context of these eight major cities have direct relevance to smaller municipalities.

A FRAMEWORK

This chapter introduces the major themes that are interwoven throughout this book. It begins by illuminating the central issues faced by urban governments in Canada (and elsewhere) and by showing how many of these issues are played out through the very real events of local politics and governance. These issues are:

- the importance of economic development for ensuring vital cities;
- the challenges of financing urban government;
- the goal of fostering and sustaining livable cities, where people can live and work safely and with a basic level of comfort and urban pride;
- the encouragement of democratic life in the urban milieu; and
- the need for political and administrative reform to provide institutional foundations that will enhance the capacity of cities to better address all of these issues.

The following chapters contain basic information and an explanation of various, often competing, conceptual approaches to the study of urban systems, structures, and processes. In most cases, we attempt to provide a deeper appreciation of alternative lenses through which these issues can be viewed. However, on many topics we take a stand, arguing in favour of our own position. In particular, we express our distinctive views on several foundational issues:

- Municipal governments are integrally entangled in a variety of **co-production** and partnership arrangements with a wide range of voluntary and business organizations. This perspective is incorporated as part of our basic conception of the local state.
- The push toward more citizen-centred government, particularly responsiveness to the multicultural diversity of cities, is (and should be) at the heart of revamping policy processes and service delivery.
- The resources and policy levers available to urban governments in Canada are often inadequate for grappling with the issues that they face.
- The need for restructuring is critical to **metropolitan governments** in the late 1990s. There is, however, no single reform solution that will ensure cost savings, economic development, or better governance in every case. Rather, reform must be pursued with careful reference to local conditions.
- Finally, urban governments need to be studied and analyzed as governments — not simply as service providers — that have a central role in the social and cultural fabric and in the democratic life of the nation.

This chapter proceeds to put these issues in the context of some of the fundamental debates about local government's place in **civil society**, in the overall framework for governance of the federation, and in the global economy.

Before proceeding to an in-depth examination of urban government in Canada, a sense of what urban Canada is and how it has developed is essential. This will help you to understand the importance of these debates and challenges. This chapter starts to build this awareness by introducing some basic information about the development of urban Canada and the Canadian cities that will be our particular focus. The rest of this book builds on this introduction.

THE MAJOR CONTEMPORARY ISSUES

Why should the firing of two officials from a local economic development corporation interest us (see Box 1.1)? Learning a little more about the nature of OCEDCO and its relationship to the metropolitan government serving Ottawa-Carleton can help you to see this event as illustrating many of the challenges facing urban governments and the evolution of Canadian cities more generally.

The Importance of Economic Development

Most obviously, this vignette illustrates the priority accorded to urban economic development. More particularly, it shows the anxiety that civic leaders now experience about how to generate development at a time when the economy is increasingly global and knowledge based and when economic uncertainty and the mobility of capital have made the existing economic base of many of our cities more precarious. We will be dealing with these challenges throughout this book as we examine how specific Canadian cities deal with economic development in this era of global competition. Are all of our metropolitan areas global cities or do some occupy primarily a regional niche? How do politicians and civic staff view their city's economic base and prospects? What types of policies do they control that really influence the course of local economic development?

Beyond the desire to be a winner in an increasingly competitive economy, we have to ask why economic development is so important an issue for city governments. Chapter Three, Legacies of Historical Development, shows that concern about local government's role in attracting and supporting commerce has been long standing, as have been some of the fundamental debates about what constitutes the best approach to doing so. But why the urgency for metropolitan governments to put in place an economic development strategy for the late 1990s? Why not let natural competitive advantage and the apparent tendency for firms to locate in compatible clusters (e.g., "Silicon Valley North" in the Ottawa region) be the stimulants of economic growth? Underlying our vignette are two reasons for anxiety-driven action. One is the increasing financial squeeze faced by urban governments. The second reason stems from the perception that the right kind of economic development will foster the livability of metropolitan areas at a time when demographics and other factors, such as increased environmental awareness, are changing the use of time and space in the city.

The Fiscal Squeeze

As you will see, the fiscal squeeze is an integral part of the policy and management environment of major Canadian cities. Both our treatment of the historical context, in Chapter Three, and our detailed examination of the financial

---

BOX 1.1 ECONOMIC DEVELOPMENT FOR THE 90S

In mid-1995, the Board of Directors of the Ottawa-Carleton Economic Development Corporation (OCEDCO), the agency responsible for undertaking economic development initiatives on behalf of the Regional Municipality of Ottawa-Carleton, abruptly fired its two senior executive officers. In the words of the OCEDCO board's chair, a local business leader, "the firings are an acknowledgement that the region's steady-as-she-goes approach to economic development isn't working."

Source: Paraphrased from Patrick Dore, "Business Group Fires Top Official," *Ottawa Citizen*, August 12, 1995, p. A2.

---

resources and fiscal capacity of urban governments, in Chapter Nine, examine long-standing assertions by urban governments in Canada that there is a fiscal gap between their ability to raise revenues and required expenditures. Frequently, these assertions have been coupled with attacks on the property tax as the main independent base of revenue for urban governments in Canada. The contemporary period has been characterized by heightened concerns about the financial situation of urban governments, causing them to renew pleas for fiscal reform and revisit the priority of municipal economic development initiatives. This angst has stemmed from two developments.

First, the traditional property tax base of municipal governments has become much more fragile. Changing economic circumstances have resulted in the decline or closure of established businesses, leading to a loss of industrial and commercial property tax revenues which were once thought to be assured. Commerce has generally become more mobile, leaving municipal governments to contend with firms relocating to other cities, sometimes in other countries, or being much more footloose when deciding where to locate new growth.

The second factor has been the impact on urban governments of the federal and provincial governments' efforts to deal with their debts and deficits. Cutbacks and changes to transfers from the federal to provincial governments, especially in areas related to social spending, have contributed to decreasing provincial–municipal grants. In addition, provincial governments have sometimes used the approach of downloading costs and responsibilities for particular services to the local level. In some cases, urban governments find themselves having to fill the gap left when a provincial government simply ceases to be involved in a particular activity. Increased pressure on municipal governments to support shelters for the homeless and the victims of domestic violence are a case in point. In other cases, provincial governments have directed new municipal undertakings more openly. In Ontario, for example, municipal governments howled loudly about the impact on their policing budgets as a result of having to assume responsibility for security in provincial courthouses around the province in the mid-1980s.

As illustrated in Chapter Five, Politics, Elections, and Representation, and in the discussion of the budget process in Chapter Nine, the increasingly strained financial circumstances of urban governments have not been accompanied by a decrease in the demand for urban services. The impact of cutbacks in programs and services by other levels of government, the efforts of diverse elements of the urban population to have their voices heard and their needs in the urban environment met, and the reluctance of some segments of the population who have traditionally benefited from the services provided by city governments to accept less make for hard financial choices. The situation is made even more complex as urban politicians and administrators contemplate the spectre of taxpayer revolt. No wonder, then, that economic development strategies for the 1990s assume great importance.

Fostering and Sustaining Livable Cities

City governments have traditionally devoted a significant share of their financial resources to the construction of new **urban infrastructure**, in the form of roads, water and sewer lines, and facilities to house fire and police services. Before World War II, urban services were often extended to respond to the physical growth of the city. Important motivators for city officials were the prevention of public health problems and the facilitation of the local economy's functioning (Weaver, 1977). The postwar period saw the doctrine of planned urban development come to the forefront. Land-use regulation, one of the established areas of municipal government activity, became subsumed under proactive efforts to guide the nature and geographic direction of urban growth by city governments' development of long-term official plans.

The history and more contemporary issues of land-use planning in Canadian urban centres are dealt with at various points in this book. The history of planning debates is covered in Chapters Three and Eleven, the latter focussing on the creation of sustainable and livable communities. The links between land-use planning and the entire enterprise of urban government are dealt with in Chapters Four and Seven, which discuss the structures and systems and the policy and administrative processes of urban governments respectively.

What you need to know, by way of introduction, is that some of the dominant assumptions about the desirable characteristics of urban development are increasingly being called into question. Intensifying public debates about consumer preferences for certain types of housing, the relationship between workplace and living place, urban transportation priorities, and desirable urban amenities mirror debates within the planning profession, often between professional planners representing the land development industry and those working for urban governments. We are now seeing more widespread awareness that the commuter city, ringed by tracts of predominantly single-family houses, may not be the best way ahead. In addition, new needs are being voiced by aging baby boomers, women who seek a more hospitable urban environment, Aboriginal people in cities, and others. New visions of urban livability are central to local political discourse. These visions are also increasingly important to the attraction of new capital, since firms rank livability criteria high in location decisions. Modifying existing patterns can, however, be a somewhat scary prospect. This is particularly the case over the short term as those in urban government contemplate the immediate political and economic costs and uncertainties associated with making these changes. The capacity of metropolitan regions to pursue policies of sustainable development over the long run has sparked intense debates about the restructuring of political boundaries and institutions.

The Encouragement of Civic Democracy

In revisiting our vignette from Box 1.1 one more time, the central question we now consider is, Who made the decision to fire the two OCEDCO executives? Look again at the nature of OCEDCO's mandate (the agency responsible for economic development for the region) and at who chaired its board (a local business leader). To give a little more detail, the agency was established by the Regional Municipality of Ottawa-Carleton as a **quasi-autonomous municipal government organization** for economic development. Approximately 95 percent of its annual budget comes from the regional municipality, with the remainder coming from membership fees paid by local firms, revenues from OCEDCO events, and other sources. As our vignette suggests, the agency is overseen by a board, appointed by regional council. The board consists of a majority of people from the business community, plus six members of regional council. The head of the board traditionally has been selected from the business members, as was the case at the time of the firings.

This arrangement points to some of the fundamental issues of political representation and accountability that will be part of our examination of city governance. At this stage, we can foreshadow our exploration of these issues by asking, Why did the elected council of the Regional Municipality of Ottawa-Carleton not exert more influence over the operation of OCEDCO when it provided the lion's share of its budget? Why was not a broader cross-section of the community represented on the board of OCEDCO?

Together, these questions lead us to one of the classic debates about local government: Who does local government serve? Is local government more, or less, democratic than other levels of government? Some of the theoretical lenses through which these questions may be viewed are discussed in Chapter Two. Some of the dimensions of historical debates about local political representation and accountability in Canada will be discussed in Chapter Three. It is important to consider the contemporary political and management practices of Canadian urban governments in the context of these historical debates because they have created a powerful conventional wisdom about why things are as they are.

There are also new issues of representation and accountability which we will explore. These include different perspectives concerning what is really the source of vitality for local political life and governance. Is the action at the street or neighbourhood level rather than in the corridors of city hall? In the diverse, multicultural city, what is the role of different interest groups in local politics and governance? Can we make urban government more effective by reforming municipal boundaries, amalgamating local governments, creating **two-tier governments** for metropolitan areas, developing new ways of electing councils, or having fewer (or more) councillors? Throughout the textbook, we will be exploring what the recent experience of inquiries into urban government reform and the reform initiatives themselves suggest about these questions.

THE CONTEXT OF CANADIAN CITY GOVERNANCE: CENTRAL DEBATES

If the issues of encouraging local democracy, fostering economic development and the creation of livable cities, and providing a sound fiscal base for city governance are now at the forefront, what is the context in which they are confronted? We suggest that there are three levels at which this question should be addressed:

- historical and continuing debates about the place of local government in Canadian confederation;
- changing perspectives concerning the role of cities in the international context; and
- debates about the structure and internal operations of city governments, including the question, Who does/should city hall serve?

As the rest of this text illustrates, the position you take at each level of debate shapes your image of city government. This, in turn, will guide your views about whether or not urban governments have the ability to deal with the central issues facing cities and your thinking about what public policies and management practices urban governments should embrace. The sketch of each of these debates given in this chapter is embellished as we proceed through the book.

Local Government and the Canadian Confederation

Section 92(8) of Canada's Constitution Act assigns responsibility for municipal institutions to provincial governments. Section 92 provides provincial governments further power to determine the sources of municipal revenue. These arrangements mirror the provisions of the 1867 British North America Act, which the Constitution Act superseded.

The fact that there was no change in the constitutional treatment of local government from 1867 to 1982 may seem surprising given the very high concentration of Canada's population in large cities, the wealth accumulated in them, and the importance of city governments as sites of public policy and administration. For example, the metropolitan areas of Toronto, Montreal, and Vancouver each had 1991 populations larger than six Canadian provinces. The annual budget of Metropolitan Toronto is larger than that of the smaller provinces as well.

The unchanged constitutional context of Canadian city governments requires us to repeat the old chestnut that urban governments are still considered creatures of the province. This view of urban governments raises the prospect that provincial governments will continue their practice of treating even the largest of our cities as if "father knows best" (O'Brien, 1975). As we discuss in greater detail in Chapter Eight, Intergovernmental Relations, this vision of local government has prompted scholars to assess possible implications of the formally subservient role accorded city governments in the Canadian intergovernmental arena (Dupré, 1968; Feldman and Graham, 1979; Boswell, 1996). It has also prompted efforts by scholars of local government and local governments themselves to develop counter-arguments, asserting that the municipal level should have a more equal footing with the federal and provincial governments.

In shaping our own perspective about the place of urban governments in the Canadian constitutional context, we can see that this situation results in tension concerning how urban governments are seen. Are they to be thought of primarily as agents of provincial government, carrying out provincial directives and dealing with the consequences of provincial government actions (or inaction)? Alternatively, do they have a more independent base of action stemming from their independent democratic base as elected governments? As you will see, this tension pervades the course that Canadian urban governments pursue, individually and as they attempt collective action. As voters and those with vested interests watch urban governments, public understanding of urban governments' capabilities is sometimes subliminally, sometimes openly, shaped by this same tension.

Cities in the International Context

Our earlier discussion of the multi-faceted challenges of contemporary economic development drew our attention to some of the impacts of **globalization** on Canadian cities. Looking beyond economic development, we have to consider two basic questions when thinking about each of our chosen cities in the international context:

• What are the dimensions of international influence on their development and governance?
• What initiatives do we see city governments taking to deal with the challenges of globalization and internationalization?

DIMENSIONS OF INTERNATIONAL INFLUENCE

In her assessment of the challenges facing cities today, Margit Mayer argues, "There are larger social and cultural differences between midtown Manhattan and the South Bronx than between Manhattan and Frankfurt" (Mayer, 1991, p. 110). Broadly speaking, we can think about these international commonalities in terms of the physical form of modern urban development (e.g., the internationalization of architecture), the growth and increasing speed of international travel and communication, and the globalization of markets and increasing mobility of capital among the cities of the world, which we discussed earlier. Looking within the modern city, Mayer also argues that we can find new distinctions among the population. Supplementing and perhaps supplanting traditional differences we attribute to socio-economic class, ethnic origin, or length of residence, Mayer suggests that we now have cities divided between those participating in the new global order and those who are not. This second group, she argues, are nonetheless buffeted by the impacts of this new metropolitan, international world (Mayer, 1991, p. 109).

Certainly, the idea that large cities exist within an international trading order and are subject to cultural and other influences that cross borders is not new. Our more extended discussion of Approaches to the Study of Urban Governance, in Chapter Two, deals with this question more extensively. Also, as you will see in Chapter Three, there have been powerful international influences on the shape of Canadian city government.

In both the broader sense of urban development and in the more focussed context of urban governance, we need, however, to be precise in thinking about the international influences on contemporary Canadian cities. Our chosen cities are by no means identical in the international context.

Among them is our national capital and four provincial capitals. From the standpoint of governance, they bring different attributes into the international arena than those that are not capitals. The complexity of governing a Canadian capital city, as evidenced by federal–local relations in the Ottawa-Hull area and by provincial–city relations in the case of provincial capitals, sometimes puts capital cities at a comparative disadvantage, domestically and internationally (Graham, 1992, p. 143). By the mid-1990s, Canada's capitals had perceived enough common interest, related to their unique role, to form a Capital Cities Network complete with its own constitution.

Our chosen cities are also distinguishable in terms of their airports and other transportation links. These make Vancouver, Toronto, Montreal, and perhaps Halifax more at the centre of international networks of physical interaction between people and among goods and services than the others, although Winnipeg is intent on becoming an international hub for air freight. Thus the pervasiveness of international influences may be greater in these cities, especially if they are also centres for media and communication.

Finally, we must be sensitive to the different roles each of our cities plays as the centre of its own region. Each city government will be preoccupied by particular issues, depending on the nature of the forces that pull people from its hinterland. Is there a surplus or shortage of people coming to the city in search of employment? What are the impacts on city social services of new arrivals from the hinterland, let alone from overseas? Is there a significant demand on the city to provide regional leadership in the provision of particular goods and services — regionally focussed media, tourism, professional sports, and recreational outlets, for example? In considering these and other aspects of our cities' regional roles, it is important to think about how these pressures complement, contradict, or merely co-exist with the international dynamic. Specifically, one should be sensitive to the interplay of international, regional, and local influences on urban government.

CITY GOVERNMENT INITIATIVES IN THE INTERNATIONAL ARENA

By way of introduction, let's assume that the changing global environment and the opportunities and threats it holds have broadened the focus of contemporary Canadian city governments to "think globally, act locally." For any Canadian urban government coming to consensus that this is the way forward, the debate has really just begun. The hard question is, What can urban governments do to steer their cities to prosperity and civility in the new environment while avoiding urban decline? Our review of the constitutional position of urban governments suggests that their scope for policy and other actions is severely limited by provincial governments' control over local government powers and operations. Also many key policy levers, vis-à-vis the international order, reside with the federal government, with its responsibility for international trade, monetary policy, and the conduct of foreign affairs. If physical location is less important for firms in the new economy, how do local governments compete in the traditional activity of offering serviced lands for industrial or business purposes? When the existing tax base of many cities is more fragile than in the past and financial pressures are mounting on all levels of government, how can tax competitiveness be offered up as a location incentive?

As you will see in Chapters Ten and Eleven, which deal with economic development and creating sustainable and livable communities, urban governments in Canada have adopted a variety of approaches to dealing with these challenges. These include the establishment of focussed international relationships with twin cities (Smith and Cohn, 1990, p. 7), the selection of particular sectors as targets for international marketing and exposure (as exemplified by Toronto and Vancouver's pursuit of the film industry), and the development of locally-based consortia of public and private organizations to take up the international challenge (e.g., Ottawa-Carleton Research Institute, Ottawa Tourism and Convention Authority). Part of our analysis will focus on the effectiveness of these and other approaches.

RETHINKING CITY GOVERNMENT
Canadian Cities and Metropolitan Reform

Urban planning has become inextricably linked with urban politics and reform. The rapid urbanization that followed the end of World War II greatly outpaced the capacity of local government systems to service and manage this growth. The pressures created by rapid population growth and the need to provide modern urban services led to both the rise of urban planning and significant changes to the political boundaries and structure of urban governments in Canada. Added to this mix were the challenges facing provincial and local governments to find an appropriate way to finance urban growth and development and, beginning in the 1960s, to meet increasing public expectations about access to the institutions of city government.

Beginning with the creation of Metropolitan Toronto in 1953, Canada has been an acknowledged leader among western democracies in urban government reform (Smallwood, 1971; Sharpe, 1995, pp. 11–31). More recently, Canada has become a great battleground over metropolitan reform. The nature of these reform efforts across the country has varied, as you will see from its more extended treatment in Chapters Three and Four. Basically, however, urban government reform efforts have attempted to align the functions of urban governance with some notion of a metropolitan model in which the unity of the agglomeration is recognized and reflected in area-wide arrangements (Sharpe, 1995, p. 13).

Within this broad definition, the metropolitan reform of Canadian urban governments has had many different dimensions:

- from voluntary co-operation to provincially imposed structural reform;
- from the establishment of two-tier metropolitan or regional governments, with local municipalities and an over-arching government responsible for specific area-wide functions, to the creation of large unitary cities; and
- from approaches that have been selective in the functions receiving metropolitan focus to those that have involved comprehensive reform (Sancton, 1994).

No single approach has predominated, however, as a course of reform.

It has been suggested that the golden age of metropolitan reform in Canada ended in the early 1980s, as doctrines of comprehensive planning for local government began to fall into disrepute and as various provincial governments began to experience or anticipate voter reaction against reforms or reform proposals (Feldman and Graham, 1979; Plan Canada, 1984).

The 1900s, however, have witnessed considerable rethinking of past reforms and intense pressures for further reform in many city-regions. The results of this rethinking range from slow, methodical tinkering to sweeping, dramatic changes. For example, a variety of amendments to the City of Winnipeg Act, since the establishment of a "**unicity**" in 1970, have altered what some saw as the innovative aspects of the original reform related to public participation and political accountability. Further, one Winnipeg community, Headingly, asked the Manitoba government to give it independence from the unicity arrangement in 1994, claiming that it resulted in excessive service costs to its residents. The province complied with this request. In 1995, anxiety over the role of Metropolitan Toronto and the governance of the Greater Toronto Area prompted the Ontario provincial government to establish the Greater Toronto Area Task Force (the Golden Task Force). In a dramatic move just over a year later, the Ontario government ignored the recommendations of the Golden Report and announced unilaterally that the six lower-tier municipalities would be merged into one "supercity" of Toronto. The province attempted to execute the forced amalgamation in a swift manner, over loud protests from area politicians and the public.

Beyond raw parochial politics, these developments may reflect growing interest in an alternative perspective on reform. This is known as **public choice theory**, namely that different co-existing local governments can provide a market of tailored services, catering to different needs, tastes, and consumer price preferences. By doing so, a range of independent local governments can exist across an urban agglomeration, which are more reflective of the needs of different segments of the population and thereby satisfy goals of efficient democracy.

As will be seen, public choice theory has been the subject of considerable academic interest and criticism, particularly in the United States but also in Canada. At least one Canadian commentator has argued, however, that this approach has so far received inadequate attention from those actually undertaking reforms (Sancton, 1994, p. 42).

It will be evident in the following chapters that the story of urban government reform in Canada is a rich one. This introduction to the subject and our further treatment is intended to help you focus on one central question: Does the political and territorial structure of urban governments affect their ability to deal with the major challenges they now face and the specific nature of the policy and management responses they use to do so?

Canadian Cities and Management Reform

In the 1990s, considerable attention has been paid to the need to re-invent the management of Canadian urban government. This has stemmed, in part, from the broader preoccupation with re-inventing government, which has been the subject of a host of recent books and inquiries, such as the federal government's Public Service 2000 exercise in the early 1990s (Seidle, 1993; Swimmer, Hicks, and Milne, 1994). The re-inventing government approach has focussed on making the internal operations of government more responsive and cost-effective. Debates have also continued to rage about the role of private sector management practices in public sector management (see, for example, Savoie, 1995; Borins, 1995). Rather than being mere followers of the experience of senior governments in management reform, however, Canadian cities have in many respects been the real leaders and innovators.

As you will see in Chapters Three, Four, and Seven, there are many important differences in the history and contemporary development of management structures and practices in Canadian urban governments. There are also major differences between city governments and their federal and provincial counterparts. Chapter Three, for example, explores the legacy of the turn-of-the-century municipal reform era. Its emphasis on taking the politics out of local government and introducing a professional management ethos into city hall had significant impact on local government structures, some of which remains today. In short, notions of managerialism are not new to Canadian urban governments, but the meaning of the term has changed as new ideas and prescriptions for better urban government have emerged.

The apolitical ideal of the turn of the century has, to some degree, been replaced with an understanding that urban governments are inherently political and that this must be factored into structures and processes of urban government management. Perhaps ironically, emphasis of some of the modern prescriptions has been to urge urban politicians to be more rational in their approach to policy and management issues while simultaneously acknowledging their legitimate political role.

The contemporary period of reflection regarding the management of urban government began in the 1970s with the publication of Plunkett and Betts' book *The Management of Canadian Urban Government* and various other research initiatives, some of which were funded by provincial governments and the short-lived federal Ministry of State for Urban Affairs as they sought the holy grail of modern urban government management (Hickey, 1973; McAllister, 1979).

The Plunkett and Betts text serves as an excellent example of the new effort to merge the rationality of modern management, especially systems management, with the essentially political environment of city hall. Supporting Banfield and Wilson's assertion that "Whether one likes it or not, politics, like sex, cannot be abolished" (Banfield and Wilson, 1963, pp. 20–21, quoted in Plunkett and Betts, 1978, p. 18), the authors build their extended prescriptions for urban government management on the following perspective:

> By looking at local government organization in terms of a system, it is possible to identify the specific elements involved and their inter-relationships in the total process of management.... The importance of a model of this kind lies not so much in the fact that it conforms to all of the realities of the practical world but that it focuses attention on the processes that need to be developed. It emphasizes a planned process of management and it helps to clarify the needs of an organization that must respond to a changing environment. (Plunkett and Betts, 1978, p. 202)

In Chapter Seven, we will be paying particular attention to the extent to which this paradigm of general management has taken hold. What are the approaches Canadian city governments use to ensure that policy issues are not viewed in isolation from one another? How are policy decisions related to the management of the budgetary process? These are some of the central questions raised by modern discussions of municipal management.

There are other elements of the contemporary urban management agenda which we will also be exploring. These include the notion that citizens are also customers of the design and delivery of various urban services, and concern that urban services be provided in the most cost-efficient or cost-effective manner. Both of these tie into the deployment and management of human resources by urban governments. The fact that the largest share of urban operating budgets is dedicated to salaries of municipal employees also means that the human side of city hall is increasingly regarded through a financial lens. Chapter Seven deals with human resource management in this context. In Chapter Four, we also deal with the influence of some of the contemporary debates about urban management practices on the structures and systems of urban government.

As in our thinking about Canadian cities and metropolitan reform, our consideration of the issues and debates concerning the internal management of city governments leads us to one central question: How can we evaluate urban management practices? This encapsulates the question of what evaluation criteria we might use, as well as the obvious issue of how urban government management actually performs. We will offer more thoughts concerning this question as we proceed.

Rethinking City Government: Does It Matter?

Our description and assessment of the range of ideas and debates about rethinking urban government would be relatively dry and perhaps arcane if we did not infuse it with the *realpolitik* of city hall and the fundamental questions underlying everything that follows in this text. In a very real sense, two fundamental questions underlie the realpolitik and the specific cases that we will offer as vignettes:

- What is the role of urban government?
- Whose interests should local government serve?

These questions are not conclusively resolved. Indeed, they may never be. What we attempt to do, however, is to understand the differing perspectives concerning city government and its management.

THE FOCUS

As already indicated, we have deliberately focussed on eight Canadian **census metropolitan areas**. The term "census metropolitan area" (CMA) is used by Statistics Canada to denote urban regions with a minimum population in their urbanized core of 100 000 and which may have areas on their periphery whose population is heavily dependent on the urban labour market. As of the 1991 census, there were a total of 25 CMAs in Canada. We will be referring to some of these other CMAs as we proceed. As we will discuss in more detail in Chapter Four, the boundaries of a CMA do not define the boundaries of local government units. The concept does, however, provide a good sense of Canada's city-regions, in demographic terms.

Each of our selected sites, as shown in Table 1.1, is very important as a population centre in the province in which it is located. All have grown in population since the 1986 census, although at different rates. Population growth exceeded 10 percent in Calgary, Ottawa-Hull, Toronto, and Vancouver. Table 1.2 starts to hint at the complexities of governing our major metropolitan areas. In only three instances, Calgary, Edmonton, and Winnipeg, does the central city have over 50 percent of the total CMA population. This is very significant in both Calgary and Winnipeg, as a result of their strong unicity political arrangements. All of our selected areas have a bigger land area than Prince Edward Island. These variations in land area and population density set the stage for our later discussion of urban government reform and the challenge of making our cities livable in the context of their natural, as well as their built, environments.

As the rest of this text shows, these urban centres have different histories which have contributed to their particular political and administrative structures. They also exhibit similarities and differences in the ways they have grappled with the central challenges facing Canadian urban governments. In the context of the challenges and debates just outlined, we can now begin our more detailed examination of contemporary city governance in Canada.

TABLE 1.1 SELECTED METROPOLITAN AREAS: BASIC POPULATION FACTS

Census Metropolitan Area (CMA)	Population 1991	Percentage Population Change 1988–91	National Population Rank 1991	1991 POP as % of Prov. POP	Can. POP
Calgary	754 033	12.3	6	29.7	2.8
Edmonton	839 924	8.5	5	33.0	3.1
Halifax	320 501	8.3	13	35.6	1.2
Montreal	3 127 242	7.0	2	45.3	11.5
Ottawa-Hull	920 857	12.4	4	9.1	3.4
Toronto	3 893 046	13.4	1	38.6	14.3
Vancouver	1 602 502	16.1	3	48.8	5.9
Winnipeg	652 354	4.3	7	59.7	2.4

Source: Statistics Canada, "Population and Dwelling Counts: Census Metropolitan Areas and Census Agglomerations," Catalogue 93–303, p. 5. Reproduced with permission.

TABLE 1.2 SELECTED METROPOLITAN AREAS: SETTLEMENT PATTERNS 1991

CMA	Central City POP as % of CMA POP	Number of Dwellings	Land Area km²	Population Density per km²
Calgary	94.3	276 973	5 085.84	148.3
Edmonton	73.4	307 345	9 532.48	8.1
Halifax	35.7	119 450	2 503.10	128.0
Montreal	32.5	1 242 469	3 508.89	891.2
Ottawa-Hull	34.1	352 411	5 138.34	179.2
Toronto	16.3	1 373 056	5 583.51	697.2
Vancouver	29.4	612 962	2 786.26	575.1
Winnipeg	94.6	252 934	3 294.82	198.0

Source: Statistics Canada, "Population and Dwelling Counts: Census Metropolitan Areas and Census Agglomerations," Catalogue 93–303, pp. 32, 34, 35, 38, 39, 43, 44, and 45. Reproduced with permission.

CONCLUSION

You should now have an understanding of the basic issues and themes to be explored in greater detail as we proceed. The five challenges for urban governments discussed at the beginning of this chapter — economic development, urban public finance, encouragement of democratic life, sustaining livable cities, and political restructuring — come to life through our exploration of the historical context and the contemporary world of urban politics and government. We have also reviewed some of the fundamental debates about local government's place in our lives. We move immediately to a fuller consideration of these debates as we delve into theoretical approaches to the study of local government.

BIBLIOGRAPHY

Bach, Sandra and Susan D. Phillips. (1997). "Constructing a New Social Union: Child Care Beyond Infancy?" In *How Ottawa Spends 1997–98: Seeing Red*, edited by Gene Swimmer. Ottawa: Carleton University Press.

Biggs, Margaret. (1996). *Building Blocks for Canada's New Social Union*. Ottawa: Canadian Policy Research Networks.

Borins, Sandford. (1995). "The New Public Management Is Here to Stay." *Canadian Public Administration*. 38(1): 122–32.

Boswell, Peter G. (1996). "Provincial–Municipal Relations." In *Provinces: Canadian Provincial Politics*, edited by Christopher Dunn. Peterborough, ON: Broadview, pp. 253–74.

Dupré, J. Stephan. (1968). *Intergovernmental Finance in Ontario: A Provincial–Local Perspective*. A study for the Ontario Committee on Taxation (Smith Committee). Toronto: Queen's Printer for Ontario.

Feldman, Lionel and Katherine Graham. (1979). *Bargaining for Cities: Municipalities and Intergovernmental Relations — An Assessment*. Montreal: Institute for Research on Public Policy.

Graham, Katherine. (1992). "Capital Planning/Capital Budgeting: The Future of Canada's Capital." In *How Ottawa Spends: The Politics of Competitiveness*, edited by Frances Abele. Ottawa: Carleton University Press, pp.125–50.

Hickey, Paul. (1973). *Decision Making Processes in Ontario Local Government*. Toronto: Ministry of Treasury, Economics, and Intergovernmental Affairs.

McAllister, Anne B. (1979). *An Approach to Manpower Planning and Management Development in Canadian Municipal Government*. Toronto: Institute for Public Administration of Canada.

Mayer, Margit. (1991). "Politics in the Post-Fordist City." *Socialist Review* 21(1): 105–24.

O'Brien, Allan. (1975). "Father Knows Best: A Look at the Provincial–Municipal Relationship in Ontario." In *Government and Politics of Ontario*, edited by Donald MacDonald. Toronto: MacMillan of Canada, pp. 154–71.

Plan Canada (1984). Special Issue on the Golden Age of Planning. In *Ontario 1966–1975: Ontario Planned?* 34: 3–4.

Plunkett, T.J and George M. Betts. (1978). *The Management of Canadian Urban Government*. Kingston, ON: Queen's University Press.

Sancton, Andrew. (1994). *Governing Canada's City-Regions: Adapting Form to Function*. Montreal: Institute for Research on Public Policy.

Savoie, Donald J. (1995). "What Is Wrong With The New Public Management?" *Canadian Public Administration*, 38(1): 112–21.

Seidle, Leslie F. (1993). *Rethinking Government: Reform or Reinvention?* Montreal: Institute for Research on Public Policy.

Sharpe, L.J., ed. (1995). *The Government of World Cities: The Future of the Metro Model*. Chichester, UK: John Wiley.

Smallwood, Frank. (1971). "Reshaping Local Government Abroad: Anglo-Canadian Experiences." *Public Administration Review* 30: 521–30.

Smith, Patrick J. and Theodore H. Cohn. (1990). "Municipal and Provincial Paradiplomacy and Intermestic Relations: British Columbia Cases." A paper presented to the Canadian Political Science Association. Victoria, BC.

Swimmer, Gene, Michael Hicks, and Terry Milne. (1994). "Public Service 2000: Dead or Alive?" In *How Ottawa Spends 1994–95: Making Change*, edited by Susan D. Phillips. Ottawa: Carleton University Press, pp. 165–204.

Weaver, John C. (1977). *Shaping the Canadian City: Essays on Urban Politics and Policy, 1890–1920*. Toronto: Institute of Public Administration of Canada.

CHAPTER TWO

◆

APPROACHES TO THE STUDY OF URBAN GOVERNANCE

INTRODUCTION

Theories of urban governance cannot be deduced simply by taking theories of the nation-state and sizing them to fit. As Warren Magnusson (1985a, p. 51) notes, "local governments are not just national governments writ small." His observation is apt in both the Canadian and international contexts. In reality, local governments are distinct political entities whose character, management, and politics are shaped by the constitutional limits on their powers, by the configuration of local political economies, and by the interests and identities active on the local stage. The lenses that we use to focus upon urban phenomena determine to a large degree what we see and how we explain and evaluate what we see. Indeed, the particular lens we are predisposed to use may influence the kinds of questions that we ask in the first place. In this chapter, we outline the four main theoretical approaches to urban governance that have dominated or are rising in the field. These are public choice theory, **community power studies, political economy perspectives**, and **feminist approaches**.

This chapter is somewhat different from the others because it is based on a review of the theoretical literature, enriched by observation, rather than on a combination of primary and secondary sources. It is also more international in its reach. We do not have home-grown theories of local government in Canada, although Canadian urban scholars are fully engaged in theoretical debates (see, for example, Andrew, 1992; Filion, 1995; Frisken, 1991; and Magnusson, 1985b).

Our intent is not to advocate a particular theoretical perspective but to better understand the view that each affords us. After reviewing the theories, we will compare how each would respond to the basic debates laid out in Chapter One:

- What is the appropriate role of urban government in relation to the other spheres of government in Canada?
- What is the relationship of urban governance to international developments?
- Whom does local government really serve?
- What is the most efficient and effective structure for urban governance?

In the concluding section, we outline the basic parameters of our conception of urban governance. This provides a bridge from the theory to the practices of urban governance examined in later chapters.

PUBLIC CHOICE
The Theory

Public choice theory, which developed in the United States beginning in the late 1950s, uses an economist's tools to understand urban government. It takes the essence of local government to be the delivery of packages of goods and services and assumes that efficient service delivery results from competitive markets. A highly deductive and normative approach, public choice is built upon three elements: individuals, public goods, and organizations.

According to public choice theory, decision making has to be examined at the level of the individual. As decision makers, individuals are assumed to be rational and self-interested utility maximizers; they strive to attain their preferred mix of urban goods and services at a price they are willing to pay in taxes or user fees. Individuals dissatisfied with the services they receive may voice their concerns to the city council and administration. However, a critical assumption — developed by Charles Tiebout (1956) and often called the "Tiebout hypothesis" — is that individuals may also vote with their feet by moving to another municipality which better provides their preferred service and tax package.

In understanding how local governments respond to individuals' preferences, we must also consider the nature of the goods being provided (Bish, 1971). Goods have different characteristics: some are private goods that can be packaged for individual use via a price mechanism, while others are public goods (e.g., clean air) that are not divisible and cannot exclude use by specific individuals, even if those individuals do not pay for the goods. Therefore, goods have different boundaries or scales at which they are best produced. For example, the production of clean drinking water is best matched to the natural boundary of the watershed from which water is collected. Major parks that draw from a large region would be governed best by a jurisdiction that includes most of the users; otherwise, people outside the governing area could use the park without contributing taxes to it, creating a negative spillover or externality. A neighbourhood park with very localized use, in contrast, can be effectively governed at a very local level.

Public choice advocates also argue that we must analyze the delivery of a good according to its two basic components of production and provision. Production is the technical process of making or rendering goods or services, while provision is the collective process that determines how and how much of a service will be provided to residents (see Parks and Oakerson, 1989). For example, a municipality may provide, but not directly produce, garbage collection through contracts with a private company or with a neighbouring municipality. Alternatively, it may both provide and produce the service directly by operating its own fleet of garbage trucks.

The third element in public choice theory is the organization. Local governments, as organizations, provide the means for citizens to communicate their preferences for goods and services to politicians and administrators. The criteria for evaluating the effectiveness of organizations are how efficiently they provide the desired services and how responsive they are to the preferences indicated by citizens. Preferences are signalled through a variety of means including lobbying, informal contact with public officials, and, of course, voting in elections. Because politicians are also self-interested utility maximizers whose main preference is to gain and keep elected office, they will respond to the majoritarian preferences. The signalling of citizen preferences is naturally most efficient in units of homogeneous population, usually physically smaller jurisdictions.

The greatest criticism of local government levied by public choice theorists is that municipalities are inefficient because they usually act as monopoly providers. As monopolists, governments have little incentive to innovate or lower their costs (Bish and Warren, 1972). Bureaucrats, too, are self-interested individuals who, by maximizing the discretionary budget of their departments, substitute administrative values for citizen preferences (Niskanen, 1991). This leads to an oversupply of goods and services (Niskanen, 1991). More efficient government can be achieved by separating the provider (demand articulation) role of a municipality from its producer (supplier) role. When politicians and bureaucrats are in a position of buying services on contract, for instance, they have an incentive to get the best price and to measure and report more accurately on value for money attained. Not surprisingly, then, many of the mechanisms for contracting out, vouchers, and other means of creating quasi-markets, recommended by Osborne and Gaebler in their popular 1992 book *Reinventing Government*, have long been endorsed by public choice economists.

The normative nature of public choice has some very clear implications for governing structures and boundaries. Although public choice theorists argue that there is no single ideal structure that is optimal for every local government (since the appropriate jurisdictional framework is partly dependent on the natural boundaries of the services being provided and on the specific preferences of citizens), a "polycentric" structure is generally much better than a consolidated single jurisdiction for a metropolitan area (Ostrom, Tiebout, and Warren, 1961, p. 831). There are several reasons why multiple jurisdictions are seen to be more effective: they allow citizens to send clear signals about preferences to their governments; they encourage competition among municipalities; they provide for territorial flexibility, (specialized units, such as water or hydro districts, that govern a single good according to its natural boundaries may co-exist alongside more traditional multipurpose municipalities); and the proximity of multiple municipalities enhances the possibilities for contracting out. Intergovernmental co-ordination can be achieved in this polycentric form through contracts or through special councils (in the United States, sometimes called councils of government) that serve as forums for discussing common problems. These councils are not a second tier of government as they have no formal authority over the members (Bish, 1971, p. 77). Public choice theory is also unequivocal about what services local governments should not deliver. It makes a strong case that income redistribution from wealthier to poorer areas and citizens is not the proper role of local governments. If one municipality carried out income redistribution within its own boundaries, there would be a strong incentive for poor people residing elsewhere to migrate in and for richer residents to exit to communities where they would not be forced to bear such costs. Thus redistribution, a public good workable only with large-scale boundaries, is the proper role of senior governments.

The Critique

Public choice theory has been strongly criticized on at least two fronts. The first set of criticisms challenge the theoretical premises of the models, starting with the basic assumption that individuals are, in fact, rational utility maximizers (Keating, 1995, p. 124) and the underlying premise of the Tiebout hypothesis that mobility is costless for citizens (Rose-Ackerman, 1983, p. 74). Other critics have challenged the assumptions about the ways in which efficiency is assessed and the presence of competition across municipalities. As argued by Keating (1995, p. 125), "[m]erely because smaller jurisdictions have lower costs does not mean that they are more efficient." Based on an extensive literature survey, Dowding and colleagues (1994, p. 787) conclude that there is virtually no worthwhile evidence to support the implication that the greater the number of jurisdictions, the greater the competition among them.

The second type of challenge has been on empirical grounds. Since this is a normative theory for which the implications are deduced from the theoretical premises, early public choice theorists saw little need for empirical testing. In recent years, however, the theory has been subjected to extensive empirical analysis, producing contradictory findings. Lowery and Lyons (1989, p. 537) found little support for the assumptions that citizens in fragmented urban areas feel more satisfied with their local government or that fragmentation reduces delivery costs. A complicating factor is that citizens, particularly in a fragmented system, have relatively limited knowledge about the level and costs of services provided by their municipalities and therefore cannot accurately base decisions to move on comparisons of service packages. Other evidence suggests that people relocate primarily for reasons related to job and family rather than the level of urban services (Percy and Hawkins, 1992).

To many critics outside the United States, the theory is seen as ethnocentric: it excessively generalizes from American experience where the ideological span of politics is very narrow and racial politics are central (Keating, 1995, pp. 127-888; see also Frisken, 1991). Small homogeneous communities can be seen as a way of rationalizing, enclaving, and justifying racial and social segregation by the white middle class in suburbia (Newton, 1975). This criticism has not been lost on Canadian observers. Andrew Sancton has argued, however, that the full potential of public choice theory, as an approach to local government reform, has been given inadequate attention in the Canadian context (Sancton, 1994). Nonetheless, public choice has received some attention in the Canadian context. For example, it has been applied to the study of service markets in contracting out by Canadian urban governments (McDavid and Schick, 1987) and is beginning to be used as a serious challenge to aficionados of one-tier unitary urban government.

COMMUNITY POWER

Community power studies encompass a variety of perspectives, including **elite**, **pluralist**, **growth machine**, and **regime theories**, all of which are concerned with the question, Who has influence at city hall?

Elite-Pluralist Debates

Since the 1950s, pluralists have battled elite theorists in attempts to assess empirically who governs our cities. Both share a common methodological approach based on case studies of individual cities in which power is measured according to the reputation or position (in elite theory) of pre-eminent individuals in the community or by determining who participated in decision making (in pluralist theory). From the perspective of elite theory, urban areas are run by small groups of prominent notables who are interconnected politically, economically, and socially and who determine power behind the scenes, thereby subordinating the position of elected and administrative officials (Judge, 1995, p. 15). Indeed, in his classic reputational study of Atlanta published in 1953, Hunter found that virtually all of the small powerful cadre who shaped policy in the city were senior executives in key businesses. While highly influential, they were seldom visible in community, local business, or other civic associations. These roles were left to a secondary but less powerful group of notables. The only elected official to be included as part of Atlanta's elite was the mayor.

Although elite theorists differ slightly on the nature and composition of elites, how they rule (by consent, right, or duplicity), and how they evolve (Harding, 1995, p. 37), most agree that the main sources of power in cities are ownership of real property and control of key industries (Dye, 1986). James Lorimer has advanced a similar argument in the Canadian context (Lorimer, 1978). Consequently, urban elites are composed primarily of large landowners, real-estate developers, bankers, and heads of large corporations who share a consensus around the imperatives of economic growth and development.

There are two main critiques of this approach. The first concerns its reputational methodology. Critics argue that asking who has a reputation for influence pre-ordains identifying an elite cadre. The second criticism is that the way in which elites exercise their power is not explained well.

In contrast, pluralists, using similar empirical case studies (often of the same cities), argue that not only is power fragmented and diffused, but that such decentralization is desirable. Rather than focussing on reputation for power, most pluralists argue that it is necessary to look at who actually took part in and had influence over particular decisions on an issue or sector-specific basis. Unlike elite theory, pluralism does not posit that certain groups will a priori be barred from political influence. Later pluralists (often called neo- or post-pluralists) have recognized, however, that political resources and opportunities are unequally distributed among individuals and groups and that certain actors, usually representing business interests, enjoy systemic advantages.

The classic example of pluralist analysis is Dahl's 1961 study of New Haven, in which he tried to assess the process of influence at work in three issue areas:

urban development, public education, and political nominations. In direct contradiction of Hunter's earlier study of Atlanta, Dahl found that influence was
fragmented: participants who were influential in one issue were not the same
people who were significant in the other issues and did not represent the same
social strata or groups. But participation itself was stratified. There was a small
stratum of people who were politically active in at least some issues compared
with a much larger group who were not active at all.

The findings of Dahl and other early pluralists have been challenged on a
number of grounds, the most serious of which are that the methodology drives
the findings and that the results are context bound. By studying issues that are
reputed to be issues and already part of a public decision-making process, pluralists ignore the other — elite — face of power (Bachrach and Baratz, 1962).
Issues get on the political agenda and come to open political debate, many elite
theorists argue, only when such issues do not threaten the fundamental interests
of elites. The second critique confronts pluralism on its own premise that the
nature of urban issues and the environment of policy making affect the shape of
politics (Yates, 1977). As contexts change, so too should the nature of influence
over policy-making. Thus studies of urban policy making in the 1980s and 90s
have uncovered systems of "hyperpluralism" rather than the stratified pluralism
of the 1950s and 60s. In hyperpluralistic systems, power is so splintered among a
diversity of groups that government is weaker than the pressure groups system
(DeLeon, 1992; Savitch and Thomas, 1991). Under these circumstances, urban
governments have trouble getting anything done.

Growth Machines

Case studies of influence that were the hallmark of both early elite and pluralist
theories are no longer popular. But the community power approach has spun off
variations that are very much alive in the late 1990s. The concept of "growth
machines" developed by John Logan and Harvey Molotch (1987) continues the
debate over who controls and who benefits in urban politics. The growth
machine perspective shares with elite theory a focus on individual actors and
groups, particularly the activism of entrepreneurs as a critical force in shaping
urban politics and development (Logan and Molotch, 1987, p. 52). It is more
expansive than its antecedent because it is concerned with broad decision-making over economic development, not just with decisions made by governments.
It also borrows from political economy a recognition of the importance of the
structural determinants of local economies. It is more limited, however, by its
focus on economic development rather than including redistribution or other
issues of urban life.

A growth machine is a coalition of local interests built around the property
development industry that acts out of its vested interests to espouse an ideology
of value-free development and the notion that markets alone should determine
land use (Logan and Molotch, 1987, p. 32). The model is built on the primacy
of land as a commodity and makes a distinction between the value of land as *use*
(e.g., the value of a home or office building accrues primarily to the occupants

and users) versus its value as *exchange* (the financial gain that can be made from property as an asset). At the core of an urban growth machine is a small group of property owners, called **rentiers**, who try to maximize their rental income by intensifying the use to which their land is put. They are also important intermediaries between the corporate elite and local citizenry. These rentiers are closely allied with other growth interests including developers, financiers, construction companies, development-dependent professionals (e.g., lawyers and engineers), utility companies, and the local media. Occasionally, universities, professional sports clubs, and labour unions may join in as auxiliary members of the machine to press for general economic growth and specific redevelopment ventures.

While campaigns favouring selective or even anti-growth strategies may be waged by neighbourhoods and other citizen organizations, they are seldom successful in the face of the highly mobilized and well resourced machine. Due to its ongoing interactions with and significant campaign contributions to city councils, the property industry has systemic power (Logan and Molotch, 1987, p. 62). Consequently, local governments usually strongly support growth, couching their support in both symbolic politics and the public interest of providing new jobs, expanding the tax base, and paying for urban services (Logan and Molotch, 1987, p. 33). If the urban policy-making system works to the advantage of the powerful growth machines and to the detriment of more marginalized groups, some serious concerns about the limits of democratic politics in urban areas are obvious.

Although concerns about the dominance of the property industry have been raised in Canada and elsewhere, the applicability of the growth machine model to countries other than the United States has been questioned. In the United Kingdom, for instance, the central government has had a much greater impact on the distribution of development than in the United States, where parochial rentiers have been central. Moreover, in the United Kingdom, as in Canada, intergovernmental relations and public–private partnerships are increasingly important to urban development. Such factors have made it more difficult for business to play one city administration against others in a bid for subsidies and development incentives. In addition, the emphasis on property as the key commodity ignores other critically important factors in locational decisions (Harding, 1994). In spite of globalization, capital may not be as footloose as Logan and Molotch suggest, and factors other than cheap land — such as quality of life, a highly educated workforce, and proximity to universities and research laboratories — are increasingly critical in decisions of where to locate, particularly for technology-dependent industries. These criticisms, however, do not seriously detract from the central implication of the model, that the property industry and its allies are the key players in urban governance.

Regime Theory

Regime theory rose to prominence in urban studies, as it did in other fields of political science, in the 1980s. While it shares the view of the growth machine school, that business enjoys a privileged role in urban politics, the intent of regime theory is not to identify a particular elite or cadre that exerts control over city hall. Rather it seeks to identify how and under what conditions often competing interests join together to achieve public policy goals. In this sense, regime theory is a more sophisticated understanding of *governance* — the capacity to act collectively to accomplish public policy goals — in contrast to the earlier models that attempt to explain how *governments* act and who influences them. Its importance is that it recognizes the interdependence of government with not only business but the voluntary sector and other interest groups as well.

An "urban regime" is defined as the informal arrangements by which public bodies and private interests function together in order to be able to make and carry out governing decisions (Stone, 1989, p. 6). A regime is not just any informal, politically stable group, however. By definition, it is one with access to institutional resources which enables it to play a role in policy making. As Stone notes in his study of Atlanta, the particular actors involved in an urban regime vary from one city to the next, as well as over time, depending on the underlying political economy. This affects both the scope of institutions required to mobilize the resources necessary to make and implement governing decisions and the degree of co-operation needed among them. The underlying premise is that modern governance is built on complexity and fragmentation so that no one actor or set of actors can readily dominate or easily impose their will on society (Stoker, 1995, p. 58). This complexity also limits the capacity of the state to act alone. While the state is considered by regime theorists to be the key player and as having relative autonomy (rather than being a mere arbiter of interests on an issue by issue basis as many pluralists would argue), it often needs to mobilize communities of interest and co-ordinate resources in order to achieve its public policy goals. Regime coalitions do not form on the basis of ideology or grand visions of the city's future. Instead, they represent attempts to accomplish relatively manageable tasks. Leadership, not raw power, is the critical factor in bringing coalition partners together. While participants may seek to further their own self-interests, once a relationship of co-operation, trust, and mutual support has been forged, the maintenance of the relationship becomes a valued asset in itself. This stands in contrast to both elite theory and pluralism in which hierarchy (in elite theory) and political bargaining (in pluralism) are the driving forces behind coalition-building.

The capacity of a regime to accomplish the governing tasks it sets itself depends on three elements: the composition of the regime, the nature of the relationships among the members, and the resources that the members bring or can access (Stone, 1989, p. 2). Regimes may have different political orientations and modes of governing. Several different types, in addition to pro-growth models, have been identified including:

- growth management coalitions that use planning and other regulations to limit or direct growth;
- social reform regimes that concentrate on community rather than business development; and

- fiscally conservative caretaker regimes that focus on the provision of core services but attempt to limit the role of government in every respect (DiGaetano and Kiemanski, 1993, pp. 59–60).

There are decisive advantages to regime theory in understanding community power. First, it focusses attention on the interdependence of urban government business, and the voluntary sector. Second, by looking at the capacity of governing coalitions, it forces us to examine the ability of governments both to make decisions and to implement them. Third, since regime theory makes no normative propositions (i.e., that the development industry will always dominate) it requires empirical analysis of particular locales and politics. But regime theory also has two important limitations. In contrast to the earlier pluralists or elite theorists, regime theorists do not offer a well developed methodology for empirical analysis, although the growing body of case studies of urban and other regimes is instructive. Second, regime theorists, themselves, note that the capacity and actions of a city's governing regime cannot be adequately analyzed in the absence of a broader view of the political economy.

POLITICAL ECONOMY

From the perspective of political economy, the problem with community power studies is that they address only the mechanisms of the *process* of decision making (Castells, 1977, p. 247). In contrast, political economy asserts that analysis of decision making cannot tell the whole story because the urban state has only a limited degree of autonomy for decision making in the first place, due to the nature of a capitalist economy. Political economy perspectives focus on the structural conditions of economic relations, specifically the processes of capital accumulation, production and consumption, and the conflicts generated by these forces. These processes set the parameters for decision making by urban governments and other political agents. In addition, a political economy lens contributes to a deeper understanding of the changing character of capitalist economies and of how cities fit into restructuring of the global economy. While there are a number of different streams within political economy, we will briefly review two: the earlier neo-Marxist analyses, as developed largely by David Harvey (1973) and Manuel Castells (1977; 1978), and the more recent **regulation school** which explains the implications for cities of the transition to a **post-fordist** economy. The latter explores the economic, social, and political developments stemming from the shift away from the manufacturing-based assembly-line economies most closely associated with the rise of mass production in the era of Henry Ford. In contrast to the public choice and community power schools previously discussed, political economy has been more heavily influenced, at least in its early stages, by European rather than American scholars.

Neo-Marxist Perspectives

From a neo-Marxist perspective, urban politics are explained using the twin concepts of capital accumulation and class struggle (Harvey, 1989, p. 59).

Accumulation by various fractions of capital occurs at the expense of the working classes, inevitably producing class conflict. The role of the state is to provide the general prerequisites for the production of capital (such as a healthy labour force and transportation systems) and to maintain social order. While the state has a degree of relative autonomy from the interests of capital, its continued authority rests on economic growth and thus it responds to capital's demands for a more efficient urban environment. The process of capital accumulation is inherently unstable, however. For example, original investment in the built environment often becomes a spatial barrier to reinvestment in other forms. "Under capitalism there is, then, a perpetual struggle in which capital builds a physical landscape appropriate to its own condition at a particular moment in time, only to have to destroy it, usually in the course of a crisis, at a subsequent point in time" (Harvey, 1989, p. 83). Class struggle is critical in shaping the flows of capital within and across urban regions. For instance, if capital can switch production to areas where the working classes are more compliant, it is likely to do so. The process of suburbanization can also be seen as a product of capital accumulation. According to Harvey, suburbanization is actively encouraged because it sustains a demand for products, thereby facilitating the accumulation of capital, and because white-collar suburbs reinforce community rather than class consciousness. And this fragmentation of class consciousness serves the interests of capital.

Castells (1977) extends this analysis by shifting the focus to the processes of consumption. He introduces the concept of "collective consumption" which refers to the services that, while consumed individually, are usually provided by the state due to the scale and complexity of their management. These include transportation, education, recreation, public housing, and urban planning. Collective consumption activities are important because they often serve as an independent basis for the development of social cleavages. In contrast to many neo-Marxists, Castells does not see the state as passive, primarily responding to the demands of capital, but as playing an increasingly key role in organizing a labour force to meet the needs of capital. As the state becomes more involved in collective consumption, it becomes the target of political demands by a wide range of social movements, which themselves come to play an increasing role in urban culture and politics (Castells, 1983).

Major contributions of neo-Marxist perspectives have been to focus our attention on urban services, situate urban policy in the context of economic structures, and define urban politics in terms of content rather than locale. They have also generated an understanding of urban policy as encompassing complex patterns of non-local institutions and non-governmental bodies. The main criticism of neo-Marxist analyses of urban issues is that they are too structural and overly deterministic, tending to downplay the relative autonomy of the state. For this reason, other less structural approaches, such as regulation theory which developed in the 1970s and 80s, have tended to supplant traditional structural neo-Marxism.

Regulation Theory

Regulation theory provides an account of changing economies in a global context, and the emerging role of cities in them, and links political with social and cultural change in this economic context. Two concepts are key to regulation theory: the concept of a regime of accumulation and a regime of regulation. A regime of accumulation refers to the stabilization of relations among production, consumption, and investment. A stable regime of accumulation can be identified when "rough balances between production, consumption, and investment, and between the demand and supply of labour and capital allow economic growth to be maintained with reasonable stability over a relatively long period" (Painter, 1995, pp. 277–78). This stabilization does not mysteriously happen but is the result of a regime of regulation, which is defined as the set of institutional, social, and cultural relations and practices that promote the compatibility between production and consumption. Contradictions of capital are inherent in this model, and a regime of regulation never permanently resolves these but merely adapts to reduce the more acute crises.

Much of regulation theory has concentrated on explaining the implications of the fundamental shift that began in the mid-1970s from fordism to post-fordism as a mode of regulation. Fordism promoted the emergence of a strong middle class through production of standardized consumer products and high manufacturing wages, which allowed workers to purchase the goods they produced. National governments played a key role in planning economic life and sustaining economic growth; they supported the welfare state and developed a compromise between capital and labour that gave significant recognition to unions (Jenson, 1989). Local governments, however, were in a subordinate position, often serving merely as administrative units in channelling growth, providing infrastructure, and managing urban renewal. Low density suburban development was encouraged and often funded by senior governments because it increased consumption (e.g. the purchase of a second car) (Filion, 1995, p. 48). Urban governments made optimistic projections of growth and held the technical rationality of urban planning in high esteem. Differences among cities and distinctiveness of local culture, however, were diluted due to the upper hand of senior governments and look-alike suburbanization.

With the oil crisis of 1973–74, the fordist model of accumulation and regulation began to unravel. Productivity declined and economic growth slowed as attention was directed toward controlling production costs, especially wages. Cost cutting in the private sector reverberated in the public sector, resulting in a shrinking of the welfare state and a less interventionist role by government in the economy. The result was a downward spiral of both consumption and production. More flexible forms of production replaced large-scale factories and the availability of high-wage manufacturing jobs declined, leading to polarization of the labour market into high-end knowledge workers and low-end retail/service, often part-time, workers. This transition is usually referred to as post-fordism, and it has had significant effects on the social and spatial division within and competition among cities.

First, the segmentation of the labour market has made cities increasingly differentiated socially, culturally, and spatially. On the one hand, the preference for specialty gourmet goods by high-income consumers has created concentrations of specialty stores, and preferences for classy and safe neighbourhoods have produced walled enclaves of expensive homes. Disenchantment with the conformity of suburbs has also encouraged gentrification of working-class neighbourhoods (with the spillover effects of displacing existing residents and increasing housing prices), a reduced faith in urban planning, and a greater desire for neighbourhood influence on policy making. On the other hand, conditions are quite different in the marginalized parts of the city, where there is a lack of affordable housing, a growing informal economy, and the rise of self-help institutions, such as housing co-operatives and voluntary employment centres, to replace a retreating state (Mayer, 1995). New political actors, such as groups representing squatters and street kids, have appeared on the political scene to contest definitions over quality of life with more traditional community and business associations.

Second, urban governments can no longer support infrastructure for suburbanization and have begun to press for the intensification of development (Filion, 1995, p. 50). In the interests of cost cutting, they also increasingly have adopted private sector management styles that emphasize contracting out and entrepreneurship and begun to undertake only minimal provision of the services of collective consumption. In addition, they have engaged in partnerships with the private sector, to build facilities and promote economic development, and with the voluntary sector, to provide the social services that they feel they can no longer afford (Mayer, 1995, p. 232).

Since the post-fordist regime of regulation is still in the process of unfolding, many contradictions are evident. Most notable is the mismatch between enduring consumer preferences for low-density, single-family housing and the inability of urban governments to pay for the infrastructure required to support this type of development. Another challenge is to provide the means for political participation of both the traditional insiders and the outsiders representing a variety of new urban social movements (Mayer, 1991, p. 119).

On the national stage, more attention is being focussed on urban governments because nation-states have become "hollowed out," having lost their ability to control their domestic economies and to manage the compromise between capital and labour. In the global picture, large cities are increasingly competing directly with one another for economic development, often using their quality of life as a strong selling point.

The study of post-fordism has moved political economy models in the direction of a greater focus on the political agency of various actors, as well as greater consideration of macroeconomic conditions. Yet many critics argue that the perspective does not go far enough, that it is primarily historical and still does not give sufficient attention to the role, capacity, and choices made by governments (Goodwin, Duncan, and Halford, 1993, p. 85). It is also suggested that regulation theory's analysis of post-fordism needs to take into account differing constitutional regimes (Garber and Imbroscio, 1996), that is, the policy levers that are available to cities under the institutional arrangements and rules established largely by provincial governments.

FEMINIST PERSPECTIVES

Feminism's contribution to the study of cities has been to enhance our understanding of the links between urban spaces, social identities, and social practices (Jacobs, 1993, p. 835). In addition, it has demanded a closer examination of consumption and production activities and provided a strong critique of urban planning.

Gender, Space, and Identity

Feminism brings gender into urban analysis by focussing on how the effects of public policy may have differential impacts according to gender, and examining how gender relations are structured and represented by state institutions (see Phillips, 1996). The difficulties inherent in liberalism, public choice theory, and traditional urban planning practices, feminists argue, are the assumption of a universal citizen — an individual without gender, class, race, age, or community — and the notion that everyone experiences the city in more or less the same way. From a feminist perspective, however, the world is pervasively shaped by gendered relations which can be institutionalized in government, organizations, culture, and public policies. How we use urban spaces or how safe we feel walking to our cars in the parking garage or using the neighbourhood park may very much depend on gender.

A second contribution of feminism is that it emphasizes the importance of the concept of space. Space is not merely a bounded physical locale and a contextual background to people's actions. Feminist analysts see space as constitutive of these actions (Kobayashi et al., 1994, p. xxix; see also Massey, 1994, p. 264). All spaces are gendered to some degree and, once in place, the gendered nature of a space influences how people experience it. Feminist geographers have shown how the activities of production and reproduction have created gendered spaces in the city and how this has influenced urban form. Suzanne MacKenzie (1988), for example, shows how the creation in the late 1800s of work spaces away from home reinforced the distinction between public and private spaces in people's lives and affected urban form by establishing purely residential areas to which women became more or less confined.

Feminism has also helped to focus attention on **identity politics**. Identity is a political point of departure and a motivation for action, rather than a set of objective needs. As Jenson (1994, p. 55) notes, "[t]hese ideas about who we are . . . are never fixed in time, nor do they fall from the sky. They are created out of the political actions of groups and individuals who work to make themselves heard, their positions represented, and their demands met." The formation of identities is also closely tied to the construction of space.

In practical terms, these twin concepts of space and identity encourage students of urban politics to look beneath broad categories of business and the community to the particularities of specific identities, and to pay attention to difference. Increasingly, urban politics is characterized by a politics of difference — one which is necessarily a politics of identity because it is based on a vision of "a heterogeneous public that accepts and affirms group differences" (Young, 1990, p. 10). A politics of difference is also concerned with voice, that is, with participation in political processes that includes some measure of power. The mode of representation under a politics of difference shifts from traditional representation by elites, whether elected or interest group elites, to direct representation and participation by people who personally share in the experiences of the social and cultural groups for whom they claim to speak. Feminist analysis of urban space and identity has made a contribution that extends beyond the distinction between women and men. At least in recent work, it has shown sensitivity to other dimensions of social and political identity, such as culture, sexual orientation, and tenure of residence.

Feminism and Urban Research

Feminism offers important challenges to research methodologies in urban policy and planning processes. Feminists reject the insistence on objectivity that has been at the heart of theories of rational planning. What is required from a feminist perspective is more grounded research that develops a deeper understanding of different communities and spaces. Feminists argue that we, as analysts, need to learn to ask the right questions rather than having ready answers. The researcher must recognize that she or he may not be asking the same questions, let alone coming up with the same answers, as people touched by the analysis. Not surprisingly, then, feminists have been vocal critics of traditional planning (see Hendler, 1994, p. 26). They argue for developing closer, more caring relationships between planners and the communities for and with whom they plan. They also advocate democratizing policy processes so that people, especially marginalized communities, can be engaged in meaningful ways.

Can we identify what a city built on feminist principles would look like? Caroline Andrew has ventured to outline the basic elements:

- a wide variety of services offering genuine choices for different communities;
- elimination of violence against women and children with a public agency so mandated and a well developed network of services;
- friendly neighbourhoods with lively streets oriented to pedestrians rather than cars;
- mixed land use involving close spatial proximity of residences, services, and work;
- an active social housing policy producing a mix of housing including co-operatives, transitional homes, and suitable housing for the elderly;
- a first-class public transportation system;
- good, accessible daycare;
- encouragement of community-based economic development that provides meaningful jobs for women, co-ordinated with training opportunities and daycare;

- democratized planning processes that work with communities rather than planning for them; and
- concern for a healthy environment (see Eichler, 1995, p. 17).

Two main criticisms are often levied at feminist approaches. First, many observers would note that the city described above would be appealing not only to women and that advocates for such a city are not uniquely found among feminists. The importance of gender as the central defining aspect of urban life is thus contested. A related criticism is that because feminism is so focussed on gender dimensions and urban design, it misses many of the larger questions concerning urban economics and broad governance issues.

THE ESSENTIAL DEBATES ABOUT URBAN GOVERNANCE

How do these four theoretical perspectives inform the basic debates about urban governance that we set out in Chapter One? As you will see, there is no consensus on these issues, but rather varying, and sometimes directly opposing, views.

What Is the Role of Urban Government in the Context of the Canadian Constitution?

Can we conclude from these theories that municipal governments should be granted a greater degree of autonomy and more policy levers by senior levels of government? While none of the theories are specifically designed to respond directly to this question, they do, by implication, offer some important observations. The extent to which greater autonomy is judged to be desirable depends, in part, on how we define the essence of what local government does. In both public choice theory on the right end of the political spectrum and in much of neo-Marxism on the left, there is a bias toward seeing cities primarily as the providers of goods and services. When seen in this light, the primary goals of efficiency and customer satisfaction in service provision can be achieved by reconfiguring some structures of urban government and changing the relationships between service producers and providers. No new policy levers would be required however.

In contrast, feminists and some political economy and community power theorists refuse to limit the definition of urban politics to the provision of goods and services. As a globalized economy accentuates the need for cities to compete internationally, cities are increasingly constrained in their efforts at economic development. In addition, feminists focus our attention on urban space and how we live our lives in urban settings. Although government-provided social services and the capacity to address issues of diversity are important, in many cases provinces, not local governments, have control over these functions. From a feminist or political economy vantage point, there is a clear case to be made for granting more autonomy and policy levers to urban governments so that they can develop more locally sensitive solutions to urban problems and enhance the opportunities for economic development.

What Is the Relationship of Urban Government to International Forces?

The four theories we reviewed attempt to link the global to the local in varying degrees. At one extreme, public choice is the most locally focussed, declaring its spatial interest as the outer boundary for the marketing of urban services. At the other extreme, the post-fordist scholars argue that the forces of global economic restructuring have fundamentally altered the economy, politics, and space of cities. The result has been to place large cities in more direct competition with one another, thus elevating their economic and political importance relative to the province or nation-state. From both post-fordist and feminist perspectives, this has produced more spatially differentiated areas within cities and given rise to new urban social movements that are dramatically affecting the content and process of political representation.

Whom Does Local Government Really Serve?

Again the theories are divided on the democratic nature of urban politics. Pluralists and public choice theorists start from the position that there is no inherent ideological or structural bias that predetermines who will have influence. In sharp contrast, elite, growth machine, and political economy perspectives detect an underlying power imbalance at city hall in favour of the property development industry. Feminists point to the failure of urban governments to understand and plan for the differences among citizens, especially differences based on gender and culture. Regime theorists would demand that we have a closer empirical look at coalitions of interests. While they do not deny the possibility of an influential business-oriented growth coalition, they note that due to the complexity of urban issues, governance almost always requires working with outside partners and allies, both in the private and voluntary sectors. The specific configuration of governing coalitions, however, may vary from one city to the next.

Which Structures and Management Processes Are the Most Efficient and Effective?

Can we conclude from these theories that one structure of urban government is clearly preferable to others? Specifically, can we determine whether a consolidated, single-tier structure is more efficient and effective than a system of multiple municipalities or a two-tier government in a metropolitan area? The theorists are, in fact, quite divided on the issue. On the one hand, political economists, who look to urban governments to provide the services of collective consumption and to regulate social control, tend to favour a stronger, more unified governing structure. They view fragmentation as weakening the role of urban governments relative to federal and provincial governments, which does not serve them well in a globalized economy. Public choice theorists, in contrast, present a strong case that having many relatively homogeneous units and special districts is both more efficient and more democratically responsive. The political economist would counter, however, that public choice tends to reduce the citizen to a mere consumer of services and equates politics with market activity. This debate leaves the question of an optimal governing structure unresolved.

Summary

It is obvious from the differing responses to these four questions that the debates on urban governance are indeed lively ones. There is no consensus that would allow us to offer generalized prescriptions for the governance of cities. We can merely draw a few general observations from these theories: there is a growing recognition of the link between global forces and local responses, the property industry is an important player, and the diversity of cities requires them to re-evaluate what they provide and how they provide it.

THE CONCEPT OF URBAN GOVERNANCE

In many respects, the contending propositions and differing views presented by the four theories discussed above raise more questions than they answer. In fact, the very definition of what constitutes an urban area and what governing apparatus should be considered part of the **local state** are left open to question. Most of the theories either do not address these questions or equate local governance with municipalities and take the geographic boundary of the urban area as equivalent to the jurisdiction boundary of the municipality (Magnusson, 1985, pp. 576–77). Our approach is to focus on urban *governance* — defined as the collective capacity to set and achieve public policy goals — rather than simply on the institutions of urban government. This involves several conceptual distinctions.

First, the terms "municipality" and "city" are imprecise ways of describing the geography of urban agglomerations. We discussed this in terms of Statistics Canada's perspectives in Chapter One. As discussed in more detail in Chapter Four, we use the concept of a "city-region" to define the territory in question. City-regions are characterized by several things: they contain a variety of communities with different identities but have a sense of cohesiveness, they are economically interdependent units, and there is an interest and a capacity for managing growth (Greater Toronto Area Task Force, 1996). As illustrated in later chapters, the functional boundaries of urban regions change over time as regions grow, and the arrangements for governance vary enormously across the eight urban regions we examine. Second, most approaches to local governance focus simply on municipalities as the governing apparatus, but this is too limited a view of the local state.

The Local State

Our model of urban governance consists of three main parts.

MUNICIPAL GOVERNMENT

Municipal government is the most easily identified part of the local state. In its simplest form, it consists of a mayor and council who preside over an administrative structure with responsibility for a range of local functions. But few city-regions in Canada are governed by just a single municipality. Many have not only a series of municipalities, but a second tier of regional government with its own council and administration. Municipal functions are split between governments operating at the municipal and regional levels. Both are essential parts of the core governing institutions.

SPECIAL PURPOSE BODIES

The second component of the local state is bedevilling to many and befuddling to all. Local special purpose bodies are the agencies, boards, and commissions charged with responsibility for single purpose functions at the local level. While their territorial jurisdiction is usually coterminous with a municipality (or small group of municipalities), most special purpose bodies have a degree of autonomy from, and an arm's-length relationship with, municipal councils because they have their own legislative basis and often are directly elected (Richmond and Siegel, 1994, p. 7). Their accountability relationships to municipalities and directly to the public vary greatly but often are less than open or obvious.

VOLUNTARY ASSOCIATIONS

The third partner in urban governance is the voluntary sector. People familiar with rural or small-town life are accustomed to relying on the volunteer fire department or recreation committee to carry out important functions within the community. In contrast, one of the dominant characteristics of the emerging modern city government in the post-World War II era was the professionalization of the civic service. Municipal governments and local special purpose bodies expanded the range of expertise and size of their staff in order to meet increasingly complex service requirements and preferences. But voluntary associations continued to deliver a wide range of urban services, working alongside and sometimes under contract with municipalities.

In the late 1990s, in most cities, this pattern of urban service delivery is under enormous pressure in the face of significant fiscal constraints. Urban governments are turning many programs, which they once provided directly, over to voluntary organizations. The range of services now provided by the voluntary sector in cities is enormous. It can include maintaining park and recreational facilities, operating community centres and co-operative housing, providing language training and immigrant settlement programs, protecting the environment, and running food banks.

The roots of the groups actively engaged in these and other functions remain in the community. But their responsibilities for delivery of urban services place them in a new relationship with municipal governments and special purpose bodies. It is a relationship of co-production. In some cases, this is based on financial transfers, as the local state attempts to cut costs by supplying core or project funding to local groups, who then supply the voluntary labour. In other cases, the relationship is also rooted in policy and other forms of guidance. For example, in the recently amalgamated Halifax Regional Municipality, retaining the 33 voluntary fire brigades in the rural and semi-rural parts of the region was essential to the financial viability of the reform. These departments will now, however, be directed by the municipality's professional fire chief and be involved in the municipality's fire protection training program. Regardless of the basis of the co-production relationship, it is characterized by strong mutual dependency. The lines of authority and responsibility between these organizations and the core of the local state are increasingly blurred and shifting. As a result, we characterize them as the phantom arm of the local state.

CONCLUSION

The four theories discussed in this chapter create the basis of a dialogue — indeed, often a vigorous debate — about the nature of politics, local economies, and appropriate governing structures for city-regions. In the following chapters, we will not consistently follow or advocate one perspective over another. Rather we will continue to use some of the debates raised by the theorists. As will be evident, however, our conception of urban politics does not equate urban governance with merely ensuring the efficient provision of services related to collective consumption. Nor does it assume that all politics is about property. The issues that arise in urban politics can also be interpreted as addressing questions of quality of life and difference related to a diversity of cultural and social communities. They thus involve fundamental debates over representation and participation in decision-making processes.

Our model of urban governance which consists of three main parts — municipal (and regional) governments, special purpose bodies, and the voluntary sector — has not been advanced by any of the four theories previously discussed. While our model shares the notion of interdependence of partners with regime theory, we see these three elements not as coalitions but as essential parts of the governing apparatus that are common, albeit in different specific forms and combinations, to all of the city-regions we study.

The main point in examining these differing approaches to the study of urban governance is to recognize that the assumptions you start with determine, to a large degree, both the questions you find compelling and the answers you find convincing.

SUGGESTED READINGS

Andrew, Caroline. (1992). "The Feminist City." In *Political Arrangements: Power and the City*, edited by Henri Lustiger-Thaler. Montreal: Black Rose Books. This chapter offers a critique of urban planning from a feminist perspective and describes a city the form and policies of which were designed according to feminist principles.

Castells, Manuel. (1977). *The Urban Question*. London: Edward Arnold. Castells develops the concept of collective consumption within a neo-Marxist framework.

Dunleavy, Patrick. (1980). *Urban Political Analysis*. London: The Macmillan Press. Dunleavy applies the concept of collective consumption to developing a framework for the analysis of urban policy.

Judge, David, Jerry Stoker, and Harold Wolman. (1995). *Theories of Urban Politics*. London: Sage. This comprehensive collection of essays provides a good overview and critique of public choice, community power, and political economy perspectives.

Mayer, Margit. (1995). "Urban Governance in the Post-Fordist City." In *Managing Cities: The New Urban Context*, edited by Patsy Healey et al. Chichester, UK: John Wiley & Sons. pp. 231–49. An excellent discussion of regulation theory and the implications of post-fordism for urban life.

BIBLIOGRAPHY

Andrew, Caroline. (1992). "The Feminist City." In *Political Arrangements: Power and the City*, edited by Henri Lustiger-Thaler. Montreal: Black Rose Books, pp. 109–22.

Bachrach, P. and M.S. Baratz. (1962). "Two Faces of Power." *American Political Science Review* 56: 947–52.

Bish, Robert L. (1971). *The Public Economy of Metropolitan Areas*. Chicago: Rand McNally College Publishing.

Bish, Robert L. and Robert Warren. (1972). "Scale and Monopoly Problems in Urban Government Services." *Urban Affairs Quarterly*, September, pp. 97–122. .

Castells, Manuel. (1977). *The Urban Question*. London: Edward Arnold.

———. (1978). *City, Class, and Power*. New York: St. Martin's Press.

———. (1983). *The City and the Grassroots*. University of Berkeley: California Press.

Dahl, Robert A. (1961). *Who Governs? Democracy and Power in an American City*. New Haven: Yale University Press.

DeLeon, R. E. (1992). *Left Coast City: Progressive Politics in San Francisco, 1975–1991*. Concise: University of Concise Press.

DiGaetano, Alan and John S. Klemanski. (1993). "Urban Regimes in Comparative Perspective: The Politics of Urban Development in Britain." *Urban Affairs Quarterly* 29(1): 54–83.

Dowding, Keith, Peter John, and Stephen Biggs. (1994). "Tiebout: A Survey of the Empirical Literature." *Urban Studies*, 31(4/5): 767–97.

Dye, Thomas R. (1986). "Community Power and Public Policy." In *Community Power: Directions for Future Research*, edited by Robert J. Waste. Newbury Park, CA: Sage Publications, pp. 29–52.

Eichler, Margrit. (1995). "Designing Eco-City in North America." In *Change of Plans: Towards a Non-Sexist Sustainable City*, edited by Margrit Eichler. Toronto: Garamond Press, pp. 1–23.

Fagan, Robert H. and Richard B. Le Heron. (1994). "Reinterpreting the Geography of Accumulation: The Global Shift and Local Restructuring." *Society and Space* 12: 265–85.

Filion, Pierre. (1995). "Fordism, Post-Fordism and Urban Policy-Making: Urban Renewal in a Medium-Size Canadian City." *Canadian Journal of Urban Research* 4 (1): 43–72.

Frisken, Frances. (1991). "The Contributions of Metropolitan Government to the Success of Toronto's Public Transit System: An Empirical Dissent from the Public-Choice Paradigm." *Urban Affairs Quarterly* 27(2): 268–92.

Garber, Judith A. and David L. Imbroscio. (1996). "'The Myth of the North American City' Reconsidered: Local Constitutional Regimes in Canada and the United States." *Urban Affairs Review* 31(5): 595–624.

Goodwin, M., S. Duncan, and S. Halford. (1993). "Regulation Theory, the Local State, and the Transition of Urban Politics." *Society and Space* 11: 67–88.

Greater Toronto Area Task Force. (1996). *Report of the Greater Toronto Area Task Force.* Toronto: Queen's Printer for Ontario.

Harding, Alan. (1994). "Urban Regimes and Growth Machines: Towards a Cross-National Research Agenda." *Urban Affairs Quarterly* 29(3): 356–82.

Harvey, David. (1973). *Social Justice and the City.* London: Edward Arnold.

———. (1989). *The Urban Experience.* Oxford: Basil Blackwell.

Hendler, Sue. (1994). "Feminist Planning Ethics." *Journal of Planning Literature* 9 (2): 115–27.

Hunter, Floyd. (1953). *Community Power Structure.* New York: Anchor Books.

Jacobs, Jane. (1993). "The City Unbound: Qualitative Approaches to the City." *Urban Studies* 30(4/5): 827–48.

Jenson, Jane. (1989). "'Different' But not 'Exceptional': Canada's Permeable Fordism." *Canadian Review of Sociology and Anthropology* 26(1).

———. (1994). "Understanding Politics: Contested Concepts of Identity in Political Science." In *Canadian Politics*, 2nd ed., edited by James P. Bickerton and Alain-G. Gagnon. Peterborough, ON: Broadview Press, pp.54–74.

Judge, David. (1995). "Pluralism." In *Theories of Urban Politics*, edited by David Judge, Gerry Stoker, and Harold Wolman. London: Sage, pp. 13–34.

Keating, Michael. (1995). "Size, Efficiency, and Democracy: Consolidation, Fragmentation, and Public Choice." In *Theories of Urban Politics*, edited by David Judge, Gerry Stoker, and Harold Wolman. London: Sage, pp. 117–34.

Kobayashi, Audrey et al. (1994). "Introduction." In *Women, Work, and Place*, edited by Audrey Kobayashi et al. Montreal: McGill-Queen's University Press, pp. 1–25.

Logan, John R. and Harvey L. Molotch. (1987). *Urban Fortunes: The Political Economy of Place.* Berkeley: University of California Press.

Lorimer, James. (1978). *The Developers.* Toronto: James Lewis and Samuel.

Lowery, David and William E. Lyons. (1989). "The Impact of Jurisdictional Boundaries: An Individual-Level Test of the Tiebout Model." *Journal of Politics*, February, 51(1): 73–97.

Lyons, W. E. and David Lowery. (1989). "Governmental Fragmentation Versus Consolidation: Five Public-Choice Myths about How to Create Informed, Involved, and Happy Citizens." *Public Administration Review*, November/December, pp. 533–43.

MacKenzie, Suzanne. (1988). "Building Women, Building Cities: Toward Gender Sensitive Theory in the Environmental Disciplines." In *Life Spaces: Gender, Household, Employment*, edited by Caroline Andrew and Beth Moore Milroy. Vancouver: UBC Press, pp. 13–30.

Magnusson, Warren. (1985a). "The Local State in Canada: Theoretical Perspectives." *Canadian Public Administration* 28(4): 575–99.

———. (1985b). "Political Science, Political Economy, and the Local State." *Urban History Review* XIV(1): 47–53.

Massey, Doreen. (1994). *Space, Place, and Gender*. Minneapolis: University of Minnesota Press.

Mayer, Margit. (1991). "Politics in the Post-Fordist City." *Socialist Review* 21(1): 105–24.

———. (1995). "Urban Governance in the Post-Fordist City." In *Managing Cities: The New Urban Context*, edited by Patsy Healey et al. Chichester, UK: John Wiley & Sons, pp. 231–49.

McDavid, James C. and Gregory K. Schick, (1987). "Privatization versus Union–Management Co-operation: The Effects of Competition on Service Efficiency in Municipalities." *Canadian Public Administration* 30: 472–88.

Newton, Kenneth. (1975). "American Urban Politics: Social Class, Political Structure, and Public Goods." *Urban Affairs Quarterly* 11(2): 241–63.

Niskanen, William A. (1991). "A Reflection on Bureaucracy and Representative Government." In *The Budget-Maximizing Bureaucrat: Appraisals and Evidence*, edited by André Blais and Stéphane Dion. Pittsburgh: University of Pittsburgh Press, pp.13–32.

Osborne, David and Ted Gaebler. (1992). *Reinventing Government*. Reading, MA.: Addison-Wesley Publishing Company.

Ostrom, Vincent, Charles M. Tiebout, and Robert Warren. (1961). "The Organization of Government in Metropolitan Areas: A Theoretical Inquiry." *American Political Science Review* 55: 831–42.

Painter, Joe. (1995). "Regulation Theory, Post-Fordism, and Urban Politics." In *Theories of Urban Politics*, edited by David Judge, Gerry Stoker, and Harold Wolman. London: Sage, pp. 276–96.

Parks, Roger B. and Ronald J. Oakerson. (1989). "Metropolitan Organization and Governance: A Local Public Economy Approach." *Urban Affairs Quarterly* 25(1): 18–29.

Percy, Stephen L. and Brett W. Hawkins. (1992). "Further Tests of Individual-Level Propositions from the Tiebout Model." *The Journal of Politics* 52(4):1149–57.

Phillips, Susan D. (1996). "Discourse, Identity, and Voice: Feminist Contributions to Policy Studies." In *Policy Studies in Canada: The State of the Art*, edited by Laurent Dobuzinskis, Michael Howlett, and David Laycock. Toronto: University of Toronto Press, pp. 242–65.

Richmond, Dale and David Siegel, eds. (1994). *Agencies, Boards, and Commissions in Canadian Local Government*. Toronto: Institute of Public Administration of Canada and Intergovernmental Committee on Urban and Regional Research.

Rose-Ackerman, Susan. (1983). "Beyond Tiebout: Modeling the Political Economy of Local Government." In *Local Provision of Public Services: The Tiebout Model after Twenty-Five Years*, edited by George R. Zodrow. New York: Academic Press, pp. 55–84.

Sancton, Andrew. (1994). *Governing Canada's City-Regions: Adapting Form to Function*. Montreal: Institute for Research on Public Policy.

Savitch, H.V. and J.C. Thomas. (1991). "Conclusion: End of the Millennium Big City Politics." In *Big City Politics in Transition*, edited by H.V. Savitch and John Clayton Thomas. Newbury Park, CA: Sage, pp. 1–13.

Smith, Michael Peter and Richard Tardanico. (1987). "Urban Theory Reconsidered: Production, Reproduction, and Collective Action." In *The Capitalist City: Global Restructuring and Community Politics*, edited by Michael Peter Smith and Joe R. Feagin. Oxford: Basil Blackwell, pp. 87–110.

Stoker, Gerry. (1995). "Regime Theory and Urban Politics." In *Theories of Urban Politics*, edited by David Judge, Gerry Stoker, and Harold Wolman. London: Sage, pp. 54–71.

Stoker, Gerry and K. Mossberger. (1994). "Urban Regime Theory in Comparative Perspective." *Environment and Planning C: Government and Policy* 12: 195–212.

Stone, Clarence. (1989). *Regime Politics*. Lawrence, KA: University Press of Kansas.

Tiebout, Charles M. (1956). "A Pure Theory of Local Expenditures." *Journal of Political Economy* LXIV: 416–24.

Waste, Robert J. (1986). "Community Power and Pluralist Theory." In *Community Power: Directions for Future Research*, edited by Robert J. Waste. Newbury Park, CA: Sage Publications, pp. 117–38.

Yates, D. (1977). *The Ungovernable City: The Politics of Urban Problems and Policy Making*. Cambridge, MA: MIT Press.

Young, Iris Marion. (1990). *Justice and the Politics of Difference*. Princeton, NJ: Princeton University Press.

CHAPTER THREE

◆

LEGACIES OF HISTORICAL DEVELOPMENT

INTRODUCTION

This chapter discusses the historical development of urban Canada and its governments. We show how the past has influenced the present day and provide an opportunity for speculation about how the legacies of the past might influence the future.

Our treatment of history is more thematic than descriptive. We do not, for example, provide a summary of the evolution of local government legislation and policy in each province and territory; neither do we provide a history of each of our chosen cities. There are numerous sources that provide rich descriptive and analytic detail in both of these contexts (Magnusson and Sancton, 1983; Brownstone and Plunkett, 1983; Colton, 1980; Tindal and Tindal, 1995). Instead we examine the history of Canada's urban governments in terms of four defining legacies:

- The legacies of our intellectual history. It is important to have a sense of how Canadian scholars and other observers have conceived and articulated their views about the role and purpose of local government in the country. In Chapter Two, we explored different perspectives that might be used to analyze the contemporary structures and politics of urban government. Our treatment of the intellectual history of urban government, in this chapter, provides insight into why some of the analytical perspectives discussed in Chapter Two have been more evident than others in public discourse about urban government.

- The legacies of settlement. Without undertaking exhaustive histories of individual cities, we illustrate how some of the geographic characteristics, the origins of settlement, and the social and economic history of individual cities, and the Canadian urban system more broadly, have influenced today.

- The role of key events in shaping subsequent urban politics and government. Urban Canada has evolved, but our chosen cities have also been shaped by various defining moments, which altered the course of their governments at the time and also produced a legacy. We will review some of these to illustrate this point.

- The legacies of urban reform. No treatment of the history of urban government and politics in Canada would be complete without a review and assessment of the impact of different visions about urban reform. Three streams of reform are important. They focus respectively on inculcating a managerial ethic into urban government, injecting populist influence and energy into urban politics and government practices, and emphasizing the alteration of the political boundaries and functional responsibilities of urban governments. Our discussion of urban reform in this chapter takes us up to the end of World War II. Discussion of more recent initiatives occurs in later chapters.

After reading about these various legacies, you will see the difficulty in determining precise cause and effect through the prism of history. Contemporary institutions of urban government in Canada have been shaped by a complex interplay among the legacies of settlement; the impact of key events; the pressures exerted by the imposition (rather than the organic development) of local government structures, beginning in colonial times; and by varying visions of urban reform. There has often been a tension between the imposition of local government structures and natural development, based on patterns of urban settlement and urban life. That persistent tension also exerts an influence on how debates about key issues, such as sustainable development and economic development in cities, are played out today.

The intellectual underpinnings of these contemporary debates may be more obscure. It is important to understand the legacies of earlier thinking about local government in order to have informed discussions about the past and its influence on today and the future. Analyses of local government have tended either to romanticize its role or disparage it. Both perspectives have implications for more recent debates and initiatives regarding urban reform.

THE LEGACIES OF OUR INTELLECTUAL HISTORY

> Toronto, Godly, cleanly and British; Ottawa with a fresh beauty and growing strength typical of the youthful Dominion . . . Montreal, regal and superb; quaint and medieval Quebec; loyal Saint John and martial Halifax complete a galaxy of deep-rooted, prosperous, and expanding cities which is justly the pride and glory of the sturdy young "Giant of the North.". . . The future of the Dominion of Canada is assured. Its growth into a mighty nation, a clean-limbed and worthy rival of its great and generous American neighbour, can be foreseen by those who do not claim prophetic vision. The forward impulses in this expansion of the Dominion will emanate from her magnificent cities . . . . (Nelson Company, 1905:1, quoted in Weaver, 1977, p. 5)

Quaint as this urban imagery may be, we can see a number of the central themes in the conceptualization of Canadian cities and their governments embedded in it. In this section, we will explore these themes. They concern the **origins debates** about the roots of local and urban government in Canada, specifically, the influence of British tradition and government (progenitor of "the youthful Dominion") and the urban heritage of Canada's "great and generous American neighbour" (Weaver, 1977). They also concern debates about the role of cities and city governments in generating economic prosperity and originating other forward impulses. We will examine the urban government and enterprise debate.

A final theme in the traditional discourse about urban government in Canada concerns its role in our democratic life. These debates are, in part, rooted in different conceptions of the origins of urban government. As you will see, they are also vitally connected to the legacy of urban government reform.

The Origins Debate

Treatments of the origins of Canadian local government, as we know it today, have tended to emphasize two foundational elements. The first is the requirement of an essentially colonial administration to have some form of district administration over the pre-Confederation colonies. It pre-dates notions of local democracy, whereby local governments would have independent elections and an independent ability to raise revenues, as well as designated authority for local affairs (Sharpe, 1981, pp. 28–39). It still has a historical legacy.

The early roots of local administration are found in the military-dominated administrations of the French and English colonial authorities. During the French regime, successive governors oversaw the affairs of New France using the principle of centralized control. By 1647, a system of electing local officers to *syndics d'habitation* had been established in places like Quebec, Montreal, and Trois Rivières. In 1663, Frontenac permitted election of a board of civilian aldermen in Quebec. Both initiatives were viewed with suspicion by authorities in France. Frontenac was specifically forbidden from continuing the board of aldermen. These developments prompted one observer, K.G. Crawford, to state categorically, "There may be said to have been no municipal government in Canada during the French regime" (Crawford, 1954, p. 19). This sums up the conventional wisdom about the French period.

The British initially adopted military administration as their model for colonial government as well. Contemplating expanded and orderly settlement of their new holdings, the British began to survey townships along the St. Lawrence River in 1783. The idea of creating townships as units of local identity and government was far from the minds of the British however. This is evident in their practice of numbering, rather than naming, the new townships (Lightbody, 1995, p. 60).

The second foundational theme is the emergence of municipal institutions with the additional elements of democratic self-rule, independent elections, and revenues. This generally has been attributed to two developments: the arrival of settlers from New England, with experience in and a taste for local democracy, and the fruition of the English reform movement, through passage of the Reform Act in 1832 and the first modern piece of legislation affecting English local government in 1835 (Isin, 1995a, pp. 75–76 and Isin, 1992). Scholars of local government in Canada have put varying emphasis on the influence of democratic reform, the anti-democratic views of elite family compacts, and the requisites of colonial administration and protection from American intrusion on the evolution of our local government system (Shortt, 1913; Brittain, 1951; Crawford, 1954). This is especially true in interpretations of the evolution of local governments in the remaining British colonies, after the American Revolution. Regardless of emphasis, these developments are generally recognized as contributing to the rebellions of Upper and Lower Canada in the 1830s, as well as the drive for responsible government in Nova Scotia. An important legacy of these political upheavals was the passage of new municipal legislation by colonial legislatures, most notably the 1849 **Baldwin Act** in Ontario, which has had a seminal influence on the development of local government to the present.

The Baldwin Act is significant because it was the first piece of legislation to create a uniform system of municipal government over an entire province. In very specific terms, it created a two-tier system of county government for the part of the province settled at that time. The approach of having counties deal with local activities of area-wide importance and more local town, villages, and townships assume other local responsibilities lies at the root of municipal organization in many other provinces as well. As we examine later efforts to reform local government, the question of how to sustain local democracy and responsiveness to community needs while providing for the efficient delivery of services becomes evident. The two-tier county system, first established in Canada under the Baldwin Act, represents the starting point for dealing with the "democracy-efficiency trade-off."

Other principles embedded in the Baldwin Act, which were applied elsewhere, are as follows:

- Municipal councils should receive delegated authority from the provincial legislature and are subject to its control. This led to the often used description of municipal governments as "creatures of the province."
- Urban and rural governments should be separated and have different powers. This principle was born, in part, out of recognition that the needs of cities were different from smaller settlements or rural townships. It was also a reflection of the suspicion and antipathy with which cities were regarded. As we shall see, this had lasting effects.
- The local right to vote should be restricted to property owners. This reinforced the orientation of municipal government to providing services to property and has had a lingering impact on participation in local political life, even after the franchise was widened.

In a recent critique of the written history of local government in Canada, Engin Isin argues that many of the historical overviews written in the latter half of the twentieth century mistakenly adopt the Anglocentric view of earlier writers. Beginning with the 1887 Ontario Royal Commission to Inquire into Municipal Institutions, a popular view was developed that "Anglo-Saxons did not merely engraft their own principles upon the municipal system established by the Romans in Britain, but brought with them the gem of our free municipal system" and that, under French rule, "the establishment and development of municipal institutions worthy of the name was evidently impossible" (Isin, 1995, p. 76, quoted from the original).

These views are not only ethnocentric. They also reflect a romanticized view of the role of local government in Canada which has perhaps obscured two other scholarly interpretations of its roots. The first is that local governments were established by colonial governments and sustained by their provincial successors essentially to download responsibility for the imposition of unpopular taxes. This is essentially a more sophisticated interpretation of the colonial administration concept. Warren Magnusson argues that this is a legacy of both the British system of local government and the tradition of royal administration in France, contributing to the unpopularity of local government in New France, which lingered well beyond the advent of British rule (Magnusson, 1983, pp. 4–5). He also argues that the local court system (known as Courts of Quarter Sessions) as well as the boards to regulate local markets and local police boards, established by the British in part to respond to the need for local rule before the legislative reforms of the 1840s and 50s, had regulatory and somewhat negative functions. These have tainted the more rosy view of local government as a popular democratic instrument. Certainly the potential tax consequences of the establishment of local government are still part of our political life and lore. Higgins writes of them as being an integral part of the antipathy toward local government in Nova Scotia and Newfoundland (Higgins, 1986, pp. 33–40). As late as 1995, residents in a number of smaller communities in Newfoundland were simply "walking away" from their local governments by refusing to pay local taxes or produce candidates for local elected office. In the larger urban context, taxpayer perceptions about the needless expense of two-tier metropolitan governments reflect a similar legacy.

The final defining vision of urban government in our intellectual tradition is that it exists as a more positive instrument, but not necessarily as an instrument of popular will. Instead the image of city government as a corporation emerges. This image defines local government both as an institution and in terms of the interests it serves. The corporate character of local government has urban roots. Its history begins with the granting of a royal charter to Saint John, New Brunswick, in 1785. That charter established the city and set out key elements of its political and administrative structure. It constituted a "body corporate and politic" of qualified inhabitants to both select and serve as holders of elected and appointed office. Ownership of property and other restrictions limited eligibility to about one-quarter of the city's inhabitants (Isin, 1995, p. 62). The charter delegated civic responsibilities and permitted the passage of local by-laws, as long as they did not contradict the higher colonial authority (Isin, 1995, p. 63).

The restrictions on participation in the Saint John government and the delegated and circumscribed nature of its authority are two characteristics that permeated other city incorporations, which began to follow after a hiatus of over 50 years. Beginning in the 1830s, we see the gradual spread of incorporation to centres like Montreal and Quebec (1832), Toronto (1834), Halifax (1841), and Ottawa (1855). Incorporation of cities west of Ontario occurred relatively more quickly after settlement. Winnipeg was incorporated in 1873, Calgary in 1884,

Edmonton in 1892, and Vancouver in 1886. The legacy began as a matter of fact and of intellectual interpretation that city governments were there to serve the specific interests of qualified electors, who were people of status and means. Use of the tool of incorporation raised the prospect that city government would do more than undertake to maintain local order. Instead it could serve as the public analogue to private corporations and devote itself to the public service of local enterprise.

Incorporation, and its legacy of restricting the role of urban government and participation in it, co-exists in a tension with the liberal democratic ideal and the legacy of seeing local governments as administrative agents of the larger state to inform, and sometimes bedevil, the conceptions of city politics and government we have today. As late as 1996, assertions of the pre-eminent role of business in urban government and the argument for special treatment were still being made.

From the standpoint of intellectual history, we see the impact of incorporation on the **metropolitan thesis**. This much-discussed conception of Canada's development is rooted in the legacy of Harold Innis's staples theory of development and focusses on the economic and ecological relationship between urban centres and their hinterland (Innis, 1956). Its economic foundation lies in the idea that cities are the gathering points for entrepreneurs and capital. This potent urban mix generates enterprises and infrastructure (such as railways), which extend the influence of the city into the surrounding region. Urban

---

BOX 3.1 OTTAWA BOARD OF TRADE WANTS ELECTED BUSINESS SEATS ON COUNCILS

The main lobby group for local business isn't satisfied with having the ear of Ottawa Mayor Jacquelin Holzman and Regional Chair Peter Clark. The Ottawa-Carleton Board of Trade wants a seat set aside on each municipal council for an elected representative of the business community.

"We think the time is right to look at this idea," says the board's president, Willy Bagnell, who unveiled the board's 1996 action plan Tuesday. "There was a time when the business community had a greater say in running local government."

Holzman said she sympathizes with business and is intrigued by a special councillor for the sector. "I would never discount it," she said, noting that in some city wards the commercial constituents have been neglected by councillors "who represent the very narrow interests of the residential population."

But Clark and other municipal politicians denounced the idea as a blatant bid for more power by a special interest group. Such a change would require legislation at Queen's Park.

Source: Excerpted from Randy Boswell, "Ottawa Board of Trade wants elected business seats on councils," *Ottawa Citizen*, January 24, 1996, pp. A1–A2. Reproduced with permission of the *Ottawa Citizen*.

enterprises import raw materials from the hinterland and export both finished goods for sale and a prevalent vision of the city as an important market centre and the centre of economic progress. Over time, the hinterland becomes increasingly dependent on the central city. The ecological formulation of the metropolitan thesis places more emphasis on city–hinterland interdependence. Rather than seeing the city as dominating the relationship and exploiting its hinterland, the ecological view sees the relationship more as mutually supportive and symbiotic (Careless, 1954, pp. 16–21; Davis, 1985, pp. 95–114).

The metropolitan thesis has also had an important influence on the emergence of Marxist and neo-Marxist analyses of urban development and government (see, for example, Leo, 1995). This has extended to critical assessments of the formative role of the development industry in urban Canada (see Lorimer, 1978, and Sewell, 1993). Its contribution in this context comes through its focus on the role of urban capital as an important link with both urban places and the development or expansion of urban space.

In summary, scholars and other observers have viewed the development of local and urban government in Canada as having diverse roots. Assessments of how and why local government emerged have been sometimes celebratory, sometimes more conspiratorial in tone. Viewing this from a historical perspective will inform our thinking about current debates concerning whether urban politics, based on liberal democratic principles, is dead.

THE LEGACIES OF SETTLEMENT

For students of urban history and contemporary urban government, the *Historical Atlas of Canada* is a gold-mine. It shows the natural development of urban Canada, based on settlement and the emergence of an urban economy. Its maps and other illustrations, plus the accompanying commentary, show the transformation of Canada from "a thinly populated, marginally viable group of colonies in 1800 to the consolidated Canada of the 1890s, poised for industrial expansion" (Matthews and Harris, 1987, Preface), and the equally dramatic shifts in population and life as Canada emerged as a highly urban country over the twentieth century.

Works such as the *Historical Atlas* and geographers' treatments of the evolution of the Canadian urban system show us the pattern of settlement in individual cities and the changing role of different cities in the fabric of Canada over time (Bourne and Ley, 1993; Preston, 1991; Yeates, 1994). For example, Winnipeg has changed from a national railway transportation hub to a predominantly regional centre. It is now focussing its economic future by assuming a central role in air freight transportation networks. The general assessment in the geographic literature is that Toronto has eclipsed all other cities as Canada's national urban centre, Montreal has experienced a decline in this regard, and Vancouver is ascending due to its role as the gateway to the Pacific Rim (Preston, 1991, p. 174).

But how do such developments relate to urban politics and government? Many of the issues that emerge on the urban political agenda and the manner with which they are dealt are affected by a lag between the legacies of earlier times and present realities. This discontinuity can be seen in the way issues are framed and in the institutions and processes that urban governments (and, in some cases, provincial governments) use to deal with them. In later chapters, we will explore how much of a lag really exists in various urban centres. First, we have to consider the link between early settlement and contemporary urban issues and the institutions and processes of urban government.

In many instances, important political and economic legacies are tied to the physical setting of Canadian cities. For example, consider the role of water in our urban evolution. Not only was water critical in determining the location of many major Canadian urban centres (e.g., deep protected harbours for Halifax and Vancouver; the confluence of important rivers in the case of Montreal, Ottawa, Winnipeg, and Calgary), it also influenced the long-standing separation of urban political boundaries within the metropolitan areas that evolved in each case. Only recently, for example, do we see the provincial government of Nova Scotia amalgamating Halifax and Dartmouth. In the Montreal area, consolidation of lower-tier political boundaries has been contained within the North Shore, with the **amalgamation** of several municipalities to form the City of Laval in 1965 and other amalgamations within the confines of the Island of Montreal and the South Shore. The situation is even more remarkable in the case of Ottawa and Hull, which are separated by a river demarking a provincial border, although as a 1988 commission on local government in the Regional Municipality of Ottawa-Carleton noted, "Ottawa-Carleton-Outaouais, taken together, is a functional economic entity . . . . Superimposed on this physical and economic reality is a grid of political boundaries, an historic legacy which does not reflect the way that the metropolitan area actually functions today" (Ottawa-Carleton Regional Review, 1988, p. 1).

It is worthwhile to think, in a similar way, about the influence of cities' early social and economic bases on contemporary urban government. There are at least three such legacies. First, the social and economic history of Canadian cities has influenced their physical layout and patterns of settlement. In some cases, topographical features have supported social predilections. We see, for example, evidence of local elites' preference for seizing the heights. In one of our cities, Ottawa, this is rendered simply in the distinction between lower town, as the long-time place of residence for the French working class, and upper town (Taylor, 1986). In greater Montreal, Westmount and Outremont were preferred locations for English- and French-speaking elites respectively; while in Calgary, the well-off initially congregated in Mount Royal. Upon death, Toronto's elite have traditionally been buried on Mount Pleasant.

Such preferences have a modern planning legacy, which suggests the continuing social differentiation in cities based on the concentration of those in higher socio-economic groups in areas with greater natural beauty or potential. For example, the model city of the Town of Mount Royal, located on the other side of Mount Royal from Westmount, was opened up in the 1930s for upwardly mobile families who hadn't yet made it to the other side. In Calgary, the original Mount Royal is a neighbourhood in transition. The local well-to-do, however, still exhibit a noticeable preference for hillside development which, in some cases, has extended beyond the city limits. In some cases, waterfront industrial areas have been targeted for redevelopment, and gentrification has resulted. Perhaps the most notable example of this has occurred in Vancouver with the redevelopment of False Creek. Thus, in the Vancouver area, we see both continuing preoccupation with the heights (the area in the City of West Vancouver known as the British Properties, which climbs up a rather steep mountainside and has the most expensive house prices in Canada) and the redirection of personal wealth to other areas with natural attraction.

One implication of this for urban governments is the potential for highly fragmented political representation and the articulation of interests based primarily on socio-economic cleavages. Another legacy has been structural fragmentation of governments in some of our metropolitan areas along socio-economic lines. In the Montreal Urban Community (MUC), for example, both the City of Westmount and the Town of Mount Royal are fiercely independent, resisting amalgamation with the City of Montreal or expansion of the role of the MUC. Either of these outcomes can increase the potential for differences within a single metropolitan area, thus affecting how urban politics are practised, how municipal administrations are structured and carry out their work, and how exclusionary or inclusive the policies and other initiatives of urban governments are. For some, such differences reflect the vitality and true role of local government. For others, the fragmentation of urban government, based on socio-economic class and the existence of enclave municipalities or electoral wards, is less positive. Our discussion of public choice in Chapter Two should help you form views concerning which side of the argument is more compelling.

The impact of the socio-economic history of our cities on their urban governments must also be considered through a somewhat wider lens. Specifically, how has the history of settlement and urban development influenced the big policy issues and preoccupations of urban governments. Writing about Vancouver, Gutstein states: "In the early years most citizens agreed that what was good for the CPR was good for Vancouver. During the twentieth century the CPR's influence waned, but city government continued to be strongly affected by business (Gutstein, 1983, p. 189).

Rapid population growth and high demand for housing in the Toronto area following World War II was a major factor in the creation of Metropolitan Toronto and in the subsequent preoccupation of Metro and Toronto area governments with land-use planning and development issues (Kaplan, 1982; Feldman, 1974; Friskin, 1988). The oil and gas boom years in Alberta had a similar impact on the governments of Calgary and Edmonton. In Calgary, the focus was on expansion of the city's political boundaries, through **annexation**, to keep pace with rapid growth (Feldman and Graham, 1979). In Edmonton, contending ideas of whether to manage growth through annexation of suburban and rural municipalities by the city or to allow existing municipalities to remain sparked an all consuming political battle between the City of Edmonton and its municipal neighbours, lasting from 1979 until 1981 (Plunkett and Lightbody, 1982, pp. 162–63). The dust remains stirred up from the Edmonton annexation fight.

We also can see examples of significant delay in urban government's recognition of important historical aspects of urban settlement. For example, the City of Winnipeg has only recently begun to involve its large Aboriginal population in initiatives related to the physical development of the city, especially in the city core, and in cultural and economic affairs. We now see the inclusion of Aboriginal people in the development of and activities at the valued juncture of the Red and Assiniboine rivers, and in other community economic development initiatives (Fielding and Couture, 1997). Africaville, the traditional Black settlement in Halifax, was razed in the urban renewal blitz of the 1960s without thought to the implications for its inhabitants or for Canadians of African origin more generally. Interestingly, a review of city politics in Halifax, published in 1983, makes no mention of the Africaville redevelopment whatsoever (Cameron and Aucoin, 1983). As of the early 1990s, however, the legacy of the razing of Africaville was assuming increasing prominence in the City of Halifax's political agenda (Africaville Genealogy Society, 1992).

In summary, then, the natural topography of cities and historical preferences and patterns of settlement by residents influence urban political boundaries, political traditions, and the agendas of urban governments.

DEFINING MOMENTS

In considering the legacies of settlement, we focussed on the effects of physical geography and demographics on urban governments. However, we must not ignore another aspect of history: the influence of key events on the shape of our cities and their urban governments. For our purposes, key events include both developments affecting cities generally and events that have altered the course of a particular city's government and politics.

Broad Trends

In some cases, our cities have been transformed by important technological breakthroughs. For example, the advent and changing roles of trains, planes, and automobiles in shaping urban life have been significant. The building of railroads provided the raison d'être or significantly augmented the importance of places like Winnipeg, Calgary, Edmonton, and Vancouver. Location of the headquarters of Canadian Pacific and Canadian National (as well as many of CN's predecessors) in Montreal was one of the cornerstones of that city's economic and political prominence, at least until the 1960s. In virtually every Canadian city, the railway station was central to the urban core. The vitality of the station area was embedded in debates about development of the central core of Canadian cities, through the urban redevelopment boom of the 1960s and into the present. For example, the fate of the old CPR station in Winnipeg was an important issue into the mid-1990s. Its reincarnation as a centre for Aboriginal people reflects recognition of the changing role of core areas in some of our cities, as well as a somewhat more inclusive urban politics.

The advent of the airplane further opened up Canadian cities to one another, to previously remote but resource-rich areas in the North and the interior, and to the world. Aside from the implications of speedier movement of people and goods for local economies, the location and development of airports emerged as an important issue for local governments, as well as for their provincial and federal counterparts. Debates over second airports and airport expansion were particularly sharp in Montreal, Toronto, and Vancouver during the 1970s (Feldman and Milch, 1982; Massey, 1972). As recently as 1995, the fate of the municipal airport in Edmonton was the subject of a hot referendum campaign, as part of the 1995 municipal election.

The importance of the automobile in the establishment of suburban Canada began to be documented by the early 1960s (Carver, 1962; Clark, 1966). The automobile did not create the suburban phenomenon. In Canada, as elsewhere, we had pre-World War II railway and streetcar suburbs, such as the previously mentioned Town of Mount Royal on the island of Montreal. The automobile did, however, have the important effect of enabling the suburbs to spread out (Rybczynski, 1995, p. 194). They spread farther away from the central city and sprawled from within, inducing further reliance on car travel for everyday errands as well as journeying to work.

We must also acknowledge the role of economic benchmarks in shaping urban government and politics. For example, cycles of boom and bust have influenced the spending priorities and capacities of urban governments. This is the case for both controllable and demand-driven expenditures. Periods of economic

---

BOX 3.2 THE REVENGE OF THE BICYCLE

The resurgence of the bicycle has been a notable aspect of urban life in more recent times. We see municipalities, such as the City of Ottawa, establishing Bicycle Advisory Committees to promote and ensure safe cycling. The Regional Municipality of Ottawa-Carleton established a bicycle pool, which provides access to bicycles for employees, as they travel on civic business. As a mode of transport with political ramifications, the bicycle has a longer urban legacy. As Nelles and Armstrong (1977) recount in their treatment of the battle for Sunday public transit in the City of Toronto, the bicycle had a role to play. The manufacture of affordable bicycles (by a Methodist-dominated company) rendered the middle class Protestant bias of city politicians of the day irrelevant. Access to this affordable mode of travel gave working people an opportunity to leave the confines of their neighbourhoods on Sunday, to seek fresh air and recreation, regardless of the municipal prohibition against streetcars on Sunday.

difficulty have also contributed to important developments in urban governments' relations with one another and with the other levels of government. For example, during the Depression of the 1930s, the mayors of Canada's largest cities first banded together to form what is now the Federation of Canadian Municipalities to lobby the federal government for legislation and other measures to alleviate the social desperation, caused by economic hardship, in cities. Soaring welfare costs during the recession of the early 1990s prompted earnest, if unsuccessful, efforts by Ontario municipalities to reform the provincial–municipal finance system in the province (Siegel, 1992).

Beyond boom and bust, we see Canadian urban governments (as well as others around the world) experiencing or considering the impact of other economic, social, and technological developments — free trade, free skies, increasing mobility of capital, changing patterns of immigration, increased participation of women in the labour force, the internationalization of discourses on politics, economics, and society via television, fax, and the Internet. These are all phenomena that have affected life in our cities and, more specifically for our purposes, urban political life and governance.

The Shock Factor

Students of public policy are often tempted to embrace theories that emphasize the gradual or incremental development of policy and the institutions that contribute to its fruition. We must not become so caught up in the broad sweep of history, however, that we forget the influence of very specific one-time events on the development of our cities. These are the one-time shocks felt long after their first impact. Our selected cities show evidence of both positive and more difficult events of this nature.

Among our cities, we can see at least three examples of one-time good news events that have definitively shaped their urban politics and government, as well as their urban milieu more generally. Queen Victoria's choice of Ottawa as Canada's capital, in 1856, was surely a defining moment for the Ottawa-Hull area and its governments. The decision had long-term, generally positive effects on the physical planning of the area and on the municipal financial base (Knight, 1991; Graham, 1992). For Vancouver and Calgary, their selection as host cities for a world's fair and the winter Olympics, respectively, gave them a new international image and local physical infrastructure, which shaped each city's economic development strategy and physical development well after the event itself.

We see the long-term impact of less welcome events as well. For example, the explosion of a munitions ship in Halifax harbour in 1917 razed a large area and caused many deaths and injuries. The resulting social and economic cost for Halifax is fairly easy to deduce (MacLennan, 1991). One additional effect of this disaster was that the City of Halifax undertook the first urban public housing initiative in Canada. Its public housing partnership with the federal government set a precedent for other cities and other times (Weaver, 1977, p. 30).

In Winnipeg, it is frequently suggested that the 1919 General Strike had a significant impact on the modern political history of that city, primarily by polarizing local politics along class lines (Wichern, 1983, pp. 39–44). Andrew Sancton suggested that, in Montreal, the violence associated with the Montreal police strike of 1969 led to the creation of the metropolitan government, the Montreal Urban Community (MUC) (Sancton, 1983, p. 80). Provincial imposition of the MUC over the City of Montreal and other area municipalities has significantly shaped the political dynamic of the Montreal area ever since. Montreal and the suburban municipalities that make up the MUC have fought over control of the metropolitan council, assessment reform, and the distribution of services, among other things.

In addition to these one-time events, the institutions of urban government have been subject to concentrated periods of political pressures for reform. As mentioned in the introduction, urban reform has been conceived in different ways and has had different impacts. We now turn to an overview of **urban reform movements** and their legacy for contemporary practices and reform ideas.

URBAN REFORM MOVEMENTS

Efforts to reform urban politics and government in Canada have been multi-dimensional. Broadly speaking, advocates of urban reform have placed varying emphasis on three initiatives: administrative managerialism, political populism, and rationalization of urban political boundaries and service responsibilities. These three streams of reform have sometimes flowed together and sometimes moved apart. Regardless, they have exerted significant influence on urban government today.

The Managerial Reform Movement

Most followers of contemporary government are aware of the intensification of efforts, in recent times, to make government operate more like the private sector. In the context of national governments we might think of the election of the Thatcher Conservatives in the United Kingdom in 1979, the establishment of the President's Private Sector Survey on Cost Control (the Grace Commission) in 1982, by U.S. President Reagan, and the establishment of the Task Force on Program Review, by the newly elected Mulroney government in 1984, as ushering in the current period of interest in private sector-oriented managerial reform (Savoie, 1994).

The idea of making the public sector operate more like the private is certainly not confined to recent times, in the case of our federal and provincial governments (see Royal Commission on Government Organization, 1962). However, the **managerial reform movement** has generally been stronger and more sustained at the municipal level in Canada. The roots of managerialism are partially embedded in the emergence of municipal governments as corporate entities, discussed earlier. Urban Canada's managerial reform movement was fertilized and brought into full flower in the early part of the twentieth century. One contributing factor was rapid urban population growth and an increasingly diverse urban population. This resulted in pressure for more diverse and technologically sophisticated urban services. Equally important, however, was the emergence of a gospel of urban reform. Canadian proponents of management reform were heavily influenced by the emergence of an urban reform movement in the United States.

The turn-of-the-century urban reform movement proclaimed a succinct diagnosis of the ills of urban politics and government. City politics were understood to be corrupt, subject to the evils of political gamesmanship, and increasingly pulled away from the essential mission, namely, the efficient administration of services to property and public protection. Whether these were real features of Canadian urban government of the time or were transplanted perceptions, based on the U.S. urban scene, has been the subject of debate (see, for example, Plunkett and Betts, 1978, pp. 98–106). Regardless, the reformers' diagnosis led to some strong prescriptions, some of which have had a lasting effect. They centred on reform of the political and administrative structures of urban governments to make them apolitical. Efficiency was seen as the foundation of a sound local economy, the engine of good urban life.

At the political level, manifestations of reform included the following:

- The removal of responsibility for key urban services, such as planning and policing, from the direct control of municipal councils. They were vested in apolitical agencies, boards, and commissions, some of which exist to this day (Richmond and Siegel, 1994).
- Establishment, in Ontario cities, of a strong political executive in the form of a board of control. Members of this board were elected at large, thereby removing them from the temptation to practise the evils of ward-based politics. The board of control (with the mayor as chair) oversaw matters related to the budget, personnel, and municipal property. It took a two-thirds vote by full council to overturn decisions of the board. This represented a significant hurdle, since controllers were included in the full council vote. By the 1990s, boards of control had virtually disappeared from the Ontario municipal scene. The single remaining board, in the City of London, no longer had the power of the two-thirds override requirement. Despite this, the legacy of the board of control has persisted in many Ontario urban centres, as similar responsibilities have been assigned to executive committees of council. More recent developments in this regard are discussed in Chapter Six.
- In many cities, especially the western cities, the abandonment of ward-based representation in favour of at-large elections. The intent was not only to free council from the corruption, patronage, and special interests that were thought to be associated with ward politics, but to squash labour's quest for power and the threat of mobilization by poor Europeans settling in the major cities (Masson with LeSage, 1994, p. 274). Calgary and Edmonton did not return to a ward system until the 1960s, and Vancouver still maintains an at-large system. In other cities, such as Toronto, large strip ward systems were developed by the reformers that permitted dominance by people reflecting a business or, at least, a middle-class ethos.

The municipal reform movement also brought about long-lasting changes in the administration of Canadian urban governments. Chief among these was the recruitment of professional city managers to oversee the full orbit of municipal operations. Again this idea was imported from the United States. The city manager model of municipal administration was intended to introduce technocratic expertise and professional detachment from politics into city hall. The city manager was retained to run the show, with council operating as a board of directors, generally ratifying the proposals of the manager and supporting the administrative apparatus he (until recently, city managers were always male) chose to put in place. The first city manager in Canada was hired by Westmount, Quebec, in 1913. In some major western cities, notably Calgary and Edmonton, the idea of managerial pre-eminence was broadened by the establishment of a committee of senior administrators (plus the mayor), known as the Board of Commissioners, to oversee the municipality.

Today most major Canadian cities have a city manager, usually called a Chief Administrative Officer or Chief Commissioner. As you will see in Chapter Seven, they are usually supported by a formal committee of senior managers. Over time, the pure city manager model, envisioned by the turn-of-the-century reformers, has become more politically sensitized. In general, the continuing legacy of the turn-of-the-century managerial reform movement has been that reform of the structure and internal operations of urban governments remain very much at the forefront of recent explorations of how to re-invent or rethink urban government (Siegel, 1993).

The Rise of Populism

Earlier we discussed the role of democratic ideals in the formation of Canadian local government. At the outset, the predominant ideal was perhaps more anti-colonial than democratic. The emphasis was on local government as an agent of self-rule, rather than widely participatory rule. Restrictions in the municipal franchise were a factor. These restrictions were both broad, for example, the general disenfranchisement of women, and, more specifically, a reflection of the corporate conception of local government.

Despite these caveats, it has been suggested that the period between Confederation and the rise of the managerial reform movement in the 1890s represents an early epoch of vital local democracy. Plunkett and Betts (1978, p. 101) argue that: "it would be true to say that in Ontario and Quebec, especially after 1867, democratic elements were relatively strong. And although property qualifications still narrowed the electorate down considerably, clear lines of responsibility existed to inhabitants. There was in fact a simplicity and direct-ness in civic life not since recaptured." The end of this golden age is attributed to the efforts of the municipal reform movement to take the politics out of local government and the increasingly active control of municipal affairs by provincial governments. Regardless of the cause, formal democratic participation in urban government in the twentieth century has been low, if measured only by the standard of voter turnout at municipal election time.

Important developments in **urban populism** between the early part of this century and the contemporary period are rooted in participation outside the traditional definitions of municipal electoral politics. For example, the 1919 Winnipeg General Strike was primarily about broader issues of labour rights, social justice, and economic well-being. Nonetheless, it shaped electoral politics in the City of Winnipeg and the agenda of its city government well past the middle of the century, as formal urban parties and other alliances were cemented along class lines (Kiernan and Walker, 1983, pp. 223–24). Similar issues and, arguably, the shock effect of the Winnipeg General Strike and a later general strike in the City of Oshawa cast a shadow over the practice of urban politics in other Canadian cities as well. For example, business leaders and municipal politicians in Toronto worried throughout the Depression about the emergence of unions as an active force in municipal politics. This, however, did not materialize (Magnusson, 1983, p. 108).

In addition to the lack of movement concerning expansion of the local franchise and reform of local ward boundaries, the rise of urban populism in the period from the early twentieth century to the end of World War II was stifled by the effects of the urban managerial reform movement. The establishment of numerous agencies, boards, and commissions to oversee key local functions was an important factor. In some cases, these special purpose bodies were made less responsive and accountable to the general public because they were captured by special interests. For example, the City of Vancouver's town planning commission was established in 1925, in response to pressure from the Vancouver Board of Trade, the Association of Property Owners (an organization of the largest property interests in the city), and other real estate interests. Once established, the commission submitted all drafts of the first master plan and zoning by-law for the city for vetting by the Association of Property Owners before sending them to the public domain (Gutstein, 1983, p. 195).

Not until the post-World War II period did major changes in the political structures of Canadian urban governments and the reshaping of public participation in local affairs take place, resulting in urban representation and politics as we now know them. This contemporary period is discussed in Chapter Five.

CHANGING URBAN FORM AND FUNCTION

If, as Plunkett and Betts suggest, a golden age of urban populism existed from Confederation until the end of the nineteenth century, the first golden age of reconceptualizing urban political boundaries and structures did not occur until the 1950s. Experimentation with new forms of metropolitan government and the re-alignment of responsibilities of urban governments among different levels or tiers at the local level consumed a major part of Canada's urban agenda, beginning with the establishment of Metropolitan Toronto in 1954. As we discuss in the next chapter, various approaches have been used to reform the structure and functions of urban governments in Canada in this golden age of reform. They reflect different conceptions of how to balance the trade-off between the public's access to their urban governments, the need for democratic accountability, and pressures for the efficient development and delivery of services in urban areas.

There are, however, two important characteristics of this particular aspect of urban reform, prior to the contemporary period, which are worth noting. These are the changes in the structures of urban government in light of population growth and the changes in the functions and finances of urban government in response to society's needs.

Growth and Urban Political Arrangements

In Chapter One, we discussed the pattern of population growth in our selected cities. To some extent, this growth was the result of migration from rural to urban Canada, supplemented by the arrival of immigrants from abroad. Population growth within existing urban boundaries was a factor in the development of urban-style housing on the edges of cities. The need to provide urban services to such developments and, in some cases, to industrial and other commercial ventures located outside city boundaries was sometimes in conflict with the traditional ethos of local politicians in rural areas. In addition, it was often beyond the technical or financial capabilities of a rural administration. The sometimes uneasy co-existence of the overspilling urban population with long-time rural residents added fuel to this mix. Until after World War II, the prevalent way of dealing with urban growth beyond existing city boundaries was through the process of annexation of the urbanized part of adjacent municipalities by city governments or, in some cases, by total amalgamation, whereby the entire adjacent township, village, or town was absorbed by its urban neighbour.

Debates about annexations and amalgamation were frequently contentious, as they are today. Annexation and amalgamation proposals were as problematic for the provincial politicians, who, in various ways, controlled their approval, as they were for the locals (Crawford, 1954). In some instances, rural municipalities were able to successfully resist losing territory or existence to urban centres. The patchwork of urban and suburban municipalities that persisted in the Halifax area until 1995 is one manifestation of this. Fierce resistance to annexation of suburban municipalities by the City of Montreal was historically based on French-English language cleavages and the preference of different language groups to live in their own preserves (Sancton, 1983, pp. 65–66). The persistence of social and political fragmentation in the greater Montreal region is indicated by the fact that the Island of Montreal consists of 29 municipalities, while the greater region consists of no less than 135 separate municipalities.

Looking at the pre-World War II period, there are two lasting consequences of the focus on annexation/amalgamation as the likely political consequence of urban population growth and overspill. The first is that this was seen as the dominant, if problematic, solution. As late as 1954, the year after the new era of political/functional reform was inaugurated with the creation of Metropolitan Toronto, Crawford's (1954) definitive work, *Canadian Municipal Government*, discussed amalgamation as the only approach to dealing with urban population growth. Clearly, the time was ripe for trying different approaches.

Second, we see the seeds of some of the approaches to major reform in the contemporary period born out of reluctance or downright resistance to annexation/amalgamation in earlier times. For example, beginning in 1914, a number of metropolitan special purpose bodies were established in the Vancouver area. These dealt with area-wide issues and service provision in matters such as sewerage and drainage, water, and public health (Gutstein, 1983, p. 194). The Montreal Metropolitan Commission was established in 1921 to supervise the financial health and borrowing of fifteen municipalities on the Island of Montreal, with a view to avoiding unwanted amalgamation with the City of Montreal. The fear was that the financial difficulties being experienced by some area municipalities would force them into amalgamation with the city with the rich tax base.

It is important to remember that these alternatives emerged as much from the **apolitical ideal** of urban managerialism as from a need to deal with urban growth. The lack of democratic accountability inherent in these approaches is now subject to considerable criticism. While the tide may have turned against the apolitical ideal, the establishment of alternative structures has proven difficult.

Changing Functions and Finances

As we approach the end of the twentieth century, we are experiencing a major public debate about the role of government generally and the preservation or reconstruction of the foundations of the Canadian social welfare state. As in the case of the contemporary effort to reform public management, much of the attention in the debate about our social safety net has focussed on the roles, responsibilities, and capacities of our federal and provincial governments. The consequences of our fiscal and social policy dilemmas are perhaps most evident on the streets and in the shelters of Canadian cities. There we see in starkest relief the faces of the unemployed, the elderly, the homeless, and others in dire straits. Urban governments have been whip-sawed as they work at the end of the chain of government cutbacks and revenue constraints. Urban governments' social assistance, public health, public housing, and other community-based programs have suffered or been eliminated.

In the context of history, the current situation is ironic. In earlier times, the effect of massive social and economic dislocation was to galvanize city governments. Urban political action had two distinguishing elements. First, city mayors, their councils, and other civic leaders successfully brought provincial governments and the federal government into joint action to deal with the problems at hand. In some cases, this started with a one-off initiative, such as the movement to provide public housing in response to the Halifax explosion. It was unique but seminal as a model for urban public housing initiatives across Canada. In other instances, cities banded together. Lobbying by the Dominion Conference of Mayors for public employment schemes and other forms of social relief in cities are a major case in point. The results of urban-based initiatives to alleviate the effects of the Depression may have varied from place to place, but they began the process of intergovernmental fiscal entanglement affecting urban affairs and urban governments. They also started the major expansion of urban government functions beyond the traditional focus on provision of services to property and the protection of public order to include a range of social initiatives and community-based programs, such as recreation and expanded public health activities. Expansion of the domain of urban government beyond its traditional responsibilities would be much more notable after World War II. In periods of prosperity, this would occur as a result of an expanded social conscience and demands for increasingly sophisticated and varied services by a public conditioned to expect activist government. It is important to understand, however, that the roots of urban governments' willingness and ability to undertake new functions in this later period stem, at least in part, from the outcome of an earlier period. That period was characterized by social and economic challenges of a similar magnitude to those we face today, when different prescriptions regarding the role and capabilities of urban government predominate. Today, urban governments are preoccupied with the reduction of public spending on social programs and the disentanglement of urban finance from the coffers of other governments. We also find the rhetoric of back to basics — emphasis on the provision of services to property and public protection — increasingly echoing through city halls. Therein lies the irony, when we think about the present in light of the history of urban governments' structure and finance.

CONCLUSION

This chapter has illustrated the diverse and important foundations of urban government and politics in Canada today. Some of these, such as the influence of location and topography, are so evident that we risk overlooking them or trivializing their importance. Others, such as the interpretation of urban government and politics by scholars and other observers, are more remote from our everyday observation and thought. All are important and contribute to our perceptions of urban government and politics and their development in real life. In the next chapter, we will begin to see how history has influenced the contemporary period by deepening our understanding of urban government and politics today.

SUGGESTED READINGS

Bunting, Trudi E. and Pierre Filion, eds. (1991). *Canadian Cities in Transition.* Toronto: Oxford University Press. A collection of essays, written mainly by geographers, that provides an excellent overview of theories and approaches to understanding the evolution and development of Canadian cities. Several chapters also address specific policy issues such as housing and planning.

Clark, S. D. (1966). *The Suburban Society.* Toronto: University of Toronto Press. A ground-breaking sociological study of suburban life in Canada.

Matthews, Geoffrey and R. Harris Cole. (1993). *Historical Atlas of Canada,* Vol. II. Toronto: University of Toronto Press. This volume examines Canada's transition from a rural to an urbanized country.

Stelter, Gilbert A. and Alan F. Artibise, eds. (1986). *Power and Place: Canadian Urban Development in the North American City*. Vancouver: University of British Columbia Press. A bibliography of Canadian urban studies to 1980.
Weaver, John. (1977). *Shaping the Canadian City: Essays on Canadian Politics and Policy*. Toronto: Institute of Public Administration of Canada. A historical examination of the rise of the urban reform movement early in the twentieth century.

BIBLIOGRAPHY

Africaville Genealogy Society. (1992). *The Spirit of Africaville*. Halifax: Formac Press.
Bourne, Larry S. and David Ley, eds. (1993). *The Changing Social Geography of Canadian Cities*. Montreal: McGill-Queen's Press.
Brittain, Horace. (1951). *Local Government in Canada*. Toronto: Ryerson Press.
Brownstone, Meyer and T.J. Plunkett. (1983). *Metropolitan Winnipeg: Politics and Reform of Local Government*. Berkeley: University of California Press.
Cameron, David M. and Peter Aucoin. (1983). "Halifax." In *City Politics in Canada*, edited by Warren Magnusson and Andrew Sancton. Toronto: University of Toronto Press, pp. 166–88.
Careless, J.M.S. (1954). "Frontierism, Metropolitanism, and Canadian History." *Canadian Historical Review*, vol. 35: 1–21.
Carver, Humphrey. (1962). *Cities in the Suburbs*. Toronto: University of Toronto Press.
Clark, S.D. (1966). *The Suburban Society*. Toronto: University of Toronto Press.
Colton, Timothy. (1980). *Big Daddy*. Toronto: University of Toronto Press.
Crawford, Kenneth Grant. (1954). *Canadian Municipal Government*. Toronto: University of Toronto Press.
Davis, Donald F. (1985). "The Metropolitan Thesis and the Writing of Canadian History." *Urban History Review* XIV (2): 95-114.
Feldman, Elliot J. and Jerome E. Milch. (1982). *Technocracy versus Democracy*. Boston: Auburn House.
Feldman, Lionel David. (1974). *Ontario 1945–73: The Municipal Dynamic*. Toronto: Ontario Economic Council.
Feldman, Lionel David and Katherine A. Graham. (1979). *Bargaining for Cities: Municipalities and Intergovernmental Relations*. Montreal: Institute for Research on Public Policy.
Fielding, Jeff and Gerry Couture. (1997). "Economic Development: The Public's Role in Shaping Winnipeg's Future." In *Citizen Engagement: Lessons from Local Government*, edited by Katherine A. Graham and Susan D. Phillips. Toronto: Institute of Public Administration of Canada.
Friskin, Frances. (1988). *City Policy-Making in Theory and Practice: The Case of Toronto's Development Plan*. Local Government Case Studies #3. London: University of Western Ontario, Department of Political Science.
Graham, Katherine. (1992). "Capital Planning/Capital Budgeting: The Future of Canada's Capital." In *How Ottawa Spends: The Politics of Competitiveness*, edited by Frances Abele. Ottawa: Carleton University Press, pp. 125–50.
Gutstein, Donald. (1983). "Vancouver." In *City Politics in Canada*, edited by Warren Magnusson and Andrew Sancton. Toronto: University of Toronto Press, pp. 189–221.

Higgins, Donald J.H. (1986). *Local and Urban Politics in Canada*. Toronto: Gage.

Innis, Harold A. (1956). *Essays in Canadian Economic History*. Toronto: University of Toronto Press.

Isin, Engin. (1992). *Cities without Citizens. Modernity of the City as a Corporation*. Toronto: Black Rose Books.

———. (1995). "The Origins of Canadian Municipal Government." In *Canadian Metropolitics: Governing Our Cities*, edited by James Lightbody. Toronto: Copp Clark Publishing.

———. (1995a). "Rethinking the Origins of Canadian Municipal Government." *Canadian Journal of Urban Research*, 4(1): 72–92.

Kaplan, Harold. (1982). *Reform, Planning and City Politics: Montreal, Winnipeg, Toronto*. Toronto: University of Toronto Press.

Kiernan, Matthew and David Walker. (1983). "Winnipeg." In *City Politics in Canada*, edited by Warren Magnusson and Andrew Sancton. Toronto: University of Toronto Press, pp. 222–54.

Knight, David B. (1991). *Choosing Canada's Capital: Conflict Resolution in a Parliamentary System*. Ottawa: Carleton University Press.

Leo, Christopher. (1995). "The State in the City: A Political-Economy Perspective on Growth and Decay." In *Canadian Metropolitics: Governing Our Cities*, edited by James Lightbody. Toronto: Copp Clark Publishing, pp. 27–50.

Lightbody, James, ed. (1995). *Canadian Metropolitics: Governing Our Cities*. Toronto: Copp Clark Publishing.

Lorimer, James. (1978). *Developers*. Toronto: James Lorimer & Co.

MacLennan, Hugh. (1991). *Barometer Rising*. Toronto: McClelland and Stewart.

Magnusson, Warren and Andrew Sancton, eds. (1983). *City Politics in Canada*. Toronto: University of Toronto Press.

Massey, Hector J. (1972). *People or Planes*. Toronto: Clark.

Masson, Jack. (1985). *Alberta's Local Governments and Their Politics*. Edmonton: Pica Pica Press.

Masson, Jack K. with Edward C. LeSage. (1994). *Alberta's Local Governments*. Edmonton: University of Alberta Press.

Matthews, Geoffrey and Cole R. Harris. (1987). *Historical Altas of Canada*. Toronto: University of Toronto Press.

Nelles, H.V. and Christopher Armstrong. (1977). *The Revenge of the Methodist Bicycle Company: Sunday Streetcars and Municipal Reform in Toronto: 1888–1897*. Toronto: Peter Martin Associates Ltd.

Ottawa-Carleton Regional Review Commission. (1988). *Phase II, Functions and Finances*. Toronto, ON: Queen's Printer for Ontario.

Plunkett, T.J. and G.M. Betts. (1978). *The Management of Canadian Urban Governments*. Kingston, ON: Queen's University Press.

Plunkett, T.J. and J. Lightbody. (1982). "Tribunals, Politics, and the Public Interest — The Edmonton Annexation Case." *Canadian Public Policy* VIII (2): 207–21.

President's Private Sector Survey on Cost Control. (1984). *A Report to the President*. Washington, DC.

Preston, Richard E. (1991). "Central Place Theory and the Canadian Urban System." In *Canadian Cities in Transition*, edited by Trudi E. Bunting and Pierre Filion. Toronto: Oxford University Press, pp. 148–77.

Richmond, Dale and David Siegel, eds. (1994). *Agencies, Boards, and Commissions in Canadian Local Government*. Toronto: Institute of Public Administration of Canada.

Royal Commission on Government Organization (Glassco Commission). (1962). *Report*. Ottawa: Queen's Printer.

Rybczynski, Witold. (1995). *City Life*. Toronto: HarperCollins.

Sancton, Andrew. (1983). "Montreal." In *City Politics in Canada*, edited by Warren Magnusson and Andrew Sancton. Toronto: University of Toronto Press, pp. 58–93.

———. (1994). *Governing Canada's City-Regions: Adapting Form to Function*. Montreal: Institute for Research on Public Policy.

Savoie, Donald. (1994). *In Search of a New Bureaucracy*. Toronto: University of Toronto Press.

Sewell, John. (1993). *The Shape of the City*. Toronto: University of Toronto Press.

Sharpe, L.J. (1981). "Theories of Local Government." In *Politics and Government of Urban Canada* 4th ed., edited by Lionel D. Feldman. Toronto: Methuen, pp. 28-38.

Shortt, Adam. (1913). "The Beginning of Municipal Government in Ontario." In *Transactions of the Canadian Institute*, edited by Adam Shortt and Arthur G. Doughty 7: 409–24.

Siegel, David. (1992). "Disentangling Provincial–Municipal Relations in Ontario." *Management*. Fall, Institute of Public Administration of Canada.

———. (1993). "Reinventing Local Government: The Promise and the Problems." In *Rethinking Government*, edited by Leslie Seidle. Montreal: Institute for Research on Public Policy, pp. 175–202.

Taylor, John. (1986). *Ottawa: An Illustrated History*. Toronto: James Lorimer & Company.

Tindal, C.R. and S.N. Tindal. (1995). *Local Government in Canada*, 4th ed. Toronto: McGraw-Hill Ryerson.

Weaver, John C. (1977). *Shaping the Canadian City: Essays on Urban Politics and Policy, 1890–1920*. Toronto: Institute of Public Administration of Canada.

Wichern, P.H. (1983). "Historical Influences on Contemporary Politics: The Case of Winnipeg." *Urban History Review* XXII (1): 39–44.

Yeates, Maurice. (1994). "The Windsor–Quebec Corridor." In *Canadian Cities in Transition*, edited by Trudi E. Bunting and Pierre Filion. Toronto: Oxford University Press, pp. 178–208.

CHAPTER FOUR

◆

THE CHALLENGE OF GOVERNANCE: STRUCTURING THE METROPOLIS

INTRODUCTION

This chapter deals with contemporary approaches to the structure, form, and functions of urban governments. As noted in the previous chapter, Canada has an extensive history of local government restructuring and reform. Some legacies of the past should be kept in mind as we look at the contemporary period:

- The notion that urban and rural are different and should be kept separate as units of local government are established. This is one legacy of the Baldwin Act of 1849.
- Our inheritance from the turn-of-the-century urban reform movement, specifically the creation of local special purpose bodies, operating at arm's length from municipal councils, and the emphasis on managing urban growth through annexation/amalgamation or through the creation of special purpose bodies whose mandate crossed municipal boundaries.
- The legacies of settlement, as settlement patterns reflected the social differentiation in cities.

The evolution of contemporary urban form and structure is inextricably linked to the challenges of urbanization. Local circumstances have generated pressure for reform. This pressure has been rooted, to varying degrees, in what Lithwick has termed the problems *of* the city (i.e., spatial growth and growth management) and problems *in* the city (i.e., including issues of equity of service and access to urban government) (Lithwick, 1970, pp. 14–17).

The political saga of contemporary reform also varies from location to location. Important factors influencing the course of reform include historical legacies and attitudes, both at the local level and within provincial governments; the fiscal environment; the constellation of public interest groups contesting local issues; and contemporary public opinion.

As you will see, efforts to reform urban government in Canada have taken different forms and had different outcomes. Political and public reaction has been mixed. Across our cities, you can see examples of reform that have been relatively uncontroversial (Calgary, Halifax, and Vancouver); instances where restructuring has been hotly contested, but where there has been some (sometimes significant) movement (Edmonton and Winnipeg); and instances of apparent gridlock (the Greater Toronto Area, the Greater Montreal Region, and Ottawa-Carleton). If the Ontario government has its way, the Greater Toronto Area and the Ottawa-Carleton region will undergo significant change.

Before describing the course of contemporary urban reform and restructuring or assessing outcomes, we must consider three essential ingredients in contemporary urban reform and restructuring:

- conceptions of the urban region;
- perceptions of what constitutes appropriate local or urban functions; and
- conceptions of what the appropriate institutions of local authority are and the nature of the mandate they should be given.

The art of cooking provides a good analogy for thinking about how urban governments become structured. First, there are the basic ingredients — the three listed above. Just as there are different kinds of flour, sugar, and other basic cooking ingredients, so we see variations across the country in the ingredients for the structuring of urban areas. These basic ingredients and their variations will be explored as the chapter proceeds.

The real art of cooking is reflected in the fact that different chefs can use similar ingredients to prepare dishes appealing to different tastes. The art of the good cook is to prepare a very palatable dish, which either reinforces existing taste preferences or induces us to try something new.

The same challenge exists for proponents of **urban restructuring**. In this case, the skill of the "chef" lies in an ability to marshal convincing evidence about the need for reform and the merits of specific proposals. The final section of this chapter will explore the outcomes of contemporary efforts to do this in our selected cities. Equally important as having evidence and the ability to conceive a grand recipe for reform is the requirement to sway public and political opinion about the merits of reform proposals. The grandest confection is worthless if no one will partake.

THE BASIC INGREDIENTS
Conceptions of the Urban Region

City-regions are not defined by natural boundaries. Because they are wholly the artifacts of the cities at their nuclei, the boundaries move outward — or halt — only as city economic energy dictates (Jacobs, 1984, p. 45).

> [A] metropolitan area consists of a central city, several suburban cities (residential or industrial or both, and of various sizes) and, in the interstices between the cities, villages and unincorporated places. . . . What makes it a unity, to the extent that it is one, is a common orientation — cultural and political, perhaps, but mainly economic — toward the central city. (Banfield and Wilson, 1966, pp. 7–8)

> The Task Force has based its definition of the GTA (Greater Toronto Area) on three criteria: **commutershed**, or the web of commuting patterns that help delineate an economic region; cohesiveness, by which we mean the sense of relationship and common citizenship that transcends local boundaries; and anticipated development, which dictates that areas of future urbanization be

THE CHALLENGES OF GOVERNANCE: STRUCTURING THE METROPOLIS 67

included for the purposes of planning and managing growth. (Greater Toronto Area Task Force, 1996, p. 24)

The reason there are no "Welcome to" signs at **Edge City** is that it is a judgement call where it begins and ends. (Garreau, 1991, p. 6)

DEFINING THE URBAN REGION: WHAT'S IN A NAME?

Where do any of our cities end? Are cities always densely built up? Can we really speak of the city, or is the reality of our urban life that we live in complex urban regions? Answers to these questions are found in the different conceptions of urban development and the reach of cities as quoted above.

Most certainly, the concept of "the city" is a misnomer. The conception of the metropolis that emerges from the previous quotes, as well as from observation, is one of a city-region. Perhaps the most fundamental element of the city-region is that it contains a variety of places — communities with a social or political identity — and a variety of spaces — urban, suburban, and even rural. Garreau, in his book, *Edge City* (Garreau, 1991), goes so far as to suggest that the notion of the "central city," implicit in earlier conceptions of the urban region, should be called into question, as nodes of settlement that contain both residential development and significant employment spring up around established central cities. Writing in the American context, Garreau adopts a definition of an edge city that includes the criterion that it has "more jobs than bedrooms" (Garreau, 1991, p. 7). In the Canadian context, we might ask if places like Laval (Montreal), Kanata (Ottawa), and Surrey (Vancouver) are moving into the edge city category.

There are some other important elements of the conception of the urban region. First is the significance of economic interdependence as a criterion for defining the boundaries of the urban region and for holding it together. Second is the notion of some common orientation or cohesiveness among the region's population. This is somewhat more complex and abstract than the binding ties of economy. It is, however, clearly important when one thinks about governing the urban region.

Finally, most of the conceptions of the city-region before us show a preoccupation with the need to understand and manage the dynamics of urban growth and containment. Jacobs and Garreau, respectively, refer to changing urban boundaries linked to economic fortunes and to the fluidity of an edge city's boundaries. The Greater Toronto Area Task Force's (also referred to as the Golden Task Force, after its head) definition of the Greater Toronto Area (GTA) demonstrates preoccupation with planning and managing anticipated development.

What does all this mean for the course of urban politics and management? The complexity of urban regions, in Canada and throughout the world, has resulted in a need to reconcile their spatial development and their common orientation with other elements of local political and social life. In short, there is a need to reconcile the complexities of city-regions' spatial form with the functions of urban servicing and with the development of a constructive civic society.

SPATIAL GROWTH PATTERNS

When thinking about the spatial form that different urban regions take, it is important to think of the influence of natural and other historical factors on the pattern of urban development and the influence of policy decisions. To a considerable degree, the patterns of development and the influence of policy are intertwined. It is largely a question of when governments have chosen to intervene. For example, a Restricted Development Area, imposed around Fish Creek in Calgary in the mid-1970s, was a policy response to the perceived need to protect a natural environment from rapid urban growth (Feldman and Graham, 1978, pp. 75–80). In other cases, topographical features have proved immutable and have been a dominant influence on urban spatial development without the early intervention of policy. In this context, we can think of the long-time separation of Halifax and Dartmouth. Until they were amalgamated in April 1996, these two cities eyed each other across the waters of Halifax harbour.

Economic history has also played an important role in the early spatial form of what have become Canada's urban regions. For example, Oshawa, now considered part of the GTA, was, until the early 1980s, much more distinct from Metropolitan Toronto than it now is. It was separate not only in a spatial sense but was seen as its own economic and political node (Ontario, 1972), tied to the automotive industry and centre of the Regional Municipality of Durham, established in 1974. New Westminster was initially separated from Vancouver in a physical sense and had its own economic niche (Gutstein, 1983, p. 193).

Finally, we want to remember the role of early market towns, on the periphery of burgeoning cities, as nodes of growth in the modern period of complex urbanization. In this context, we might think of the Town of St. Albert, near Edmonton; places like Cooksville and Streetsville, which are now part of Mississauga, which is itself part of the GTA; and places like Ste. Hyacinthe and the forerunners to the present City of Laval, which are part of the Montreal urban region.

Contemporary Urban Form and Governance

What spatial form do our urban regions now take? How have we connected form and other aspects of "urbanness" to governance? This has been the central challenge of urban reform and restructuring in the contemporary period. Over 30 years ago, Banfield and Wilson noted, "No metropolitan area has a general purpose government serving the whole of it" (Banfield and Wilson, 1966, p. 8). As recently as 1996, the Golden Task Force on the GTA, various municipal governments in the area, and the government of Ontario struggled with the question of defining appropriate units of local government and intergovernmental arrangements for an area extending from Lake Ontario to Lake Simcoe, on the north–south axis, and from Port Hope to Hamilton Bay, on the east–west axis. Commentaries on Vancouver deal variously with the Greater Vancouver Regional District, the Vancouver Census Metropolitan Area, the Lower Mainland, and the "Pacific Fraser" region (Oberlander and Smith, 1993, p. 331). The Montreal region is more than the area under the jurisdiction of the Montreal Urban Community (MUC). We must include Laval and the South Shore as well.

In thinking about spatial configuration as one of the essential ingredients in our recipe for urban reform and restructuring, it is useful to consider three conceptual models: **central urban growth**, **nodal urban growth** and a **spread growth model** of urban spatial development (IBI Group, 1990, S-1, cited in Frisken, 1993, p. 170).

- The central model describes an urban area with intense and dense population and commercial growth in its core. The amount of space outside established urban boundaries devoted to urban development is relatively small.
- The spread model perhaps best reflects the Canadian postwar urban experience. It describes the creeping or the galloping city, with land on the outskirts being absorbed for relatively low density residential purposes and some commercial purposes, largely of a service or industrial nature.
- The nodal model describes designated growth centres within the overall urban region, most often the central city and a few designated suburbs or edge cities. The nodes are connected, perhaps by transportation and other communication links. They may or may not be connected in terms of water and sewer systems and the other underpinnings of physical urban development. An aerial view of a city-region established on the nodal model would show substantial green spaces separating the nodes.

These distinctions are obviously ideal types. Figure 4.1 shows them in their pure form.

In reality, our chosen cities show a tendency to reflect one form more than the others. One might argue that the course of urban development in every case following World War II was a reflection of the spread model. This was certainly the pattern of development in places like Winnipeg, Calgary, the Greater Toronto Area, and Ottawa-Carleton.

FIGURE 4.1 IDEAL MODEL

 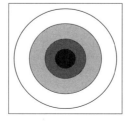 

Nodal Model   Spread Model   Central Model

BOX 4.1 MISSISSAUGA ON NODAL GROWTH

COMPACT DEVELOPMENT

The nodal form of development builds on existing communities and their infrastructure. It provides for continuing population and employment growth in the suburban and the central built-up areas, while stressing compact, mixed-use communities which would favour urban transit, walking, and cycling for many trips. It also recognizes the rural areas that exist with the GTA.

The nodal form also provides the greatest range of choice in terms of population density and housing types, community size and character, suburban and downtown living styles, transportation modes, and integrated delivery of services.

Source: Submission to the GTA Task Force by the City of Mississauga, "Running the GTA Like a Business," *Report of the Greater Toronto Task Force*. Toronto: Queen's Printers for Ontario, 1996, p. 113.

There has, however, been increasing interest among planners and other urban policy makers in the nodal form. As early as the mid-1970s, when Calgary was absorbing new land faster than any other city in Canada, city planners promoted the idea of focussed nodal growth as part of the city's 1978 General Plan review. It was an idea whose time had not yet come.

During the same period in Ontario, the emphasis was on reform to create modern units of political responsibility through the establishment of regional governments, mostly around Toronto. But political restructuring was overtaken by provincial support of water service and sewer arrangements, which promoted spread growth (Frisken 1993, pp. 171–77; Ontario, 1974). This is the physical and urban growth pattern that did occur, with the contemporary challenges of governing the Greater Toronto Area being one result. Ironically, what we now see in the GTA are efforts by outlying municipalities, many of which are essentially Metro Toronto suburbs, to solidify their political survival by arguing that they are or should become growth nodes.

The GTA case illustrates the potency of the mix of our three basic ingredients in the recipe for local government reform and restructuring. We now proceed to consider the other two basic ingredients of urban reform and restructuring.

The Functions of Urban Government

Box 4.2 shows the extensive range of functions assigned to local government in Canada.

BOX 4.2 MAJOR FUNCTIONAL RESPONSIBILITIES OF CANADIAN LOCAL
GOVERNMENTS

Public education — elementary and secondary
Policing
Fire protection
Animal control
Roads — construction and maintenance, traffic control, parking, and
street lighting
Public transit
Water supply
Electricity and natural gas supply
Sewage — collection and treatment
Solid waste — collection and disposal
Land-use planning and regulation
Building regulation
Economic development and promotion
Public libraries
Parks and recreation
Public cultural and heritage facilities
Business licensing
Emergency planning
Social services — income support, personal social services, and social
planning
Public health — health inspection, promotion, and planning

In developing a very similar list, Sancton made the important point that
there are significant variations in the responsibilities assigned to the local level
among the provinces and among cities within the same province (Sancton
1994, p. 11). In one unique arrangement, the government of British Columbia
retains responsibility for public transit within the Vancouver area. The most
extensive local involvement in social services is found in Ontario. In other
places, the provincial government has assumed full responsibility for administering income support, assisted by the federal government, under the Canada
Health and Social Transfer (CHST).

THE CONTEMPORARY PERIOD

It is important to understand that the assignment of functions to the local level
has changed over the years. The contemporary period has been characterized by
considerable turbulence as provincial governments have assumed some functions and assigned others to the local level. An overview of some important
examples of functional re-alignment illustrates this.

Quebec

The Quebec Union of Municipalities was perhaps the first locally focussed organization in Canada to suggest the link between functional re-allocation and the **downloading** of additional financial obligations to the local level. It objected vigorously to provincial reforms in 1990 and 1991 that opened the local property tax base to school boards as a means of financing newly devolved responsibilities for financing school maintenance and, almost simultaneously, shifted additional responsibilities from the provincial to the local level for public transit, roads, and policing. In Quebec, the re-alignment of provincial and local government responsibilities continues to be on the table. The 1996 Quebec Budget took up the theme of provincial local re-alignment, as well as the prospect of other structural reforms at the local level involving the fusion of municipalities.

Nova Scotia

The government of Nova Scotia undertook a so-called service exchange initiative in 1992, announcing it would assume full financial and administrative responsibility for social services and devolve further responsibility for transportation to the local level (Task Force on Local Government, 1992). When the Halifax Regional Municipality was officially launched on April 1, 1996, the province assumed supervision of former local social services staff involved in administering income support programs. It also assumed responsibility for the full cost of these programs, while decreasing transportation grants to the new municipality.

Ontario: Crombie and "Who Does What?"

The Nova Scotia initiative is similar to proposals made in the early 1990s for the re-allocation of functions and finances between the provincial and local levels in Ontario. Negotiations on the exchange of responsibility for social services and transportation were intense between 1991 and 1993, when the Association of Municipalities of Ontario rejected a draft agreement which would have brought about such a change. The rejection stemmed from the specifics of the financial arrangements proposed rather than from rejection of the principle that functions should be re-allocated (Tindal and Tindal, 1995, pp. 203–204). This illustrates the strong link between functional reform and fiscal reform, which has accompanied re-allocation of functional responsibilities between the provincial and local levels in Quebec, as well as in the other cases cited.

Election of a new Conservative government in Ontario in 1995 prompted the most extensive review of provincial and local responsibilities yet undertaken in Canada. Shortly after the election, the government tabled a 1995 Fiscal and Economic Statement and a Savings and Restructuring Act, 1995, to implement sweeping changes to governance in Ontario. In jurisdictions with two-tier regional governments, the Savings and Restructuring Act provided for more fluid migration of functions from regional to area municipalities and vice versa.

In May 1996, the Minister of Municipal Affairs appointed a panel, chaired by former mayor of Toronto and federal Cabinet Minister David Crombie to spend the next six months developing recommendations concerning "who does what" to govern Ontario. This unique exercise had no process of public consultation, nor did the panel undertake research to support its deliberations. Instead it looked at previous studies and reports on the issues included in its mandate.

By December 1996, the "Who Does What?" panel had made numerous recommendations. It advocated changing the property tax system, a new municipal act, greater municipal responsibility for the costs of policing and many physical services, overhauling education governance and financing, assumption of all responsibility for income support and family and children's services by the province, and an approach to restructuring the GTA and other regional and county governments.

The speed and breadth of the panel's recommendations caused alarm in municipal quarters. This was quickly overshadowed, however, by the government's pronouncements on many of these same issues. These were rendered during "mega-week" in January 1997. Particularly surprising was the government's intention to increase local governments' funding responsibility for social services and public health to 50 percent of the total and to transfer downward the full responsibility for social housing. This distribution of responsibilities had not been the subject of any prior public discussion. A period of intense negotiations ensued between the province and municipalities. These culminated in the May 1997 announcement by Ontario that it would revert to funding arrangements for social services similar to those previously in place.

The Nature of the Local State

The final basic ingredient is the local state itself. Our conception of the local state was first introduced in Chapter Two. It consists of two elements, both of which are discussed more fully in Chapter Seven:

- municipal government — the mayor and council; and
- special purpose bodies — agencies, boards, and commissions with responsibility for single purpose functions at the local level. These range from education to policing to public transit, to name just a few.

It is also important to remember the strengthening trend of entanglement of both elements of the local state with the voluntary sector. We have characterized this sector as the phantom arm of the local state. We discuss the voluntary sector more fully in Chapter Six. It includes:

- Neighbourhood associations that have roots in a geographic territory.
- Issue-oriented groups and identity-based social movements that build social communities of interest which are not primarily geographically centred. These groups are born in a political capacity, representing their constituencies, and in a service role, engaging in the delivery and co-production of an increasingly wide range of services.
- Local service clubs such as the Kiwanis and Rotary.

In addition to these voluntary groups, highly organized, sophisticated, and well-resourced business associations are active across a range of issues. They use a variety of means to get the attention of local councils and special purpose bodies.

Conclusion: The Basic Ingredients

You now have a basic sense of the spatial, functional, and institutional aspects of cities and their governments — the three basic ingredients for reform and restructuring. But, as the introduction to this chapter indicated, the process of reform and the environment in which it is attempted are crucial to actual outcomes. A review of the efforts to reform and restructure our selected cities will illustrate this point.

RESTRUCTURING THE METROPOLIS

Taking a snapshot of the current state of urban reform and restructuring across our selected city-regions, we find some interesting variations. In three cases, the Greater Toronto Area, the Greater Montreal Region, and the Ottawa-Carleton Region, the prospect and process of reform have been accompanied by a debate about what should be done to develop local solutions, as opposed to relying on provincial government intervention. In the Halifax area, provincial government action has recently resulted in dramatic restructuring. This followed many years of failure by the voluntary inter-municipal Metropolitan Authority to achieve progress on key environmental and servicing issues, partly as a result of political parochialism. In other places, we see tentative steps toward locally generated reform. In Edmonton, for example, current initiatives are occurring in the shadow of a tradition of inter-municipal squabbling and suspicion between the central city and its surrounding municipalities. Finally, our selection of urban regions includes places that are adapting readily to the challenges of growth and changing political realities without much controversy. Winnipeg, Calgary, and Vancouver fall into this category. The complex web of inter-municipal arrangements in the Vancouver region belie the idea that unitary structures, such as those found in the other two cities, are a requirement for relatively smooth urban reform.

Examination of the history of urban reform and the nature of contemporary initiatives in each place suggests some possible explanations concerning why we find these variations and commonalities across the country.

The Greater Toronto Area

METROPOLITAN TORONTO

In Chapter Three, we noted that annexation and amalgamation were the common solutions to the challenges of urban growth and overspill prior to the end of World War II. The crush of urbanization in the Toronto area immediately following that war initially portended business as usual. However, in a departure from past practice, the government of Ontario spurned a 1953 annexation bid by the City of Toronto. Instead it established a two-tier federal arrangement for governing this rapidly growing area.

The Municipality of Metropolitan Toronto came into existence in 1953. Its initial mandate was to plan for the entire metropolitan area (plus territory beyond its formal boundaries) and to develop the sophisticated urban infrastructure required to service the region's rapid and substantial growth. "Metro," as it became known, oversaw construction of major water, sewer, and transportation networks in its early years. The conventional wisdom is that Metropolitan Toronto was a resounding success. Sharpe has described it as "a jewel in the crown among metro authorities around the world" (Sharpe, 1995). The Toronto region grew and prospered. The provincial government made periodic adjustments to the metropolitan arrangement in the wake of royal commissions appointed to review the arrangement in the mid-1960s and 70s. The major change in this period was a reduction in the number of lower-tier municipalities to six and assignment of responsibility for social services and policing to the upper tier. This occurred in 1967. At the same time, a system of designating the number of seats on Metro council to lower-tier municipalities based on their population was put in place. This shifted the power on Metropolitan Toronto Council from the City of Toronto to the suburban boroughs (Frisken, 1993, p. 165).

EMERGENCE OF THE GREATER TORONTO AREA

The apparent success of the Metro model was a factor influencing the province's decision to establish regional governments, modelled on the same lines, in a number of urban regions in Ontario. Between 1971 and 1974, Metropolitan Toronto became ringed with three regional municipalities: Peel, York, and Durham. A fourth, Halton, was also part of the Toronto commutershed.

From the mid-1970s until the early 1990s, the Greater Toronto Area experienced significant population and economic growth. The urban region was transformed, both physically and in terms of the social and demographic characteristics of its population. Locally and within the government of Ontario, awareness grew of the interconnectedness of life and governance in the GTA. In 1988, the provincial government established its own Office for the Greater Toronto Area, headed by a deputy minister. The objective of this initiative was partly to coordinate work among the five regional municipalities on issues such as transportation and solid waste disposal for the GTA. It also paralleled the emergence of major political fault lines within Metropolitan Toronto and between Metro and its surrounding regions. Contentious issues included:

- How to maintain and enhance the prosperity of the entire GTA, in light of the enhanced ability of companies to change locations and move capital in the new global economy.
- How to achieve prosperity of the central city (the City of Toronto) and the central region (Metro) in light of the emergence of strong edge cities, in places like Mississauga, Brampton, and Oshawa.
- How to finance future growth and development in the GTA, given problems with the existing system of local government finance and significantly different recipes for reform advocated by different municipal governments in the GTA.

- The emergence of notable social differences in terms of the living circumstances and lifestyle preferences of people who reside in the centre of the GTA and on its periphery. The phenomenal development in the outlying area of the GTA was reflected in the designation of its own telephone area code in the early 1990s. The "905 Belt," as it became known, provided strong support for the provincial Conservative Party in its 1995 Ontario election win, presumably on the basis of the tax cut and other "small c" elements of the party's platform.
- Tensions within Metropolitan Toronto itself. Beginning in 1989, the members of Metro Council were directly elected. Political tensions between Metro and the lower-tier councils, particularly the City of Toronto Council, escalated. City council's perception of a suburban bias on the part of Metro Council and the persistently thorny issue of property tax reform, which pitted the central city against the suburbs in Metro, induced the City of Toronto Council to put a question calling for the dissolution of Metro on the 1994 municipal election ballot.

The Golden Task Force

These factors compelled the provincial government to act once again. It established the Task Force on the Future of the Greater Toronto Area on April 1, 1995. The Golden Task Force, as it became known, reported to the newly elected Conservative government of Ontario in January 1996. Its report made recommendations regarding the issues identified above. Its approach to restructuring the GTA also reflected some of the prevailing trends in thinking about local government and provincial–local relations.

The key principles underlying Golden's recommendations include:

- The structuring of urban servicing responsibilities based on the principle of subsidiarity — in other words, provided by the lowest level of government that has the capacity to do so (Golden, p. 146).
- The disentanglement of provincial funding and policy responsibilities between the provincial and municipal levels (p. 142).
- Greater freedom of action to municipalities through provincial legislation that establishes local governments and sets out their roles and responsibilities (p. 157).
- Making the municipal revenue system, particularly the property tax system, equitable and sensitive and able to provide for revenue sharing across an integrated urban region, such as the GTA (pp. 73–110).

The Golden Task Force also made recommendations concerning the political organization of the GTA. Most important were its recommendations to replace the five existing regional governments with a single Greater Toronto regional government, with a more limited number of functions (p. 166). This government would be headed by an indirectly elected Greater Toronto Council. It was also recommended that local municipalities be strengthened, consistent with the principles summarized above and by reducing the number of special purpose bodies in various localities (p. 166 and pp. 147–49). The task force suggested, however, that special purpose bodies made up of volunteers should be retained.

Response to the Golden Report

When members of the Golden Commission met with the newly elected premier of Ontario to discuss their report, they all sported campaign-style buttons that read "Implement the Sucker!" (Jack Diamond, 1996). This gesture was prompted by a number of factors influencing the possible implementation of the reforms the commission proposed or, for that matter, any other changes to current governing arrangements for the GTA. There was no political consensus among GTA municipalities about the Golden Task Force proposals, although some agreement did exist about the need for reform.

In late fall of 1996, the waters became murkier as the Minister of Municipal Affairs floated the trial balloon that he was in favour of reforming Metropolitan Toronto to create one large "supercity," eliminating the six lower-tier municipalities. He stated, "Amalgamating and having one city would give Toronto tremendous international recognition and presence when dealing with trade and other issues." The minister also believed that a single-tier Toronto would have a better chance of attracting the 2008 Olympics (Wright, 1996, p. A1).

From the beginning, this proposal caused a political firestorm within Metro, as local mayors and the chair of Metropolitan Toronto debated proposals and counter-proposals for reform. In short, everyone had his or her own solution for the GTA's governance. Competing research and argumentation were habitually used by all sides. It was as much a war of numbers as of words. Every side claimed considerable cost savings would be realized if its proposal were adopted. This made it difficult for the public to reach concensus about the need for reform and the shape it should take.

In December 1996, the "Who Does What?" Panel made its pronouncement on the GTA. It recommended consolidation within Metropolitan Toronto (although not necessarily a single city), consolidation of municipalities elsewhere in the GTA, and the creation of a regional services board for the GTA. It would consist of representatives from Toronto plus those from newly amalgamated municipalities outside the Metro boundary. The panel offered no blueprint for municipal amalgamation elsewhere in the GTA. It simply advocated the idea and recommended that the province immediately appoint an implementation commissioner to establish the Greater Toronto Services Board and direct the dismantling and amalgamation of local governments throughout the area by January 1, 1998. The Crombie panel further exacerbated the provincial government's political difficulties by asserting strenuously that restructuring of local government within Metropolitan Toronto should not occur without implementing the full package of its GTA recommendations. In the words of David Crombie, "I want them to staple the GTA to Metro" (De Mara and Moloney, 1996, p. A1).

In summary, the provincial government was confronted with three basic choices by the end of 1996:

- The GTA Task Force recommendation — dismantling upper-tier regional governments throughout the GTA and creating a GTA Council with a limited set of functions.
- Its own trial balloon — eliminating lower-tier governments within Metropolitan Toronto and letting GTA governance and reform in the "905 Belt" evolve.
- The "Who Does What?" Panel recommendation — creating a single government for Metro and appointing an implementation commissioner to establish a GTA Services Board for overseeing the major servicing issues in the GTA and to design and implement single-tier amalgamations throughout the GTA.

In terms of the political calculus involved, choosing from these seems delicate indeed. Metropolitan Toronto is home to major corporate interests, as well as significant population. Some of the government's most powerful ministers, including the Minister of Municipal Affairs and Housing, come from metro ridings. However, the government's significant political support in the "905 Belt" is at least as important as the central city in this calculus (Walkom, 1996, p. B4)

In January 1997, the provincial government introduced legislation to eliminate lower-tier governments within Metropolitan Toronto and create a new megacity. The rest of the GTA was left untouched, although all municipalities would be affected by the wholesale shift in municipal functions stemming from "mega-week."

Within Metropolitan Toronto, this plan was highly controversial and was subject to mounting attacks from many quarters. Local mayors and councils were upset that the province would not consider holding any public vote on the change. Undaunted, most area municipalities undertook their own referenda or opinion polls. In each case, the majority of citizens voicing their opinions were opposed to the supercity plan. The minister responded to this result by suggesting that people did not understand what they were voting for. Numerous public meetings and other protests were held. In addition, Crombie himself and the Metro Toronto Board of Trade began to criticize the government. They argued that the government was trying to do too much too quickly without adequate evidence of the benefits (James Rusk, 1997, p. A1). The cost savings that the province suggested would accompany this change were subject to dispute, with two of the country's largest accounting firms offering competing sets of cost estimates. Finally, the government found itself in legal difficulties. In its rush to seal the change, the Ontario government had appointed three trustees to oversee the affairs of all of Metro's municipalities until the new city came into being in 1998. The province appointed these trustees prior to passage of the legislation creating the new supercity, effectively kneecapping local democracy throughout Metro. Shortly thereafter, the courts overturned these appointments, ruling that the government had acted *ultra vires*. In another extraordinary development, the

Speaker of the provincial legislature found the government in contempt of the legislature for sending a pamphlet to all Metro's residents speaking of the reform as a fait accompli, before the legislation had been passed. The Minister of Municipal Affairs apologized. All of this indicates that the march to reforming Metro would not be as smooth and fast as the province had thought. Nonetheless, Bill 103, the City of Toronto Act, came into law on April 21, 1997. The new Toronto would be launched on January 1, 1998, subject to Ontario winning a court challenge by area municipalities against the legislation.

The Greater Montreal Region
EARLY DEVELOPMENT OF THE MONTREAL URBAN COMMUNITY

Similar stresses and strains accompany the realization of reform in the Greater Montreal Region, which now includes 135 municipalities. These municipalities include the Island of Montreal, with its 29 area municipalities and the over-arching government of the Montreal Urban Community (MUC); the relatively new but dynamic edge city of Laval (established in 1965 by amalgamating 14 small rural villages on Île-Jésus, it is now the second largest city in Quebec); and a number of municipalities on the South Shore of the St. Lawrence River and twelve adjoining Regional County Municipalities (RCMs), established following legislation by the Quebec government in 1979 (Trepanier, 1993, p. 64; Tindal and Tindal, 1995, pp. 132–33).

The MUC itself has had a somewhat more checkered history than Metropolitan Toronto. It was established by the government of Quebec in 1969 as a two-tier federal arrangement. However, the upper tier was not given a significant range of authority. Its major function, initially, was policing. In its early years, other initiatives, such as regional planning and assessment reform, were made difficult by the political dynamic on the MUC Council between representatives of the City of Montreal and the suburban mayors sitting on the council. The suburbs were very protective of their turf and suspicious of any attempts by then mayor of Montreal, Jean Drapeau, to use the MUC for his own and the city's ends. Under the legislation establishing the MUC, suburban mayors effectively had a veto on the MUC Council, which they used to block metropolitanization (Sancton, 1983, p. 80).

Provincial reforms to the MUC were undertaken in 1982. To a significant degree, they responded to a suburban perspective. Among these reforms was the establishment of a bipartite commission structure to replace the former MUC Executive Committee. Each of five permanent commissions was designated with responsibility for a specific set of MUC functions. Under legislation, the chair and vice-chair of each commission were to be drawn equally from both Montreal and suburban representatives on the MUC Council. This approach to managing the affairs of the MUC, and the re-affirmation of the principle that the MUC would only be assigned responsibilities agreed to by its constituent municipalities, made MUC politics more harmonious but sustained the MUC as a relatively weak metropolitan structure (Trepanier, pp. 75–78).

The Montreal City Region: Economy and Governance

In the aftermath of the MUC reforms of the early 1980s, the broader Montreal urban region has faced significant challenges. Perhaps chief among them has been coping with major recessions and issues of poverty and differential development within the region itself. In a relative sense, Laval, the South Shore, and the western parts of the MUC have sustained themselves or, particularly in the case of Laval, prospered. In contrast, the central and eastern districts of the City of Montreal have high chronic unemployment, abandoned industrial sites, and related problems of urban decay and dislocation.

Facing these problems, the local community has been understandably preoccupied with economic development issues, as has the government of Quebec. It is generally recognized that the Montreal region is the engine of the province's economy, and its political make-up makes it centrally important to any provincial government.

Parallel with the development of various strategies for the economic improvement of the region, the Task Force on Greater Montreal, established by the Minister of Municipal Affairs in 1992, made recommendations about structural reform of the urban region, designed to deal with the problem of differential development. The task force's report (the Pichette Report), released in 1993, recommended that a Montreal Metropolitan Region be established. The boundaries of the new region would correspond to those of the Montreal Census Metropolitan Area and would be adjusted as the definition of the Montreal CMA changes in the future. The task force proposed that the region be governed by an indirectly elected regional council with responsibility for, among other things, creation of a regional land-use plan; economic development; and the planning and co-ordination of services such as transportation, policing, and environmental services.

New Inter-municipal Services Areas (ISAs) would take responsibility for inter-municipal co-ordination on joint service issues and have the power to borrow to make capital improvements. The ISAs were, in part, an outgrowth of the task force's decision not to recommend any amalgamations of lower-tier municipalities in the region (Sancton, 1994, pp. 87–89).

Aftermath of the 1993 Regional Proposals

The recommendations to formalize local governance over the entire Montreal urban region generated considerable controversy at the local level. They also created similar political dilemmas for the Quebec government to those made by the Golden Task Force. Upon assuming the premiership in 1996, Lucien Bouchard designated one of his most senior Cabinet members as Minister Responsible for the Montreal Region. The minister took a plan to create a single metropolitan region to Cabinet shortly thereafter, but it was rebuffed (Cherney, 1996, p. A8). Instead the minister was redirected to focus his attention on creating an economic development commission for the region. The link between economic development and the need for political restructuring is still being promoted by local business interests, however.

The political balance is delicate within the provincial government and in terms of the provincial–municipal and inter-municipal relationship. As with the GTA, future developments will confirm whether or not this is the recipe for gridlock in terms of reform and restructuring in the contemporary context.

Ottawa

THE REGIONAL MUNICIPALITY OF OTTAWA-CARLETON

The Ontario government established the Regional Municipality of Ottawa-Carleton (RMOC) in 1969, as the first of the two-tier arrangements building on the success of Metropolitan Toronto. Initially dominated by the City of Ottawa, whose entire council sat on regional council, the RMOC also consisted of growing suburban municipalities, two very small urban municipalities, and extensive, primarily rural townships. The regional arrangement was fine-tuned in the mid-1970s, following the report of a review commission (Mayo, 1974), but the essentials of political representation, based on indirect election of regional council, and the retention of a startling mixture of lower-tier municipalities remained.

By the mid-1980s, the Regional Municipality of Ottawa-Carleton had become a large and complex municipal operation. A regional Official Plan was in place. The RMOC had overseen development of extensive regional water, sewer, and transportation networks and created sophisticated departments of social services and health. Its annual budget was approaching $1 billion.

The political dynamic of the time was telling. Members of regional council, who were elected primarily to hold office at the local level, showed a strong tendency to criticize the regional arrangement as if they were not implicated in its very work. In the mid-1980s, a committee of the RMOC Council was struck to recommend restructuring reforms. It foundered, however, as a result of its members' inability to consider amalgamating lower-tier municipalities or other boundary changes.

The province of Ontario stepped in. A series of three commissioners was appointed to examine various aspects of reform in Ottawa-Carleton (Bartlett, 1986 and 1988; Graham, 1990; Kirby, 1992). As a result of their recommendations, the Regional Municipality of Ottawa-Carleton Act was amended in 1992 to provide for direct election of regional council. Regional ward boundaries were drawn across the boundaries of local municipalities to promote a broader perspective among regional councillors. This reform was particularly contentious among the mayors of local municipalities, who were angered at being excluded from regional council. Anxiety about the system of local government in the region was fuelled by reductions in provincial–municipal grants; campaigns by local business groups for simplification and less government at the local level; concerns about the future of the regional economy, in light of reductions in direct federal government employment in the region; and concern that the provincial government would impose a "made-in-Toronto solution" to local government, following the provincial election in 1995. The prospect of finding a local solution was hindered by the requirement that any locally generated restructuring proposal must have the support of a triple majority — a majority of regional council and the majority of lower-tier councils representing a majority of the region's population.

CONTEMPORARY REFORM INITIATIVES

These pressures resulted in a variety of local efforts to explore reform. Local municipalities initiated talks on service sharing and several considered possible amalgamation. The City of Ottawa prepared a formal report and held a symposium on alternative governance of the region, laying out four one-tier options for the Ottawa region (City of Ottawa, 1996).

The regional municipality had little option but to be drawn into the debate. In November 1996, the region released a report advocating a streamlined two-tier structure, with a significant reduction in the number of lower-tier municipalities. This prompted all local mayors, excluding the mayor of the City of Ottawa, to caucus and announce that they were working on a scheme that would replace the regional municipality with an inter-municipal co-ordinating body and the existing eleven lower-tier municipalities with three or four new ones. Perhaps because of its preoccupation with Toronto, the provincial government stepped back in Ottawa-Carleton, sending somewhat mixed signals to local officials. The minister indicated that an earlier April 1997 deadline for local agreement was no longer firm. At the same time, however, he appointed a facilitator to help reach a local agreement, suggesting the province still wanted to see something happen. As a result, local politicians confronted three challenges: what model of reform to adopt, whether to press ahead to implement the chosen approach as of the fall 1997 municipal election, and how to meet the requirement for public consultation·and engagement in coming to these decisions. Faced with these challenges, local politicians began to grasp for help from a citizens' panel, a representative group of local citizens who would come to judgement on the best model of reform and engage the rest of the public as it went about this process.

The Halifax Regional Municipality

ORIGINS OF REFORM

The Halifax case illustrates an example of decisive provincial action to bring about major urban government reform. It would be a mistake, however, to think that the amalgamation of the cities of Halifax and Dartmouth with the Town of Bedford and the County of Halifax occurred overnight. Instead this dramatic reform, which resulted in the creation of a municipality with a land area larger than Prince Edward Island, had a long gestation period.

The 1974 Report of the Royal Commission on Education, Public Services, and Provincial–Municipal Relations in the Province of Nova Scotia (the Graham Commission) recommended sweeping changes in the division of provincial and municipal government responsibilities, creation of a new system of single-tier counties in the province, and an overhaul of the system of local government finance. Although this massive report landed with a distinct thud at the time, it proved to be a seminal document for recent reforms in the Halifax area and for other changes in the Nova Scotia local government system.

Twenty years after release of the Graham Commission Report, the Nova Scotia government decided to proceed with amalgamation of the cities of Halifax and Dartmouth, the Town of Bedford, and Halifax County Municipality. This decision was influenced by concern within the provincial government and locally (as expressed by the local business community) that the Halifax region emerge as the "capital" of Atlantic Canada and as a competitive player in the changing global economic environment.

It was also affected by public dissatisfaction over an ineffective two-tier arrangement. The Halifax-Dartmouth Metropolitan Authority was established in 1962 to co-ordinate and provide a number of physical and transportation services. It was also given a permissive planning function — it could do regional planning, but there was no requirement for conformity by member municipalities. Its council was indirectly elected, consisting of representatives from four member municipalities. It was constantly beset by internal political wrangles over financing its work and different visions about priorities. It never really took up the regional planning function and proved to be particularly ineffective in dealing with major challenges, such as the environmental clean-up of Halifax harbour. Its only success was the establishment of a metropolitan public transit system.

In light of all of this, the provincial government commissioned a review of the Halifax region. The 1993 Report of the Municipal Reform Commissioner on the Halifax Region (the Hayward Report) recommended that the province establish a single-tier municipal government with a directly elected mayor and council. It also recommended that the external boundaries of Halifax County be set as the boundaries of the new municipality. Issues of community participation and accountability were to be dealt with through the development of an electoral ward system and the establishment of community councils, consisting of three or more councillors from contiguous wards, with some powers regarding planning decisions and the establishment of special area tax rates.

Local area councils opposed the Hayward proposals. They claimed that amalgamation was being railroaded through, and collaborated to commission their own study, which recommended more of a consortium approach to inter-municipal co-operation. However, a newly elected provincial government (headed by John Savage, the former mayor of Dartmouth) acted on the reform commissioner's recommendations.

THE 1994 REFORM

In October 1994, the Nova Scotia government announced establishment of the new Halifax Regional Municipality. Key elements of the amalgamation were as follows:

- Elimination of most of the existing local special purpose bodies, except the police commission. The Hayward Report also recommended continuation of the Halifax Water Board. This was left for consideration by the new municipality's council.

- Retention of 33 volunteer fire departments in the suburban and rural parts of the municipality. This was both a political and economic necessity. Volunteer fire brigades were seen by provincial officials as pillars of community life. The prohibitive expense of establishing a completely professional fire department throughout the area would have been sufficient to scuttle the reform.
- Announcement of intention to re-align provincial and municipal government responsibilities. This was modelled on the previously discussed provincial policy of service exchange.
- Appointment of the former municipal reform commissioner to oversee the amalgamation, which was to result in the launch of the new municipality on April 1, 1996.

The structure and political dynamic of the new municipality are still emerging. The first council was elected from 23 wards. The long-time mayor of the City of Halifax, Walter Fitzgerald, won election as the first mayor. It is unclear whether the new council will avail itself of the option, available through the legislation establishing the new municipality, to set up community councils.

The establishment of the Halifax Regional Municipality provides an example of a provincial government administering a strong dose of medicine to municipalities unable to bring about significant reforms themselves. The difficulties of generating regional reforms at the local level are also evident from the Toronto, Montreal, and Ottawa-Carleton cases. In another urban region, Edmonton, we see tentative steps to develop local approaches to reform, in part to avoid the heavy-handedness of the past.

Edmonton

THE HISTORICAL CONTEXT

Until recently, local government reform and restructuring in Alberta has emphasized the geographic expansion of cities, through annexation, to accommodate urban growth. Of the province's two major cities, Edmonton's outward expansion has been much more contentious than Calgary's. This can be attributed to the persistence of historic settlements on the periphery of the Edmonton region, most notably the City of St. Albert and Town of Fort Saskatchewan, and the County of Strathcona's zealous defence of its assessment-rich "refinery row," which brings significant financial benefit.

Many of the nineteen Edmonton-area municipalities were drawn into an extended, expensive, and extremely bitter annexation battle, which began in 1979 when the City of Edmonton applied to annex over 180 000 ha, including the entire County of Strathcona and City of St. Albert. The magnitude of this attempt is indicated by the fact that Edmonton only occupied 32 000 ha at the time of its application (Tindal and Tindal, 1995, p. 142). The affair came to an official end in 1981, when the provincial Cabinet awarded Edmonton 35 000 ha in a compromise decision that retained the existing local government structure in the region.

CATALYSTS FOR CHANGE

The legacy of this annexation battle still affects inter-municipal relations in the region. A number of provincial reforms, particularly since Ralph Klein became Alberta premier in December 1992, may, however, serve as catalysts for local innovation. The first was a new perspective on regionalization by the provincial government. It disbanded one set of regional institutions, the regional planning commissions. These organizations, including the Edmonton Regional Planning Commission, had been established following World War II to co-ordinate land-use planning on a regional basis. These special purpose bodies had boards made up of representatives of the councils of their member municipalities. In the urban regions of Calgary and Edmonton, the planning commissions had come to be viewed as ineffective, doing little more than rubber stamping proposals from member municipalities. At the same time, the provincial government did not turn its back on the notion of regionalization. Indeed, it signalled endorsement of the concept through creation of regional health boards to manage the allocation of health-care resources on a regional basis.

The other catalyst for change was the passage of the Alberta Municipal Government Act in 1994. This act is discussed more fully in Chapter Eight on intergovernmental relations. It is important in this context for two interrelated reasons. First, it was the mechanism for replacing the regional planning commissions with a more localized planning process. Equally important, the new legislation also imposed requirements on municipalities to co-ordinate planning and develop means for resolution of planning disputes.

These developments have contributed to the establishment of a new voluntary planning organization for the Edmonton area. The Capital Regional Forum was established in 1995. It is unique in the sense that it operates by consensus. Only with agreement of its members will the forum take up an issue. Resolution of issues is also to be achieved through consensus-style decision making.

It is too early to assess the Capital Regional Forum's success. Thirteen of the 19 municipalities in the Edmonton region initially agreed to participate. Three of the four rural municipalities, however, refused to become charter members. Nonetheless, the Capital Regional Forum provides an example of an innovative local attempt to deal with the challenges of urban growth and governmental co-ordination. It is at the opposite end of the spectrum from the grand designs of amalgamation that characterize current reform initiatives in other parts of the country.

Winnipeg, Calgary, and Vancouver: Stable Approaches to Governing Urban Regions

The story of urban reform and restructuring in the rest of our selected cities has a different text. In Winnipeg, Calgary, and Vancouver, we find examples of relatively stable approaches to governing urban regions. This should not be attributed to lack of urban growth or other challenges. Calgary and Vancouver have been among the most dynamic urban regions in Canada in terms of population growth, economic change, and physical development. In the period following World War II, Winnipeg has been more stable in these terms. It has, however, faced significant challenges in terms of revitalization of its central core and the accommodation of a growing population of urban Aboriginal people. Compared to the city-regions we have reviewed in more detail, the structure of urban government in these three regions is notably less contentious from both a political and more public perspective. However, they do have differing structures.

WINNIPEG

Following its restructuring into a large single-tier "unicity" in 1972, Winnipeg has been extensively studied by academics and other city-regions contemplating reform and restructuring. (See, for example, Kaplan, 1982; Plunkett and Brownstone, 1983.) The provincial legislation establishing the new arrangement replaced a two-tier metropolitan structure, with twelve area municipalities and a metropolitan council, elected from wards that crossed local area boundaries. The long-time mayor of the City of Winnipeg, Stephen Juba, had carried out a relentless campaign against the metropolitan model. Further, the provincial government of the day had cause for concern that differences in the financial health of the twelve local municipalities were contributing to significant inequities in local services.

The initial unicity arrangement has been widely cited as an example of bold structural reform. This is not only because of the move to a single tier. In addition, the architects of the reform proposals had recommended:

- creation of an exceptionally large city council to govern the city (50 members);
- creation of an executive structure for the new council that resembled Cabinet-style government; and
- an innovative approach to citizen involvement in neighbourhood decision making, through the establishment of Resident Area Advisory committees (RAGs) and thirteen community committees of councillors from different sections of the city with power to deal with selected local matters.

The 1972 reform was also accompanied by the administrative unification of major urban services, the establishment of a uniform property tax rate for the entire city, and the legislative mandate for Winnipeg to produce a development plan that would reflect Winnipeg's mandated land-use control over an additional zone outside its formal boundaries (Frost, 1996).

The concept of single-tier government for Winnipeg had become well accepted by the time its enabling legislation was first reviewed in 1976. This review and a subsequent review committee, which reported in 1986, resulted in changes to Winnipeg's governing legislation to make the institutional arrangements accompanying unicity more conventional. Since 1972, the size of council has been reduced significantly, from 50 councillors plus the mayor, to fifteen councillors plus the mayor. The community committees have been reduced from thirteen to five and the resident advisory groups have been seriously weakened. Critics have argued that these changes, plus the marked decline in spending in the urban core immediately following unification, all symbolize unicity's failure (Gerecke and Reid, 1992). Nonetheless, the unicity arrangement appears to be well entrenched in Winnipeg. The only spoiler has been the community of Headingly, which the Manitoba government permitted to secede from Winnipeg in 1992. The rationale was that Headingly was more of a rural community, not requiring urban services such as those found throughout the rest of Winnipeg.

The future of unicity will be determined by the way Winnipeg and the Manitoba government propose to deal with increasing urban overspill, particularly beyond the city's northern boundary. Restiveness about the need for community sensitivity, in the face of the abandonment of the institutional approaches to community government put in place in 1972, may also be a future challenge. For the moment, however, the fundamentals of unitary government in the City of Winnipeg appear secure.

CALGARY

Calgary has had unitary urban government since it was founded. There has been virtually no pressure from either local or Alberta government sources to depart from this tradition. Instead changes in Calgary's government have taken the form of internal adjustments to political arrangements, such as the size of council and ward boundaries, and management reforms. The pattern of dealing with urban growth through annexation is also very well established and uncontentious.

In short, Calgary is much richer as a site to explore in the context of its internal management and the city's approach to the creation of a livable region, from land-use, social, and economic development perspectives, than as a hotbed of urban reform and restructuring.

VANCOUVER

The relative tranquillity of Vancouver as a site of significant reform and restructuring cannot be attributed to local preferences for single-tier or other "simple" arrangements. Indeed, the government of the Greater Vancouver Regional District (GVRD) and, increasingly, the entire lower British Columbia mainland is characterized by considerable institutional complexity. The conventional wisdom is that regional reform and restructuring in the Vancouver region have been relatively uncontroversial because of "the politics of gentle imposition" (Tennant and Zirnhelt, 1973, pp. 124–38).

As discussed in Chapter Two, urban growth and the challenges of providing urban services to this dynamic region have long been accompanied by a willingness to embrace special purpose bodies for the regional planning and delivery of services, ranging from water and sewer to public health. The somewhat subtle move to a more comprehensive regional approach began in 1967 with the provincial government's creation of the Greater Vancouver Regional District (GVRD), as one of the network of regional districts established throughout British Columbia. The key characteristic of these arrangements that distinguishes them from two-tier governments in Ontario is that they have very few provincially mandated responsibilities. Vesting responsibility for major urban services in the GVRD was left to the discretion of its member municipalities.

In the fifteen years following the creation of the GVRD, its board, consisting of designated members of local councils, became the replacement for long-standing organizations such as the regional water and sewer boards, various local health and hospital boards, and the Lower Mainland Planning Authority. This occurred under the rubric of tidying up the previous array of special purpose bodies rather than the creation of a government per se (Sancton, 1994, p. 65).

One of the functions that the British Columbia government initially assigned to the GVRD was the development of a regional land-use plan. This was achieved through the 1975 Livable Region Plan, adopted by the GVRD Board. Planning was removed from the GVRD's mandate in 1984 as part of the province's move, in an atmosphere of considerable political rancour, to reduce the influence of local government. Demonstrating considerable local political support, the GVRD retained its mandate for a regional planning function. The geographic boundaries of the GVRD have expanded since its inception; however, we still see the difficulty of aligning governing arrangements with the full urban dynamic on the British Columbia lower mainland.

At present, the GVRD consists of a 32-member board, five of whom are members of the City of Vancouver Council. Its jurisdiction covers eighteen municipalities and three unincorporated electoral areas. Aside from public health and hospitals, the GVRD has never been assigned any responsibility for social services, although it does have a social planning advisory committee. The establishment of new regional health boards in British Columbia affects the GVRD's role in this area. Another important challenge facing the Vancouver city-region relates to transportation planning. Although the GVRD has worked with the provincial government on a transportation process, the province continues to play the dominant role, buttressed by its direct control over operation of public transport in the Vancouver area.

Despite the fact that it has a current annual budget of approximately three-quarters of a billion dollars and approximately 1000 employees, it is debatable whether the GVRD sees itself or is perceived by the public as a regional government. The relative absence of high profile politics at the GVRD Board reinforces a different image. Regardless, there is little pressure for change in the concept or the structure of the GVRD.

Conclusion

This overview of contemporary debates about and reforms to the political boundaries, institutions, and functions of selected Canadian cities illustrates important elements affecting reform. They include the following:

- The prevailing political culture, both at the provincial and local levels.
- The extent to which proposed reforms are seen to benefit the population at large or to result in significant redistribution or targeting of benefits.

- The extent to which the provincial government has room to manoeuvre. In many instances, reform has occurred early in a provincial government's mandate.
- The presence of a widely recognized "urban problem," be it related to management of growth, economic development, environmental sustainability, or social or demographic issues.

Ironically perhaps, disposition to change on the part of urban governments themselves is not on this list. The cases we have reviewed indicate a greater tendency for urban governments to resist changes in boundaries, the distribution of functional responsibilities, and governing institutions at the local level than to embrace them. Even in instances of agreement about the need for change, recipes for reform have had many local variations. Indeed, it appears that the skills of a master chef are needed to work magic on these basic ingredients of urban reform in order to achieve success.

SUGGESTED READINGS

Garreau, Joel. (1991). *Edge City*. New York: Doubleday. An examination of the rise of new centres with both housing and employment at the periphery of traditional cities.

Kaplan, Harold. (1982). *Reform, Planning, and City Politics: Montreal, Winnipeg, Toronto*. Toronto: University of Toronto Press. The experience of these cities is compared using a form of systems analysis that builds on the works of Talcott Parsons.

Lustiger-Thaler, Henry, ed. (1992). *Political Arrangements: Power and the City*. Montreal: Black Rose Books. Case studies of urban reform using political economy and feminist analysis.

Plunkett, T.J. and Meyer Brownstone. (1983). *Metropolitan Winnipeg: Politics and Reform of Local Government*. Berkeley: University of California Press. A detailed examination of the development and implementation of the unicity model.

Sancton, Andrew. (1994) *Governing Canada's City-Regions: Adapting Form to Function*. Montreal: Institute for Research on Public Policy. An examination of perspectives on reform in different centres and an exploration of the role of public choice in contemporary thinking about urban restructuring.

BIBLIOGRAPHY

Banfield, Edward C. and James Q. Wilson. (1966). *City Politics*. New York: Vintage Books.

Bartlett, David. (1986, 1989). *Report of the Ottawa-Carleton Regional Review*, Vols. 1 & 2. Toronto: Queen's Printer for Ontario.

Cherney, Elena. (1996). "Region Needs More Co-ordinators New Board-of-Trade Chief Says." *The Gazette* [Montreal], September 20, p. D8.

Committee of Review, City of Winnipeg Act (P. Taraska, Chairman). (1976). *Report and Recommendations*. Winnipeg: Government of Manitoba.

De Mara, Bruce and Paul Moloney. (1996). "Name GTA Czar, Crombie Urges." *The Toronto Star*, December 7, pp. A1, A32.

Diamond, Jack. (1996). "New Terms of Reference for Municipal Government." Address to the CAMA–IPAC–PCM Seminar, March 5, Hull, Quebec.

Feldman, Lionel. (1974). *Ontario 1945–1973: The Municipal Dynamic*. Toronto: Ontario Economic Council.

Filion, Pierre. (1992). "Government Levels, Neighbourhood Influence, and Urban Policy." In *Political Arrangements: Power and the City*, edited by Henri Lustiger-Thaler. Montreal: Black Rose Books, pp. 169–83.

Frisken, Frances. (1993). "Planning and Servicing the Greater Toronto Area." In *Metropolitan Governance*, edited by David Rothblatt and Andrew Sancton. Berkeley, CA and Kingston ON: Institute of Governmental Studies Press and Institute of Intergovernmental Relations, Queen's University.

Frost, Richard. (1996). "The Winnipeg Experience from Two Levels to One." Presentation to the civic symposium Seizing the Future. April 1996, Ottawa.

Garreau, Joel. (1991). *Edge City*. New York: Doubleday.

Gerecke, Kent and Barton Reid. (1992). "The Failure of Urban Government: The Case of Winnipeg." In *Political Arrangements: Power and the City*, edited by Henri Lustiger-Thaler. Montreal: Black Rose Books, pp. 123–42.

Graham, Katherine A. (1990). *Report of the Electoral Boundaries Commission for Ottawa-Carleton*. Toronto: Ministry of Municipal Affairs.

Greater Toronto Area Task Force. (1996). *Report of the Greater Toronto Area Task Force*. Toronto: Queen's Printer for Ontario.

Gutstein, Donald. (1983). "Vancouver." In *City Politics in Canada*, edited by Warren Magnusson and Andrew Sancton. Toronto: University of Toronto Press, pp. 189–221.

Hayward, William C. (1993). *Interim Report of the Municipal Reform Commissioner*. Halifax: Government of Nova Scotia.

IBI Group and Associates. (1990). *Greater Toronto Area Urban Structure Concepts Study, Summary Report*. Toronto: The Greater Toronto Co-ordinating Committee.

Jacobs, Jane. (1984). *Cities and the Wealth of Nations*. New York: Random House.

Kaplan, Harold. (1982). *Reform, Planning, and City Politics: Montreal, Winnipeg, Toronto*. Toronto: University of Toronto Press.

Kirby, Graeme. (1992). *Ottawa-Carleton Regional Review Commission: Final Report*. Toronto: Ontario Ministry of Municipal Affairs.

Lithwick, Harvey. (1970). *Urban Canada: Problems and Prospects*. Ottawa: Central Mortgage and Housing Corporation.

Mayo, Henry. (1974). *Report of the Ottawa-Carleton Review Commission*. Toronto: Ministry of Treasury, Economics, and Intergovernmental Affairs.

Nova Scotia Task Force on Local Government (W. Hayward, Chair). (1992). *Report*. Halifax: Nova Scotia Department of Municipal Affairs.

Office of the Chief Administrative Officer, City of Ottawa. (1996). *One-Tier Government Option for Ottawa-Carleton*. Ottawa: City of Ottawa.

Ontario. (1972). *Proposal for Local Government in an Area East of Metropolitan Toronto*. Toronto: Queen's Printer for Ontario.

Ontario. (1996). *A Guide to Municipal Restructuring*. Toronto: Ministry of Municipal Affairs.

Ontario Fair Tax Commission. (1993). *Fair Taxation in a Changing World.* Toronto: University of Toronto Press.

Plunkett, T.J. and Meyer Brownstone. (1983). *Metropolitan Winnipeg: Politics and Reform of Local Government.* Berkeley: University of California Press.

Rusk, James. (1997). "Municipalities Face Financial Crisis, Board of Trade Says." *The Globe and Mail,* January 25, p. A1.

Sancton, Andrew. (1983). "Montreal." In *City Politics in Canada,* edited by Warren Magnusson and Andrew Sancton. Toronto: University of Toronto Press, pp. 58–93.

———. (1994). *Governing Canada's City-Regions: Adapting Form to Function.* Montreal: Institute for Research on Public Policy.

Sharpe, L.J. (1995). "Is There a Case for Metropolitan Government?" Paper presented at the conference Urban Regions in a Global Context. Toronto, ON: University of Toronto.

Tennant, Paul and David Zirnhelt. (1973). "Metropolitan Government in Vancouver: The Politics of Gentle Imposition." *Canadian Public Administration,* 16: 124–38.

Tindal, Richard C. and Susan Nobes Tindal. (1995). *Local Government in Canada.* Toronto: McGraw-Hill Ryerson.

Trepanier, Marie-Odile. (1993). "Metropolitan Government in the Montreal Area." In *Metropolitan Governance,* edited by David Rothblatt and Andrew Sancton. Berkeley, CA and Kingston, ON: Institute of Governmental Studies Press and Institute of Intergovernmental Relations, Queen's University, pp. 111–52.

Walkom, Thomas. (1996). "Harris Landed Two Tiers of Grief." *The Toronto Star,* December 27, p. B4.

Wright, Lisa. (1996). "Leach Nails Megacity's Clout." *The Toronto Star,* November 2, p. A1.

◆
POLITICS, ELECTIONS, AND REPRESENTATION

INTRODUCTION

It has become fashionable to argue that urban politics is dead or, alternatively, that it was never truly alive in the first place. As Mark Gottdiener (1987, p. 13) asserts, "the very heart and soul of local politics has surely died. A form without content remains." Death is indicated by very low levels of voter turnout and by a lack of public debate over fundamental issues of social justice and visions of the future for metropolitan areas. An autopsy reveals multiple causes of death including a loss of community, particularly in the central cities; the handing over of political issues to professional managers; the intervention of senior levels of government which dictate local policy and control resources; and powerful multinational corporations that have created social, economic, and geographic restructuring (Gottdiener, 1987, p. 14; cf. Clarke and Kirby, 1990). Urban governments then cannot and perhaps have never performed the democratic functions attributed to them (Magnusson, 1981, p. 61).

This perspective, which is shared by public choice, growth machine, and many political economy theories alike, derives largely from the view that the central role of urban government is to control and service property in an efficient manner. As the politics of property, virtually all conflict can be located on a pro-anti-development spectrum (Sancton, 1983, p. 295). There is seen to be little scope for other kinds of issues, no need for fundamental debates about quality of life, and minimal interest by citizens, as long as things work reasonably well.

This chapter argues that the reports of the death of urban politics are premature. As we noted in Chapter Two, the view that cities are technocratic providers of services is a myopic view of the nature of urban life. In fact, the politics of everyday life can be the most important arena in which debates about social justice and quality of life are played out. The attempt to understand political participation and citizen engagement by focussing almost exclusively on elections — and therefore concluding that, due to low voter turnout, citizens regard urban issues as irrelevant to their lives — is too narrow a perspective on the nature of representation. At the municipal level, electoral politics are only a small part of — and arguably not the most important vehicle for — political participation. In addition to the chance to vote, residents in most cities can appear before council or a council committee to make their concerns and viewpoints heard. **Plebiscites** are a frequent means of testing public opinion on important matters. Community associations, social movements, and interest groups provide ongoing means of citizen involvement and mechanisms for lobbying governments on issues of concern to both geographic and social communities. Finally, urban governments have been pioneers in establishing innovative means of public participation, which afford citizens the opportunity to partake in developing a vision of the future for their communities and increasingly to participate in budgeting exercises and the redesign of governance structures. With this wealth of ongoing opportunities to voice one's opinion, voting may seem like a mere blip in the overall process of representation.

Our analysis of representation and politics in Canadian cities begins with an examination of the more traditional democratic machinery involving elections, **open government** and plebiscites. In the following chapter, we discuss the additional means for citizen engagement in politics through interest groups and public participation exercises.

MUNICIPAL ELECTIONS AND VOTING

Municipal elections differ from provincial and federal ones in several ways. First, municipal elections are held at fixed intervals, every three years in eight provinces and the territories and every four years in Quebec and Newfoundland. In addition, they are always held on a specified date as set by the provincial Municipal Act (e.g., the second Monday in November). This imposes a large degree of regularity and predictability on the timing of and preparation for electoral campaigns. Second, the mayor is elected at large which greatly enhances the legitimacy and credibility of the position, and in all major cities except Vancouver, councillors are elected on a **ward** or constituency basis. In fact, the mayors of Canada's major cities are elected by more people than the prime minister of the country. For example, 526 300 people are eligible to vote for the regional chair of Ottawa-Carleton while an average of only 57 500 people can vote for the prime minister (depending on his or her specific riding). Third, municipal ballots are generally crowded since not only are the mayor and council elected, but school board trustees and certain agencies, such as parks boards and utilities commissions, are elected as well. This makes for long lists for the voter to sift through. Finally, few cities have political parties, so ballots do not bear party labels next to a candidate's name as easy identifiers. Collectively, these characteristics put a greater onus on the municipal voter to know the candidates as individuals and to know a variety of candidates for different positions. This complexity is often pointed to as one explanation for low voter turnout in municipal elections.

Voting Rules and Turnout

When first established in Canada, municipal elections were not intended to be expressions of local democracy but to protect the interests of property. Thus the rules were designed to exclude the riff-raff. In the 1800s, most municipalities had relatively high property requirements for voter eligibility and even higher ones for candidate qualification. Women were not eligible to vote in most municipalities until well into the twentieth century, although there had been some earlier provisions for widows and unmarried female property owners. The rules governing municipal elections have been liberalized rather slowly. As late as 1952, a property or tax-paying qualification was still required in seven provinces (Higgins, 1986, p. 319). Until 1962, Montreal had a very complex set of franchise rules that had been imposed by the province under conditions of trusteeship. One-third of council was appointed by designated institutions such as universities and trade unions, one-third was elected by property-owners, and one-third was elected by all householders (Sancton, 1983, p. 68). Not only did this scheme protect the propertied class, but it bolstered Anglophone representation on council. In Alberta municipal elections before 1983, a candidate's occupation could be shown on the ballot. This subtly discriminated against new candidates because it allowed incumbents to list their occupations as mayor or alderman (Masson with LeSage, 1994, p. 306).

Today the franchise has been made universal, and the rules regarding who can vote and who can run as a candidate are very straightforward. As set out in provincial municipal acts, the general requirements are simply that a voter be a Canadian citizen, 18 years of age, and meet a residency requirement (which varies from three months in Halifax to one year in Montreal and is six months in the other cities). Owners of property or businesses, whether resident in the city or not, are also allowed to vote but may only cast one vote. For the 1993 election, Vancouver further relaxed some of the rules to ensure that homeless people were eligible to vote simply by signing a card at the polling station verifying age, citizenship, and residency.

In most provinces, the eligibility rules for candidates are the same as those for voters. While candidates must qualify as eligible voters in the municipality, in most cases (except Montreal and Halifax), they do not have to live in the wards in which they are running. Several provinces disqualify anyone who is in default of taxes or other dues payable to the municipality. Nova Scotia goes further in disqualifying anyone who has been convicted of a criminal offence in the past five years or has ever been convicted of two offences. In most cities, a small deposit (usually $100) and/or a certain number of signatures in support of a nomination (e.g., 250 for mayor in Winnipeg) are required as a means of discouraging frivolous contenders. This is to deter people like Wretched Ethyl, Zippy the Circus Chimp, and Sage Advice who have run for mayor in recent Vancouver elections.[1]

The low level of voter turnout in civic elections is widely decried and given as evidence that municipal politics is boring. The average turnout in elections in the larger cities is about 40 percent, compared roughly to between 73 and 75 percent at the provincial and federal levels respectively (Clarke et al., 1991, p. 37; McCormick, 1996, p. 365). As Higgins (1986, p. 313) notes, low turnout is not a recent phenomenon and, contrary to popular belief, there is little evidence among the eight cities in our study that turnout has declined substantially in recent years. As shown in Table 5.1, the level of voter turnout tends to be quite variable depending on particular issues and candidates, whether there is a general sense among the electorate of a need for change, and whether there are also critical plebiscite questions on the ballot. There have been occasional surprises that have caught even city clerks off guard. For example, at least ten polling stations in three wards ran out of ballots in the 1992 Edmonton election when voter turnout at those stations exceeded 85 percent (*Edmonton Journal*, 1992, p. A1).

In 1996, Ontario revised its Municipal Elections Act to allow municipalities greater power in determining various aspects of the voting process, including opting for new forms of voting such as by telephone, computer, or mail. While a common election day will remain, it is anticipated that greater flexibility in voting method may increase voter turnout.

There is no single explanation, but rather a combination of reasons, for the relatively low level of voting in municipal elections. First, because municipal elections occur at fixed times, they lack the suspense and anticipation that build up when a federal or provincial government calls an election. Second, there tends to be a strong return of incumbents and a high proportion of acclamations, especially in smaller municipalities, thus reducing the competitiveness of civic elections. Third, in the absence of parties that provide a shorthand way of understanding what a candidate stands for, voters need to invest considerable effort in learning about their mayoral and council candidates (as well as school board and candidates for other special purpose bodies) on an individual basis. Thus, many people feel that they simply do not know their candidates well enough to bother voting. Fourth, municipal elections have traditionally been fought on very narrow grounds, with the focus being on property taxes, servicing issues and, sometimes, specific planning issues. Candidates for municipal office have generally steered away from higher order issues, such as how to preserve or build a vibrant city in the context of a changing economic and social order. There is a connection between city governance and these higher order

TABLE 5.1

VOTER TURNOUT IN CIVIC ELECTIONS IN THE EIGHT MAJOR CITIES 1974–1995

City	1974	1985/86	1988/89	1990/91	1993/94/95
Halifax	38.9	33.0	—	40.1	43.7*
Montreal	—	49.8	—	30.0	47.5
Ottawa	36.3	40.6	33.2	40.3	38.4
Toronto	31.0	36.7	31.0	43.0	37.0
Winnipeg	34.9	34.0	34.0	58.4	53.5
Edmonton	48.1	33.8	36.4	51.6	50.3
Calgary	46.0	37.3	48.6	34.2	23.4
Vancouver	31.6	49.2	43.3	51.7	34.7

* First election following amalgamation of area municipalities into Halifax Regional Municipality.

issues, but it is, as yet, poorly understood by many candidates for local office as well as voters. In addition, the media in most cities have shown a distinct lack of interest in urban politics, although this is beginning to change. Finally, as noted above, urban politics provide a variety of other means besides elections for participating in civic affairs through open council meetings, interest groups, and organized public participation exercises.

Wards

The biases inherent in an electoral system may serve to privilege certain groups or classes over others. A municipal electoral system based on wards tends to increase representation of geographically concentrated communities, such as poor or ethnic communities, while at-large elections favour the middle class. The shape of wards also affects representation because a large strip-like ward that cuts a swath across neighbourhoods tends to dilute the voting strength of class or ethnic communities. The turn-of-the-century reform movement stamped a bias on Canadian municipalities in favour of at-large elections, which were designed to break up the influence of parties and "boss" politics (even though parties and ward bosses had never been particularly influential here). Consequently, this system under-represented the growing diversity of minority populations (Anderson, 1979). Gradually, municipalities have converted to ward systems so that, by the late 1990s, the only major Canadian city that continues to use at-large elections is Vancouver.

A ward system divides the city into geographic constituencies, the number, size, and shape of which are determined by council. The underlying principles are, first of all, to make wards roughly equivalent in population and, second, to reflect communities of common interest with boundaries that correspond to socio-economic and ethnic communities, although the latter principle is often debated. Wards are usually designed in a block-shaped manner because long, narrow, and twisted boundaries create a public perception of a biased approach favouring particular interests. Their boundaries are reviewed periodically (usually following a general election) to enable appropriate adjustment for population growth and shifts to be made.

PROS AND CONS OF WARD SYSTEMS

The arguments in favour of a ward system are, first of all, that wards make elections less complex by shortening the long lists of candidates and permitting voters to get to know their local candidates better, thereby making more informed choices. In an at-large system, the length of the ballot can sometimes be horrendous, a factor that is said to contribute to voter apathy. In the 1996 election, for example, Vancouver voters were asked to select one of 58 choices for mayor, ten of 58 names for council, and among 54 candidates for the parks and school boards — in all, 170 names on the ballot. Beginning in 1993, the order of names on the ballot was determined by random lot, rather than by alphabetical order, because evidence exists that when confronted with a lengthy ballot voters are more likely to select from the beginning and end of the list.

A second advantage of a ward system is that it ensures every area of the city has a representative on council, thus empowering communities. In contrast, Vancouver's at-large system has produced highly uneven geographic representation. For instance, in 1996, nine of the city's eleven councillors lived in the more affluent west end or southwest corner of the city, while only two were from the poorer east side. Wards make it easier for citizens to mobilize around community concerns and for anti-business voices to be heard. It is not surprising that the business community generally prefers an at-large system that allows them to define the public interest in terms of economic development and expansion.

Another issue relates to costs. Because a candidate has to run a city-wide campaign, at-large elections are argued to be more expensive and to encourage big spending over community activism. Finally, wards are said to enhance accountability because people know who to call if they have a problem or concern.

The main case against a ward system is that it increases parochialism. Councillors focus on local issues that they know will sit well with their own constituents rather than legislate with the bigger, city-wide picture in mind. Log-rolling — whereby a councillor gives support to another councillor on one issue in exchange for support of his or her pet concerns — is easier in a ward system, and this results in one neighbourhood's issues being traded off against others. Thus the locale-based bargaining and compromises involved in a ward system are argued to make policy making more time consuming and less efficient (Masson with LeSage, 1994, p. 295).

Questions of fair and adequate representation related to the ward system are currently important in two major cities: Edmonton and Vancouver. In Edmonton, the issue is one of ward design. Edmonton did not convert to a ward system until 1968. The initial system consisted simply of four gigantic strip wards running north and south, which were oblivious to ethnic communities or socio-economic cleavages, with three aldermen elected from each. In 1980, council increased the number of wards to six, with two people representing each, but there remain a number of serious problems with this system. The most significant is that the wards are enormous, ranging from 84 000 to 120 000 people, and are very heterogeneous. Heterogeneity tends to promote dominance by the middle class because it has higher rates of voter turnout. In addition, with two representatives battling over who attends each function in the ward, there is considerable duplication of effort. No one person is accountable, and thus accountability can be sloughed off (Masson with LeSage, 1994, p. 297). An alternative proposal, advocated by reform-minded Councillor (and later Mayor) Jan Reimer, is a system of twelve single representative constituencies, which would leave council at its existing size. However, the business community and conservative councillors have opposed such changes, and the public has not shown a strong interest.

In Vancouver, the issue is more fundamental: whether to have wards at all. The ward system was abandoned in Vancouver in 1936 as a result of a plebiscite. The absence of wards is cited as a major factor in sustaining the long-standing dominance of the conservative civic party, the Non-Partisan Association (NPA) (Tennant, 1980). In the past 50 years, there have been five more plebiscites on the issue: wards were turned down in 1973 but supported by a majority in 1978, 1982, 1988, and 1996 (but with insufficient support to reach the requisite 60 percent for approval). Although the conservative NPA has always opposed a ward system, in 1981 a new left-leaning mayor, Mike Harcourt, asked the province to amend Vancouver's Charter to implement a ward system. However, the provincial Social Credit government, conservative ally of the NPA, refused to legislate the change. Instead the Minister of Municipal Affairs insisted on another plebiscite with a 60 percent pro-ward vote necessary to make the change (ironic given that in the 1995 Quebec referendum, it was assumed that a mere 50 percent plus 1 would be sufficient to break up the country). The ensuing two plebiscites in 1982 and 1988 fell just short of this threshold at 57 and 56 percent, respectively, favouring the re-establishment of wards. In 1993 the provincial New Democratic government under Premier Harcourt altered the rules to allow Vancouver's council to change the city's electoral system by a majority vote of council. By this time, however, conservative forces again controlled council and were not interested in a ward system which probably would have disadvantaged incumbent conservatives. Although, NPA Mayor Philip Owen agreed to put another question on the ballot in the 1996 election, he reinstated the 60 percent decision rule.

This time the question was more complicated. It asked voters to select among ward, mixed (some councillors elected at-large and some by ward), and proportional representation systems. While 56 percent of voters again supported a ward system, the results did not meet the 60 percent rule and are not binding on council anyway.

Because the issue of electoral wards and their boundaries goes to the heart of how people are represented, the issue will be a central one as two-tier systems are restructured and municipalities amalgamated in the late 1990s.

Who Gets Elected?

OCCUPATIONAL BACKGROUNDS

One of the big differences between municipal councils and federal or provincial legislatures is the occupational background of candidates. As shown in Table 5.2, the most common backgrounds for urban councillors are in public service, business, education, and community organizations. In comparison with the federal scene, there is a marked dearth of lawyers. This composition reflects the strong role that business plays in urban development issues. It is also a result of the historical legacy that the job of municipal councillor was that of a "gifted amateur" and was considered to be a part-time position. Until the 1980s, even in some major cities, council was still viewed as part-time work, and was therefore well-suited to the entrepreneur (Sancton and Woolner, 1990, pp. 484–90). Councillors in the large urban centres now treat their positions as full time, but salaries do not reflect this. Although there is no concrete evidence, the comparatively low salaries may deter many lawyers and other high-income professionals from seeking municipal office.

TABLE 5.2

COUNCILLORS' OCCUPATIONS PRIOR TO ELECTION IN THE EIGHT MAJOR CITIES

Occupation	No. of Councillors
Public servant*	29
Business person	27
Community activist	20
Educator	11
Lawyer	8
Journalist/Broadcaster	7
School trustee	4
Politician	3
Police officer	3
Social worker/Nurse	3
Accountant	3
Scientist/Engineer	3
Farmer	2
Physician	1
Environment	1
Coach	1

* The majority were municipal public servants, but this includes administrators with community centres and universities.

TABLE 5.3

COUNCIL AND MAYORAL SALARIES FOR MAJOR CANADIAN CITIES, 1996

City	Council Salaries	Expenses	Mayor's Salary
Halifax	$38 000	$12 520	$57 562*
Montreal	$30 309	$10 103	$89 513
Ottawa	$40 000	$13 333	$78 500
Toronto	$42 571	$10 750	$67 615
Winnipeg	$46 987	$15 505	$88 100
Edmonton	$44 322	$14 626	$88 644
Calgary	$30 581	$15 291	$91 746
Vancouver	$35 347	$ 3 928	$89 154

* Salary for the mayor of Halifax, before amalgamation.

Note: Under the federal Income Tax Act, one-third of local politicians' salaries are tax exempt.

WOMEN IN LOCAL POLITICS

Another distinctive feature of urban politics is the much greater proportion of women represented than in provincial legislatures or the federal House of Commons. While women held only 18 percent of the seats in the House of Commons in 1993 (up from 13 percent in the 1988–93 session), they held 25 percent of council seats in the eight major cities in 1996. In addition, four cities — Edmonton, Winnipeg, Toronto, and Ottawa — had women mayors between 1992 and 1996. In general, there are significant differences in representation of women according to city size and region. Women tend to have greater success in larger urban centres and capital cities than in smaller ones, and in western cities than in Atlantic Canada (Brodie, 1985, p. 19i; Maillé, 1990, p. 13; Trimble, 1995, p. 97).

The greater representation of women in urban politics compared to the federal and provincial spheres raises two interesting questions. First, why do women seek and win electoral office in greater numbers in the municipal arena? There are three standard answers to this question. The first is that the proximity of municipal councils minimizes travel and thus reduces conflicts with family responsibilities of which women still shoulder a greater share than men (Maillé, 1990; see Bashevkin, 1996, pp. 483–85 for an overview). Second, it is less expensive to run for municipal office, and parties, often a barrier to the recruitment of women, are less prevalent (Brodie and Vickers, 1981, p. 323; Maillé, 1990, p. 14). Third, the core subjects of urban politics — housing, education, and neighbourhood issues — are argued to be of greater interest to women due to their traditional roles in private life. In her recent work, however, Linda Trimble challenges all of these explanations. The primary reason that women run for municipal office in great numbers, she suggests, is because urban government matters.

TABLE 5.4

REPRESENTATION OF WOMEN AND MINORITIES ON COUNCILS OF THE MAJOR CITIES, 1996

City	No. of Women	No. of Visible Minorities	Council Size (including mayor)
Halifax	0	1	24
Montreal	15	0	51
Ottawa	5	0	11
Toronto	3	0	17
Winnipeg	4	0	16
Edmonton	2	0	13
Calgary	5	0	15
Vancouver	5	2	11

Women become involved in city government because of its profound influence on their lives; that is, women choose city politics because it is powerful in ways that matter to them. Politics at the city level — "politics where we live" — is arguably more tangible, more immediate, and more rewarding than political action at the federal and provincial levels. (Trimble, 1995, p. 110)

The other intriguing question is, Do women bring a distinctive approach to politics that influences the nature of politics in council? This question is difficult to answer definitively, but a cursory look at the political ideologies of the women mayors of the major cities reveals little consistency. For example, Jan Reimer (mayor of Edmonton from 1989 to 1995) and Barbara Hall (elected mayor of Toronto in 1994) both have their roots in social services and the New Democratic Party, and both gave social issues a priority in their campaigns. In contrast, Susan Thompson (elected mayor of Winnipeg in 1992 and re-elected in 1995) comes from a business background and, like Jacquelin Holzman of Ottawa, is a conservative, pro-business mayor. Former Toronto mayor June Rowlands has best been described as an enigma who ran (and lost to Hall) on a tough law and order platform. Perhaps the only lesson that can be drawn from the striking differences among these mayors is that there is considerable danger in gender stereotyping.

MINORITY REPRESENTATION

In sharp contrast to the success of women in winning elected office in the major cities, visible minorities are poorly represented. Of the total number of 158 council seats in the eight major cities, only three are held by visible minorities. One reason for such under-representation that is sometimes given is that minority communities are not sufficiently concentrated geographically to have voting strength in numbers. But this is a less than compelling case. In Vancouver, a city without wards and with a large Asian population (constituting 40 percent of the city's population), there were only two Asian members of council in each of the 1993–1996 and 1996–1999 terms. Another possible explanation is that without a party machinery, there is no proactive recruitment of a diversity of candidates. Thus potential candidates from minority communities have more limited access to financial backing. Even in Montreal, however, which has a well developed civic party system and a multicultural population (15 percent of the island's population are of Asian, Aboriginal, and African descent), only one of the 51 candidates nominated in 1994 by the winning Vision Montreal Party came from the cultural communities. Moreover, even when nominated, many minority candidates say they feel like they have been mere window-dressing, rather than having been taken as serious candidates (Aubin, 1994, p. B1). It seems clear that electoral politics has not been made sufficiently attractive and accessible to minority communities. This stands in sharp contrast to the United States where African-Americans have been very successful in winning mayoralties and the black vote is a powerful element in many large cities (Stone, 1989). While minority communities may play an important behind-the-scenes role — attending nomination meetings, for example, to ensure the preferred candidate gets nominated — a more visible role is being demanded as part of the recognition of the cultural and social diversity of Canada's cities. Councils, civic parties, business associations, and community organizations will need to respond.

Campaigning: What Does It Take to Get Elected?

In most cities, the key to getting elected is name recognition. The absence of party labels means that voters do not have shorthand monikers for associating a candidate with an underlying platform or ideology. Candidates whose names are most familiar to voters therefore tend to have the upper hand. This is one reason that incumbents, whose names have become known through the media over several years, have such an advantage in municipal elections. Lawn signs, billboards, television ads, and brochures are all widely used to ensure that voters feel very familiar with a candidate. Door-to-door canvassing is also critical but requires an extensive team of volunteers to be effective in large centres. Of course, successful candidates also need to run on the issues that are important to voters and present their issues in a way that will separate them from other contenders. By far the most universal issues are preventing tax increases and promoting economic growth, although there often are hot issues particular to a specific ward or city. A candidate's stature is enhanced by endorsements from individual community leaders, key organizations, such as the Chamber of Commerce, and large unions, depending on one's political orientation. Finally, the ability to appeal to and get out the ethnic vote is increasingly important and candidates often work through the leadership of ethnic associations (see Masson with LeSage, 1994, p. 320).

Susan Thompson's successful race for the mayoralty of Winnipeg in 1992 demonstrates the extent to which urban political contests are being run more professionally and increasingly like federal and provincial campaigns. Thompson's success can be attributed to several tactics (Flood, 1992, p. A1). First, she had an experienced campaign manager who had been the electoral strategist for the provincial Tories. Her team started by running focus groups to identify the most important issues in the minds of citizens. The overwhelming response was that citizens were angry at taxes and the councillors who had voted for tax increases. Thus, a "no tax increase" campaign by a political outsider was launched. Thompson concentrated on meeting people in the streets rather than doing media interviews. Perhaps more importantly, an extensive, high quality ad campaign was run in both the print and broadcast media and on strategically located billboards. Other mayoral candidates with less money and less backing from the business community never successfully competed in the advertising game.

Susan Thompson spent $174 000 on her campaign. This is about average for a mayoral race in a major Canadian city. As shown in Table 5.5, the leading contenders for mayor in the major cities spent anywhere from $66 000 in Calgary, where Al Duerr was a shoe-in, to $267 000 in Toronto on their campaigns in recent elections. This compares with average per candidate spending of $65 000 (exclusive of direct spending by the parties) to contest a seat in the federal parliament (Stanbury, 1996, p. 374). The real estate industry remains the largest contributor to municipal campaigns. In fact, an investigation conducted by *The Globe and Mail* in 1990 found that 75 percent of campaign contributions to Toronto politicians came from the real estate development industry (Ferguson and McInnes 1991, p. A3).

Concerns that election spending may be running out of control and that the public should be informed about who makes campaign contributions have prompted most major Canadian cities (with the exception of Halifax) to implement election expense by-laws. Generally, these by-laws require disclosure of all campaign expenses and contributions above a fixed minimum, which ranges between $100 and $300. While these by-laws enhance the transparency of campaign financing, most of them — with the exception of Winnipeg and some Ontario cities — do not impose ceilings on the amounts that any particular donor may give and do not limit the total money that a candidate can spend. Nor do they allocate free public broadcast time, as does federal expense legislation. The by-laws, however, do allow us to check who is supporting candidates, a particular concern related to the possibility that developers might attempt to buy influence through their contributions.

Violations of election expense legislation are beginning to be taken seriously. Charges of illegal fundraising were recently brought against both Mayor Pierre Bourque and his Vision Montreal Party. While an investigation by Quebec's chief electoral officer in early 1997 vindicated the mayor, seven charges were filed against the party: two for illegally funnelling money into its coffers and five for paying volunteers after the 1994 election without approval of the party's official agent. Fines ranged from $100 to $10 000 for each of the seven counts (Derfel, 1997, A1, 8).

TABLE 5.5

CIVIC ELECTION EXPENSES
(FOR ELECTIONS 1993-1995)

City	Minimum Spent by Successful Councillors	Maximum Spent by Successful Councillors	Mayor's Campaign Expenses
Halifax*	—	—	
Montreal	$ 33	$282 204	N/A
Ottawa	$3581	$ 18 521	$173 085
Toronto	$ 100	$ 38 751	$267 374
Winnipeg	$6408	$ 27 100	$174 342
Edmonton	$8089	$ 28 086	$204 885
Calgary	$2808	$ 28 677	$ 65 726
Vancouver	$9293	$ 42 528	N/A

* No campaign disclosure requirements.

THE ROLE OF POLITICAL PARTIES

In contrast to the United States or the United Kingdom, political parties have played a very limited role in urban politics in Canada. The question of whether urban politics would be more visible, interesting, and accountable with more active and direct involvement of parties is strongly debated. We need to be clear, however, as to what is meant by party politics. Conceptually, there are three types of political systems in local government in Canada. The first model is the **extended party** system in which provincial or national parties are directly involved at the local level. While this is the most common model in the United States and the United Kingdom, it has been quite rare in Canada. The main concern with direct involvement of senior parties is that federal and provincial issues and the public's attitudes to these parties will spill over into the local arena. This may hurt local candidates if the provincial or national parties are in political trouble or may detract the focus from local issues.

Although limited, national and provincial parties have shown some interest in urban politics. Beginning in the 1920s, Winnipeg has had active involvement of the Communist Party, the Co-operative Commonwealth Federation (CCF), and later the New Democratic Party (NDP), although this has waned somewhat in recent years. In general, the NDP has been the most visibly active party in municipal elections and Toronto the most sought after territory. A significant event for national parties came in 1969 when both the Liberals and New Democrats ran aldermanic candidates in Toronto and the Liberals ran a strong candidate, Stephen Clarkson, on their ticket for mayor. The party candidates fared poorly, however, and Clarkson's resounding defeat dampened the Liberals' enthusiasm for local politics. In the mid-1980s, some Toronto-area Conservatives strove to make the party more active in Metro politics, but the idea created sufficient dissension within the party that the group, PC Metro, merely backed "small-c" conservatives rather than running officially (Illingworth, 1995, pp. 23–24). Although the NDP has remained the most active in the city with an identifiable NDP caucus in council, many NDP candidates in the 1994 Toronto election chose to distance themselves from the party label due to dissatisfaction over the Rae government's social contract. It seems that official ballot support by national and provincial parties does not significantly help municipal candidates get elected in Canada. Today most provincial and national parties work behind the scenes, giving financial support and lending political strategists, organizers, and canvassers to officially non-partisan candidates.

The second model is the **civic party**. These parties are unique to the city. They run slates of candidates on party platforms, take responsibility for campaign financing, are active to some degree between elections, and have longevity over successive elections. The only cities in Canada that currently operate under civic party systems are Montreal and Vancouver. Montreal could be said to be a truer example of a civic party system because not only do the parties run on organized platforms, but, once elected, they evoke party discipline in how the councillors vote. While Vancouver's NPA is the country's oldest civic party, it is a somewhat looser coalition whose members frequently do not vote as a block. Nor do Vancouver electors tend to vote a straight party ticket (Tennant, 1980). Although Winnipeg has also had a long history of anti-socialist local parties that have dominated councils since the General Strike of 1919, these parties, including the Winnipeg-in-the Nineties (WIN) coalition that was active in the mid-1990s have clung vigorously to a public persona of being non-partisan. A debate over whether city hall is any place for party politics has been a backdrop to Winnipeg elections in recent years (Walker, 1983, p. 234). In contrast to true civic parties, most of these so-called **alphabet parties** like WIN are transient, disappearing after an election or two and then reforming with different people and a new name.

The third model and most popular one in Canada is the **non-partisan party system** in which candidates run as and, once elected, vote as independents. Although candidates may have behind-the-scenes campaign assistance from national or provincial parties and may ally themselves with a "reform" or a pro-business agenda, the strategy is to achieve sufficient name recognition as independents to win. Although independent councillors often join together as voting blocks which frequently are formed along lines of personal friendship rather than ideology, they have no ongoing commitment to vote with a block (Kay, 1982). The non-partisan system is deeply rooted in Canadian municipal politics and shows little sign of being displaced in favour of a more fully developed civic party system. Moreover, greater direct involvement by provincial or national parties seems to be a non-starter in an era of general mistrust of professional politicians and parties. However, as we will see below with a closer look at Calgary and Edmonton, official non-partisanship does not necessarily mean that urban politics is dull.

Politics on the Ground: A Closer Look

Urban politics cannot be fully appreciated by dealing only with the theoretical arguments about the nature of politics and role of parties. The politics in each city is different depending on historical factors, the part played by particular individuals, and the economic situation faced by that city, among other things. In this section, we explore further the role of parties by focussing on the two extremes: Montreal with a long-established practice of civic parties, and Calgary and Edmonton in which non-partisanship is the norm. Following this examination, we focus our attention more directly on the pros and cons of civic parties.

MONTREAL: A CIVIC PARTY SYSTEM

Why have civic parties developed and been sustained in Montreal in a manner that is rare in Canada? Three distinct factors about Montreal politics provide partial explanations. The first factor is simply the stamp of history. Jean Drapeau created the Civic Party in 1956, albeit the party was not a democratic political machine in the modern sense, and he used it to run city hall for almost 30 years. This political machinery required that successful contenders to the

Drapeau administration also organize themselves into parties. Second, Montreal council has evolved into a quasi-parliamentary system, including a cabinet structure and an official leader of the opposition. At 51 seats in 1996, the Montreal council is the largest in Canada (with the exception of the 57 member council of the new City of Toronto) and thus lends itself to both party organization and discipline. A powerful executive committee, whose members are appointed by the mayor from his own party, operates as a cabinet, giving the mayor extensive powers for policy formation. A third explanation for the well defined party system in Montreal has been a relative lack of interest by provincial parties. In fact, during his long tenure as mayor, Drapeau did not encourage a provincial interest. It is speculated that during the years of the first Parti Québecois (PQ) government, Drapeau made a deal that he would stay out of the sovereignty debate if the PQ did not interfere in Montreal politics (Sancton, 1985). In the 1970s and 80s, the PQ did lend considerable support and party organizers to Drapeau's opposition and eventual successor, the Montreal Citizens' Movement (MCM), but both levels kept an official distance between them (Quesnell, 1994, p. 595; Sancton, 1985, p. 75). Consequently, there has been sufficient political space between provincial and urban politics in Quebec to allow the emergence of a well developed multi-party system.

The longevity of Drapeau's Civic Party can be attributed to Drapeau's three personae: a Quebec nationalist, a populist, and an astute political strategist. As a nationalist, Drapeau's goal was to "show the whole world the achievements of French Canadians" (Chorney and Molloy, 1993, p. 71). To this end, he set about building internationally recognized mega-projects, such as the Métro (subway system) and Place des Arts, and attracting spectacle events that included Expo '67, the establishment of the Expos baseball team, and the 1976 Olympic Games. This international focus and mega-project orientation was also an astute political strategy because, until the mid-1970s when the costs became a nagging concern, it unified disparate sectoral, language, and ethnic interests by giving Montrealers an identity distinct from English Canada and a sense of having a world-class city of which they could be proud (Ruddick, 1992, p. 272).

Jean Drapeau was also a populist. Dubbed "Mr. Montreal," he sought to maintain a direct link with the people by appearing regularly on a local television station and personally answering letters from his extensive fan club (Leveillee, 1986, p. 122). Mayor Drapeau, however, was not a proponent of participant democracy. Indeed the struggle to open up city hall and democratize the party system has been a consistent theme in Montreal politics. Under Drapeau, the Civic Party was constituted as a caucus party so that only current and former councillors could belong. As Henri Lustiger-Thaler (1993, p. 15) suggests, it was "a select group of acolytes protectively ringed around the Mayor." Backbench councillors who were not members of the powerful executive committee had little say and were expected to vote according to the dictates of the executive. Citizens also had few opportunities to be heard.

While Drapeau's pursuit of an international stature for Montreal transformed the city, it ignored the everyday needs of people for affordable housing, jobs, recreation, and green space. By the late 1960s, this inattention to the quality of living conditions began to spark a multitude of citizen committees that challenged the administration. In the atmosphere of growing polarization that characterized Quebec politics in the early 1970s, a successful opposition coalition, the MCM, emerged. In contrast to the Civic Party, the MCM was a mass membership party, composed of an alliance of progressive forces including labour leaders, feminists, nationalists, socialists, and members of the PQ and NDP, drawn from both francophone and anglophone communities.

From the outset, the MCM laid out a well defined policy agenda under the banner "Une ville pour nous." It switched the focus of economic development from internationalism to a new localism. Central tenets of the MCM's original platform were grassroots democracy and decentralization of power through the creation of neighbourhood councils that would have real decision making power and would directly deliver some services.

Although the MCM took one-third of the seats in the 1974 election, the next ten years were uneasy ones because the party was internally divided. Given its roots as an urban social movement, the MCM was torn by a tension common to many movements-turned-parties: a tension between the ideologues, who want to remain true to founding principles and concentrate on building a strong grassroots movement, and the pragmatists, who want to ensure electoral success (Thomas, 1995; Milner, 1988). The party's transformation came in 1982 when a new technocratic backer, Jean Doré, set it on a pragmatic election-oriented course.

Just before the 1986 election, Jean Drapeau announced his retirement, resulting in an easy victory for the MCM. Re-elected again in 1990, Doré and the MCM made some significant changes in both policy and process. They brought in the first true land-use master plan in the city's history (Marson, 1995, p. 41); reorganized municipal apparatus (including instituting the first committees of council); created a policy for ethnic communities and a program for women's equality; established a new waste recycling program; and made city hall more accessible to citizens (Quesnel, 1994, pp. 600–601). To its surprise, the business community was generally pleased with the direction of the MCM's policies and found that its members were usually well received at city hall (Peritz, 1990, pp. A1, A4). Many former MCM supporters, however, were bitterly disappointed by the party's record in office. For them, being in power had ruined the MCM's social base movement with the result that it acted like "a fairly ordinary political party" and had not gone as far as the grassroots expected in empowering citizens (Roy, 1990, p. 155; Lustiger-Thaler and Shragge, 1993, p. 29).

During the MCM's second term, council became increasingly tumultuous. The official opposition changed five times in three years. Both the left and the right fractured. In 1989, dissident councillors on the left quit the MCM to launch two new political organizations, the Democratic Coalition and Ecology Montreal, which merged in preparation for the 1994 election. Without Drapeau, the Civic Party had become a doddering version of its former self and in 1994 joined with the fledgling Montrealers' Party led by former Quebec justice minister Jerome Choquette.

The 1994 election was hotly contested with eleven candidates for mayor, including a representative from the White Elephant Party. To the surprise of the media, the winner was Pierre Bourque and his Vision Montreal, which won 39 of the 51 seats while the MCM was reduced to only six seats. Vision Montreal has been described as "a ragtag party that rambles across the ideological spectrum and lacks a basis consensus" (Siblin, 1997, p. A1). Bourque, who had been director of the Botanical Gardens, promised voters a rose garden, both literally and figuratively. Not only would he create gardens and green space, but he promised to cut spending, lower taxes, offer simplicity in government, and encourage a new value system based on voluntarism — all the populist buzzwords of the 1990s.

Bourque's administration has failed to live up to his grand election rhetoric, however. One of the most controversial aspects of Bourque's administration is his return to the autocratic governing style of Drapeau. Not only did Bourque attempt to dismantle the public consultation machinery created by Doré, but his party rammed several controversial land-use decisions through committee, ignoring public opposition. In early 1997, Bourque faced a near caucus revolt sparked by his attempt to oust two members of the executive committee. He was prevented from doing so by the courts, which ruled that the city's charter does not give the mayor the right to fire executive committee members.

What should be evident from this review of 40 years of partisan politics in Montreal is that the civic party system cannot be easily classified into pro- and anti-development. The internal and inter-party dynamics involving splintering and merging have been more complex than this. It is also evident that there is growing volatility in Montreal politics for two main reasons. First, Montreal's economic problems are enormous and will require powers greater than those possessed by the city to solve them. Second, the "politics of difference" which encourages cultural communities to seek their own voice, has become critical. The language division in Montreal historically has been reinforced by class and geographic cleavages (the working-class francophones in the east end of Montreal versus the middle-class anglophones on the west island). But increasingly the city's diverse allophone population is also pressing to be heard, and Montreal's parties have had a poor record in making room for them. In this atmosphere of diversity and greater distance between the economic development interests of Montreal and the sovereignty goals of the PQ government, calls for Montreal to become a "city-state" were seriously made in 1996 (Came, 1996, p. 22).

CALGARY AND EDMONTON: DIFFERENCES IN NON-PARTISANSHIP

At the opposite end of the spectrum from Montreal are the non-partisan councils as exemplified by Calgary and Edmonton. Although non-partisan systems often focus electoral campaigns on ward issues, this does not mean that city politics are necessarily dull. Indeed, the contrast between Calgary and Edmonton shows the vast differences in styles that may exist between councils and reveals just how heated non-partisan politics can become. Calgarians showed such bovine contentment with their incumbent mayor and aldermen in the 1995 election that one local columnist inquired whether somebody had been slipping Prozac into the Glenmore Reservoir (Baird, 1995, p. B1). In sharp contrast, Edmonton council has been characterized in recent years by a left-right split and enormous interpersonal animosity. In this discussion, we explore two questions: Why does non-partisanship continue to be the predominant form in Canada, and how do we explain the difference in political styles between non-partisan systems?

As discussed in Chapter Three, one of the legacies of the reform movement that swept the United States in the early 1900s and was exported to Canada was the attempt to make civic politics more business-like. Parties were seen as a corrupting influence on city administration, a notion which had some merit in the United States at the time. The principles of apolitical councils gained favour in Canada in spite of the fact that parties had not taken hold here. In particular, the business community saw non-partisan elections as a means of dispelling labour's quest for power and militating against a perceived threat from large numbers of eastern Europeans settling in the major cities (Masson with LeSage, 1994, p. 274). The influence of the American reform movement was felt most strongly in the west. Alberta was particularly receptive to the ideas of municipal non-partisanship at the city level because an anti-party tradition permeated provincial politics.

Non-partisan politics is also reinforced by council structures and practices. In Calgary, for example, there is no executive committee (although an agenda-setting committee has begun to emerge) and the mayor does not pick the membership of the standing committees of council. Aldermen self-nominate to sit on the four standing committees and a nomination committee (composed of the four committee chairs and the mayor) makes the actual selection, trying to accommodate every member's first and second choices. The committees then elect their own chairs and these change every year. These practices mean that the mayor has little opportunity to create a cadre of insiders who think and vote as he or she does. Even if parties or coalitions were to develop, their coherence would be countermanded by council practices.

Another explanation as to why parties have never taken hold in Calgary and Edmonton is that the highly developed system of community associations provides a satisfactory conduit of communication between the grassroots and councillor, thus fulfilling an important role of civic parties. Dating back to 1917, both cities have an extensive system of neighbourhood associations, staffed totally by volunteers and organized into area councils and a city-wide federation (Bowler and Wanchuk, 1986). At the ward level, councillors meet regularly with representatives of the community associations, who keep them informed about emerging concerns in the community and lobby for action on particular issues. Candidates who ignore ward issues in favour of partisan or city-wide issues do so at their peril.

In general, provincial and federal parties have tended to stay out of the cities' elections, although several have lent behind-the-scenes support. No candidate has been officially sponsored by a provincial or federal party in Alberta since the 1940s (Masson with LeSage, 1994, p. 283).

In spite of their similarities as non-partisan councils, there are some striking differences in the politics of Calgary and Edmonton. In part, these differences reflect the distinct political cultures or personalities of each. While Calgary is generally characterized as private sector oriented, white collar (with its head offices of the petroleum and other industries), entrepreneurial, and politically conservative, Edmonton is described as public sector oriented, blue collar (with the servicing end of the oil and gas industry), and liberal. In the early 1990s, Calgary pulled ahead of Edmonton in economic development, with lower unemployment and a more diversified economy, partly because Edmonton bore the brunt of provincial government cutbacks (*Alberta Report*, 1994a, p. 13). These factors, as well as some council-specific variables, have given rise to a relatively uniform centre-right council in Calgary and a deeply split, often rancorous council in Edmonton.

Calgary politics in recent years have been described as extremely dull and the election of the mayor a virtual coronation. Beginning in 1980, Mayor Ralph Klein won three easy terms with a high of 90.1 percent of the popular vote in his last attempt. He was followed by Al Duerr, who also coasted to three victories, slightly topping Klein's record in the popular vote. The aldermanic races have been equally uncompetitive, and in recent elections, it has been rare for an incumbent not to get re-elected. Not surprisingly, voter turnout was appallingly low at 23 percent, the worst since 1974 when the city began to keep records.

Why was there a lack of lively debate? Are Calgarians uninterested in city politics? Rather than jump to this conclusion, we suggest that several other factors contributed to dull campaigns and low voter turnout. First, in a climate of overall prosperity, surveys indicate that residents of Calgary are very happy with the services they receive from the City and feel that their council is doing a good job. Going into the 1995 election, even the media concluded that the mayor and aldermen had earned their high approval ratings (Baird, 1995, p. B1). Second, there is a fairly clear politics–administration dichotomy. A strong administration resolves the details of issues before they are presented to council so that it need not get mired in operational detail; council in turn tends to stick with policy, leaving the daily administration to the administration. Finally, there was no important plebiscite issue on the ballot in 1995 to entice voters out regardless of their specific candidate choices.

Edmonton tends to take a distinctive political course compared to the rest of Alberta. In contrast to Calgary, no mayor since William Hawrelak (1951–59, 1963–65, 1974–75) — a mayor twice forced to resign due to questionable real estate deals — has been able to win three terms in office in Edmonton. What has distinguished Edmonton from its southern sister since the 1970s is the considerable electoral success of the labour and progressive reform movements. Whenever they have become too strong, however, a pro-business backlash has followed. Jan Reimer, whose political roots were in an urban reform group, was elected mayor in 1989 after serving as a councillor for nine years. The media immediately labelled her as socialist and anti-business — labels that were not well deserved — and gave the city the nickname "Redmonton."

A political low was reached with the 1992–95 council, which became infamous for its internal fractiousness. This was not merely an ideological split but frequently was personal and petty. In fact, the bickering got so heated near the end of a twelve-hour marathon session in September 1994 that one councillor, angry that her by-law to control cats had been pushed off the agenda, doused another member, who had helped to dispose of her pet project, with a pitcher of water (*Alberta Report*, 1994c, p. 16). A major contributor to the general enmity on council was that it fell into the trap of trying to micro-manage the city's $1.5 billion enterprise, producing laboriously long meetings that were "larded with minutiae," and creating disputes over minor details while ignoring the big picture (*Alberta Report*, 1994b, pp. 16–17).

In the 1995 election campaign — as often happened in the past when the left got too strong — an organized effort was mounted by the business community to unseat Reimer and to push a strong pro-development agenda. Given the city's economic decline relative to Calgary, this election was very much about a broad vision for the future. Bill Smith, a tire retailer and ex-Edmonton Eskimo football player, ran on a traditional boosterism line, promising to sell Edmonton as a place to invest, cut property taxes, promote job creation, and ensure greater accountability of the city administration. The voters, who had grown tired of council's antics and had a general disposition to throwing out the incumbents, turned out in great numbers: there was a 50 percent turnout, the highest since 1966. In the end, Reimer lost to Smith by only 1 percent and only five of twelve incumbent councillors were returned.

This brief comparison suggests that while non-partisan systems force all electoral candidates to pay close attention to ward issues, there may be significant differences in the nature and dynamics of non-partisan councils and elections. As the case of Edmonton reveals, the term "non-partisan" does not imply the absence of politics.

The Pros and Cons of Civic Parties

The comparison between Montreal and the western cities raises an important question: Do locally organized political parties have an appropriate role in municipal politics? The case against civic parties is argued on several grounds. First, it is argued that the issues are usually apparent to voters because they relate primarily to service delivery. Parties do little to enhance debate about these service and technical matters. Second, the accountability relationship in municipal government is a direct one between individual councillors and voters. The councillor cannot promise a party platform that he or she cannot deliver nor hide behind the party when achievements fall short of election promises (Kaplan, 1982, p. 380). Third, non-partisan councils are better able to work together and resolve differences because their members are not automatically divided by party lines (Siegel, 1987). Finally, harmonious intergovernmental relations are argued to be improved by the absence of parties because a provincial government is less likely to punish a city that elects a council whose majority is of a different political persuasion than the governing provincial party (Tindal and Tindal, 1995, p. 278).

The case in favour of civic parties, especially in large urban centres, dismisses as archaic the narrow view of politics as being merely about the development of property and technical administration of services. While issues related to the scale and nature of development remain important, urban politics increasingly is also about quality of life in its broadest sense, including debates about democracy, protection of the environment, and the distribution of costs and benefits of services. On this premise, several advantages of parties are put forward. First, parties help voters to understand fundamental debates over the values associated with urban life because they present coherent, but simplified platforms. They tend to focus politics on issues rather than personalities and get their message out by using the media more effectively. Second, parties are better equipped to recruit a diversity of candidates to run on a slate, thereby potentially enhancing the representation of councils. Third, parties have greater resources for door-to-door campaigning which tends to increase voter interest and turnout (Masson with LeSage, 1994, p. 280). Fourth, civic parties are more likely to accomplish the things they set out to do because they can count on the votes of their members in council. The political leadership of a council majority deters council from becoming staff-led, which is a problem often faced by non-partisan councils (Siegal, 1994, p. 11). Finally, proponents of civic parties claim that they enhance accountability by pinpointing political responsibility (Masson with LeSage, 1994, p. 281). In a non-partisan system, power tends to be dispersed so that councillors can avoid responsibility by claiming council out-voted them. But in a party system, with its attendant discipline, party members can be held directly responsible for the actions of their party.

The debate over the advantages of civic parties sharply divides both scholars and practitioners. In an increasingly complex policy environment and with politicians' serious lack of credibility in the eyes of the public, the debate remains an important one.

OPEN GOVERNMENT AND DIRECT DEMOCRACY
Government in a Fishbowl

Citizens' opportunities to participate in municipal government are not confined to elections but are ongoing as a result of the principles of open government. Indeed many councillors say that municipal government feels like life in a fishbowl. Three specific conventions contribute to this openness: municipal councils are required to have open meetings; the public has the right to be heard, either by council or its committees; and plebiscites afford the opportunity for the public to be consulted directly on substantive issues.

Transparency and openness were not founding principles of municipal government (O'Connor and Smithers, 1994, pp. 1.2–4). Councils often met in special or informal, closed meetings so that they could discuss all the ramifications and political sensitivities of an issue in private and then move to an open session where a motion or recommendation could be presented and voted on with minimal public discussion. Over the past 25 years, however, there have been decisive initiatives by municipalities, supported by the provinces, to provide legal sanctions against such practices. Municipal councils passed by-laws and provinces amended their municipal acts to require that all regular meetings of council and committees be open to the public unless the discussion involves issues related to a limited number of matters, such as the disposal or purchase of real estate and personnel matters, in which the protection of privacy is required (Ontario Ministry of Municipal Affairs, 1992).

Along with an increased standard of transparency have come controversy and several lawsuits over what constitutes a meeting of council. While Ontario's legislation does not prohibit councillors from meeting socially, it does restrict purportedly social occasions from being used as a guise to discuss public business. The boundary between private and public is often ill-defined, however. For example, in 1996 a councillor from the RMOC created a furore of allegations about secret deals when she hosted a private dinner party for other RMOC members of council a few days before a major budget meeting (Adam, 1996a, p. B1). Only more conservative politicians were invited, excluding others on the basis that there were not enough chairs. Although the hostess and guests claim it truly was a social event with no budget or other council business discussed, the timing and selectiveness of the event attracted media attention. Undoubtedly, there is reduced public tolerance for quiet retreats, workshops, and even social events that occur behind closed doors.

The public also has a right to make representation to council or committees simply by giving notice. The agendas of council and committee meetings are publicized in advance in the local newspapers and/or on the community television channel that broadcasts council meetings. The meetings open with a question period in which councillors may pose questions of personal interest or on matters raised directly by their constituents. In most council chambers, it is not unusual to see a full house of citizens when particularly sensitive issues are being discussed. Council votes are, by law, transparent as municipal acts contain prohibitions against secret (and thus anonymous) voting.

The application of provincial Freedom of Information laws to municipalities in the 1990s has further augmented the public's ability to hold local governments accountable and has reversed the common law perspective that access was merely a privilege. With exceptions to protect personal privacy, this legislation clearly establishes that access to information held by municipal governments and boards is a right and should be the prevailing practice.

Plebiscites

Most provinces allow councils to consult the public directly on important issues through plebiscites. Although they are not binding, the results of a plebiscite are usually difficult for a council to ignore. Municipalities can undertake a plebiscite on any matter that is a municipal question. This has permitted plebiscites on a wide range of issues including local prohibition, Sunday shopping, fluoridation, boundary issues and ward systems, market-value assessment of property taxes, and the future of facilities, such as the municipal airport in Edmonton. Indeed the issue of what constitutes a municipal question has been interpreted very broadly. In 1994, for example, the City of Toronto sparked a controversy with Metro when it planned a plebiscite asking, "Are you in favour of eliminating the Metro level of government?" Metro took the City to court claiming that it had no authority to ask the question because issues of regional government are outside the city's jurisdiction, and additionally that the question was biased. The court disagreed with Metro, saying that the question was an appropriate one for the municipality and, because the results of plebiscites are not binding, the city can engage its electors in this form of direct democracy.

Following the introduction of legislation to create the new megacity of Toronto, in late 1996, councils of the six local municipalities facing extinction held their own plebiscites on the issue. In the interests of timeliness and keeping costs down, however, they used mail-in ballots rather than official polling booths. The plebiscites held no sway with the province as both the premier and the Minister of Municipal Affairs were emphatic that they had no intention of recognizing these votes.

The law places an onus on municipalities to ensure that any plebiscite question is put fairly to the people. The question must be neutral, clear, simple, and direct. Timing is also important and most plebiscites are held (and in many provinces required to be held) in conjunction with elections. This timing is not only a cost-saving measure but tends to increase voter turnout, which is essential if the plebiscite is to be viewed as a legitimate test of public opinion. There are few guidelines for government spending and provision of information. While voters need adequate information about both sides of a plebiscite issue, the extent to which the city may act as an advocate for one side is somewhat contentious. The general guideline has been that the city should provide background information and encourage people to vote, but that the information officially provided should be as neutral as possible. However, councillors, as individuals, are free to act as advocates in promoting one side over the other (Boyer, 1992, p. 80). Because third parties have no restrictions on spending (i.e., by business, lobby groups, and other interested parties), they may be significant players, spending a considerable amount in advertising in favour of their preferred result.

In addition to council-initiated plebiscites, some provinces' municipal acts have provisions for **petitions** which allow citizens to force a plebiscite. In British Columbia and Alberta, councils must submit plans for financing long-term capital debt (not payable out of the current year's budget) to the public (Masson with LeSage, 1994, p. 302). An advertisement regarding the proposal must be posted and/or published in the local newspaper, and if a petition against it is filed within fifteen days, the proposal must go to a general plebiscite. Because plebiscites related to increasing a city's debt almost surely would be lost in the no-tax-increase environment of the 1990s, municipalities have looked to more creative ways of financing capital projects. This legal requirement explains, in part, the extensive use of public-private partnerships in several provinces in recent years. In Alberta, citizens have also been able to force plebiscites on other policy issues, although they have rarely been successful. Under the 1994 revisions to Alberta's Municipal Government Act, however, it is now almost impossible to succeed with petitions in larger urban centres. The minimum numbers of petitioners required in a municipality has been raised from 5 percent to 10 percent of the population, and the signature collection must be completed within 60 days. In Calgary or Edmonton, this would mean that sponsors of a petition would need to collect 65 000 valid signatures — more than 1000 per day for two months.[2]

There is mixed support for direct democracy by plebiscite (Cronin, 1989; Boyer, 1992). Critics argue that the process of representative democracy already works well because citizens get to hold their municipal politicians accountable and vote on issues at regular, relatively short intervals. Councils may use plebiscites to shirk their leadership obligations in deciding difficult issues. A second concern is that most public policy issues are too complex to be clearly and simply divided into a yes/no decision format. People may vote without knowing much about a plebiscite issue and without much informed debate, being swayed by glitzy advertising. If there is a low voter turnout, a small but vocal minority may end up deciding the vote. Another important issue relates to who takes responsibility for failed actions. For example, if the public votes against all proposals for waste management strategies, what does the council do? And not least, plebiscites are expensive. For instance, in the case of the referendum on the new Toronto supercity, one of the six participating municipalities, the City of Toronto, set aside $1 million for its share of the cost (De Mara, 1996, p. A9).

Proponents of direct democracy argue that we should have more faith in and respect for the integrity of citizens. Elections are as much about personalities as they are about issues. People vote for a particular candidate for a plethora of reasons so that elections are seldom accurate expressions of opinion on specific public policy issues. Petitions and plebiscites are valuable because they impel councils to make decisions on contentious matters which they might otherwise try to avoid. Because the vote is brought closer to the people, the decisions that result from plebiscites have greater legitimacy, particularly for issues on which the population is deeply divided. Finally, plebiscites are argued to have a useful role in citizen engagement. Not only do they educate people about issues, but, because voters have the opportunity to express their opinions directly, they enhance the sense of political efficacy and reduce alienation. The use of plebiscites is unlikely to fade, but their continued use will be a trade-off between the cost and populist sentiment for greater direct control over politicians.

Protecting Ethical Conduct: Conflict of Interest Rules

Trust in government requires that elected officials be — and be seen to be — beyond reproach in the conduct of their public affairs and in the relationship between their private and public lives. Concerns about avoidance of **conflict of interest**, particularly conflict related to **pecuniary interests**, are critical in municipal government, not because local politicians are inherently more corrupt than provincial or federal ones, but due to the nature of civic affairs. So much of the deliberations of councils involve the disposition and development of real property and rules regarding the conduct of business (e.g., licensing, zoning, and contracting). The possibility of conflict between this public agenda and the private lives of elected officials is considerable because municipal politics disproportionately attracts people with roots in the property industry, and many councillors, especially in smaller centres, continue to work at their primary jobs or businesses.

A conflict of interest occurs when a public official is involved, directly or indirectly, in an activity or interest that will or may influence his or her decisions in office (City of Vancouver, n.d.). The existence of a conflict of interest is not necessarily the result of intentional wrongdoing, but may be merely the collision of one's private life with public office in ways that produce the possibility of personal gain.

Historically, the common law and early conflict of interest legislation designed for municipalities were ineffective in dealing with serious allegations of involvement of councillors with land developers (Sypnowich, 1991, p. 150). Penalties for an elected official acting in a conflict of interest were severe, potentially resulting in the setting aside of a decision made by the official, requiring the offender's seat to be declared vacant, and even disqualifying him or her from running for office for seven years (O'Connor and Smither, 1994, pp. 9–18). But the laws were also ambiguous with vague definitions of the nature of pecuniary interest and kinds of declarations required. Consequently, the courts were reluctant to convict offenders, producing a void of enforcement.

In the 1990s, many municipalities, their associations, and provinces have developed or passed proposals to modernize the common law and existing conflict of interest legislation to give them real teeth. The intent of conflict of interest rules is not to prevent people with a stake in their communities from holding public office, but to present clear guidelines as to the situation in which they must declare their private interests and abstain from decision making (O'Connor and Smither, 1994, p. 9–2). Current proposals require councillors to:

- declare, according to specific guidelines, the existence of (although not necessarily the value of) their real property, assets, and outside income, as well as that of their spouses and minor children (although this does not need to be declared separately);
- declare (initially orally and later in writing) the nature of the pecuniary interest when she or he is facing a situation of a conflict of interest; and
- in conflict situations, refrain from participating in the council's discussions or voting on the matter (Union of British Columbia Municipalities, 1995; Ontario Ministry of Municipal Affairs, 1992).

The penalties are not for having a conflict of interest in the first place, but for failure to disclose the conflict or withdraw from decision making accordingly. Increased public scrutiny and lack of tolerance for using public office for personal advantage have made the issues and rules surrounding ethical conduct a high priority in municipal governance. The chance of a "Wild Bill Hawrelak," who was turfed from office as mayor of Edmonton by the courts in 1959 for gross misconduct in a land deal, being re-elected (as he was a few years later) is highly unlikely today.

Conclusion

Politics concerns the trade-offs in values that underpin the decisions we make about the future of urban life. The traditional view of urban politics focusses overwhelmingly on delivering services efficiently and on either promoting or preventing development. There is little question that decisions about land use, economic development, and the delivery of services continue to be a big part of what urban governments do. Battles over particular developments, such as the construction of the Spadina Expressway in Toronto or the destruction of Africaville in Halifax, have become legendary in both the literature and urban lore. Under the pressures of globalization, the issues surrounding the debates over development have become more expansive. Today development issues include broad visions for the economic future of city-regions and questions concerning how cities can become more competitive internationally. Increasingly this debate also includes issues of municipal autonomy and relationships with the provincial and federal governments. We noted, for example, that the 1995 election in Edmonton was a hard fought battle over a vision of how a city in decline could re-establish its economic base. In Montreal, a central dimension of the 1994 election was how it could strike a better fiscal deal with the province in order to begin to address some of its economic problems.

In our view, this is the reason why the substance of urban politics has broader importance. This view was first and is still most eloquently expressed by Jane Jacobs. The central issue in cities, argues Jacobs (1961), is accommodating and encouraging diversity, in both a physical and cultural sense. As we also saw in this chapter, debates over multiculturalism, language and cultural communities, integration of new immigrants, and promotion of racial tolerance are also the stuff of urban politics. As cities become the sites at which the shrinking of the welfare state is put to the test of deciding which specific programs or services to cut, issues of redistribution across classes and specific groups are becoming more critical. While these questions relate to economic development, they concern the quality of life more broadly. In spite of the fact that local governments often do not have the requisite levers or authority to deal with many of these quality of life issues, they nevertheless remain part of local political debates.

It is important to recognize that politics is not only about outcomes but about the nature of representation itself. Who gets to speak for whom, on what issues and with what degree of influence? As discussed in this chapter, debates over representation and the practices of local democracy figure prominently in many Canadian cities. The question of the ward system in Vancouver has been a lively debate for the past three decades; concerns regarding the appropriate role of political parties have been a backdrop to elections in Winnipeg; and the tension between autocratic mayoral styles and the public's desire to open up the policy and planning process to citizens has been a recurring theme in Montreal politics. Given the centrality of such fundamental debates, it is evident that urban politics is far from dead.

This does not mean that the patient may not be ailing, however. Globalization and the growing class division between the wealthy and the poor are creating a two-class society composed of locals and elites (Lasch, 1995, p. 28; Mayer, 1995). Under globalization, the new elites are highly mobile (likely to move from one international city to another) and oriented to the international scene through their business, entertainment, and personal ties. In contrast to the traditional, often philanthropic, elites who tended to be leaders in community life and politics, these new elites have little attachment to place. They prefer to live in homogeneous communities of walled suburbs and private schools, are less dependent on public services, and are less tolerant of differences across society. Thus they are less willing to make sacrifices for the community and are not strong participants in local civic affairs. As Christopher Lasch argues, "[t]he new elites are at home only in transit, en route to a high-level conference, to the grand opening of a new franchise, to an international film festival, or to an undiscovered resort. Theirs is essentially a tourist's view of the world — not a perspective likely to encourage a passionate devotion to democracy" (1995, p. 6). If Lasch is correct in his analysis, the challenge of urban politics in the coming decades will be to reconnect the placeless elites with communities and to encourage their participation in local politics.

NOTES

1. Vancouver requires no fee and only two supporting signatures to register as a candidate. Many of the joke candidates among the 58 contenders for mayor in the 1996 election were signed up in a local pub (in exchange for free beer) by a former member of the Rhinoceros Party. While incumbent Philip Owen won the 1996 election with 53 percent of the popular vote, Mr./Ms Sage Advice actually placed sixth (taking 340 votes) and Mr. Chimp came in ninth with 264 votes.

2. A Canadian municipality that has led the way in experimentation with direct democracy is Rossland, BC, a city of 3700 in the southern Kootenay region. In 1990, the city adopted a constitution which enables residents to force a referendum or initiate legislation with a petition containing the signatures of 20 percent of the population. Voters' interest has been strong with an average of 60 percent voter turnout on the proposals to date. While proposals for approving pay raises for council members were defeated, residents voted with a clear majority to accept a $100 property tax increase to improve the water quality. "Power to the Politicians," *Alberta Report*, June 6, 1994, p.16.

SUGGESTED READINGS

Clarke, Susan E. and Andrew Kirby. (1990). "In Search of the Corpse: The Mysterious Case of Local Politics." *Urban Affairs Quarterly*, 25(3): 389–412. This article challenges the argument made by Gottdiener and others that urban politics is dead.

Magnusson, Warren. (1981). "Community Organization and Local Self-Government." In *Politics and Government of Urban Canada*, edited by Lionel D. Feldman. Toronto: Methuen, pp. 61–86. In this essay, Magnusson revisits the classical debates about whether local government is more democratic and closer to the people than other levels of government.

O'Connor, M. Rick and Michael J. Smither. (1994). *Open Local Government*. Toronto: Municipal World. A highly recommended book, especially for the practitioner, dealing in depth with issues surrounding conflict of interest, open meetings, and other conventions of open government.

Ruddick, Susan. (1990). "The Montreal Citizens' Movement: The Realpolitik of the 1990s?" In *Fire in the Hearth: The Radical Politics of Place in America*, edited by Mike Davis, Steven Hiatt, Marie Kennedy, Susan Ruddick, and Michael Sprinker. London: Verso, pp. 287–316. Students will find Ruddick's essay a useful example of the application of a political economy framework to urban politics, as well as an insightful comparison of the politics of Drapeau and Doré.

Siegel, David. (1994). "Politics, Politicians, and Public Servants in Non-partisan Local Governments." *Canadian Public Administration*, 37(1): 7–30. Essential reading for students who want to explore the relationship between politicians and municipal public servants in more depth. It lays out the comparison between the dynamics of municipal councils and parliamentary systems in a clear cogent manner.

BIBLIOGRAPHY

Adam, Mohammed. (1996). "Private Dinner Party for Councillors Leads to Secrecy Charges." *Ottawa Citizen*, January 10, pp. B1-2.

Alberta Report. (1994a). "It's Calgary All the Way," June 15, p. 13.

———. (1994b). "Red Faced in Redmonton," September 12, pp. 16–17.

———. (1994c). "Aldermania," October 17, p. 16.

Anderson, James D. (1979). "The Municipal Government Reform Movement in Western Canada, 1880–1920." In *The Usable Urban Past: Planning and Politics in the Modern Canadian City*, edited by Alan F.J. Artibise and Gilbert A. Stelter. Toronto: Macmillan, pp. 73–111.

Aubin, Henry. (1994). "Montreal Lags Behind in Allowing Minorities a Share of Power." *The Gazette* [Montreal], October 29, p. B3.

Baird, Dan. (1995). *The Calgary Herald*, September 16, p. B1.

Bashevkin, Sylvia. (1996). "Political Parties and the Representation of Women." In *Canadian Parties in Transition*, 2nd ed., edited by A. Brian Tanguay and Alain-G. Gagnon. Toronto: Nelson Canada, pp. 479–95.

Bowler, Vaughn and Michael Wanchuk. (1986). *Volunteers: Edmonton Federation of Community Leagues*. Edmonton: Lone Pine Press.

Boyer, Patrick. (1992). *The People's Mandate*. Toronto: Dundurn.

Brodie, Janine. (1985). *Women and Politics in Canada*. Toronto: McGraw-Hill Ryerson.

Brodie, Janine and Jill Vickers. (1981). "The More Things Change... Women in the 1979 Federal Campaign." In *Canada at the Polls: 1979 and 1989*, edited by H. R. Penniman. Washington DC: American Enterprise Institute, pp.322-336.

Came, Barry. (1996). "Storm Warnings." March 4 *MacLean's*, pp. 18–22. .

Chorney, Harold and Andrew Molloy. (1993). "Boss Politics in Montréal and Québec Nationalism Jean Drapeau to Jean Doré: From the Pre-modern to the Post-modern." In *Québec State and Society*, edited by Alain-G. Gagnon. Toronto, ON: Nelson Canada, pp. 64–79.

Clarke, Harold D., Jane Jenson, Lawrence LeDuc and Jon H. Pammett. (1991). *Absent Mandate*. 2nd ed. Toronto: Gage.

Clarke, Susan E. and Andrew Kirby. (1990). "In Search of the Corpse: The Mysterious Case of Local Politics." *Urban Affairs Quarterly*, 25(3): pp. 389–412.

Cronin, Thomas E. (1989). *Direct Democracy: The Politics of Initiative, Referendum, and Recall*. Cambridge, MA: Harvard University Press.

De Mara, Bruce. (1996). "Now Angry Hall Takes Gloves Off." *The Toronto Star*, December 18, p. A9.

Derfel, Aaron. (1997). "No Charges against Mayor." *The Gazette* [Montreal], January 21, pp. A1, A8.

Edmonton Journal. (1992). "Edmonton Election May Be in Doubt," October 20, p. A1.

Ferguson, Jack and Craig McInnes. (1991). "Election Renews the Quest for More Open Government." *The Globe and Mail*, October 15, p. A3

Flood, Gerald. (1992). "Novel Campaign Pays Off." *Winnipeg Free Press*, October 30, p. A1.

Gottdiener, Mark. (1987). *The Decline of Urban Politics: Political Theory and the Crisis of the Local State*. Newbury Park, CA: Sage.

Higgins, Donald J.H. (1986). *Local and Urban Politics in Canada*. Toronto: Gage.

Illingworth, Dick. (1995). "Party Politics at Local Level Unless Voters Start Voting." *Municipal World*, August, pp. 23–24.

Jacobs, Jane. (1961). *The Death and Life of Great American Cities*. New York: Vintage Books.

Kaplan, Harold. (1982). *Reform, Planning, and City Politics: Montreal, Winnipeg, Toronto*. Toronto: University of Toronto Press.

Kay, Barry J. (1982). "Urban Decision-Making and the Legislative Environment: Toronto Council Re-examined." *Canadian Journal of Political Science*. XV, 3: 553–74.

Kiernan, Matthew J. and David C. Walker. (1983). "Winnipeg." In *City Politics in Canada*, edited by Warren Magnusson and Andrew Sancton. Toronto: University of Toronto Press, pp. 222–54.

Lasch, Christopher. (1995). *The Revolt of the Elites and the Betrayal of Democracy*. New York: W. W. Norton.

Leveillee, Jacques. (1986). *Montreal after Drapeau*. Montreal: Black Rose Books.

Lustiger-Thaler, Henri. (1993). "On Thin Ice: Urban Politics in Montreal." *City Magazine* 14(2): 15–17.

Lustiger-Thaler, Henri and Eric Shragge. (1993). "New Politics in Montreal." *City Magazine*, 14(2): 28–31.

Magnusson, Warren. (1981). "Community Organization and Local Self-Government." In *Politics and Government of Urban Canada*, edited by Lionel D. Feldman. Toronto: Methuen, pp. 61–86.

Maillé, Chantal. (1990). *Primed for Power*. Ottawa: Canadian Advisory Council on the Status of Women.

Marson, Jean-Claude. (1995). "MCM and Planning." *Plan Canada*, January, 41.

Masson, Jack with Edward C. LeSage Jr. (1994). *Alberta's Local Governments: Politics and Democracy*. Edmonton: University of Alberta Press.

Mayer, Margit. (1995). "Urban Governance in the Post-Fordist City." In *Managing Cities: The New Urban Context*, edited by Pastsy Healey et al. Chichester, UK: John Wiley & Sons. pp. 231–49.

McCormick, Peter. (1996). "Provincial Party System, 1945–1993." In *Canadian Parties in Transition*, 2nd ed., edited by A. Brian Tanguay and Alain-G. Gagnon. Toronto: Nelson Canada, pp. 349–71.

Milner, Henry. (1988). "The Montreal Citizens' Movement, Then and Now." *Québec Studies*, 6: 1–11.

O'Connor and Smither. (1994). *Open Local Government*. Toronto: Municipal World.

Peritz, Ingrid. (1990). "Flip-Flop in the MCM." *The Gazette* [Montreal], October 30, pp. A1, A4.

Quesnel, Louise. (1994). "Party Politics in the Metropolis: Montreal 1960–1990." In *The Changing Canadian Metropolis: A Public Policy Perspective*, vol.2, edited by Frances Friskin. Berkeley and Toronto: Institute of Governmental Studies Press and Canadian Urban Institute, pp. 581–612.

Roy, Jean-Hugues. (1990). "Promises: The MCM's Credibility Gap." In *Montreal: A Citizen's Guide to Politics*, edited by Jean-Hugues Roy and Brendan Weston. Montreal: Black Rose Books, pp. 152–55.

Ruddick, Susan. (1990). "The Montreal Citizens' Movement: The Realpolitik of the 1990s?" In *Fire in the Hearth: The Radical Politics of Place in America*, edited by Mike Davis, Steven Hiatt, Marie Kennedy, Susan Ruddick, and Michael Sprinker. London: Verso, pp.287–316.

Sancton, Andrew. (1983). "Conclusion: Canadian City Politics in Comparative Perspective." In *City Politics in Canada*, edited by Warren Magnusson and Andrew Sancton. Toronto: University of Toronto Press, pp. 291–317.

———.(1985). *Governing the Island of Montreal: Language Differences and Metropolitan Politics*. Berkeley, CA: University of California Press.

Sancton, Andrew and Paul Woolner. (1990). "Full-Time Municipal Councillors: A Strategic Challenge for Canadian Urban Government." *Canadian Public Administration*, 33(4): 482–505.

Siblin, Eric. 1947. "Bourque Breaks New Ground." *The Gazette* [Montreal], January 18, p. A1, A14.

Siegel, David. (1987). "City Hall Doesn't Need Parties." *Policy Options*, June.

———. (1994). "Politics, Politicians, and Public Servants in Non-Partisan Local Governments." *Canadian Public Administration*, 37(1): 7–30.

Stanbury, W.T. (1996). "Regulating the Financing of Federal Parties and Candidates." In *Canadian Parties in Transition*. 2nd ed., edited by A. Brian Tanguay and Alain-G. Gagnon. Toronto: Nelson, pp. 372–402.

Synowich, Marcia. (1991). "Promoting Ethical Behaviour for Municipal Councils," *Canadian Public Administration*, 37(1): 7–30.

Tennant, Paul. (1980). "Vancouver Civic Politics 1929–1980." *B.C. Studies*, 46: 3–27.

Thomas, Timothy. (1995). "New Forms of Political Representation: European Ecological Politics and the Montreal Citizens' Movement." *Canadian Journal of Political Science*, XXVIII (3): 509–31.

Trimble, Linda. (1995). "Politics Where We Live: Women and Cities." In *Canadian Metropolitics*, edited by James Lightbody. Toronto: Copp Clark, pp. 92–114.

Whelan, Robert K. (1991). "The Politics of Urban Redevelopment in Montreal: Regime Change from Drapeau to Doré." *Québec Studies*, 12: 155–69.

CHAPTER SIX

INTEREST GROUPS AND PUBLIC PARTICIPATION

INTRODUCTION

In 1996, residents on the two sides of the Ottawa River lined up against each other over the issue of whether to add a third lane to the Champlain Bridge, one of five bridges linking Ottawa and Hull. A loose coalition called Communities before Cars was quickly formed by west-end Ottawa residents who feared an increase in traffic in their neighbourhoods. This group led a vigorous lobbying campaign that included letter writing, phoning, holding protests, and even using the courts in an attempt to halt the planning process. In the end, the National Capital Commission (NCC), in an effort to appease people on both sides of the river, decided to build the third lane but not to use it for a least a year (Adam, 1996, pp. A1–2). Still dissatisfied with this outcome, Communities before Cars launched legal action against the NCC.

Vancouver's Downtown Eastside Residents' Association (DERA), which represents the area around East Hastings and Main streets, once known as skid row, has evolved over the past 25 years from a conflict relationship with the city to being a partner in development. DERA had always been a strong advocate for decent, affordable housing to its poor population, but by 1990 the association had itself become one of the largest landlords in the downtown eastside (Hasson and Ley, 1994, pp. 197, 204).

In the City of Winnipeg's attempt to involve the public in the creation of a new economic development strategy between 1989 and 1995, city staff found it relatively easy to get the participation of the business community and suburban residents, but they were initially perplexed over how to include the Aboriginal, transient, and poor residents of downtown — people who seldom come to public meetings (Couture and Fielding, 1997). Cleverly, city officials turned to the primary and most trusted points of contact that these marginal populations have with the civic administration: public health nurses were thus recruited to ask their clients some fundamental questions about the downtown and their experiences living there. Although the overall response from the clients was limited, the ingenious approach yielded some valuable insights, created opportunities for future contact, and helped establish a co-operative working relationship between two disparate units — planning and public health — with the civic administration.

What do these vignettes tell us about urban governance? Collectively, they point to the important ways outside of the electoral arena in which citizens can participate in the political process: through collective action with other citizens, and through occasions when the government reaches out to learn from the public using exercises in citizen engagement. More specifically, the first example shows the ability of local communities to mobilize with great speed as interest groups, often managing to achieve a considerable impact on policy outcomes. In fact, cities are often portrayed as being overrun by single issue politics and "NIMBYism" (the not-in-my-backyard syndrome) (Lightbody, 1995, p. 296). The preponderance of interest groups, particularly NIMBYs, is argued to produce fragmentation of urban culture and, ultimately, the ungovernability of cities.

But the cases also show that it would be a serious fallacy to equate all citizens groups operating at the local level with expressions of mere single issue or reactionary protest politics designed to stop some development. Citizen groups do not merely react to narrow interests based on self-interest. Groups like DERA have an increasingly important role in the co-production of urban services. Indeed the importance of voluntary organizations in the delivery of services has led us to characterize them as the phantom arm of the local state. This also offers an alternative perspective to the ungovernability thesis: citizen groups are a vital means of self-government and help to create strong democracies — democracies that depend upon and respect pluralism, civic education, and citizen participation (Barber, 1984). As Jane Jacobs notes, "[a] city's very wholeness in bringing together people with communities of interest is one of its greatest assets, possibly the greatest" (1961, p. 119).

We must remember, too, that not all interest groups on the local stage are organizations of individual citizens. As the growth of machine and political economy perspectives discussed in Chapter Two remind us, by far the most organized, well resourced, and consistently effective lobbyists are business associations and developers. They are also increasingly involved in co-production with urban governments and are defining their scope of interest in very broad terms. In particular, business is taking the lead in pressing the economic development agenda on behalf of cities. For instance, in many cities in Ontario that are facing restructuring, the **boards of trade** are pushing for simplified one-tier political systems as part of an overall economic development strategy.

Finally, the last example is illustrative of the long-standing practice by urban governments of engaging citizens through **public participation** exercises. Public participation has gradually expanded over the past 25 years from formalized hearings surrounding official land-use planning to covering broader issues related to budgeting, economic development, and political restructuring. Innovative methods have been developed to reach out to diverse urban populations.

This chapter expands the analysis of representation and political participation begun in Chapter Five with the intent of developing a fuller understanding of the ways in which citizens and citizen groups are involved in urban politics and community life. We begin our discussion by examining the types of interest groups and **social movements** that are regular and featured actors in urban politics and then explore some of the means they use for effective advocacy to urban governments. In the second section, we explore the evolving art and environment of public participation in Canadian cities.

INTEREST GROUPS AND SOCIAL MOVEMENTS

Collectively, interest groups and social movements perform three crucial roles in the political process and in society (Phillips, 1995). First, they *represent* the identities, interests, and concerns of their memberships and communities with a view to changing public policy, educating the broader public, and influencing the behaviour of society at large. Representation is equally as vital to the well established business community as it is to fledgling associations of new immigrants or poor people, although the latter may have much farther to go in gaining access to political debates. Indeed, citizen groups may need to introduce new discourses about issues in order for their concerns to be recognized as legitimate and political. Second, as discussed in more depth in Chapters Nine and Eleven, many citizen and business organizations are increasingly involved in the co-production of and direct *delivery* of a wide variety of services to their communities. The third basic role of citizen groups is as a basis for *engagement*, which reinforces citizenship through participation as well as representation. Here the similarities between business and citizen groups break down. Business associations depend more on representation through their leadership and are often content being staff-led organizations, whereas citizen groups rely on getting people to act, even to protest when necessary. Because citizens generally have little political clout as individuals, they depend upon collective action to gain influence. Groups thus provide opportunities for people to get engaged: in coming together to debate and clarify societal values and policy issues, in identifying as members of a broader community, in enhancing a personal sense of political efficacy, and in working for the benefit of fellow citizens.

Citizen Groups: A Conceptual Map

There is a wide diversity of citizen-based interest groups involved in urban politics and government. To a considerable degree, this reflects the different ways citizens organize for political activity, locally and more broadly. Within any Canadian city, we find:

- **neighbourhood associations** that have roots in a geographic territory;
- **issue-oriented groups** which build social communities of interest that are not primarily geographically based;
- identity-focussed grassroots organizations of national social movements; and
- site-specific protest groups, often called NIMBYs.

NEIGHBOURHOOD ORGANIZATIONS

Neighbourhood or community organizations (variously called associations or leagues) are citizen groups oriented toward improving or maintaining the quality of life in a geographically delimited residential area (Logan and Rabrenovic, 1990, p. 68). Community associations are not recent phenomena in Canadian cities. The first official community based organization in Canada was started in Edmonton in 1917 when one of the city's commissioners, an American by birth, imported the idea of a community league to organize the citizens of Jasper Place, a new residential area on the edge of the city.

Many neighbourhood organizations started out as ratepayer associations, designed to protect the privilege and investment of property owners, but over the years were converted into more inclusive organizations including homeowners and tenants with a broader range of concerns over quality of community life, not just protecting property values. The longevity of these associations is striking. For example, in Calgary, where community associations started at about the same time as in Edmonton, all but three of the original associations remain (Davies and Townsend, 1994, p. 1742).

Emphasis on the value of community organizing was further augmented in the 1960s with the popularization of the lessons of Saul Alinsky's (1971) "rules for radicals." Alinsky was a community activist in Chicago from the 1930s through 1950s who stressed and developed techniques for community empowerment. Gradually, urban governments themselves got directly involved in helping neighbourhoods do their own community development, often creating Community Development departments as part of the land-use planning function. This encouraged the emergence of local community leadership. Today a number of Canadian cities, notably Edmonton, Calgary, and Ottawa, have highly developed city-wide systems of community associations operating under umbrella structures; other cities, such as Vancouver and Toronto, have a range of fledgling to very strong neighbourhood organizations, although they are not systematically organized in the same way.

Like the neighbourhoods they represent, associations vary enormously in their characteristics, levels of activity, and relationships with government, but several features are common. First, neighbourhood organizations represent the concerns of their communities on a broad range of issues on an ongoing basis in the land-use and social planning process. The civic administration actively encourages this participation and routinely consults with or invites community association representatives to sit on advisory councils or task forces because they are regarded as the experts on neighbourhood issues. Community associations thus generally do a good job providing two-way communication between the city and neighbourhoods. People trust their community associations, more so than they trust politicians, whether they directly participate in the associations or not (Berry et al., 1993, p. 177). Residents tend to perceive community associations as credible, non-partisan sources of information about neighbourhood issues and feel that their leadership is directly accountable.

Community associations do more than lobby or consult with local governments. They are increasingly engaged in co-production: running sports, education, and fitness programs; undertaking community environmental and aesthetic activities (e.g., parks maintenance, recycling); organizing social events (e.g., block parties and picnics); assisting in safety and security programs (e.g., block parents); and providing, independently or by contract with the municipality, charity, goodwill, and social services (Davies and Townsend, 1994). As the example of the Vancouver Downtown Eastside Residents' Association illustrates, this co-production role is becoming increasingly important as the state withdraws from the direct provision of many social services and other programs.

ISSUE-ORIENTED GROUPS

The second type of citizen group includes those public interest groups that build communities of interest and advocate on behalf of constituencies that are not primarily geographically based. While many of these groups have narrowly defined interests, such as promoting the development and use of bicycle pathways, others define their interests more broadly, focussing on such issues as environmental protection, relief of poverty, integration and support of new immigrants, or promotion of the arts and culture. The number and variety of issue-oriented groups at the local level have exploded since the 1970s. Many of them were born out of protest, specifically against construction of major freeways and other urban renewal projects (Higgins, 1986, pp. 282–7). In addition, there has been a sharp rise over the past decade in the number of groups representing ethnic, racial, and cultural communities. Issue-oriented groups are distinguishable from the NIMBY element by their relative permanency (with varying levels of infrastructure and activism at different times) and their adoption of broader goals, usually related to monitoring a city's penchant for growth, seeking improvements in the quality of urban life, and securing a voice for disadvantaged groups.

The relationship of issue-oriented groups to urban government is often an adversarial one, but there is a much greater mutual dependency than is generally supposed. These groups play a vital role as sounding boards for new policy ideas. This is true from the perspective of both local politicians and bureaucrats. These groups also help focus attention on issues and mobilize interest and participation by their diverse communities. For example, the Community Services Network, a broad coalition of over 70 community-based organizations with some connection to social development, has worked to keep the issue of the social implications of restructuring local government and provincial–municipal financial relations on the front burner in the Halifax region. Finally, many of these groups rely on the local government for funding. This is an increasingly difficult aspect of the relationship. It is also increasingly the case that issue-oriented groups are pitted against one another and against community associations and more traditional charities in the competition for funds from the local government and other sources. In 1995, for example, the City of Ottawa, gave almost $6.8 million in grants to 189 groups; by 1996, this had decreased to $6.3 million, partly as a result of cuts in provincial transfers.

THE GRASSROOTS OF NATIONAL SOCIAL MOVEMENTS

Not all citizen organizations active at the local level are specifically local in their focus or identity. Historically, nationally mobilized social movements have had their origins and strongest bases of support in urban centres due not only to the concentration of people but to cities' tolerance of diversity. The New Social Movements (NSMs), such as the women's, peace, and environmental movements, that arose in the late 1960s are no exception. The NSM practices of coalitional politics, giving voice to the disadvantaged and marginalized groups, and allowing such groups to speak for themselves have opened new debates about the nature of democratic politics. And they have had considerable success. As Hamel (1991) notes, the variety of very active social movement organizations in Montreal has reclaimed a more humanitarian city: more ecological, with a better design, and with a politics that is more open to public debate.

The gay and lesbian movements provide a good example of how the grassroots of national movements have influenced both city space and politics. In addition to policy advocacy — aimed most specifically at the police and, following the spread of AIDS, at the medical establishment — an important dimension of the gay and lesbian movements has been to create new cultural and social identities. This identity is reinforced by public events, such as gay pride parades, and in the embodiment of culture in space. In Montreal, for instance, the establishment of a gay culture has had lasting spatial and electoral implications with the development of the "Gay Village" on the east side of downtown, where gay men now account for 40 percent of the electorate (Herland, 1992, p. 156). The small but growing concentration of gay businesses in Ottawa (identified by their multi-coloured flags which are a symbol of gay and lesbian activism) is starting to revitalize a rather seedy commercial area in Centretown (Boswell, 1996, pp. A1–2). At the same time, it is sending a political message of recognition and acceptance of this often harassed segment of society.

NIMBYs

NIMBY organizations are a relatively recent phenomenon, attracting attention beginning in the 1980s. They have been characterized as reactionary protest groups, working to stop the siting of a specific facility in order to protect the group's own narrow self-interest. They are partly a reflection of the spillover effects of the siting of a public good (e.g., a highway or solid-waste dump), whereby the benefits may accrue broadly but the disadvantages are concentrated near the site locale (Wolsink, 1994, p. 854). The influence of NIMBYs has been felt most keenly in the siting of waste management facilities and group homes.

Many scholars argue that the emergence of NIMBY groups is a direct consequence of the decentralization of decision making and opening of the policy process through mandated citizen participation that occurred in the 1970s and 80s (Filion, 1992, p. 170). For instance, environmental protection and planning legislation provided new opportunities for stopping projects by providing new procedural instruments, such as public hearings and appeals to quasi-judiciary bodies. In the late 1970s, many provinces embarked on policies of de-institutionalization and privatization of psychiatric and criminal justice facilities, but they vested responsibility for siting the new decentralized services, such as group homes, detox centres and halfway houses, with local governments (Laws, 1994, p. 13). This transformed social tensions between marginalized populations and middle income groups into conflicts over the built environment, thereby situating these tensions concretely in contested locales.

NIMBY groups often mobilize quickly with minimal infrastructure and under leadership that may not be overly concerned about the long-term relations with the community or the government. Once a decision on the project in question is made, NIMBYs usually fade equally quickly. Nevertheless, they can be very effective in changing site decisions, although they may increase the fractiousness within a community. Thus NIMBYs are the subject of considerable interest to local media which love to report a good fight.

In spite of the media attention, there is some indication that the preponderance and influence of NIMBYs have been overestimated (Wolsink, 1994). This is partly because the NIMBY label is applied in a blanket fashion to any public interest group opposing a development. But environmental groups that oppose a solid-waste dump because they want to see policies directed at reuse and recycling, or a group that attempts to stop the development of a highway because it believes investment in public transit is a better policy option, are not properly categorized as NIMBY groups.

While NIMBY organizations may empower local citizens, the danger is that they elevate parochialism and use it to their advantage with neither a willingness to accommodate other concerns nor an interest in long-term relations, either with the government or their constituents. Of the community interest groups we have discussed, NIMBYs are obviously the farthest removed from the local government. Generally speaking, they are not involved in co-production nor do they receive funding from the local government. Their dominant profile in the media makes it important to understand them in the context of the wide range of other groups that have a more entangled relationship with the local government. By doing so, we get a sense of the complexity and variety of relations between local interest groups and local government.

Business Organizations

Business–government relations are the subject of considerable interest in the study of Canadian politics and public administration (see, for example, Atkinson and Coleman, 1989). Our treatment of the theory and history of urban government in Canada suggests that the business–local government relationship is centrally important to the course of urban politics and administration. As discussed in the last chapter, municipal elections are frequently contested by candidates with close ties to the local business sector. However, it is equally important to understand the nature of corporate involvement with city hall outside the electoral process.

Virtually every municipality in Canada has a chamber of commerce. In large centres, such organizations tend to call themselves boards of trade. They represent the interests of a broad cross-section of local businesses and industry, which support their work through annual membership fees. In large cities, these are highly organized, sophisticated, and well-resourced business associations. The property development industry is also highly organized (with some natural overlap in membership in the boards of trade) as large integrated local–national associations which can exercise influence at all three levels of government. For instance, the Canadian Home Builders Association, which is the voice of the residential construction industry, is organized into 80 local associations, ten provincial councils, and a national office. In addition, the Urban Development Institute represents the interests of the development industry more broadly, with a corporate membership of over 1000, including development related professionals (e.g., surveyors and architects) as well as development companies. But many developers have a large enough presence on the local scene in their own right that they do not have to work through an industry association at all. When acting as proponents of a particular project, developers tend to lobby as individual corporations.

Publicly and through less visible channels, local business associations ply the perspective of the local business community to elected officials and local bureaucrats, the media, and the public more generally. They have been active and vocal on issues of local reform and restructuring, favouring simplified municipal structures and a "back to basics" orientation to service delivery, especially in the face of fiscal constraints. Tax increases and other revenue-generating schemes that might affect local business are also a consistent bone of contention. Business associations have been strong allies of city hall in lobbying provincial and federal governments, as well as private investors, on matters of economic development. The Ottawa business community, for example, played a major role in getting better airline connections from the capital to the American cities, such as Boston and Raleigh-Durham, that are vital to the local hi-tech companies.

We are seeing new trends in the entanglement of business and urban government. Perhaps the first and most prominent development has been the increased reliance by urban governments on the private sector for the delivery of local services. Urban governments discovered "contracting out" long before their provincial and federal counterparts. Consideration of contracting out was undertaken most often in the case of garbage collection and disposal but is now common practice in a wide range of other services.

The merits of contracting out have been hotly debated (McDavid and Clemens, 1991; Graham, 1995). But the pressures on urban governments to consider this as a service delivery alternative are growing with the perception that contracting out is more cost-efficient and with the development of new business ventures that offer services to municipalities for the delivery of such things as recreation facilities, parks maintenance, and the operation of major water and sewage treatment plants. Although the beneficiaries of contracting out have been individual firms, it is local business organizations that have been active in promoting the idea, as one element of urban restructuring in tough fiscal times.

The second dimension of contemporary entanglement is the establishment of partnerships between local business organizations and the local government. As we discuss in more depth in Chapter Ten, these partnerships have become increasingly common in the field of economic development and themselves represent a form of restructuring. The model adopted in both Ottawa-Carleton and Halifax, for example, involves the creation of an economic development authority, with the municipality providing the majority of funds and the business community providing most of the activities. As discussed in Chapter Eleven, partnerships are now extending beyond economic development.

ADVOCACY AND THE LOCAL STATE

What is the key to effective political participation and advocacy by citizen organizations? Under increasingly diverse economic and social conditions and faced with a multitude of types of groups and issues, there is no one recipe for success. However, a number of consistently important factors can be identified (Woliver, 1993; Oropesa, 1989). In a recent analysis of citizen activities in Vancouver, Hasson and Ley (1994) present several instructive case studies of successful advocacy by citizen organizations.

Vancouver's wealthy upper-class neighbourhood of Shaughnessy Heights was able to preserve its English country way of life of "tasteful seclusion" against infilling in the face of a serious housing crisis in the lower mainland. It even won support from a social democratic mayor and council for a land-use plan that would force lower-income renters out of old mansions converted to rooming houses in the area. The associations of Vancouver's Chinatown were able not only to stave off massive urban renewal and freeway projects in the 1970s but, in the 1980s, transformed the city's view of the neighbourhood from a slightly distasteful area that officials disparagingly dismissed as "of significance only to the people who live there" to a beautified civic asset that was promoted for its distinctive contribution to Canadian multiculturalism (Hasson and Ley, 1994, p. 301). The Vancouver residents' association, DERA, of the adjoining downtown eastside used both conflict and joint ventures with the City to transform their area from being the most marginalized district of the city — a tax sink in the view of the planning department — to one that offered considerable amenities for its low income population.

Collectively these stories offer several lessons for citizen organizations. The first lesson is the value of effective, charismatic leadership with strong connections to the constituency. The success of DERA, for instance, was greatly assisted by two generations of charismatic and persistent leaders who knew the community intimately and had visions, consistent ideology, and tough negotiation skills. More importantly, DERA's leadership was backed by a large, active, and inclusive membership that spanned racial and income boundaries.

Second, effective citizen organizations take the lead in shaping or recasting political discourse. The leaders of the Shaughnessy Heights Property Owners Association (SHPOA) realized that it would never garner broad support outside the community by portraying itself as an affluent neighbourhood bent on preserving its privilege. Instead, it made its particular interests into city-wide ones by stressing that preserving the green space and architectural heritage of the area benefited the broader goals of creating a "livable city" (Hasson and Ley, 1994, p. 81). Similarly, one of the first tactical moves of DERA was to reshape the image of the neighbourhood from skid row, with its presumed marginality emphasizing the deviant and impoverished nature of the population, to a community focussing on its stability and loyalty (only a small minority, in fact, were transient alcoholics). Indeed one of DERA's first tasks was to rename the area from "skid row" to the "Downtown Eastside" to better suit this new identity.[1] In this struggle for identity, skilful use of the media is critical in getting an organization's message out. For instance, the media delighted in DERA's "Crummy Cockroach Haven Contest" which invited residents to nominate the "three sleaziest dives" in the district. The publicity, however, compelled the City to prosecute the winner of the contest and establish a downtown housing strategy (Hasson and Ley, 1994, p. 314).

Alliances with other organizations and with professionals outside an organization's immediate constituency are extremely valuable as bridges to broader support and enabling resources. From its inception, the community association of Chinatown–Strathcona purposefully and carefully cultivated allies outside of the Asian community and enlisted the support of non-resident professionals in planning, architecture, and law who volunteered their time as part of their personal learning experience. Many of these young professionals (notably Mike Harcourt, then a law student, and Darlene Marzari, a social planning co-ordinator with the City) went on to political careers but never lost their understanding and support for the Strathcona community. In addition, the community used the fragmentation of the government to its advantage. At the height of the community's protest against massive urban renewal in 1968, the Strathcona community invited visiting federal officials on a walking tour of the neighbourhood. "With precipitous speed, just over a week later, the city was informed that the federal government would withdraw or severely limit funds for urban renewal," effectively killing the City's plans (Hasson and Ley, 1994, p. 122). The federal government may now be less willing or able to intercede in such conflicts in the 1990s as it adheres increasingly to principles of municipal autonomy and deals with its own fiscal restraint. Nonetheless, interjurisdictional complexity or interdepartmental fragmentation within a city may present considerable opportunities for a citizen organization.

Citizen organizations must appreciate and integrate the political and cultural differences within the geographic or social community they are attempting to serve. Rarely does only one set of values permeate a community or an organization. In the case of Vancouver's Chinatown, the City has imposed its own conception of race and place on the community, assuming that this classification naturally created boundaries of inclusion and exclusion. In other words, it assumed that all residents of Chinatown were alike. But, as Hasson and Ley reveal, the community initially was not united and some of the most interesting debates took place within the community among the Chinese Benevolent Association (a very traditional organization), the Chinese merchants' associations, and the younger generation of well educated activists with ties outside the community. These potentially conflicting factions were mobilized to work collectively and supportively, in part, because the leadership was attuned to these differences and mobilized the district on a house-by-house basis using a system of block captains.

Finally, reliance on the local state to supply resources or solutions for an organization is often short-sighted. Increasingly, resources need to be found from other sources, and organizations must look to self-help and the co-production of services, as DERA has done in the provision of affordable housing. This is not an excuse for abdication of state responsibility but a recognition that the role of all governments relative to civil society is undergoing profound transitions. Interest groups are increasingly integrated into the politics and delivery of services by the local state, but the state's willingness to support advocacy or representational activities has declined dramatically.

As we think about advocacy and the local state in light of contemporary developments, we have to consider both the practice of advocacy and the trend to co-production with citizens and business organizations. In doing this, it is possible to incline toward a pessimistic view — namely that increased reliance on voluntary associations of citizens and businesses, who practice advocacy and are engaged in co-production, will encourage city governments to be clientelist in nature (dedicated to a particular function or group) and, increasingly, to be devoid of real capacity to govern. In this view, municipal governments, even in large city-regions, would see themselves and be seen by others as the focal point for the politics of pot-holes and parking rather than as vital actors in community development and democratic life. This would speak to one common theoretical conception of municipal government as a weak part of a liberal democracy. In terms of these developments, city governments would be characterized as having a "democratic deficit" resulting from crises of ungovernability and legitimacy.

Alternatively, one might take a broader view — that all of this activity by citizen and business associations combined with local governments' wide-ranging partnership and alternative service delivery arrangements represent the flowering of local democracy. Following from this perspective, the specific role of municipal governments is to be responsive to the demands made on it by the public and by new quasi-state actors. In the next section, we examine one of the important ways in which urban governments have tried to be more responsive to and learn from their various publics.

PUBLIC ENGAGEMENT
Origins of Public Participation

In addition to being on the receiving end of advocacy, city governments actively solicit the public's views through exercises in public participation. By public participation, we mean the occasions outside of the electoral process when the council and/or administration solicits input and attempts, at the very least, to learn from the public. Given the openness of local governments, with their easy access to elected officials and regular opportunities for citizens to appear before city council, it may seem surprising that local governments bother with organized public participation at all. As we argued in Chapter Five, however, urban politics is the politics of everyday life. The effects of many policies of city governments are felt tangibly and relatively immediately by citizens. Not

surprisingly then, citizens want to have a say in the policy decisions of municipal governments. The conventions of open government, rather than spawning
complacency, have created expectations that citizens will be heard. As a result,
local governments have been leaders in soliciting public engagement in major
governance decisions and innovators in developing methods for participation
that respond to changing political environments and urban populations.

Canadian municipal governments got involved in making public participation a component of their decision making processes in the late 1960s and
early 70s through two routes. The first route was through the land-use planning process and was justified on the grounds of producing better decisions
by incorporating more information into the planning process and of promoting efficiency in decision making. As cities in the 1970s proceeded with
development plans, they often encountered community groups bent on stopping a particular development at late stages in the planning process. Thus it
seemed more efficient to give citizens information about the proposed land-
use plan and get their reactions early in the process so as to prevent organized protest and appeals later on, after much time and money had already
been invested. Gradually, public participation became common practice and
was even mandated by provincial governments as a requisite part of the
development of official plans.

This planning-based perspective was counterbalanced by the community
development approach advocated primarily by community activists. The foundation of the argument that involvement of the public in decision making builds
healthier communities and nourishes democracy is much older, however. John
Stuart Mill argued in the nineteenth century that involvement of the public in
government decision making would enhance civic education and produce more
efficacious citizens. The theme of community empowerment was picked up in
this century by Saul Alinsky (1971) and his followers. In addition to developing
approaches to advocacy, they focussed on community activism and development
(Arnstein, 1969). Urban reform movements of the 1970s, which were fuelled by
these notions of neighbourhood control, met with considerable success in stopping major urban renewal projects, such as Toronto's Spadina Expressway and
the razing of Vancouver's Chinatown. In the 1990s, the importance of community organizing has been revitalized under the concept of "social capital" (a term
first used by Jane Jacobs in 1961, but made popular in the 1990s by the work of
Robert Putnam). The argument is that social capital — the informal networks of
trust built up by interactions among citizens through the voluntary process of
helping one another and participating in political activities — builds a generalized sense of trust and co-operation in society. This is argued to contribute to
more efficient and effective government and a more productive economy.

The Routinization of Public Participation

By the end of the 1970s, public participation, much to the delight and largely
because of planners, became routine — a regular, sometimes mandatory feature of
local planning. As it became routine, participation also became professionalized,

thereby becoming the almost exclusive purview of planners and a new industry of other professionals who specialized in facilitating and organizing participation exercises for governments. This professionalization is widely regarded as one of the reasons for the frequent failure of public participation. One view is that professional planners were unwilling to combine their technical expertise (which gave them control over the planning process) with communities' expertise based on popular knowledge, so their solution was to control the participation process as well (Prior, Stewart, and Walsh, 1995, p. 142). A more charitable view is that most planners were genuinely interested in making participation work, but professionalization was a natural result of making it part of their repertoire of planning techniques. A consequence of this professionalization is that governments often measure the effectiveness of participation by counting the number of people who participated, no matter how shallow their involvement. Thus, while there were many innovations and expansion of who participated over the course of the 1970s and 80s, the standardization of practices narrowed the scope and impact of participation (Howard, Lipsky, and Marshall, 1994, p. 154).

At the same time, community activists for the most part had become preoccupied not with the question of defining the kind of communities they wanted and developing lasting social capital but with the NIMBY syndrome — using community power to stop particular projects. Because the type of public participation undertaken by local governments seldom involved real power-sharing, many community activists acquired a deep sense of mistrust of planners and the planning process. To them, invited participation often seemed little more that a ritual dance of tell and sell.

These two routes to participation have produced a broad spectrum of commitment to and practices of participation, ranging from those who see it mainly as an exercise in information gathering to those who see it as a means of power sharing and creating more citizen-centred government. In our view, while public participation does not necessarily mean handing over power to citizens, it does imply mutual obligations between citizens and local governments. At a minimum, it involves two-way communication which entails some potential for influencing policy decisions and outcomes (Graham and Phillips, 1997). This requires more than sending information out by hosting a big event, such as a public meeting or open house, and more than simply gathering information in, as in a customer survey. Indeed, public participation should not be thought of as a single or even a series of techniques that can be pulled out by the local government and applied in any situation. Engaging the public is a way of doing civic business, an ongoing mode of operation for urban governments. It is an interactive and iterative process that must be well connected to political processes and must fit the appropriate techniques to a broader set of concerns and principles.

What Makes Public Participation Effective?

No one method of public participation is appropriate or adequate to every situation, but a number of guiding principles emerge from case studies of public participation in local government in Canada (Graham and Phillips, 1997).

ESTABLISHING A "CONTRACT" WITH THE COMMUNITY

As public participation became a professionalized part of land-use planning, it often became perfunctory, that is, done for every major decision without much forethought. This is usually the most common reason it fails. In such cases, the city neither fully understands nor communicates the reasons why it is engaging the public in the first place. Sometimes real options and possibilities for change are limited, but the civic administration is afraid to say this, so it allows participants to think that much more is feasible than is really the case. As Sancton (1997) notes, for example, the hearings held by the commissioner charged with making recommendations for amalgamation of the counties and municipalities surrounding London, Ontario, were "joyfully participatory" and residents made thoughtful recommendations on a wide range of issues. But their participation had minimal impact on the commissioner's report because his terms of reference were, in fact, very narrow — a detail that had never been communicated to the participants. In these situations, which have been all too common in Canadian cities, citizens naturally feel cheated by the process and conclude that it was a sham and a waste of their time. Thus the first guiding principle is that public participation be approached as a kind of "contract" with citizens in which both the potential and the limitations are identified so that people can appropriately assess whether it will be worthwhile being involved at all.

TIMING

In some instances, the goal of engaging the public is to develop a vision for the future and thus it is important to undertake the exercise before key decisions about possible futures have already been made. In developing its recent *CityPlan*, for example, the City of Vancouver consulted thousands of residents with the goal of identifying their core values and the kind of city they would like theirs to be. *CityPlan* produced a vision based on a "city of neighbourhoods" that would offer affordable housing, good jobs close to home, parks and green space, clean air and water, and more money for arts and culture (Sewell, 1997). The critics questioned, however, whether it really took a massive public participation effort, costing $1.9 million, to produce such a set of platitudes without making any hard choices (Seelig, 1995; Sewell, 1997). In contrast, policies that are presented to the public late in the decision making process often have had key options foreclosed.

Daniel Yankelovich (1991) argues that coming to public judgement involves several stages, from the awakening to the issue, through realization of the trade-offs involved, to making informed and responsible choices based on reconciling trade-offs in underlying values. Often public participation, especially polls, are taken as snapshots of public opinion at early stages when it is soft and volatile because people have not yet undertaken real deliberation about the pros and cons of choices. Furthermore, due to tight schedules for the public consultation phase, sufficient time for such deliberation is often not accorded.

The problem, then, is to determine timing that is just right — the point at which people can provide concrete suggestions and make real choices but with a range of possibilities and visions still open. Often this entails some guidelines as to what possibilities council considers to be feasible, and at what cost.

MAKING PUBLIC PARTICIPATION COMMUNITY BASED

Many urban governments struggle with the question of who the public is. In particular, three recurring issues arise in determining who should be the target set of participants:

- The value of involving groups versus individuals. Is it preferable to involve mainly organized interest groups, which have already acquired a certain degree of expertise and may have developed well thought out policy solutions (and who are likely to make themselves heard anyway), or the unaffiliated public — "ordinary Canadians" as these average citizens have come to be called?
- Breadth versus depth. Should public participation try to engage large numbers of people, even if the participation of any given individual is limited and perhaps somewhat shallow, or attempt to get intense involvement of smaller sets of people? While the advantages of reaching large numbers of people are raised awareness of an issue by the population as a whole and the opportunity for people to vent their feelings, the minimal commitment involved in going to a public meeting or responding to a customer survey seldom changes people's views or empowers communities. In contrast, small groups of participants selected by the government may be more likely to develop innovative solutions and reach a consensus, but they also run the risk of being condemned as elitist or unrepresentative by those on the outside.
- How to be inclusive. Faced with growing cultural diversity, urban governments struggle with how to reach non-white, non-middle-class communities who normally have little contact with city hall and perhaps less trust in government institutions.

Often public participation needs to do all three things at once. This involves using a variety of methods, having flexibility in how they are used, and committing sufficient time and resources. As the opening vignette of the City of Winnipeg's attempt to reach out to its downtown Aboriginal residents shows, this also necessitates having a deep underlying understanding and knowledge of the city's diverse communities and how to reach them.

Aside from the major events of big public participation exercises, much of the ongoing citizen engagement of urban governments rests on informal one-on-one contact of a city official — not necessarily a public participation professional — with customers, clients, and citizens in a variety of contexts. Often the challenge is not in making these contacts in the first place but in channelling them into and through the governing machinery in an appropriate way. In many cases, participation requires public education and building leadership capacity in the community before people can participate effectively at all. Even when the issues seem compelling and obvious, it still takes hard work to get people out and, in particular, to engage the more marginalized populations.

CONNECTING PUBLIC PARTICIPATION TO THE POLITICAL PROCESS

The legacy of the professionalization of participation is that the entire process is often run by public participation experts in isolation from council. However, politicians need to be involved throughout a process of public participation for at least two reasons. First is the interactive nature of the learning process, and second is the fact that politicians need to feel a sense of ownership of the process and to develop confidence in it. The danger of disconnecting participation from the political process is exemplified by the **constituent assembly** on political restructuring in the Regional Municipality of Hamilton-Wentworth. In 1995, a constituent assembly of 23 citizens representative of various sectors of the economy and society was established by the Regional Municipality with the mandate of making recommendations on restructuring the two-tier system and its six municipalities. For the next year, this group of volunteer citizens worked hard in subcommittees, assisted by two seconded staff, looking at all the costs and benefits of restructuring. The assembly's various activities consumed over 12 000 hours on the part of its members (Constituent Assembly on the Municipal Government System in Hamilton-Wentworth, 1996). At the end of this intensive process, the constituent assembly reached a consensus in favour of creating a single consolidated municipality in the region that would replace all of the existing municipalities. But their work as an independent assembly of citizens had taken place at a distance from the existing elected councils. Soon after the assembly began its work, politicians of the municipalities became uncomfortable with its directions and with the possibilities of amalgamation and undertook their own completely separate deliberations and consultations with constituents. Not surprisingly, the municipal politicians came up with their own report favouring a version of the status quo. The two groups could not negotiate an acceptable compromise so that at the time of publication, the decision on restructuring in Hamilton-Wentworth was awaiting adjudication by the province.

MAKING USE OF NEW TECHNOLOGIES BUT AVOIDING PUSH-BUTTON DEMOCRACY

The Internet has opened up new possibilities for communication and become a new information resource for citizens. As indicated in Table 6.1, all of the major cities have their own home pages on the Web, and interested citizens can find out a great deal about the structures, people, and current issues of their city with a little surfing. One limitation, however, is that the Internet operates almost exclusively in English. This is a source of ongoing concern for francophones in Montreal, Ottawa, and elsewhere.

Electronic mail is an easy way to ask a question of one's councillor or of a department head. The image of people sitting in front of their interactive television screens pushing buttons to vote at the same time as councils on policies and even on municipal budgets — a scenario that would have seemed like science fiction only a few years ago — is now a real possibility. While the immediacy of such home-based push button direct democracy is enticing, it is not, in itself, real public engagement. Without broader two-way dialogue and debate,

TABLE 6.1

INTERNET ADDRESSES FOR THE MAJOR CITIES

City/Regional Municipality	Address
City of Vancouver	http://www.city.vancouver.bc.ca
GVRD	http://www.gvrd.bc.ca
City of Calgary	http://www.gov.calgary.ab.ca
City of Edmonton	http://www.gov.edmonton.ab.ca
City of Winnipeg	http://www.mbnet.mb.ca/city
City of Toronto	http://www.city.toronto.on.ca
Metro Toronto	http://www.metrotor.on.ca
City of Ottawa	http://city.ottawa.on.ca
RMOC	http://www.rmoc.on.ca
City of Montreal	http://www.ville.montreal.qc.ca
MUC	http://www.cum.qc.ca
Halifax Regional Municipality	http://www.region.halifax.ns.ca

simply registering a vote may or may not be the result of a deliberative process that has included consideration of both costs and benefits.

In fact, the bulk of the technology of today's public engagement is quite low-tech, relying heavily on community television stations and community newspapers. While less glamorous, these media remain highly effective in reaching minority communities. In Vancouver, for example, the city manager's office did a series of community discussions through simultaneous translation into Mandarin on community cable TV. By most accounts, the Chinese newspapers in Vancouver now feature better coverage of city hall than the English language papers. Thus, while the Internet and other interactive technologies are additional tools for public engagement, they are not substitutes for direct personal contact with citizens and their communities.

MAKING PARTICIPATION A MUTUAL LEARNING PROCESS

A successful public participation exercise is premised on a desire to learn. This includes three components:

- Flexibility based on learning as you go. Learning means that the process needs to be sufficiently flexible, within an overall strategy, that new ideas and additional methods of participation can be tried if it appears they might be useful. Too often, public participation is undertaken on a very tight timetable so that there is no scope for following up leads and new developments without the process becoming unduly protracted.
- Transparency. People need assurances that their participation will be meaningful and will be used to inform decision making processes, even if they do not get their own way in the end. Therefore, it is important that the process

be transparent, that people can see how their input was interpreted and how it was used to inform decisions. A public record of the process is thus a basic requirement. But people also need to know that action is forthcoming and that closure can be brought to the consultation stage. As Couture and Fielding (1997) note, a pitfall in participation is that "there are too many round tables and not enough end tables."

- Building on the relationships created. While the public engagement surrounding a particular plan or policy needs to have a conclusion, the positive relationships created among city staff, community leaders, and individual citizens can be built upon as the basis of an ongoing process of more citizen-centred governance.

Current Challenges of Public Engagement

Perhaps the greatest challenge in public engagement is to respond to the rapidly changing contexts of urban and political environments. First, in a relatively few years beginning in the early 1990s, local governments have had to adopt the public participation practices that were developed primarily around official land-use planning for new policy spheres. Both fiscal pressures and new ideas about urban governance have propelled major public participation exercises in new areas including the budgeting process, economic development, alternative service delivery, and political restructuring. Second, while most cities have worked hard to make participation more inclusive rather than remaining the preserve of the educated middle class, the need to find appropriate ways of engaging diverse minority populations in which cultural norms may be very different and language a barrier, remains an ongoing challenge. Third, accommodating to and making the most effective use of technology will take some forward thinking and potentially upfront investment by municipal governments.

In addition, public participation is evolving to fit the changing philosophy of governance that is taking hold at all levels in Canada. This emerging philosophy assumes that the government does less and has less responsibility for promoting the well-being of citizens than was the norm under the Keynesian welfare state. It emphasizes reciprocal obligations between governments and citizens and responsibility-taking on the part of citizens and communities. This reciprocity gives renewed meaning to participatory democracy, but it also stresses deliberation based on informed opinion, civic education, and two-way accountability. Increasingly, there is an expectation that citizens come to the process relatively well informed (most cities will assist in this prerequisite phase of public education) and that in the process of deliberation, people be willing to take account of the interests and concerns of others. For instance, before participating in community development activities, Calgary's planning department requests that people view a video outlining the parameters of the planning process so that there are no informational gaps or misperceptions about some of the basics. The emerging philosophy of responsibility-taking has also sparked interest in the new techniques of deliberative polling (Fishkin, 1991) and citizen juries (Crosby, Kelly, and Schaefer, 1986; Kathlene and Martin, 1991).[2]

While public participation in the late 1990s is undergoing considerable innovation, it is also facing a significant backlash. Resistance to organized public participation has arisen not only as a result of its often expensive price tag, but because some populist politicians feel that councils can adequately handle citizen contact. Soon after taking office, for instance, Mayor Bill Smith of Edmonton cancelled the public participation process that had been developed as part of the budgeting process, arguing that council already had a good idea of what citizens wanted (LeSage, 1997). In Vancouver, NPA Mayor Philip Owen seemed so uninterested in connecting with the public that he earned the sobriquet "the invisible mayor" in his first term (Howard, 1996, p. A6). In many other cities, the "frills" of participation have been cancelled simply due to their cost.

In spite of a backlash and cost-cutting, public participation remains a vital part of the open government conventions of urban governance. It is an important means of enhancing the leadership, problem-solving capacity, and sense of efficacy of urban communities (Berry et al., 1993). Such efficacy is not simply a reflection of a New Age idea of feeling good about ourselves. As Margit Mayer (1995) and other political economists note, one of the adaptations of post-fordism is developing greater capacity for self-help in communities, especially disadvantaged ones. To the extent that public engagement enhances public debate and creates real opportunities for members of the public to influence the policy and planning processes between elections, it also contributes to better decisions and greater vitality of both urban governments and communities.

CONCLUSION

There has been a growing tendency in all spheres of government to affix the derogatory label of "special interest groups" to all citizen and voluntary organizations and to view them as a general nuisance to good governance. Rather than being regarded as the grassroots, citizen groups are often seen as noxious weeds. While there is little doubt that a multiplicity of lively and outspoken interest groups make policy making more complex, they nevertheless are a crucial part of democratic life. This is especially so in local government where governance increasingly depends on community associations and a wide array of other groups for co-production and delivery of services. But citizen groups and organized occasions for participation of the public are also essential counterpoints to the property development industry, which, as most models of urban government observe, has the ear of council in a way that other interests do not. Finally, groups and citizen engagement help to build resources within communities, particularly in those with limited access to institutionalized resources. When we look at the full spectrum of routes for representation in local government, the role of interest groups and public participation must be seen as part, and potentially as a very constructive part, of the bigger picture. As communities that historically have not been heard in local political discourses strive to develop their own leadership and to find their own voice, representation — both that which is sought out by governments through public participation and that which occurs uninvited through lobbying — will be increasingly complex and challenging for urban governments.

NOTES

1. On the importance of naming as a way of shaping political discourse, see Jenson (1995).
2. The deliberative polling technique brings together a group of representative citizens (usually chosen by stratified random sampling), provides them with carefully balanced background materials that discuss the costs and benefits of various choices, allows intensive discussion among participants in small groups with skilled moderators, and gives them the chance to question competing experts and politicians. When participants are then polled at the end of several days of this kind of deliberation, they can provide informed input into policy decisions. Experience with the method reveals that participants often change their views, sometimes dramatically, as they acquire information and gain perspective based on discussions with other people. Often the process is videotaped and shown on television to a wider public who thus also gain deeper understanding of complex issues. Citizen juries operate in a similar manner using the key of deliberation. Although they are quasi-institutions, juries and panels are different from traditional citizen advisory boards in at least two ways: first, citizens are randomly chosen on a representative basis rather than being self-selected, and second, the membership rotates so that views do not become entrenched and the body a staid institution unto itself. The longer term goal is to try to inculcate a sense in the public at large that it is part of their civic duty to serve on these panels from time to time, just as it is their responsibility to perform jury duty if called.

SUGGESTED READINGS

Berry, Jeffrey M., Kent E. Portney, and Ken Thomson. (1993). *The Rebirth of Urban Democracy*. Washington, DC: The Brookings Institute. A study of community associations in five American cities with well developed associational systems. The authors show how participation in community associations enhances political efficiency and trust.

Fainstein, Susan S. and Clifford Hirst. (1995). "Urban Social Movements." In *Theories of Urban Politics*, edited by David Judge, Gerry Stoker, and Harold Wolman. London: Sage, pp. 181–205. An overview of the development and role of social movements in cities.

Fisher, Robert and Joseph Kling, eds. (1993). *Mobilizing the Community: Local Politics in the Era of the Global City*. Newbury Park: Sage. A good collection of essays that provide case studies of a wide range of political mobilization in large cities, using mainly American and European examples.

Graham, Katherine A. and Susan D. Phillips, eds. (1997). *Making Public Participation More Effective: Lessons from Local Government*. Toronto: Institute of Public Administration of Canada. This collection of case studies, written by both academics and practitioners, provides an assessment of the effectiveness — with emphasis on lessons to be learned — of public participation in land-use planning, economic development, budgeting, and political restructuring, in a cross-section of Canadian cities.

Hasson, Shlomo and David Ley. (1994). *Neighbourhood Organizations and the Welfare State*. Toronto: University of Toronto Press. The authors provide detailed case studies comparing the political activities of community associations in Vancouver and Jerusalem. Both students and community activists will find the concluding chapter a useful guide for how to conduct effective advocacy to urban governments.

BIBLIOGRAPHY

Adam, Mohammed. (1996b). "Third Lane to Be Built, Not Used." *Ottawa Citizen*, October 16, pp. A1–2.

Alinsky, Saul. (1971). *Rules for Radicals*. New York: Random House.

Arnstein, Sherry. (1969). "A Ladder of Citizen Participation." *Journal of the American Institute of Planners* 35(4): 216-24.

Atkinson, Michael and William Coleman. (1989). *The State, Business, and Industrial Change in Canada*. Toronto: University of Toronto Press.

Barber, Benjamin. (1984). *Strong Democracy*. Berkeley: University of California Press.

Berry, Jeffrey M., Kent E. Portney, and Ken Thomson. (1993). *The Rebirth of Urban Democracy*. Washington, DC: The Brookings Institute.

Boswell, Randy. (1996). "The Village People." *Ottawa Citizen*, November 3, pp. A1–2.

Constituent Assembly on the Municipal Government System in Hamilton-Wentworth. (1996). *Better Municipal Government: Final Report from the Constituent Assembly*. Hamilton: Regional Municipality of Hamilton-Wentworth.

Crosby, Ned, Janet M. Kelly, and Paul Schaefer. (1986). "Citizens Panels: A New Approach to Citizen Participation." *Public Administration Review* 46 (March/April): 170–78.

Davies, Wayne K.D. and Ivan J. Townshend. (1994). "How Do Community Associations Vary? The Structure of Community Associations in Calgary, Alberta." *Urban Studies* 31(10): 1739–61.

Fainstein, Susan S. and Clifford Hirst. (1995). "Urban Social Movements." In *Theories of Urban Politics*, edited by David Judge, Gerry Stoker, and Harold Wolman. London: Sage, pp.181–205.

Fielding, Jeff and Jerry Couture. (1997). "Economic Development: The Public's Role in Shaping Winnipeg's Economic Future." In *Citizen Engagement: Lessons from Local Government*, edited by Katherine A. Graham and Susan D. Phillips. Toronto: Institute of Public Administration of Canada.

Filion, Pierre. (1992). "Government Levels, Neighbourhood Influence, and Urban Policy." In *Political Arrangements: Power and the City*, edited by Henri Lustiger-Thaler. Montreal: Black Rose Books, pp.169–83.

Fishkin, James S. (1991). *Democracy and Deliberation*. New Haven: Yale University Press.

Graham, Katherine A. (1995). "Collective Bargaining in the Municipal Sector." In *Public Sector Collective Bargaining in Canada*, edited by Gene Swimmer and Mark Thompson. Kingston, ON: IRC Press, pp. 180–200.

Graham, Katherine A. and Susan D. Phillips. (1997). "Making Public Participation More Effective: Issues for Local Government." In *Citizen Engagement: Lessons from Local Government*, edited by Katherine A. Graham and Susan D. Phillips. Toronto: Institute of Public Administration of Canada.

Hamel, Pierre. (1991). *Action collective et démocratie locale (dans les mouvements urbains montréalais*. Montréal: Presses de l'Université de Montréal.

Hasson, Shlomo and David Ley. (1994). *Neighbourhood Organizations and the Welfare State*. Toronto: University of Toronto Press.

Herland, Karen. (1992). *People, Potholes and City Policies*. Montreal: Black Rose Books.

Higgins, Donald J.H. (1986). *Local and Urban Politics in Canada*. Toronto: Gage.

Howard, Christopher, Michael Lipsky, and Dale Rogers Marshall. (1994). "Citizen Participation in Urban Politics: Rise and Routinization." In *Big-City Politics, Governance, and Fiscal Constraints*, edited by George E. Peterson. Washington, DC.: The Urban Institute Press, p. 154.

Howard, Ross. (1996). "Levity Replaced Acrimony in Vancouver Vote." *The Globe and Mail*, November 5, p. A6.

Jacobs, Jane. (1961). *The Death and Life of Great American Cities*. New York: Vintage Books.

Jenson, Jane. 1995. "What's in a Name? Nationalist Movements and Public Discourse." In *Social Movements and Culture*, edited by Hank Johnston and Bert Klandermans. London: University of London Press, pp.107–26.

Kathlene, Lyn and John A. Martin. (1991). "Enhancing Citizen Participation: Panel Designs, Perspectives, and Policy Formation." *Journal of Policy Analysis and Management* 10(1) 46–93.

Laws, Glenda. (1994). "Community Activism around the Built Form of Toronto's Welfare State." *Canadian Journal of Urban Research*, (June) 3(1): pp. 1–28.

LeSage, Edward C. Jr. (1997). "Public Participation in the Budgeting Process: Edmonton's Ongoing Experiment." In *Citizen Engagement: Lessons from Local Government*, edited by Katherine A. Graham and Susan D. Phillips. Toronto: Institute of Public Administration of Canada.

Lightbody, James. (1995). "Surviving City Politics." In *Metropolitics*, edited by James Lightbody. Toronto: Copp Clark, pp. 290–312.

Logan, John R. and Gordana Rabrenovic. (1990). "Neighbourhood Associations: Their Issues, Their Allies, and Their Opponents." *Urban Affairs Quarterly* 26,(1): 68–94.

Mayer, Margit. (1995). "Urban Government in the Post-Fordist City." In *Managing Cities: The New Urban Context*, edited by Patsy Healey et al. Chichester, UK: John Wiley & Sons, pp. 231–49.

McDavid, James C. and Eric G. Clemens. (1991). "Contracting Out Local Government Services: The B.C. Experience." *Canadian Public Administration* 38(2): 177–93.

Oropesa, R. S. (1989). "The Social and Political Foundations of Effective Neighbourhood Improvement Associations." *Social Science Quarterly*, (September) 70(3): 723–43.

Phillips, Susan D. (1995). "Redefining Government Relationships with the Voluntary Sector: On Great Expectations *and* Sense and Sensibility." Paper prepared for the National Round Table on the Voluntary Sector. Ottawa.

Phillips, Susan D. and Katherine A. Graham. (1997). "Conclusion: From Public Participation to Public Engagement." In *Citizen Engagement: Lessons from Local Government*, edited by Katherine A. Graham and Susan D. Phillips. Toronto: Institute of Public Administration of Canada.

Prior, David, John Stewart, and Kieron Walsh. (1995). *Citizenship: Rights, Community, and Participation.* London: Pitman Publishing.

Putnam, Robert D. (1995). "Bowling Alone: America's Declining Social Capital." *Journal of Democracy* 6(1): 65–78.

Sancton, Andrew. (1997). "Negotiating, Arbitrating, Legislating: Where Was the Public in London's Boundary Adjustment?" In *Citizen Engagement: Lessons from Local Government*, edited by Katherine A. Graham and Susan D. Phillips. Toronto: Institute of Public Administration of Canada.

Seelig, Michael. (1995). "Citizen Participation as Political Cop-Out." *The Globe and Mail*, February 27, p. A15.

Sewell, John. (1993). *The Shape of the City: Toronto Struggles with Modern Planning.* Toronto: University of Toronto Press.

———. (1997). "Helping the Public Participate in Planning." In *Citizen Engagement: Lessons from Local Government*, edited by Katherine A. Graham and Susan D. Phillips. Toronto: Institute of Public Administration of Canada.

Woliver, Laura R. (1993). *From Outrage to Action: The Politics of Grass-Roots Dissent.* Urbana: University of Illinois Press.

Wolsink, Maarten. (1994). "Entanglement of Interests and Motives: Assumptions behind the NIMBY-Theory on Facility Siting." *Urban Studies* 31(6): 566–81.

Yankelovitch, Daniel. (1991). *Coming to Public Judgement.* Syracuse, NY: Syracuse University Press.

CHAPTER SEVEN

◆

THE ORGANIZATION AND OPERATION OF CANADIAN URBAN GOVERNMENTS

INTRODUCTION

This chapter provides a basic road map to the ways that urban governments in Canada structure themselves and perform some central administrative and policy functions. The two functions dealt with here are strategic planning and the management of human resources. Using vignettes and case studies from our cities, we will show how turbulent the organizational and operational environment of urban governments has become. Internal restructuring and renewal have become a major preoccupation for local politicians and their staff, from senior managers to those working on the front line.

Unlike most of the changes in urban boundaries and political form, discussed in Chapter Four, changes in the organization and management of urban governments have been largely orchestrated by local governments themselves. They have been internally managed rather than provincially imposed or mediated. The changes we discuss in this chapter have, however, been shaped by three broader influences:

- the fiscal squeeze;
- changing perceptions and dominant ideologies about the role of government; and
- changing expectations about how government should perform its work.

The reduction of transfer payments to local governments from the provincial and federal levels and the challenges of raising more revenues from local sources are discussed at length in Chapter Nine. From the standpoint of urban governments' organization and operation, one important outcome of this has been pressure to downsize.

We have also seen, in recent years, the ascendance of an ideological stance favouring reduction in the role of government. In some cases, this has been entangled with concern about the fiscal squeeze. In other cases, we have seen important Canadian governments with a "small c," non-interventionist stance elected to office. The provincial governments in Alberta and Ontario are the most obvious examples. In both cases, the prevalent political ideology at the provincial level has prompted questions about what local governments should be doing and subsequent reform.

Changing expectations about how governments operate have been equally important in shaping the organizational and management agendas of Canadian urban governments. These expectations can be encapsulated in what Ken Kernaghan and others have called the **"post-bureaucratic paradigm"** (Kernaghan, 1993, pp. 636–44). Essentially, this embodies a shift from "the classical bureaucratic paradigm of public organization to a post-bureaucratic paradigm that is characterized by such emphases as innovation, risk-taking, empowerment, teamwork, client orientation, flat bureaucracies, quality, and continuous improvement" (Kernaghan, 1993, p. 636). We will examine the evidence of and the challenges associated with implementing this brave new post-bureaucratic world as this chapter proceeds.

THE ESSENCE OF URBAN GOVERNMENT'S ORGANIZATION AND REORGANIZATION

There are three essential building blocks to a city government's structure:

- council and its committee structure;
- the municipality's core departmental structure; and
- **local special purpose bodies.**

Council Structures

As the elected officials ultimately responsible for civic affairs, municipal councils usually create **standing committees of council** to oversee specific city functions. Generally speaking, there are three types of council committees.

EXECUTIVE COMMITTEES

Most of our cities have an **executive committee of council.** These committees have responsibility for overseeing many of the corporate activities of the municipality, such as personnel management, managing the municipality's property, and, in many cases, the budgeting process.

The executive committee is generally considered to be the paramount committee of council, largely because of its responsibility for the purse-strings. The mayor is, *ex officio*, typically a member of all council committees. Generally, however, the mayor is most active on the executive committee, usually assuming the chair. For other members of council, a seat on the executive committee is generally garnered through peer selection. Depending on tradition and the city's Procedure By-law, executive committee membership is determined either by formal council vote or by less formal negotiation among council colleagues. In Montreal and Winnipeg, the mayor controls membership on the executive committee.

The practice of directly electing a municipal executive committee, exemplified by the board of control model, introduced in Chapter Three, has been largely abandoned. The tensions resulting from having two classes of elected councillor brought boards of control into disrepute. The idea of direct election of the municipal executive is not completely dead, however. The City of London still has a board of control, and a 1996 agreement among municipalities in the greater Kingston area to amalgamate included the creation of a board of control as one feature of the newly expanded municipality.

STANDING COMMITTEES

Councils also divide the workload among members by assigning oversight and policy development duties to standing committees with responsibility for a particular city service or cluster of services.

The names of standing committees vary from city to city according to the functions they perform. Committee work is frequently divided along the lines of key elements of municipal responsibility and expenditure, such as social and community services, transportation services, environmental services (water, sewer, and garbage), and emergency/protective services (police, fire, and ambulance).

Many cities have traditionally had a standing council committee responsible for land-use planning. Planning committees existed because of the centrality of land use and development to the municipal role rather than because of large direct expenditures by cities on the planning function. There is a perceptible trend, however, to try to integrate urban planning more closely with the operational functions of cities. This is discussed at greater length in Chapter Eleven.

SPECIAL COMMITTEES

From time to time, councils are seized with a particular issue or problem that merits creation of a temporary or cross-functional council committee. These committees can be more eclectic in their membership, often involving members of the public and/or members of special purpose bodies as well as councillors. They are charged with responsibility for making recommendations to council on a particular issue or, in some cases, advising on the management of a particular project or initiative.

The City of Calgary, for example, has a Committee on Aboriginal Affairs, which consists of selected members of council and representatives of the Aboriginal community in the city. Even with the trend to cluster standing committee responsibilities for enhanced policy integration, **special committees of council** are still important as evidence of urban government's responsiveness and adaptability.

Assessing Council Structures

It is important to remember that the role of council committees is essentially one of providing advice to the full council. The basis for this is in law. Municipal councillors are collectively responsible for the affairs of the municipal corporation, and there are very narrow limits to the extent that these affairs can be delegated to smaller groups of councillors (or to non-elected staff). Standing committees always must have their recommendations debated at full council and be subject to a full and fresh vote, with "50 percent plus 1" of councillors determining the corporation's direction on a particular issue. In some cases, for example, the Regional Municipality of Ottawa-Carleton, executive committee decisions can only be overturned by a larger plurality of votes at the big council table.

Even in cities where there is a relatively strong executive committee, we see the contrast between the executive–legislative relationship at the municipal level and at the provincial and federal levels. With the exceptions of Montreal and, to a lesser extent, Winnipeg and Vancouver, there is no solidarity among executive committee members based on party affiliation. The open deliberations of all committees, including executive committees, are in stark contrast to Cabinet secrecy. It is not unheard of for committee members to change their votes from the committee stage when an item comes before full council.

Nonetheless, the nature of the committee structure adopted by a city council is very important. The design of council committees shapes relations among councillors, between council and the public, and between council and staff. It also influences how issues are formed, the workloads of councillors, and the efficiency with which council conducts its work.

Organizing Urban Administration: The Departmental Core

Since early urban reformers first prompted thinking on the matter, two interrelated preoccupations have predominated as Canadian urban governments have organized and reorganized their administrative apparatus:

- the extent to which council will run the administrative operations of the city; and
- the extent to which various municipal functions will be integrated under the control of one or more senior managers.

Four basic models of departmental organization and administration–council relations have been used in different cities across the country to deal with these issues. They are the **departmental model**, the **city manager model**, the **chief administrative officer (CAO) model**, and the **board of management model**.

THE DEPARTMENTAL MODEL

This approach to administrative organization and council–staff relations was prominent in many Canadian cities until the 1970s. It is important to understand its basic elements because it is the point of departure for corporate organization in many large Canadian cities. Of all the organizational models, it embodies the greatest amount of differentiation among municipal functions, at both the administrative and political levels. Essentially, each municipal responsibility (parks, public works, social services, finance, etc.) is the direct responsibility of its own administrative department head. All department heads report to city council, often through a council committee with particular responsibility for the function in question. From a management perspective, the key features of this model are that all department heads are equal in the administrative hierarchy and that each one has an independent relationship with council.

The shortcomings of this approach were trenchantly pointed out by T.J. Plunkett in the late 1960s (Plunkett, 1968). This model had a tendency to give rise to formidable bureaucratic empires, with the head of each department vying with the others for budget and new initiatives. Interdepartmental co-ordination was often very weak and there was little incentive to integrate thinking about policy issues or service delivery. Department heads were also frequently adept at co-opting council members on their particular standing committee. In short, the departmental model tended to be accompanied by political busy work and substantial bureaucratic control.

By the mid-1970s, this model was falling out of favour in many Canadian cities, although it prevailed in the City of Toronto until 1996. In different ways, the other three models offer antidotes to the problems associated with the departmental model.

The City Manager Model

The city manager model is at the other end of the spectrum from the departmental model, fostering greater administrative integration and a more hands-off role for municipal council. It arrived in Canada in the early 1900s as one of the prescriptions that municipal reformers of the day thought would professionalize city government and permit council to serve more as a corporate board of directors than as manager of the city's affairs. Councils opting for this approach hire a professional manager to oversee all administrative activities and all departments of city hall. Separate departments with responsibility for specific municipal functions may remain. All department heads report to the city manager, however, rather than to council. It is the responsibility of the city manager to frame council's agenda in the context of the administration's need for political decisions and to advise council on its strategic direction. In contrast with the departmental model, council committees operating under the city manager system are not intended to play a particularly important role.

Although it does appear to be a strong antidote to the dysfunctional aspects of the departmental model, the city manager system was slow to take hold as the organizational model of choice in Canada's largest cities. Rivalry between the manager and the elected mayor and/or council may develop if there are disagreements about who knows the city's needs best. The city manager model raises the prospect of the manager assuming the role of political boss. The limits of the management authority given to city managers have also been a concern. Councils worry that the city manager may overstep the boundaries of administrative discretion in the absence of checks and balances, such as would exist if there were other senior staff with direct access to council or more active council committees.

The complexity of urban politics and the demands of urban management may, however, have contributed to a lessening of these concerns. The city manager model is found today in the new Halifax Regional Municipality, as well as in the cities of Edmonton and Vancouver.

The Chief Administrative Officer Model

The chief administrative officer (CAO) model might be likened to a weak form of the city manager model.

The essence of this model is that a number of departments (most commonly the staff or administrative departments) report to the CAO and from there to council. Other departments (most commonly the line departments concerned with the provision of direct services by the municipality) have department heads who report directly to council and who often have their own strong relationship with council committees. The chief administrative officer is weak in the sense that he or she does not have supervisory responsibility for the major services that the municipality provides. It should be realized, however, that the CAO generally controls the budget and personnel functions, as well as various other aspects of the central administration. This gives the office of the chief administrative officer considerable leverage with other senior department heads. In contrast with the city manager system, however, disputes between a CAO and a department head can emerge which council must handle. Canada's largest municipality, the Municipality of Metropolitan Toronto, operates using this system.

THE BOARD OF MANAGEMENT MODEL

This model combines the notion that there is value in the administrative integration of related municipal functions with the concept of collective administrative responsibility by senior municipal managers.

The board of management model assigns responsibility for the management of the city's affairs to a board rather than to a single city manager. This board, often known as the board of commissioners, generally consists of three to five senior managers, each with responsibility for a cluster of city services.

Calgary is a city in which the board of management has been in place for many years. There is a Commissioner of Finance and Administration, a Commissioner of Planning, Transportation, and Community Services, and a

Commissioner of Operations and Utilities. These three are led by a Chief Commissioner, who is a "first among equals" and has designated responsibility for corporate services, human resources management, intergovernmental relations, and economic development initiatives. The City of Winnipeg has a similar arrangement. In these two cities, there is a tradition that the mayor also sits on the board of commissioners. In Calgary, the mayor chaired the commission board until 1988. In both cases, the political–administrative liaison at the commission board level is intended to enhance the link between administrative and political concerns prior to issues coming forward to full council. This is seen variously as one of the strengths of the system (Plunkett, 1968) or as a feature of the board of management system that stifles full public debate.

Local Special Purpose Bodies

Special purpose bodies, such as library boards and police commissions, are part of the urban organizational dynamic. For our purposes here, it is important to understand that local agencies, boards, and commissions are very much in view as city councils and provincial governments think about restructuring the constellation of urban government organizations. The internal organizational form of local agencies, boards, and commissions, however, is as variable as the functions they perform.

A research team studying local special purpose bodies in Canada developed a working definition suitable for our use. The definition for "local special purpose body" included these points:

• It operates in a geographic area roughly coterminous with a municipality or a small group of municipalities.
• It has a certain degree of autonomy from local governments because it is created by municipal by-law or provincial (or, rarely, federal) legislation.
• It is controlled by a separate board composed of municipal representatives and sometimes representatives of other organizations.
• Its mandate is to carry out a limited number of government-like functions.
• It does not have the right to impose taxes but receives a significant amount of its funding from the municipal government(s) (Siegel, 1994, p. 7).

Our metropolitan areas exhibit two commonalities: all have school boards and all, except Winnipeg, have police commissions. Otherwise, the range of special purpose bodies varies significantly.

THE SPECIAL PURPOSE BODY DEBATE

The use of special purpose bodies to perform local functions is controversial. As discussed in Chapter Three, many of them were established under the influence of urban reformers, who sought to remove vital local functions from political interference and corruption. Also, as suggested in Chapter Three, the local state in Canada was the first focal point for applying one of the ideas we now associate with the "new" public management — hiving off functions and activities from the central arm of government, in the name of efficiency and flexibility.

A backlash against local agencies, boards, and commissions (ABCs) emerged in the 1960s. Plunkett and Betts, for example, asserted that the proliferation of local special purpose bodies has limited effective management of local issues and is anti-democratic. In their view, the anti-democratic character of the fragmented local state reflects an unfortunate middle class bias against participation by other segments of society in local political life and reinforces the link between business and local government (Plunkett and Betts, 1978, p. 122).

Critiques such as this and mounting opposition to the remoteness of some local special purpose bodies by local politicians and the public have resulted in some contemporary reforms. For example, the establishment of regional governments in Ontario, beginning with the Regional Municipality of Ottawa-Carleton in 1969, was accompanied by the elimination of some special purpose bodies, most notably boards of health. One of the aims of the establishment of the Halifax Regional Municipality, in 1996, was to eliminate many of the special purpose bodies that had existed in the four previously existing municipalities. Some municipal politicians and councils have made municipal control over police commissions and school boards into a public issue. Tensions between councils and these high profile and big spending ABCs have mounted as local fiscal resources have become more strained.

Contemporary debates about elimination of local special purpose bodies or enhancing municipal control over them have not been totally one-sided, however. Advocates of public choice approaches to local governance see them as responsive and cost-efficient pillars of the local state. Their argument centres on the ability of special purpose bodies to fine tune the organization of local functions by permitting different geographic boundaries and arrangements for different functions. This encourages realization of economies of scale, which require different geographic and population characteristics depending on the service, and increases the responsiveness of particular services to the particular tastes of different segments of the urban population.

In a less theoretical vein, special purpose bodies are still held up as paradigms of good management and as vital sites for the conduct of local politics. Members of the Halifax Water Commission used the good management argument to avoid the fate of most other special purpose bodies in the 1996 Halifax area amalgamation.

The elected Parks Board, in the City of Vancouver, has been a lively and prominent part of that city's political life since 1890 (Gutstein, 1983, p. 211). In recent years, however, some serious questions have been raised about the level of independence exercised by the board in light of fiscal restraints and broader urban priorities. Vancouver's City Council has begun to question the board's future.

Police commissions remain in most Canadian urban centres. Along with the Halifax Water Commission, a regional police commission was retained as part of the Halifax regional reform. In at least one province, Ontario, the provincial government responded to some of the criticisms of police commissions by enlarging police commissions (although retaining minority representation for municipal governments) and changing their name to suggest a more responsive image. The 1990 Ontario Police Services Act changed the name of police commissions in the province to Police Services Boards. Municipal councils are guaranteed two of five seats on regional and metropolitan Police Services Boards. In the case of Metropolitan Toronto, Metro council has three of the seven seats. The rest of the seat selections, including the head of the board, are made by the province (Loreto, 1990, p. 235).

Conclusion: The Shape of the Building Blocks

We now have a sense of the basic building blocks forming the corporate structure of urban government in Canada. There are two important concluding observations. The first concerns terminology. The description of the various models of administrative organization has been generic. We have used terms like "city manager" and "chief administrative officer" to illustrate the differences among different approaches. The terminology used in practice may be somewhat different. Many large cities in Canada refer to their senior administrative officer as the chief administrative officer. This individual may have responsibilities akin to those of the CAO model or may be a city manager. Similarly, we see boards of management being called by different names in different places. It is important, then, to look at the specifics of the organization and responsibilities of the various elements of a city government's organization in order to gain a true understanding of how it operates.

The second concluding observation is that change is not a new phenomenon in the corporate structuring of urban governments. The relationship among the three elements of local government organization — council, administration, and special purpose bodies — has also been quite dynamic. From the end of World War II until the 1990s, it is useful to think about two periods.

Until the 1970s, one can observe a relatively high degree of political administrative integration between councils and their core administrations. This was embodied in the prevalence of the departmental model and, in the west, the board of management system. The role of special purpose agencies, boards, and commissions was generally unquestioned. This was one manifestation of the tendency to think about local government functions in isolation from one another. Roads were repaved one year, only to be dug up the next for sewer-line installation.

Beginning in the mid-1970s and into the 1980s, the chief administrative officer and city manager models began to gain pre-eminence in the larger cities. This changed the relationship of city councils to their appointed staff. The relationship became mediated by the city manager or the CAO; council was no longer to be engaged in micro-management. At the same time, the expectation existed that there would be greater administrative integration. In some cities, this extended beyond the core departmental structure to include consideration of the relationship of special purpose bodies to council and the administrative core (Municipality of Metropolitan Toronto, 1989). In the eyes of some observers, this was the nadir of "expert power" at the local level (Siegel, 1994).

The entrenched power bases of the traditional service czars, who wheeled and dealt with council under the department head system, were now challenged by the presence of senior administrators with the mandate to think horizontally across issues and services and to create a culture that valued integration throughout the city's organization. Achieving this was not always easy, although it was a prominent goal.

We are currently in the second period. The turbulent environment in which Canada's urban governments now find themselves has induced some of our cities to do much more than rearrange the managerial deck chairs. In the 1990s, organization renewal in urban government often means re-examining what local government does, re-examining how it does things, and searching for major cost savings.

These three are quite interrelated. Together, they have propelled a number of our cities to take a comprehensive review of their strategic direction and their organizations, including taking a hard look at their human resources and the attitudes of employees toward the city and the public. This chapter now proceeds to consider a sample of these reviews. They give a sense of what is really happening in today's urban government corporation.

ORGANIZATION RENEWAL AND SURVIVAL: THREE CASES

The three cities we will visit for this review are Vancouver, Winnipeg, and Halifax. They illustrate some common themes in urban corporate reform but also show how these themes play out in different contexts. The City of Vancouver has a well established tradition of partisan municipal politics and the city manager system. The independently elected Vancouver Parks Board is perhaps the paragon of local special purpose bodies in Canada — in no large part because of its management of Stanley Park. Vancouver is a charter city. Over the years, the British Columbia provincial government has exhibited strong interest in the development of the Vancouver region and has played an important role through its direct control over the public transit system, among other things. At the same time, however, the province has traditionally taken a hands-off approach to the operation of the city's affairs. Throughout the 1990s, the Vancouver region has continued to be one of the fastest growing and most prosperous of Canada's urban centres. It also has one of the most diverse populations.

The City of Winnipeg has been the site of considerable provincial government tinkering, as well as locally generated corporate reform. The establishment of unicity, in 1971, and the accompanying pressure to bring services across the city to the highest level resulted in expansion of the administrative structure from 17 to 24 departments by the early 1990s (Frost, 1996, pp. 12–13). Compared to Vancouver, Winnipeg has faced some major difficulties in its larger urban economy and in the city's own finances.

The Halifax case is quite different from the other two in that it involved creation of an entirely new civic administration to accompany the establishment of the new Halifax Regional Municipality in 1996. The challenge involved combining the administrative operations of the four municipalities which were amalgamated to form the new government. Each municipality had very distinct organizational traditions. Uncertainty among the public and staff about how the new municipality would actually respond to the needs of such a diverse region, especially in an environment of severe financial constraint, also formed part of the Halifax context.

The City of Vancouver: From Rules to Results

> The City of Vancouver is like most government organizations. Rules and processes rather than results control too much City work. While rules and consistency are necessary for our by-law related work, many of the systems we have created are slow, complex, and over-controlled. We regulate details which will be changed the moment our inspectors leave. We spend two dollars to control a one dollar expenditure. In our day-to-day operations, decisions are referred to more senior people, rather than being made by staff who are directly involved. These systems become frustrating to employees who work within them, and to the public who deal with us. They are expensive to operate. We need to change them. (City of Vancouver, 1994, p. 3)

This diagnosis by Vancouver's city manager centres on four needs: the need to focus on results, the need to de-regulate, the need to empower city staff, and the need to think smartly about city expenditures. The city's prescription for dealing with these has involved both structural and attitudinal change. Some highlights of Vancouver's recent corporate initiatives are as follows:

- Reduction in the number of city departments from eighteen to ten. Internal administrative functions, such as property administration, law, and finance, became clustered in a new corporate services department. Major planning and community services, such as social planning, health, and non-market housing, became clustered under a Planning and Community Services umbrella.
- Elimination of some senior management positions, including the deputy city manager, the Director of Housing, and the Director of Economic Development. (A distinct economic development department was no longer thought to be necessary because of Vancouver's buoyant economy).
- Creation of a new civic management team, which consists of the city manager, key department heads, and the administrative heads of the city's major agencies, boards, and commissions (i.e., the police chief, the city librarian, and the head of parks).
- A corporate commitment to reorienting the operating style of the city. The key phrases in this context are delegation; decentralization; customer consultation; teams; interdepartmental consultation; service standards and monitoring; flexibility; and empowerment of managers to coach, mentor, and support staff rather than control (City of Vancouver, 1994, pp. 6–9).
- New openness to alternative service models including technology based services; enhanced use of volunteers; regulated privatization of traditional municipal functions, such as the handing over of building permit approvals to certified construction professionals; and new emphasis on partnerships, joint delivery, and contract services (City of Vancouver, 1994, pp. 9–10).

Figure 7.1 shows the key elements of the new structure.

It should be evident that transformation in the way the city actually does its work is just as important a part of this initiative as changes in the formal management structure. It is interesting to note that the formal proposal for the city's new corporate direction distances itself from the general trend among governments to downsize: "Our objective is not to downsize but to make us more effective," said a news release highlighting the changes (City of Vancouver, 1994). Statements such as this speak to the intent of the changes. One effect, however, has been corporate **downsizing** through the reduction in the number of city departments, the elimination of some senior management positions, and the shift to co-production with the voluntary and private sectors in service delivery. The achievement of financial efficiencies through re-engineering some of the city's work processes has also been part of the plan. As we noted above, the need to do this was part of the original prescription. In our next case, the City of Winnipeg, similar elements of transformation were present, but the pressure to downsize was more direct.

Winnipeg: Organizational Transition and the Doctrine of Continuous Improvement

The dynamic flow of organizational renewal in Winnipeg is illustrated by Figure 7.2.

The main impetus for change in Winnipeg was financial. City council and management were preoccupied with a dramatic rise in assessment appeals and the unfunded liability associated with them. The city's economic vitality was also a concern. Finally, Winnipeg was facing financial pressures due to the increasing burden of social service costs by the early 1990s. City council's 1994 budget debate centred on two key issues: how to achieve the goal of a zero property tax increase in light of the fiscal and service pressures on the city, and how to reduce the city's long-term debt.

The corporate response to these challenges took the form of a significant downsizing and the simultaneous attempt to inculcate a new operating culture in the city's organization, based on the work of Edward Deming and his "principles of continuous improvement" (City of Winnipeg, 1993).

The Winnipeg transition had the following elements:

- The number of city departments was reduced from 24 to 18.
- The number of senior managers in the city was reduced from 32 to 22.
- One commissioner position was slated for elimination.
- Plans were announced to reduce city staff by an average of 23 percent across all departments. By council directive, staff reductions were to be achieved, as much as possible, through early retirement, rather than layoffs (City of Winnipeg, 1994).
- A target of $2 million in salary savings was established for the first year of the transition. Staff were also directed to "achieve significant savings" in the wage account in each of the years 1995 through 1998. (City of Winnipeg, 1994)

FIGURE 7.1 CITY OF VANCOUVER INTERIM ORGANIZATION CHART, NOVEMBER 1995

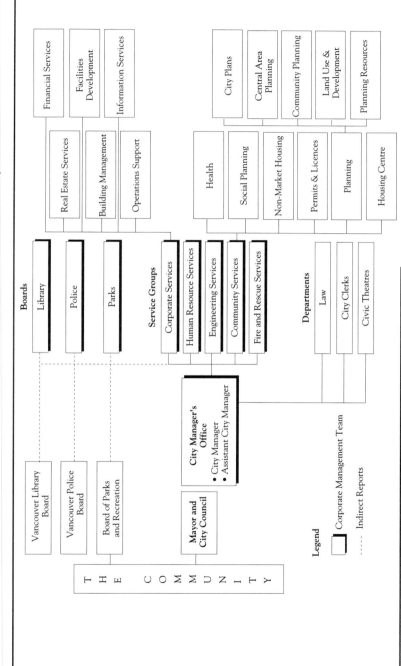

Source: City of Vancouver, *Interim Organizational Chart* (Vancouver: City of Vancouver, 1995). Reproduced with permission of the City of Vancouver.

FIGURE 7.2 THE CITY OF WINNIPEG: ORGANIZATION TRANSITION

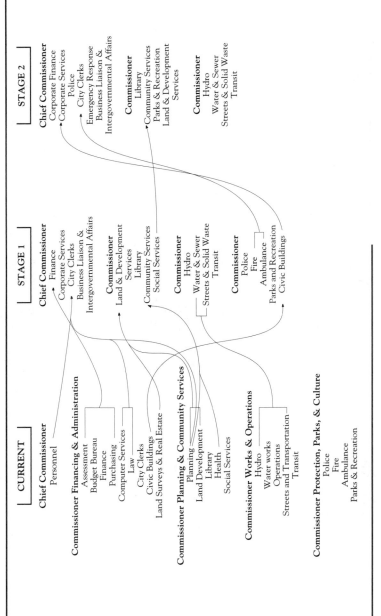

Source: City of Winnipeg, *A New Direction for Civic Administration* (Winnipeg: City of Winnipeg, 1994). Reproduced with permission of the City of Winnipeg, p. 20.

Although there is a contrast between Winnipeg and Vancouver in terms of the acknowledged motives for corporate renewal and reorganization, the two cases share emphasis on changing the way the city deals with the public, as well as the way it is structured to divide up and co-ordinate its responsibilities. Embracing the tenets of "continuous improvement," senior staff in Winnipeg have attempted, with council's guidance, to develop a vision of where the city should be. They are to use their knowledge of the current situation and agreed-upon principles for change to set the strategic direction for a leaner but more open, accountable, and responsive administration.

The City of Winnipeg is still in transition. The stage one organization is in place and significant staff reductions have occurred. Not surprisingly, some difficulties accompanied implementation. The city had a major showdown with its unions when it approached the provincial government to open up its collective agreements so that wage rollbacks could occur. (The province refused.) City staff has had to work in a very uncertain environment since the onset of the changes. Finally, the stage one reform resulted in a mismatch between the structure of the city's administration and its council organization. The council committee structure had not yet changed to reflect the new alignment of services and responsibilities among staff. The result was inefficiency in the handling of business by council committees.

Halifax: Breaking Down the Silos

Typically, city councils appoint their senior officials by by-law. This By-law of Appointment for the chief commissioner, chief administrative officer, or city manager is an important component of the employment contract that exists between the council and its most senior administrative staff member. The appointment by by-law generally sets out the responsibilities and reporting relationships pertaining to the position and its remuneration. There can be other elements of the employment contract to cover matters such as perquisites (car, professional and social memberships, and so on), leave from employment, and termination.

Traditionally, department heads and other management personnel have been considered permanent employees rather than being on contract or appointed by by-law, although this may be changing. Nonetheless, they are also appointed directly by council, often on the recommendation of the city's most senior bureaucrat.

Halifax provides a unique example of a different approach. Following its decision to create the new Halifax Regional Municipality in October 1994, the Nova Scotia government appointed a Co-ordinator of Municipal Administration with responsibility to hire the first chief administrative officer and senior department heads. These officials were all in place before the first meeting of the new Halifax regional council, following its election in December 1995. This process is interesting because it is unique but also because it is potentially informative should major municipal restructuring occur in other urban centres.

BOX 7.2 NEGOTIATING TO BE CITY MANAGER

Prior to arrival, one flamboyant city manager negotiated redecoration of his office suite, specifying that it be redone in Art Deco style. Council agreed. Dusty pink and grey paint were applied to the walls. Special Art Deco light fixtures were mounted and new white marble furniture was uncrated. The office came to symbolize the manager's style in the eyes of council, city staff, and those members of the public who were aware of it. One of the first acts of his successor, as part of the "healing process" when this individual left office, was to revert to a more traditional decor.

The administrative organizational chart of the Halifax Regional Municipality very much reflects the management philosophy of the CAO (whose position is more akin to the city manager model discussed previously) and the new senior management team's conception of the major challenges faced by the new municipality. The new corporate organization is specifically intended to "break down the silos" in terms of service delivery and, equally important, in terms of issue management. The essence of the Halifax Regional Municipality's corporate organization is shown in Figure 7.3.

The senior management team consists of three commissioners with responsibility for large clusters of operational, community, and corporate services. Their responsibilities include integration of the staff of the four original municipalities into the organization and conceptualization of the issues associated with their portfolios in a more integrated fashion. Reflecting changing tradition, the Chief of Police and Commissioner of Fire Services also sit on the management team. Until recently, these two offices were remote from city hall, but fiscal constraints and the emergence of a more holistic management philosophy are drawing more and more police and fire chiefs into the corporate fold. Recall the changes in Vancouver, for example, and re-examine Figure 7.2 to see how this issue has been handled in Winnipeg.

Establishment of a Commissioner of Policy and Planning is also significant. Although senior and prominent in the overall corporate organization, this commissioner and his or her staff have no major operational responsibilities. Instead, they are responsible for guiding the municipality in its management of strategic issues related to the region's economy, social cohesion, and environmental sustainability. This commissioner's corporate responsibility centres, initially, on developing an internal process for dealing with these major challenges. In short, this part of the organization is to be the catalyst in helping the CAO and the rest of the management team as they attempt to "break down the silos" among different services and among staff who may have come from different parts of the new municipality and may be steeped in different administrative and political cultures.

The newly elected Halifax council began to deliberate about the proposed organization and its more detailed staffing and budgetary implications over the

FIGURE 7.3 HALIFAX REGIONAL MUNICIPALITY ORGANIZATION CHART

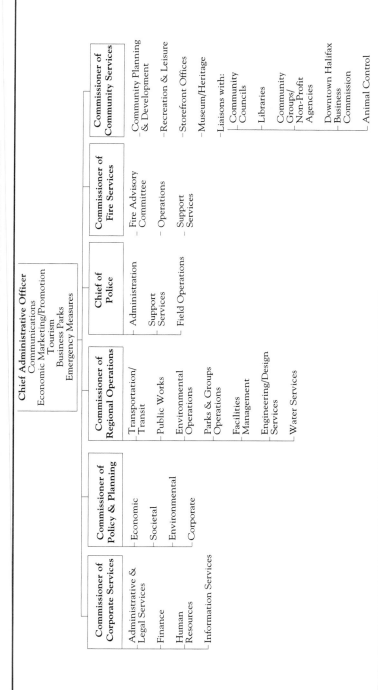

Chief Administrative Officer
Communications
Economic Marketing/Promotion
Tourism
Business Parks
Emergency Measures

Commissioner of Corporate Services
- Administrative & Legal Services
- Finance
- Human Resources
- Information Services

Commissioner of Policy & Planning
- Economic
- Societal
- Environmental
- Corporate

Commissioner of Regional Operations
- Transportation/Transit
- Public Works
- Environmental Operations
- Parks & Groups Operations
- Facilities Management
- Engineering/Design Services
- Water Services

Chief of Police
- Administration
- Support Services
- Field Operations

Commissioner of Fire Services
- Fire Advisory Committee
- Operations
- Support Services

Commissioner of Community Services
- Community Planning & Development
- Recreation & Leisure
- Storefront Offices
- Museum/Heritage
- Liaisons with:
  - Community Councils
  - Libraries
  - Community Groups/Non-Profit Agencies
  - Downtown Halifax Business Commission
  - Animal Control

Source: Office of the Chief Administrative Officer, *Halifax Regional Municipality* (Halifax: Regional Municipality of Halifax). Reproduced with permission of the Halifax Regional Municipality.

winter of 1996. Individual members of the senior management team had already been appointed; in essence, the senior personnel to be involved were a fait accompli. Council members were, however, able to debate the proposed corporate structure and related issues. Two council concerns emerged.

First, some councillors were dubious about the value of the policy and planning function, thinking it too academic for a service-oriented organization. Would this be money well spent? The chief administrative officer was able to convince council that this part of the corporate organization was central to his vision of how the corporation would plan and manage both policy and service delivery. The function was retained and the effort to break down the traditional barriers was permitted to proceed, albeit with varying levels of understanding, interest, and scepticism among council.

In addition, council displayed a major preoccupation with human resource management issues. One of the original objectives of the amalgamation was to bring about cost savings through reductions in management (Hayward, 1993). In a region with high unemployment, where a public service position has traditionally been valued, the prospect that the amalgamation would also result in downsizing for street-level workers presented a political problem for the new council, which it sought to dispense with as quickly as possible. Internal candidates from the original four municipalities were to have priority in filling the approximately 4500 positions in the new organization. At least in the beginning, downsizing was to be restricted to the management function, although all staff was feeling the stress.

Another instantaneous human resource management issue was pressure from various unions — most notably those representing police and fire personnel for region-wide wage parity — based on the top wage scale paid by the original four municipalities. Legislation establishing the new municipality stipulated that salaries of personnel would be frozen until 1997. This did not prevent an early start to the campaign for parity, which is a thorny issue for council given fiscal constraints and the political sensitivities that traditionally accompany relations between municipal councils and police and fire unions.

The organization and operations of the new Halifax Regional Municipality are still in their nascent stages. The effort to get the municipality up and running and the priority, at least among senior staff, to "break down the silos" have been the hallmarks of the corporate organization so far. How relations will function between the administrative core and council's executive structure are still evolving, as is the modus vivendi between the regional municipality and the Halifax Water Commission. We must also wait to see the extent to which elements of the post-bureaucratic paradigm take hold in Halifax.

THE IMPORTANCE OF HUMAN RESOURCE MANAGEMENT: A CONSISTENT THEME

All three of our cases illustrate the importance of human resource management in the operations of Canadian urban governments. We see cities preoccupied with managing the downsizing of staff, training and motivating remaining staff, and dealing with pressures on the municipal compensation system resulting from reorganization, amalgamation, or from decreasing financial flexibility.

Historically, Canadian urban governments have exhibited two somewhat contradictory attributes in their management of human resources. On the one hand, they have had a much longer history of collective bargaining than either the provincial or federal governments. Provincial governments have regarded municipalities' relationship to their workforce as akin to that between a private company and its employees. As a result, municipal employees have had a right to collective bargaining under provincial labour relations legislation. Union activism has been part of city governance since World War I.

The contradiction lies in the fact that, until recently, city governments have not displayed great sophistication in their labour relations practices or in other aspects of human resource management. Until the 1980s, municipal personnel departments concentrated on personnel record keeping. They did minimal human resource planning or development and had little influence within the municipal administrative organization or with councils. For example, councils frequently bypassed their personnel people when conducting union negotiations.

In recent years, however, there have been signs that the management of human resources has assumed the importance it deserves among senior municipal managers and city councils. There has been an increasing trend to professionalization of the labour–management negotiation process. City councils have been induced to do this by the financial squeeze, public criticism of municipal wages and benefits, and their own observation of collective bargaining in other parts of the public sector. Downsizing and the re-inventing government movement have also contributed to expansion of the human resource management function. Today, our cities have relatively sophisticated human resource departments, headed by a senior manager who typically is part of the corporate management team. The role of these departments varies from city to city. As a rule, however, human resource departments have an interest in and some responsibility for human resource planning, recruitment and staffing, staff development, compensation, labour relations, employee assistance, and occupational health and safety.

One noteworthy difference between local government and human resource management at the provincial and federal levels is the absence of an oversight body in the local context. In provincial governments and at the federal level, the human resource function is overseen by a public service commission, which sets basic rules for recruitment, promotion, and termination of employees and which has the power to overturn breaches of these rules. The authority of these commissions is set out in legislation. In city governments, human resource departments may try to oversee the probity of the human resource management process, but they lack similar statutory powers of oversight and control (Graham, 1995).

CONCLUSION

How can we assess the response of Canadian urban government organizations and operations to what is clearly a turbulent environment?

Our review suggests a number of important signals that urban governments in Canada are seriously attempting to be flexible in times of significant fiscal constraints and growing turbulence in their operational environments. In short, cities are trying to be innovative in their organization and operation. The impetus for this comes variously from council and senior staff. It may be induced by the policies of neighbouring municipalities or the provincial or federal governments. Public displeasure over perceived inefficiency or ineffectiveness of city operations and, in the occasional case, pure, unadulterated scandal may be the impetus for change.

The key characteristics of contemporary local government organization, as it relates to the policy and administrative processes of urban government, can be summarized as follows:

- Emphasizing structural change. The number of boxes on the administrative organization chart is shrinking, motivated by the phenomenon of corporate downsizing and the perceived need to better integrate related services. Council structures are also changing, although not always in concert with changes at the staff level.

- Becoming increasingly dynamic. The cases discussed here and other examples suggest that urban governments are now thinking about change as a process rather than as an event. The need for interim organizations to help make the transition to the final goal is increasingly recognized. Even where time pressures are severe, there is less emphasis on change by edict than in the past.

- Attempting new approaches to issue management. The reconception of senior management teams to include senior local officials who were previously not well integrated into the management process reflects this trend, as does the establishment of units like the Department of Policy and Planning in the Halifax Regional Municipality. It is also reflected in new service clusters.

- Involving more participants. Regardless of motivation, there is increasing receptivity by urban governments to co-production with the voluntary and private sectors for the delivery of service. This implies involvement by a broader range of participants in issue identification and management at the local level.

- Being preoccupied with human resource issues. These include managing the downsizing of city staff, retaining those who remain, and thinking about which elements of the post-bureaucratic paradigm can really be implemented in city operations and how this can be done. It also means dealing with pressures on the municipal compensation system resulting from reorganization or amalgamation.

In light of all this, we think that current trends in organization and corporate management among Canadian urban governments demonstrate considerable innovation. As with all innovation, we must watch to determine if the original ideas and goals of change are realized in practice. We must be mindful of the dictum:

We tend to meet any new situation by reorganizing, and a wonderful method it can be for creating the illusion of progress while producing confusion, inefficiency, and demoralization. (Petronius Arbiter, 210 BC, on Reorganization)

SUGGESTED READINGS

Graham, Katherine A. (1995). "Collective Bargaining in the Municipal Sector." In *Public Service Collective Bargaining in Canada*, edited by Gene Swimmer and Mark Thompson. Kingston, ON: IRC Press, pp. 180–200. A more extended review of recent trends in collective bargaining and human resource management in Canadian municipalities.

Peters, Guy B. and Donald Savoie, eds. (1995). *Governance in a Changing Environment*. Montreal & Kingston, ON: McGill-Queen's University Press. A review of the "new public management."

Plunkett, T.J. (1992). *City Management in Canada: The Role of the Chief Administrative Officer*. Toronto: Institute of Public Administration of Canada. A study of chief administrative officer in Canadian municipalities.

Plunkett, T.J. and G.M. Betts. (1978). *The Management of Canadian Urban Government*. Kingston: Institute of Local Government, Queen's University. The first text focussing extensively on urban management processes.

Seidle, Leslie F. (1993). *Rethinking Government: Reform or Reinvention?* Montreal: Institute for Research on Public Policy. A collection of articles and commentaries on innovation in Canadian governments, including local government.

BIBLIOGRAPHY

City of Toronto. (1995). *Toward Effective Partnerships*. Toronto.

City of Vancouver. (November 22, 1994). *Policy Report: City Management: Organization and Operating Style*. Vancouver.

City of Winnipeg. (1993). *Know Your Customer*. Winnipeg.

———. (1994). *A New Direction for Civic Administration*. Winnipeg.

Dobell, Kenneth. (1994). *Policy Report: City Management: Organization and Operating Style*. Vancouver: City of Vancouver.

Fish, Susan. (1981). "Winning the Battle and Losing the War in the Fight to Improve Municipal Policy Making." In *Politics and Government of Urban Canada*, edited by Lionel D. Feldman. Toronto: Methuen, pp. 90–101.

Frost, Richard. (1996). "Presentation to 'Seizing the Future.'" In *One-Tier Government Options for Ottawa-Carleton*. Appendix 1. Ottawa: City of Ottawa, pp. 11–17

Graham, Katherine A. (1981). "Organizational Change in Urban Governments: A Perspective." In *Politics and Government of Urban Canada*, edited by Lionel D. Feldman. Toronto: Methuen, pp. 291–316.

Graham, Katherine A. (1995). "Collective Bargaining in the Municipal Sector." In *Public Sector Collective Bargaining in Canada*, edited by Gene Swimmer and Mark Thompson. Kingston, ON: IRC Press, pp. 180–200.

Gutstein, David. (1983). "Vancouver." In *City Politics in Canada*, edited by Warren Magnusson and Andrew Sancton. Toronto: University of Toronto Press, pp.189–221.

Halifax Regional Municipality. (September 28, 1995). *Overview of the Amalgamation of the Halifax Regional Municipality*. Halifax.

Hayward, William C. (1993). *Interim Report of the Municipal Reform Commissioner*. Halifax: Government of Nova Scotia.

Kernaghan, Kenneth. (1993). "Re-shaping Government in the Post-bureaucratic Paradigm." *Canadian Public Administration* 36: 636–44.

Loreto, Richard. (1990). "Policing." In *Urban Policy Issues*, edited by Richard Loreto and Trevor Price. Toronto: McClelland & Stewart, pp. 207–39.

Masson, Jack with Edward C. LeSage Jr. (1994). *Alberta's Local Government*. Edmonton: University of Alberta Press.

Municipality of Metropolitan Toronto. (June 1989). *First Report of the Sub-committee on Special Purpose Bodies*. Toronto.

Oblerlander, Peter and Patrick J. Smith. (1993). "Governing Metropolitan Vancouver." In *Metropolitan Governance*, edited by David Rothblatt and Andrew Sancton. Berkeley, CA and Kingston, ON: Institute of Governmental Studies Press and Institute of Intergovernmental Relations, Queen's University, pp. 329–74.

Plunkett, T.J. (1968). *Urban Canada and Its Government*. Toronto: Macmillan.

Plunkett, T.J. and George Betts. (1978). *The Management of Canadian Urban Government*. Kingston, ON: Institute of Local Government.

Siegel, David. (1994). "The ABCs of Canadian Local Government: An Overview." In *Agencies, Boards and Commissions in Canadian Local Government*, edited by Dale Richmond and David Siegel. Toronto: Institute of Public Administration of Canada and Intergovernmental Committee on Urban and Regional Research, pp. 1–20.

CHAPTER EIGHT

INTERGOVERNMENTAL RELATIONS

INTRODUCTION

Upon assuming office as Alberta's Minister of Municipal Affairs in December 1992, Steve West was perplexed by one of his first duties, to approve a new logo for Killam, a small town southeast of Edmonton. Why did the minister have to be involved in a matter so trivial? The reason, he discovered from his staff, was that the provincial Municipal Government Act required that any new crest or coat of arms be approved in advance by the minister (*Alberta Report*, 1994, p. 16). In Dr. West's view, this was ridiculous: "I don't care if they want an out-house for a logo. This decision should be left to local politicians" (*Alberta Report*, 1994, p. 16). This incident prompted the minister to initiate a radical revamping of Alberta's Municipal Government Act (MGA) and related legislation with the goal of reducing unnecessary regulation and giving greater decision making and budgetary authority to municipalities. The result was to cut the size of the MGA in half and reverse the province's traditional paternalistic approach to local government.

This vignette illustrates both the essence of the traditional intergovernmental context for urban governance and its emerging direction. The common catch-phrase is that Canadian local governments are "creatures of the province," in both a legal and practical sense. Although it is too early to assess the real impact of the new Alberta legislation, its underlying philosophy may promise a better future for our cities as they govern in an increasingly complex intergovernmental milieu.

This chapter examines the urban intergovernmental relationship. We already know some of the history from Chapters Three and Four, which discussed the historical legacy of the imposition of local government systems by different provinces and the ebb and flow of structural and political reform at the local level. This chapter provides a fuller and more focussed overview of Canadian urban governments' intergovernmental relations. It deals with three aspects of the topic:

- The principles and code words underlying the relationship. We begin by getting a sense of the lexicon of intergovernmental relations.
- Contemporary issues and trends in urban intergovernmental relations including debates about the role and place of Canada's urban governments in the federation, the umbilical link between intergovernmental relations and fiscal issues, and cities' international relations in an increasingly global world.
- How urban governments manage intergovernmental relations. In this context, we will examine how our chosen cities organize themselves for this purpose. We will also look at the nature of collective local government action through municipal associations.

The Lexicon of Urban Intergovernmental Relations

As a federal nation-state, Canada has a particularly extensive history and pattern of intergovernmental relations. There is a rich body of academic literature on the subject and an equal wealth of satire and humour. In order to understand the issues that are now at centre stage on Canadian urban governments' intergovernmental agenda, it is helpful to know some of the basic principles and terms commonly used to describe the relationship between municipalities and other levels of government in the country.

Federalism

Given that Canada is a federal state, it is important to begin by tapping into the theories of **federalism**. A good starting point, for our purposes, is Daniel Elazar's conceptualization of federalism as "shared rule and self-rule" (Elazar, 1981). While this may characterize the relationship between the federal and provincial governments in Canada, it does not speak to the place of local governments in our federal system. We have two constitutionally entrenched *orders* of government in our federation, the federal and provincial. The third *level* of government, local government, derives its formal authority only as a result of delegation from the provincial order. Accordingly, from a constitutional and legal perspective, we might think of Canadian local governments as operating in a milieu characterized by shared rule, but not self-rule.

A more nuanced contrast between the federal–provincial and provincial–municipal relationship has been offered by J. Stefan Dupré. He distinguished the two on the basis of their legal status, hierarchical character, and complexity, arguing that:

- in legal terms the federal–provincial relationship is based on constitutional law, whereas the provincial municipal relationship is based on statutory law;
- in hierarchical terms, the federal–provincial relationship is one of equal to equal, whereas the provincial–municipal relationship is one of superior to subordinate; and
- in terms of complexity, Dupré described the federal–provincial relationship as being relatively simple, with one federal government and ten provinces. The provincial–municipal relationship is more complex, with each provincial government having to deal with a myriad of municipalities, ranging from the very small to the very large (Dupré, 1968, p. 1).

Dupré coined the term "hyper-fractionalized quasi-subordination," a "self-admittedly barbarous phrase" but one that has stood the test of time as a description of the provincial–municipal dimension of urban governments' intergovernmental relations (Andrew, 1995, p. 137).

Alternative perspectives emphasize the informal capacity for self-rule by local governments rather than their situation in terms of constitutional law. David Cameron (1980) and others have argued that the independent election of local councils and the fact that they have particular responsibility for the territory included in their municipality gives local governments in Canada an important foundation for self-rule and what Cameron calls "quasi-constitutional status" (see also Feldman and Graham, 1979). The interplay between the formal constitutional situation of urban governments and their quasi-constitutional capacity to act independently in the intergovernmental arena has been quite varied. There are differences among our cities based, in part, on their historical relationships with their provincial government. There are also differences over time, as different issues take centre stage on the intergovernmental agenda.

Both the quasi-subordinate and the quasi-constitutional perspectives on local government have an important element in common. They alert us to considerable entanglement among the various levels of government in a federal system, particularly between municipal and provincial governments. In fact, one of the goals underlying many contemporary provincial–municipal discussions is that of **disentanglement**.

Disentanglement

Looking back, we can see a major change in the relationship of Canadian municipal governments to the federal and provincial levels beginning with the Great Depression in the 1930s. The Depression marked the beginning of significant federal involvement in cities through the establishment of employment and other relief programs. In the period immediately following the war, Canada's social infrastructure was heavily influenced by expansion of federal roles in housing and social welfare and accompanying provincial initiatives, both in the social sector and in the major push to provide the physical infrastructure to service rapid urban growth (Magnusson, 1983, pp. 24–25). One effect of this was to entangle all levels of government in Canada in a web of shared cost programs. It also gave birth to an extensive array of intergovernmental relationships of both a provincial–municipal and tri-level nature.

By the mid-1980s, arguments began to emerge that the system was collapsing under its own weight. Governments at all levels were confronting severe fiscal challenges. Municipal governments were complaining at increasingly high decibel levels about the strictures of conditional grants. There were also concerns in some provinces, most notably Ontario and Nova Scotia where municipalities shared the cost of income support programs, that the system of local government finance was inadequate to deal with programs for which there was no apparent way to control public demand.

These pressures, perhaps combined with a political desire to go back to a simpler time, gave rise to the idea that there should be a re-alignment of responsibilities between municipal governments and their provinces. The word "disentanglement" became part of the municipal intergovernmental lexicon. Basically, it was intended to characterize an assignment of responsibilities among governments more akin to the watertight compartment image of federalism, in which the functions and responsibilities of different levels of government are much more clearly separated.

Subsidiarity

The concept of **subsidiarity** helps to determine which level of government should do what as intergovernmental responsibilities are disentangled (or entangled). Subsidiarity came into prominence as an organizing principle for assigning governmental responsibilities with the creation of the European Union. It was also articulated by the Task Force on the Greater Toronto Area as the essential principle of urban governance systems (GTA Task Force, 1996, p. 162). Basically, subsidiarity entails assigning responsibility for any particular function of government to the lowest level possible. Only if the lowest level is not capable of policy formation and delivery of this function would it be assigned to a more senior level.

The simplicity of the principle of subsidiarity masks some thorny questions. For example, must service and policy necessarily be assigned to the same government? This is not just a theoretical question. It speaks to the nature of entanglement (or disentanglement) among different levels of government. It also raises the question of whether urban governments will be involved in key functions at all, as provinces keep or re-acquire policy functions crucial to cities and then use the voluntary or private sector as the delivery agent. A second question relates to what criteria are to be used to allocate responsibilities. In particular, how might efficiency and effectiveness, which are the two criteria mentioned (but not spelled out) by the GTA Task Force, be defined? (Sancton, 1996, p. 40)

Downloading

The term "downloading" is used to refer to two manoeuvres being employed by the provincial and federal governments. Municipalities argue that both are occurring with increasing frequency. In the first instance, downloading refers to the assignment of a new responsibility to local government without a corresponding transfer of financial and other resources. Municipalities have to pick up the tab, which is sometimes a considerable one. The second type of downloading occurs when a provincial government or the federal government simply abandons a service or another activity. The assumption is that if a real need exists, someone will fill the void. Urban governments argue that an undue part of this burden will fall on their shoulders.

Downloading is very much a tri-level phenomenon. Consider the crucial functions of social services and health care. The federal government has put an absolute cap on its funding in these fields and has changed its method of funding as well. The Canada Health and Social Transfer (CHST) abandoned the federal government's role in cost sharing social assistance and significantly reduced the overall level of federal support for health care, post-secondary education, and welfare. In the no tax increase environment of the late 1990s, provincial governments found that raising taxes to compensate for federal cuts to transfers was a politically unpalatable option. The resulting financial pressure on provinces has contributed significantly to cuts to provincial–municipal transfers.

With these basic concepts in hand, we now turn to the major contemporary issues in urban intergovernmental relations.

CONTEMPORARY INTERGOVERNMENTAL ISSUES

Broadly speaking, there are four types of intergovernmental issues facing Canadian urban governments today:

- How to put some of the principles of intergovernmental relations, discussed above, into action. This includes major debates about the place and powers of urban governments within the provincial–municipal context and in the broader arena of tri-level relations.
- How city governments will relate to a fourth type of government, Aboriginal government, which is establishing an increasing presence on Canada's federal stage.
- How cities can effectively manage intergovernmental relations in the international context to enhance their presence on the global stage.
- How the intergovernmental dynamic will play out with regard to the major challenges facing cities in terms of their fiscal resources, economic development, and the need to develop sustainable and livable urban communities.

Our discussion of intergovernmental issues in this chapter will focus on the first three of these challenges. A sense of the intergovernmental dynamic related to finance, economic development, and urban livability will emerge from the subsequent three chapters.

From Principles to Action: The Provincial–Municipal Relationship

In this section, we explore how the issues surrounding **delegated (or express) powers**, disentanglement and subsidiarity, and downloading are being put into action in provincial–municipal relations in Canada.

MUNICIPAL LEGISLATION AND THE CONCEPT OF DELEGATED POWERS

The description of the traditional relationship between the municipalities and the provincial government in Alberta, in the vignette at the beginning of this chapter, typifies the provincial–municipal relationship throughout Canada. This relationship is enshrined in provincial legislation governing the role, structure, and operations of municipal governments. In each case, the cornerstone of this legislative regime is the province's Municipal Act. Historically, this and other provincial legislation affecting municipal governments (covering areas such as municipal planning, environment, social services, recreation, and culture) are restrictive rather than permissive in character. Municipal governments in Canada have been allowed to undertake only activities specifically delegated to them. They have not been able to make independent decisions on many matters, both significant (such as incurring debt) and picayune (such as a logo). They also have been restricted from keeping up with changing public policy agendas without explicit provincial approval. For example, when the movement to restrict smoking in public places arose, municipalities such as the City of Ottawa had to receive provincial permission to pass a non-smoking by-law.

Alluding to an early popular television program, Allan O'Brien (1975) characterized this situation as reflecting the notion that "father knows best."

The trend in intergovernmental relations is toward greater municipal autonomy and less restrictive provincial control. The first serious consideration of loosening provincial bonds over municipalities came in the mid-1970s when the Ontario government established a Royal Commission on Metropolitan Toronto, chaired by a former provincial premier, John Robarts. The Robarts Commission came up with a bold proposal. It argued that the government of Metropolitan Toronto had sufficient size and sophistication to warrant reducing the strictures of provincial control. Robarts recommended permissive legislation to set out broad powers and responsibilities for Metro (Royal Commission on Metropolitan Toronto, 1977). While Robarts' recommendations were ignored by the Ontario government, they encouraged Ontario and other provinces to think about mimicking the first real experiment with permissive municipal legislation in Canada, the 1994 Alberta Municipal Government Act (MGA).

If the classical image of Prometheus Bound can be seen as a metaphor for the restrictive model of municipal legislation, then the modern image of bungy cords can be viewed as a symbol for the new Alberta MGA. In the words of the minister who oversaw its passage in the Alberta legislature, the revised MGA "makes that bungy cord thin until it snaps. The municipalities become a power unto themselves" (*Alberta Report*, 1994, p. 16).

The revised act is the culmination of consultations that occurred between the province and Alberta municipalities over several years. The Alberta Urban Municipalities Association (AUMA) was prominent in this process. The innovative elements of the new legislation are as follows:

- It defines broad spheres in which municipalities are enabled to take action, a major departure from the traditional delegated or express powers approach to mandating municipal government. Furthermore, the 1994 MGA does not say what municipalities must and must not do with respect to each of these spheres.
- It eliminates 23 separate statutes that had governed municipalities, thereby collapsing traditional cornerstones such as the Planning Act and the Assessment Act. Provincial interests related to these and other activities are now set out in the MGA.
- It creates a new part-time Municipal Government Board. It consolidates the functions formerly carried out by three municipal oversight agencies: the Assessment Appeal Board, the Local Authorities Board, and the Alberta Planning Board. The part-time character of the new board reflects the significant reduction in provincial oversight procedures related to assessment appeals, annexations, and planning matters.
- It eliminates regional planning commissions, which had been part of the municipal landscape in Alberta for many years but which were viewed as ineffective in co-ordinating planning and development. The new legislation encourages co-ordination among municipalities and sets out a requirement for inter-municipal dispute resolution.

- It is the first piece of municipal legislation in Canada that permits municipalities to carry an operating deficit, although the MGA puts very strict limits on when this can occur and sets out requirements for deficit elimination.
- It smooths out the property tax assessment system, requiring municipal reassessments every two years or less. Municipalities are given greater autonomy to establish user fees and permitted to occupy expanded fields of taxation. Subject to provincial approval, Alberta municipalities can now levy entertainment, bicycle, sales, and gasoline taxes, just to name a few.
- In the case of the spheres of responsibility dealt with in the MGA itself, the province commits to intervening in municipal affairs only when there is a clear provincial interest — for example, to prevent development of an overly burdensome or unfair tax regime at the municipal level. The MGA also stresses the province's intention to have other key Alberta government departments and agencies, such as those dealing with environmental protection, agriculture, economic development, and trade, declare their broad policy interests. The objective is to leave scope for municipal activity in these areas.

It is evident that the new Alberta Municipal Government Act is a significant departure from tradition and is being followed with keen interest by other provinces. At least three other provinces have been convinced of the merits of the Alberta approach. In early 1997, Ontario also introduced a proposal for new municipal legislation moving away from the tradition of express delegated powers (Ontario Ministry of Municipal Affairs and Housing, 1997) and British Columbia announced a comprehensive three-year review of its legislation with a view to streamlining and municipal empowerment. The government of Manitoba had introduced new legislation that was a hybrid, offering broad spheres of jurisdiction on some matters and retaining the tradition of restricted delegation on others. In contrast, the government of Nova Scotia had tabled legislation retaining express delegation as the foundation for municipal responsibilities. This legislation was subsequently shelved, however, in the face of significant opposition from the province's municipalities, including the new Halifax Regional Municipality (Lidstone, 1996).

Municipal governments' enthusiasm for the new approach is somewhat tempered. As cities monitor the Alberta experiment, a key concern is how the Alberta government will define "provincial interest" over time. Will the province stand back and be quite broad and laissez-faire, or will bungy-jumping municipalities be yanked back closer to the provincial launching platform?

While Ontario is proposing to follow the Alberta model, the Ontario Savings and Restructuring Act passed in 1995 (commonly known as the Omnibus Bill) gave the Minister of Municipal Affairs sweeping powers to amalgamate, eliminate, and otherwise reform the provinces' municipalities without even having to refer legislation to the provincial legislature. There seem to be conflicting pressures to centralize and devolve at work in the Ontario context. Moreover, the events of mega-week in January 1997, discussed in the next section, abruptly reminded Ontario cities that the province views itself as firmly in control of the provincial–municipal relationship. As we shall see, however, the Ontario case does provide a cautionary tale for provincial governments.

DISENTANGLEMENT AND THE PRINCIPLE OF SUBSIDIARITY

The trend toward greater municipal autonomy has been accompanied in many provinces by efforts to determine the appropriate policy and service delivery responsibilities of the provincial government and the responsibilities of municipal governments. This debate has been felt most acutely in the area of human services, including education. Although the guiding philosophies of this sorting out of responsibilities are subsidiarity and disentanglement, the actions taken by different provinces have led to varying degrees of actual disentanglement. It is important to note, however, that the provinces had different starting points as to how entwined the delivery of services was in the first place. As we look at the seemingly compelling conceptual arguments in favour of disentanglement and three decades of experiments with it, we take a position contrary to prevailing wisdom. In our view, disentanglement as an end in itself is mistaken. Furthermore, the difficulties associated with implementing disentanglement have been underestimated and the beneficial results overrated.

EXPERIMENTS WITH DISENTANGLEMENT

The seeds of the contemporary effort to separate and simplify provincial–municipal roles and responsibilities lie in New Brunswick. In 1967, the New Brunswick government launched the Program for Equal Opportunity. This initiative was quite unlike local government reforms occurring in other provinces around the same period, which concentrated on altering local governments' political structures and territorial boundaries. In contrast, the Program for Equal Opportunity redistributed functional responsibilities between New Brunswick and its municipalities. The province assumed full control and financial responsibility for the administration of justice, welfare, public health, and education. This was intended to give New Brunswick residents equal access to a standard level of service in these four areas. At the same time, county government was abolished and provincially administered local service districts were created throughout rural New Brunswick (Feldman, 1973). This can be seen as the precursor of more recent provincial government initiatives, in British Columbia and Alberta, to use regional boards to govern health and family services.

There were other forerunners to today's disentanglement debates. The Saskatchewan government and its municipalities agreed on a formula for revenue sharing in 1978. It was intended to make municipalities less dependent on the political whims associated with provincial–municipal grants tied to a specific purpose. Following a consultation with Quebec municipalities, the Quebec Minister of Finance announced major changes to the provincial–municipal fiscal relationship in 1979. The province assumed all responsibility for funding education, removing it from the property tax base. Municipalities were thus given sole access to the property tax, as an independent revenue source, no longer having to share it with school boards. In exchange, the Quebec government significantly reduced provincial transfers to the local level and established a new approach to financing public transit in cities. These reforms were intended to address Quebec municipalities' desire for a system of finance that suited their responsibilities and gave them adequate flexibility (Lapointe, 1980, p. 272). The fact that the door was left open for Quebec school boards to access the property tax system in the future was a concern for municipalities at the time.

The issue of provincial–municipal disentanglement reasserted itself in the late 1980s. In Quebec, disentanglement became linked with downloading. Faced with increasing pressures on its coffers in 1990, the Quebec government increased the municipalities' responsibility for financing policing, public transit, and roads. Around the same time, the government announced that it would no longer give school boards grants for school maintenance and instructed them to use the property tax to make up the resulting shortfall. The Union of Quebec Municipalities viewed the so-called Ryan reforms (named after Claude Ryan, the Minister of Municipal Affairs at the time) as a direct violation of two of the principles that a 1990 Quebec parliamentary commission on Quebec's constitutional future (which had a representative of the Union of Quebec Municipalities as a member) suggested should guide the provincial–municipal relationship:

- reconnaissance institutionelle des municipalités et mise sur pied d'un mécanisme de transferts des responsabilités; and
- accompagnement des transferts de responsabilités par des transferts de pouvoirs, afin de faire correspondre les niveaux décisionnels et administratifs.

In the words of the province's municipal association, "la reforme Ryan . . . allait envenimer les relations entre les deux partenaires pour plus d'une année" (Union des municipalités du Québec, 1992, p. 18).

In two other provinces, Nova Scotia and Ontario, disentanglement has focussed on trading off functions. The exchange of responsibilities for social services and transportation has been bandied about in both cases but with different results. A provincial Task Force on Local Government (which had municipal representatives) made wholesale recommendations concerning the restructuring of Nova Scotia municipalities in its 1992 report. These included a re-allocation of functions between the province and municipal governments. The task force recommended that this occur on a "revenue neutral" basis, with the new division of labour costing neither level of government more (Task Force on Local Government, 1992).

Subsequently, the Nova Scotia government came up with its own principle of subsidiarity to underpin its proposals concerning the re-allocation of provincial–municipal responsibilities: municipal governments should provide services of primary concern to the local community, whereas the provincial government should take responsibility for services where there is a province-wide concern. This principle was to be met by a service exchange, with the provincial government assuming responsibility for social services (defined specifically as income support) and local governments assuming responsibility for local roads and policing (Nova Scotia Department of Municipal Affairs, 1993). This approach was reflected in the allocation of responsibilities between Nova Scotia and the new Halifax Regional Municipality.

There was a slight hiccup, however, in implementation. Immediately prior to the official inauguration of the new government for the Halifax metropolitan area, the Nova Scotia government seemed to get cold feet about taking on social services. The regional municipality was to be up and running on April 1, 1996. Until March 1996, senior staff of the new municipality were not certain if the provincial government would assume financial or administrative responsibility for social services. In the end, it did so. There remains a potential problem associated with the province's narrow interpretation of the social service function. A complex metropolitan area, such as the Halifax Regional Municipality, requires its social services to cover more than just income support. Accordingly, the Regional Municipality may still find itself involved in social services, especially social planning. This reflects the continuing reality of considerable provincial–municipal entanglement.

Ontario: The Road to Radical Change

Ontario is the prime example of a jurisdiction where disentanglement has become an end in itself and where the difficulties of implementation have become most evident. Interest in disentanglement arose primarily from a concern about uncontrollable and burdensome social service costs. Particularly in the area of human services, Ontario had a more entangled system of funding and delivery than many other provinces. Municipalities have been required to pay 20 percent of the cost of General Welfare Assistance for local residents. They have also administered income support and many related aspects of community social services for many years. Needless to say, this is a very big ticket item, especially in periods of economic downturn.

Provincial–municipal agreement about how to deal with this problem seemed at hand with the release of the Hopcroft Report (more precisely, the Report of the Advisory Committee to the Minister of Municipal Affairs on the Provincial–Municipal Relationship) in 1991. It developed a new vision of the provincial–municipal relationship based on three principles. First, functions would be assigned either to the provincial or municipal level as clearly as possible. Second, the province would use conditional grants only when a clear provincial interest existed. The more specific trade-off proposed that the province take over responsibility for General Welfare in return for local assumption of responsibility for some provincial roads and the cost of undertaking local property assessment. Finally, any exchange of service responsibilities would be revenue neutral for both parties.

The Hopcroft recommendations were never implemented. Provincial–municipal negotiations to identify the costs of administering various services proved difficult. Furthermore, some municipalities questioned the revenue neutrality of the exchange. Ultimately, the negotiations fell apart as a result of the imposition of Ontario's Social Contract legislation in 1993, which reduced provincial–municipal transfers part way through the fiscal year (Siegel, 1992).

The newly elected Conservative government of Mike Harris continued to pursue disentanglement. It was attracted to the idea by the desire to control costs, eliminate waste (assumed to result from the current distribution of responsibilities), and simplify government. The government's "Who Does What?" Panel made probably the most clarion call to disentangle government roles and responsibilities yet heard in Canada. The panel's December 1996 recommendations were highly reflective of the Hopcroft Report. Its basic logic was that "hard" (infrastructure) services should be the full responsibility of municipalities and "soft" (human) services be the proper function of the provincial government. Under the panel's scenario, the province would have assumed full responsibility for income support and family and children's services. In exchange, municipalities would take complete responsibility for water and sewage treatment facilities, public transit and roads within their boundaries, and a greater share of the costs of policing. The number of school boards would have been reduced, with some board functions going to municipalities and others to the province. Crombie stressed that if a choice had to be made between placing education or social services on the municipal property tax, the unequivocal preference was education. Most observers assumed that the recommendations of the "Who Does What?" Panel would be quietly and quickly implemented by the province.

In a surprise move, however, the Ontario government went in the opposite direction from that laid out by Crombie. During the span of one chaotic, historic week in January 1997, popularly called "mega-week," the Conservative government initiated massive changes to the governing and funding arrangements for education, welfare, and a wide range of other urban services, consulting neither the municipalities nor their associations. Under these reforms, education, costing $5.4 billion annually, would be removed from the property tax and become the full responsibility of the province. The number of school boards would be cut in half and the role and salaries of elected trustees reduced. The province would also assume funding of children's aid societies and women's shelters. As with the earlier initiatives, the stated intent was that the service exchange be an even trade financially; municipalities were to acquire new responsibilities equal in cost to the former education bill.

In several areas, the province and municipalities would remain and, indeed, become even more entangled through cost sharing arrangements, although municipalities would pick up a bigger share than before.

- Welfare would be funded 50–50. This includes General Welfare (up from 20–80 municipal–provincial sharing) as well as Family Benefits for single parents and support for disabled persons (which had been 100 percent provincially funded). Because welfare costs are countercyclical, rising as the economy weakens, the province agreed to set up a $700 million contingency fund to help municipalities during economic downturns.
- The municipal share of child care funding would be expanded to 50 percent (up from 20 percent).
- Long-term health care (nursing homes and home care for the elderly) would be equally cost shared rather than a provincial responsibility.

In addition, municipalities would acquire full responsibility for a number of areas previously under provincial control:

- social housing;
- ambulance services;
- public libraries;
- public transit, municipal airports, some highways, and some water and sewage facilities;
- policing in rural areas;
- property assessment; and
- community based public health (once cost shared). The province would take over immunization programs. (Ontario Ministry of Community and Social Services, 1997)

The reaction to the mega-week announcements illustrates many of the practical problems associated with disentanglement. At first, many cities welcomed the opportunity for an enhanced role in some social services. They soon discovered, however, that their actual autonomy was illusory because the province planned to maintain control over the design and delivery of most programs, merely giving up funding. As Terry Mundell, head of the Association of Municipalities of Ontario (AMO), stated in his criticism, "If we're paying, we need to have some tools" (Mittelstaedt and Rusk, 1997, p. A7). It also became apparent that the overall service exchange was far from revenue neutral, with municipalities emerging as big losers. Indeed, one Metro Toronto councillor described the new funding plan as "the biggest tax bomb in the history of Metro" (Lakey, 1997, p. A14).

The estimate of the net cost to Metro Toronto would have been about $379 million annually and to Ottawa-Carleton about $160 million (Ross, 1997b, p. A7; Adam, 1997, p. A1). These figures are probably very conservative, however. In the event of an economic recession, for instance, welfare costs could rise dramatically and demographics alone would propel expenditures on long-term care upwards. What seems evident is that the province was attempting to download those services with difficult-to-control costs, while maintaining those services, such as education, with relatively fixed or shrinking costs. The province's ultimate aim appears to be to shrink the role of the state, both provincial and municipal. The magnitude of the costs of new services loaded onto the municipal property tax will eventually force cities to significantly cut, privatize, or abandon many services. Metro Toronto would be hit disproportionately hard because, as the magnet of both domestic and international immigration it has relatively higher social expenditures than other Ontario cities (Golden, 1997, p. A21). The concern that increased property taxes and/or deteriorating quality of life in the economic engine of Ontario would seriously impair economic development in the entire province prompted the head of the Metro Board of Trade and at least one bank president to join municipal officials in denouncing the mega-week plan. These criticisms made a sufficient impression that four months after mega-week, the province reconsidered a number of aspects of the proposal. For example, it reverted to the traditional 80–20 provincial–municipal split in welfare, although there was some reduction in the specific costs which the province would cover. It also committed to repairing the province's dilapidated housing stock before any transfer to the municipal level.

Evaluating Disentanglement

Should we put our faith in disentanglement as the means of achieving greater accountability and lower costs in provincial–municipal relations? In answering this question, we would get relatively little help from urban theory as most of the theories we examined in Chapter Two do not address intergovernmental relations in depth. One exception is public choice theory. It makes an emphatic case that income redistribution must be done by senior governments in order to prevent social dumping. Although less explicit on this, political economy's focus on collective consumption would lend support for the idea that hard services and some limited social services should be provided by municipalities and most income support by the province. In contrast, feminist approaches stress the importance of human services to the quality of urban life and the need to plan for such services with full participation of local citizens. Feminists might be more supportive of local policy control over human services, as long as the viability of such services was not in jeopardy due to funding arrangements.

In our view, we should be cautious about the promises of disentanglement. First, we need to question seriously whether cost sharing and joint responsibility for a policy field necessarily produces waste and duplication of effort. In many human services, such as General Welfare versus Family Benefits, the actual programs administered by the two levels of government are quite different.

Second, we need to question the assumptions about the appropriate roles and capacities of local government inherent in disentanglement proposals. In our view, the position advocated by Crombie and Hopcroft in Ontario or the government of Nova Scotia — that cities should be primarily deliverers of hard services, rather than governments centrally involved in building citizenship and promoting social harmony — is fundamentally flawed. Responsibility for at least some policies governing the human condition are a critical means of connecting local governments to the people and are especially vital in large, culturally diverse urban areas. As Andrew Sancton (1992) argues, municipalities get out of social services at their peril. Much of the action at the local level is in the social domain; to shed a role in this area risks self-condemnation to irrelevancy. While involvement in social services is vital, the ability and desirability of placing 50 percent of the cost of all welfare services on the property tax, as the 1997 Ontario proposal does, is rightly questioned.

A third problem with most approaches to disentanglement is that they focus mainly on *government* funding and policy responsibilities but ignore the importance of the *voluntary sector* in delivery. In most social services, the voluntary sector is intimately involved in delivery, from programs like Meals on Wheels in assisting home care to literacy programs as supplements to labour market training. Yet it is overwhelmingly municipal governments, not provincial ones, that have

long-standing, close working relationships and partnerships with community organizations (Graham and Phillips, 1996). Disentanglement exercises that ignore the
centrality of the voluntary sector will likely produce greater distance and discon-
nectedness between policy and delivery, rather than greater efficiencies.

Finally, the greatest problem with many disentanglement initiatives is that
they have not been in essence about disentanglement at all. Rather, most have
become a vehicle for downloading costs to municipalities.

PROVINCIAL DOWNLOADING

Downloading is not unique to Ontario. In recent years, virtually every
Canadian city has been subject to downloading and shrinking provincial transfers to varying degrees. In some cases, the impact of the financial burden on
municipalities has been very substantial.

How have urban governments responded to the phenomenon of downloading? First, they have protested. The Quebec Union of Municipalities' disquiet
over the 1990 reforms and the AMO's intense lobbying against the mega-week
pronouncements are cases in point. Individual cities have also carried out public
campaigns against downloading and the simultaneously tight reins of provincial
control. Winnipeg, for example, published a 1991 pamphlet on the provincial–municipal relationship which placed significant responsibility for the city's
strained finances on provincial shoulders. The pamphlet concludes with a list of
eighteen areas in which civic costs are incurred as a result of provincial legislation. These items run the gamut from mosquito abatement to the requirement
that the city absorb the costs for a four-person panel to review the character of
aspiring taxi-cab drivers (City of Winnipeg, 1991, p. 6).

Second, in spite of their criticisms, municipalities and their associations have
joined provincial governments in working groups to negotiate mitigating measures for specific cases of downloading. For instance, two panels were established
in Ontario to address implementation details of the service exchange. Both
were co-chaired by the president of the AMO and had additional representation by local elected officials.

Finally, municipal governments and their associations have proposed longer
term remedies to the problems associated with downloading and the vulnerabil-
ity of municipalities in intergovernmental relations. In its 1991 Annual Report,
the Union of Quebec Municipalities, for example, advocated the principle,
"l'assurance de l'autonomie fiscale des municipalités (le gouvernement qui
dépense doit être celui qui prélève les impôts)" (Union des municipalités du
Québec, 1992, p. 18).

Municipal associations in Nova Scotia, Ontario, Alberta, and British
Columbia have proposed the establishment of a "municipal charter" as an antidote to their members' intergovernmental predicament. In general, the idea of a
charter is to enshrine the notion of partnership in the relations between municipalities and other levels of government. This implies significant intergovernmental consultation before provinces re-align responsibilities and fiscal arrangements affecting cities. The charter proposals also reflect the desire to give

municipal governments more fiscal autonomy and greater room to raise revenues, in light of their increasing responsibilities. Echoing the position of the Quebec association, the first principle in the "principled approach" to provincial–municipal relations, proposed by the Alberta Urban Municipalities Association (AUMA) in 1995, was that "property taxes should be for the 'exclusive use' of municipalities" (*Alberta Report*, 1995, p. 12).

All of these proposals reflect the real concern of municipal governments in Canada that they remain "puppets on a shoestring" as the country's federal system evolves. This concern relates to trends in provincial–municipal relations, most particularly downloading and cutbacks in provincial–municipal transfers. It also relates to concerns that cities have a voice on the national political stage. We now turn to efforts by Canada's cities to emerge from under the paternalistic arm of "father" who knows best to the big persons' world of federal–provincial relations.

Tri-level Relations

Given constitutional constraints, one of the trickiest issues for both cities and the federal government is how to develop a tri-level relationship. At various times and for different reasons, the federal government has been interested in urban affairs. Provincial governments, however, have guarded their control over municipal governments as zealously as they have protected their turf in other key provincial fields, such as education. Throughout discussions prior to patriation of the Constitution in 1982, efforts by Canada's cities to negotiate the place of urban government in our federation were immediately and firmly rebuffed by the provinces. For its part, the federal government had other priority items for negotiation at the time. It was also still recovering from its foray into urban affairs during the 1970s. The federal government's experience between 1971 and 1979 with its hapless Ministry of State for Urban Affairs (MSUA) and the prospect that a defined role for the federal government in the urban field would bleed federal coffers dry further reduced federal interest. It seems, then, that changing the role and constitutional status of urban governments was and will remain a non-issue as we continue to discuss a renewed Canadian federation.

In the Alice and Wonderland world of Canadian federalism, however, all is not as it first appears. Since patriation of the Constitution, there have been a number of significant issues and developments in the tri-level arena, including both tri-level action vis-à-vis specific cities and a significant national program established following the 1993 federal election, Canada Infrastructure Works, that affects all Canadian cities.

CITY-SPECIFIC TRI-LEVEL ACTIONS

There is a long history of federal involvement in funding urban infrastructure (Andrew and Morrison, 1995, p. 109). This tradition has been particularly strong in Atlantic Canada, although there have been examples of this practice in other provinces, notably Quebec. The most traditional vehicle for this has been regional development grants, which have wound their way from a succession of federal departments concerned with regional affairs, such as the Atlantic Canada Opportunities Agency, through the channel of federal–provincial agreements, to provide funds for the construction of water mains, sewers, and roads in various urban centres.

This tri-level focus on urban servicing continues, although in a new guise, with the national program Canada Infrastructure Works discussed below. But in recent years, another trend has emerged. Increasingly there is a new focus on harnessing the interests and responsibilities of the three levels of government to deal with particular urban problems. In some cases, these are quite specific and specialized. In others, they are more general in nature. Three examples illustrate the different situations in which this problem-solving approach has given rise to a substantive tri-level relationship:

- The problem of transporting hazardous materials within the Greater Vancouver Region led to the establishment of a tri-level task force to deal with the issue. Chaired by Transport Canada, it also had active members from the BC Ministry of Transportation and Highways and the Greater Vancouver Regional District. The task force conducted its own studies and undertook public consultation on the issue. Its 1988 report indicated consensus among all three levels of government concerning what should be done. Implementation of the report's recommendations included the establishment of an ongoing tri-level council on hazardous goods transportation in the region (Oberlander and Smith, 1993, pp. 341–42).

- In 1981, the governments of Canada, Manitoba, and the City of Winnipeg entered an agreement to undertake the Core Area Initiative. This agreement committed funding and expertise from all three governments to revitalizing the centre of Winnipeg and, more specifically, to developing the lands at the confluence of the Red and Assiniboine rivers, commonly know as "The Forks." A visit to the market, cultural facilities, and recreational open space that arose from the former railway lands attests to the success of this effort. The outcome of a similar tri-level agreement to redevelop railway lands in downtown Toronto was massive new construction, ranging from housing to Skydome.

- Concern about the future economic prosperity of the Halifax region, coupled with changes in the role of the federal government in transportation, prompted the establishment of a tri-level committee, dubbed the Gateway Committee, in the mid-1990s. It is a forum for tri-level discussion on the future of the Halifax Airport (the operation of which was transferred from Transport Canada to an independent local airport authority during the same period), the port of Halifax, and rail links to the area.

In each of these examples, the strictures of the formal constitutional relationship have been eased by the immediacy of a problem requiring tri-level collaboration. This is perhaps a reflection of the problem-oriented focus that the federal government was urged to take in dealing with urban affairs over 25 years ago (Lithwick, 1970). In dealing with urban problems, Montreal is a special case. All three governments have been involved in addressing the severe economic problems of the Montreal urban region. In this case, however, the intergovernmental dynamic is unique and the idea of federal involvement is particularly delicate. The Montreal case is discussed further in Chapter Ten.

NATIONAL TRI-LEVEL INITIATIVES: THE INFRASTRUCTURE PROGRAM

The first federal–municipal entanglement was associated with federal winter works and other employment programs that began during the Great Depression. Sixty years later, we again see a connection between a national program to undertake public works at the local level and concern about unemployment. The Canada Infrastructure Works program was implemented by the new Liberal government following the 1993 federal election as one of its Red Book campaign promises to create jobs. In their review of the infrastructure program, Caroline Andrew and Jeff Morrison contend that it was a tri-level initiative in every respect. All three levels of government shared in the cost of the program. Perhaps more importantly, Canada Infrastructure Works "could be described as a federal–provincial–municipal program because the provinces had given their approval and because municipalities had initiated it" (Andrew and Morrison, 1995, p. 112).

Initially, pressure for renewed federal involvement in funding municipal infrastructure across Canada came from the association representing municipal governments at the national level, the Federation of Canadian Municipalities (FCM). Beginning in 1983, it mounted a progressively stronger and more public lobby. The FCM campaigned that the roads and water and sewer lines in Canadian municipalities were deteriorating and could not be repaired without an infusion of money from all three levels of government. A 1985 FCM report estimated the necessary repairs would cost $12 billion, although by 1992 this estimate had been increased to $20 billion (Federation of Canadian Municipalities, 1985, 1996, p. 21). The costs of doing nothing would be catastrophic in terms of environmental degradation as well as local, provincial, and national prosperity. The worst case scenario would be that Canada's cities would become akin to some found in the Third World.

Many provincial governments shared their municipalities' concerns but argued that they could not bear the burden of funding renewal. This, together with concern about rising unemployment in the early 1990s and the tantalizing prospect that the federal government would commit money while giving provinces a large degree of discretion in infrastructure project approval, brought the provinces on board. Between the September 1993 election and the end of February 1994, all ten provinces signed agreements with the federal government to implement the program. In four provinces — Alberta, New Brunswick, Nova Scotia, and Ontario — the federal–provincial agreement provided for municipal representation on the committee to manage the agreement. In British Columbia, Manitoba, Prince Edward Island, and Saskatchewan, there were other provisions for municipal input into the operation of the program (Andrew and Morrison, 1995, pp. 120–22).

The total allocation for the program in 1993 was $6 billion ($2 billion of which was federal money), and the 1997 federal budget committed an additional $600 million from federal coffers (Canada, Minister of Finance, 1997, p. 10). Although this fell short of the FCM's estimated requirements, Canadian municipalities expressed overall satisfaction with the initiative. Larger municipal governments were particularly pleased with the impact of the program, indicating that it had permitted them to deal with their most pressing infrastructure priorities. Overall, 60 percent of the infrastructure funds went to water, sewer, and transportation projects. The remaining 40 percent went to construction or improvement of various types of community facilities and other special projects (Federation of Canadian Municipalities, 1996, p. 21).

According to the federal government's own estimates, Canada Infrastructure Works has created over 100 000 short-term and over 10 000 long-term jobs (Federation of Canadian Municipalities, 1996, p. 21). From an intergovernmental perspective, as Andrew and Morrison note, the first Canada Infrastructure Works program "has created harmonious intergovernmental relations, something that has been in short supply in Canada over the past few years" (1995, p. 133).

SUMMARY

This discussion indicates that issues involving all three levels of government in Canada can and have been addressed by tri-level collaboration. As is the case in federal–provincial relations, failure of more spectacular efforts tends to shape our prevailing image of the intergovernmental relationship. We tend to think of the Meech Lake and Charlottetown accords as symptomatic of a dysfunctional federal–provincial relationship. Many important aspects of federal–provincial relations that do work are overlooked. Similarly, considerable attention has been paid to the high profile efforts of Canadian cities to entrench the tri-level conference as one of the mainstays of Canadian intergovernmental relations or to otherwise insert themselves into the "big C" constitutional arena. The high level trilateral process, which evolved between 1969 and 1976, ended with a "crash and burn" similar to Meech Lake and Charlottetown, and municipalities' efforts to participate in later constitutional negotiations have been summarily dismissed. Nonetheless, it seems that there is considerable scope for urban governments in Canada to be effective advocates and actors in their relations with the federal and provincial levels, as the examples discussed here demonstrate.

Relations between Urban and Aboriginal Governments

A critical emerging challenge for urban governments is to forge new relationships and address intergovernmental issues with Aboriginal peoples, many of whom are establishing new forms of self-government. Urban governance issues in Canada are closely tied to Aboriginal issues for several reasons:

- There are Indian bands with urban land reserves, sometimes in the middle of major metropolitan areas. In Vancouver, for example, the Musqueam reserve is in the middle of North Vancouver. The Kahnawake Mohawk reserve is

15 km from the heart of the City of Montreal. From a geographic perspective, its 12 000 acres [4900 ha] are very much part of the Montreal urban region (Alfred, 1995, p. 2). Among our selected metropolitan areas, there are other major reserves on the edge of Calgary, Edmonton, and Halifax.

- In addition, our selected cities (as well as other cities in Canada) have large populations of Aboriginal people who are living away from their home reserve or community. For example, 45 000 people in Winnipeg identified themselves as Aboriginal in the 1991 census. The comparable numbers for our other cities were as follows: Edmonton 29 000, Vancouver 25 000, Calgary 14 000, Ottawa-Hull 7000, Montreal 7000, and Halifax 1200 (Peters, 1995, Table 3). In fact, approximately half of the Aboriginal population in Canada resides in urban areas.
- Aboriginal people in Canadian cities have higher rates of unemployment, poverty, and social difficulty than the general population. Their rates also exceed those found among the international immigrant population. In public policy terms, urban Aboriginal people who are experiencing difficulty have often fallen between the cracks. No level of government has undertaken a full obligation for meeting their needs; neither has there been significant co-ordination or co-operation among the three levels of government.
- Aboriginal peoples in Canada are pursuing their quest for self-determination and recognition. This quest has several dimensions, but two are most important for our purposes. The first is recognition by Canada and non-Aboriginal Canadians of the right of Aboriginal peoples to govern themselves. This does not imply isolationism. Instead, self-government includes the wherewithal to decide which situations warrent shared rule with other governments, as well as self-rule. The second dimension is settlement of outstanding Aboriginal land claims and recognition of other territorial interests. The settlement of outstanding claims that Aboriginal territories were taken by the Crown without clearing Aboriginal title has potentially significant impact on cities located on land subject to these claims. Municipalities in Vancouver have perhaps the greatest stake in current claims negotiations. There, and in other metropolitan areas, the issue is not whether lands improperly taken will be handed back. The issue is what redress Aboriginal peoples will receive, in terms of financial compensation and a new regime of Aboriginal land rights. Affected municipal governments want to ensure that financial settlements not result in a decrease in their financial resources and that the new land regime take their needs and interests into account.

The current era in Aboriginal affairs is commonly thought to have begun with the Oka crisis of 1990. Previously, one of our cities, Calgary, had a special committee of council on Aboriginal affairs. This practice was not widespread however. In other places, city governments had entered into contractual agreements with Indian bands for the delivery of services or for other purposes. Under the Indian Act, these arrangements require approval of the federal government. As stated above, however, urban Aboriginal issues tended to fall between the intergovernmental cracks.

There are signs that this is changing. The Royal Commission on Aboriginal Peoples, established following the Oka crisis, had urban issues among its terms of reference. It expended considerable effort in research and development of policy recommendations on issues ranging from the culture and identity of Aboriginal people living in cities to possible models of governance for urban Aboriginal people. Its final report recommended that city governments undertake special initiatives to improve relations with Aboriginal residents, including offering services in a more culturally sensitive manner. The commission also encouraged the establishment of Aboriginal institutions to provide services such as health care and post-secondary education in cities with large Aboriginal populations. Finally, it noted the possibility that First Nations with large numbers living in particular cities might opt to offer services for their membership living off-reserve. This reflects the practice of the Siksika First Nation, which provides some social services to its people who live in Calgary (Royal Commission on Aboriginal Peoples, 1996).

All of these observations and recommendations imply a growing relationship between urban governments and Aboriginal residents and governments. There are new signals that the municipal sector is increasing its focus on Aboriginal issues in light of the Royal Commission's work and other developments. For example, the City of Winnipeg, which has the largest Aboriginal population of any city in Canada, has significantly strengthened its efforts to involve its Aboriginal population in revitalization of the city's core. Associations representing municipal governments have also started to deal with urban Aboriginal issues. For example, the Union of BC Municipalities (UBCM) has been active on behalf of its membership regarding Aboriginal claims and treaty issues. The FCM now has a Standing Committee on Aboriginal Relations, which deliberates and makes representation to the federal government and national Aboriginal organizations. In 1996, it received a financial contribution from the government of Canada to establish a Centre for Municipal–Aboriginal Relations. This centre is to "identify and communicate best practices in municipal–Aboriginal relations ranging from service agreements to the creation of urban reserves" (Federation of Canadian Municipalities, 1996, p. 23).

Cities in the International Arena

In addition to working out new relationships with provincial, federal, and Aboriginal governments on the domestic scene, major Canadian cities are taking an increasingly active role on the international stage. The international activities of Canadian cities might be considered as one example of urban governments flexing their quasi-constitutional muscles. Cities are out in the international arena, dealing with one another on economic and cultural issues. The long-standing practice of Canadian cities **twinning** with those in other countries has been augmented by newer international initiatives, focussing on trade, communications, environmental issues, and the provision of development assistance. Surprisingly, much of this international intergovernmental activity has occurred without strong provincial or federal guidance or restrictions, although there have been cases of international collaboration among Canada's three levels of government (Cohn and Smith, 1995). Such international intergovernmental relations are often referred to as **constituent diplomacy**. The word "constituent" refers to the fact that these urban governments are sub-national; "diplomacy" refers to their relatively independent international role (Smith, 1992). The international dimension of cities' concerns about economic development is discussed in Chapter Ten. Here we touch on other examples of international initiatives by our cities.

TWINNING

Twinning is perhaps the most traditional and well established process for urban international involvement. Most of our selected cities have a formal twinning agreement, linking them with a partner city in another country. For example, Vancouver began its twinning program in 1944, establishing a link with Odessa. Since then, it has also paired with Yokohama, Edinburgh, Guangzhou, and Los Angeles (Smith, 1997). The City of Ottawa has a particularly well established twinning relationship with Amsterdam but is also linked formally with Georgetown, Guyana.

Cynics sometimes suggest that twinning arrangements are excuses for urban politicians and senior staff to engage in international travel. Increasingly, however, twinning initiatives are linked to the achievement of some local benefit. In the Vancouver case, for example, the agreements with Edinburgh and Guangzhou were aimed at reinforcing cultural ties for the city's Scottish and Cantonese communities. Vancouver's arrangement with Guangzhou was also intended to boost the city's profile in China from a trade perspective (Smith, 1997). Ottawa's link with Amsterdam was forged after World War II to symbolize the Canadian–Dutch connection resulting from liberation of The Netherlands by Canadian troops. It, too, has evolved into a relationship that focuses more on trade links and the exchange of expertise between the two metropolitan regions. The financial and political circumstances in which Canadian cities now find themselves suggest that twinning relationships will take on an increasingly sharp focus, as cities look to build trade relationships or to work cooperatively on matters such as the environment.

TRANSNATIONAL METROPOLITAN REGIONS: THE CASE OF CASCADIA

Canadians are well aware of their increasing involvement with their neighbours to the south. This extends well beyond the boundaries of the Canada–United States Free Trade Agreement. With most Canadians living near the Canada–U.S. border, we share concerns with people on the other side related to transportation, the environment, and local economic development. In recent years, an important cross-border initiative has been underway in the Cascadia region, which includes much of southwestern British Columbia and the states that make up the American Pacific Northwest (Artibise, 1996, pp. 27–30).

All three levels of government, in both Canada and the United States, are concerned about trans-border issues in the Cascadia region. An ongoing forum for local government exchange has also emerged as part of the Cascadia initiative. Twice each year, the mayors of Portland and Seattle meet with their counterparts from the Greater Vancouver Regional District. This Mayors' Caucus began by exploring the emergence of their municipalities as a transnational urban region. In that context, the caucus isolated two major issues for attention: transportation and the environment. It has proceeded to develop policy positions, from a local government perspective, on both. More recently, the Mayors' Caucus has begun to explore social issues, as the population in the region becomes increasingly diverse and as quality of life issues assume increasing importance for area residents and prospective newcomers (Bose, 1996).

In all cases, the emphasis has been on taking a pragmatic approach rather than establishing formal diplomatic institutions. For example, the mayors of Surrey, British Columbia and Blaine, Washington, co-chair The Border Crossing Working Group. It has worked successfully to speed up the flow of goods and people across the international border (Artibise, 1996, p. 29).

These developments suggest two reasons why the role of city governments in shaping the Cascadia region is significant. First, city governments are prominent players in the evolution of the region itself. Presumably, this will include continuing experimentation with pragmatic approaches to dealing with Cascadia's governance. The region's cities are leading, not following, in this context. Second, the urban initiative in Cascadia provides a prototype which might be useful for cities in other parts of Canada and the United States that share similar trans-border concerns.

The Issues: Conclusion

Taken together, all of the intergovernmental issues discussed here and in other chapters show the complexity of the urban intergovernmental arena. They also show how urban governments' intergovernmental policy agendas can change. This leads to an examination of the approach used by Canadian urban governments to manage their intergovernmental agenda. Given the centrality of intergovernmental relations, one might anticipate that considerable political and managerial energy is directed toward them in Canadian cities.

THE MANAGEMENT OF INTERGOVERNMENTAL RELATIONS

In the late 1970s, a review of Canadian cities' management of intergovernmental relations concluded, "Canada's urban municipal governments have not matured sufficiently as governmental institutions to participate with maximum effectiveness in the intergovernmental process. . . . [An] attribute of Canadian municipal governments which has contributed to their performance in intergovernmental affairs is their inadequate organizational and resource commitments to the effort" (Feldman and Graham, 1979, pp. 98, 116). In the authors' view, urban governments needed to dedicate specific personnel to plot intergovernmental strategy and tactics. They recommended large cities appoint an intergovernmental relations officer to assist other senior staff and council. They were also critical of municipal associations, arguing that the interests of larger municipalities tended to be sacrificed to those of rural and small town members. Have things changed?

The Emergence of a Corporate Approach

A review of our selected cities suggests that a more focussed corporate approach to managing intergovernmental relations has emerged since the late 1970s. There have been four key developments:

- Responsibility for the administrative co-ordination and management of intergovernmental relations has been formally vested in the chief administrative officer. See, for example, the City of Winnipeg's approach in Figure 7.2.
- The work of senior managers, functioning as an intergovernmental team, has become more important. Recall that many large cities had just recently abandoned the departmental model of organization in the 1970s. Several years later, those same cities have integrated corporate organizations at the senior management level. The City of Vancouver's designated corporate management team, shown in Figure 7.1, provides an illustration of this approach. In most of our cities, these exist in reality, not just on paper.
- Some urban centres, most notably the Municipality of Metropolitan Toronto and the Halifax Regional Municipality, have assigned operating responsibility for managing intergovernmental relations to their corporate planning departments.
- Councils have begun to use the corporate expertise of staff more effectively in the conduct of intergovernmental relations at the political level. In some cases, the mayor takes the political lead; in others, important intergovernmental issues are dealt with through council. Regardless, the mayor continues to have major responsibility for serving as the city's ambassador in both domestic and international relations.

Aside from these broad trends, some of our cities face unique circumstances that influence their approach to working on intergovernmental issues. For example, the City of Winnipeg does have an intergovernmental affairs office with a mandate similar to that recommended by Feldman and Graham. The Core Area Redevelopment Initiative was an important impetus for establishing Winnipeg's intergovernmental affairs group, which has a staff of eight. Beginning with the first tripartite agreement to redevelop the city's core in 1981, Winnipeg has had to manage a complex intergovernmental relationship with the government of Manitoba and several federal government departments, as well as with the federal minister whose riding includes the designated area. The Winnipeg group also has responsibility for business liaison. In the intergovernmental context, its current roles are to manage the most recent (1995) tripartite Winnipeg Development Agreement; set strategy for the city's intergovernmental relations more generally; and serve as the secretariat for interactions with the provincial government, other municipalities, school boards, and the FCM.

In at least one case, we see a city designating an intergovernmental specialist to handle a particularly crucial issue as the City of Toronto did in designating a specific liaison with the Task Force on the Greater Toronto Area. All of this suggests that large urban governments in Canada are paying more attention to the management of their intergovernmental affairs. To complete this picture, we need to look at the merits and practice of collective action by urban municipalities in the contemporary period.

The Logic of Collective Action

MUNICIPAL ASSOCIATIONS AT THE PROVINCIAL LEVEL

There is at least one organization to represent the collective interests of municipalities in each province and territory. In British Columbia, Quebec, and Nova Scotia, a single organization represents municipal interests at the provincial level (the Union of BC Municipalities, the Union des municipalitiés du Québec, and the Union of Nova Scotia Municipalities). In each of the three Prairie provinces, there is an association representing urban municipalities and another for rural and small town local governments.

In Ontario, the Association of Municipalities of Ontario (AMO) is a sort of confederation, formed in 1982 through the union of four municipal associations. AMO's working structure has continued to reflect its divergent constituencies. It has sections representing upper-tier regional municipalities and counties, and large urban, small urban, rural, and northern municipalities. Not surprisingly, this arrangement contributed to a top heavy governing structure for the full association. At its peak, AMO had a board of 82, with an executive committee consisting of twenty members. Practicality and dwindling finances prompted a reduction by almost 50 percent in the size of the AMO board in the early 1990s (Association of Municipalities of Ontario, undated).

Municipal associations in all provinces have relatively small staff complements. The largest, AMO, which represents over 650 of the 800 plus municipalities in Ontario, has a policy staff of five people, as does the Alberta Urban Municipalities Association. These and other associations rely extensively on volunteer assistance from member municipalities. Councillors from member municipalities and senior staff serve on association committees, while staff specialists from member municipalities are used as the backbone of working groups on particular issues.

Across the country, we find varying levels of sophistication and activity among municipal associations operating at the provincial level. Their common mandate is to represent the interests of their membership to the provincial government and to offer specific services to members. In the latter context, we find municipal associations brokering insurance coverage for their members, providing references to "best practices" in different aspects of municipal administration, and providing orientation sessions for newly elected councillors. The UBCM, AMO, and the Union des municipalités du Québec also offer a variety of information services and make representations related to the municipal collective bargaining relationship. In the Atlantic region, a unique organization, the Atlantic Provinces Information Centre serves this purpose (Graham, 1995, p. 190).

BOX 8.1 IT'S BUSINESS AS USUAL IN THE BOONDOCKS

They came from all over, from Kapuskasing and Coboconk, from Combermere and Calabogie. All the reeves and wardens and assorted municipal worthies from every rustic corner of Ontario crowded into the ballroom of the Royal York Hotel to hear the Minister of Small Towns pronounce their death sentence.

He did not fail them.

Yesterday, Al Leach told the annual convention of the Association of Municipalities of Ontario that he wanted heads on a platter.

"Everyone in this room knows that there are many, many municipalities out there that can't afford to stay in business," Mr. Leach said.

Source: Excerpted from John Barber, "It's Business as Usual in the Boondocks," *The Globe and Mail*, August 20, 1996, p. A3. Reprinted with permission from *The Globe and Mail*.

This commentary reflects a stereotypical view of municipal associations in Canada. They are best known for their annual conventions, which bring delegates from far and wide to pass resolutions and receive the revealed truth from provincial ministers and premiers. The difficult circumstances in which municipal governments now find themselves have caused a decreasing hospitality to provincial government messengers speaking at their annual conventions.

The contemporary reality is that municipal associations are developing greater sophistication. In Alberta where provincial staff dealing with municipal affairs has been severely cut, the AUMA is seen as an important resource by those who remain. The AUMA was directly involved in negotiations concerning the new Municipal Government Act, as was its Nova Scotia counterpart, the Union of Nova Scotia Municipalities, in the case of provincial–municipal service exchange in that province. In British Columbia, the comprehensive review of municipal legislation launched by the minister in 1997 is being carried out in collaboration with the UBCM.

Despite these and other advances, provincial associations remain secondary players in the intergovernmental activities of Canada's major urban areas. All of our selected cities have a unique place and importance in their respective provinces. Furthermore, large centres have different perspectives on some issues than their smaller or rural counterparts. Large urban centres also have more avenues for pursuing their interests at the provincial level. There is the clout of a big city mayor and the sophisticated expertise of senior city staff. In addition there is the prospect of using the collective influence of the local caucus in the provincial legislature. Red Deer has two MLAs, for example; Calgary and Edmonton have 21 each. As a result of these alternatives, we see Canada's largest urban governments participating in their provincial associations when common cause can be made with diverse municipal partners. Large urban governments also act as good municipal citizens by providing a large part of the staff expertise needed for these associations to do their work. Ultimately, how-

BOX 8.2 B.C. PREMIER HECKLED BY MUNICIPAL LEADERS

Councillors booed and heckled B.C. Premier Glen Clark during his speech Friday on the closing day of the Union of B.C. Municipalities convention. It is the first time anyone can recall a premier being booed at the annual convention, attended by councillors and regional directors. There was new unanimous condemnation this week by UBCM delegates of the province's recent decision to take $400 million out of the Forest Renewal BC fund. The government has also said it may cut grants to municipalities.

Source: Excerpted from "B.C. Premier Heckled by Municipal Leaders," *Ottawa Citizen*, September 21, 1996, p. A3.

ever, the major cities tend to go it alone in the provincial–municipal arena, lobbying the provincial government one-on-one.

THE FEDERATION OF CANADIAN MUNICIPALITIES

The Federation of Canadian Municipalities (FCM) represents Canadian municipalities at the federal level. It began as a coalition of big city mayors trying to lobby the federal government for employment relief and other forms of assistance during the 1930s Depression. After a period of decline in the 1970s, the FCM has emerged as an increasingly important force for municipal interests at the federal level (Feldman and Graham, 1979, pp. 20–21).

Although it has a somewhat larger staff than provincially-based associations, the FCM uses the same approach to developing its positions on issues. The FCM has close ties with the Canadian Association of Municipal Administrators (CAMA), with whom it shares a building in Ottawa. The FCM's major achievement in recent years has been the lobby resulting in the Canada Infrastructure Works program. It has been active on a broader range of issues as well. These include the federal government's payment of grants in lieu of property taxes, urban transportation issues, criminal justice issues, and the impact of reductions in federal social spending on the quality of life in Canadian cities (Federation of Canadian Municipalities, 1996). The FCM has also spearheaded much of the international assistance provided by Canadian municipal governments to governments in other countries.

Canada's largest cities are active members of the FCM. As noted earlier, large urban centres were particularly satisfied with the results of the Canada Infrastructure Works program. This and other federation initiatives, such as a project involving 12 of the country's largest cities to measure the impact of federal social spending cuts, will assure an FCM role in the relations between large cities and the federal government. As is the case in the provincial–municipal context, however, our cities will continue to deal directly with the federal government on issues of particular concern to them. For example, the FCM has no role in Winnipeg's Core Area Initiative or in the tri-level discussions about transportation links for the Halifax area.

INTER-MUNICIPAL COLLECTIVE ACTION

Creation of voluntary inter-municipal co-ordinating arrangements is a potentially important approach to collective action among contiguous governments in our major metropolitan areas. From a theoretical perspective, this reflects the public choice approach to achieving inter-municipal co-ordination and economies of scale in the delivery of specific services.

In Canada, we are just seeing the first tentative experiments with voluntary co-ordination. None are well institutionalized as yet. Three of these efforts illustrate the current state of voluntary inter-municipal co-ordination for collective action.

In the Greater Vancouver Regional District, a "council of councils" — consisting of every council member from all municipalities in the region — was convened several times to deliberate on the GVRD's 1995 regional growth strategy. This assembly proved useful in delivering a consistent message to all of the affected municipalities and in moving the development of the plan to conclusion (Smith, 1997). In his review of the GVRD regional growth strategy, Patrick Smith points to the success of this consensual approach. He argues that it is "biased toward agreement," in contrast to the view of the Greater Toronto Area Task Force, which rejected a similar approach in the GTA context (Smith, 1996, p. 11).

Miffed at being left off the council of the Regional Municipality of Ottawa-Carleton when the government of Ontario restructured the RMOC's electoral system in 1992, the mayors of the eleven municipalities that make up the Ottawa-Carleton region constituted themselves as the Ottawa-Carleton Mayors' Forum. This group meets regularly to discuss matters of common interest, such as further regional reform. Its deliberations are mirrored by a committee of chief administrative officers. They also meet monthly, furthering the discussions of their political leaders and dealing with joint initiatives of a more administrative nature, such as common purchasing.

Perhaps one of the boldest voluntary joint ventures is the Capital Regional Forum in the Edmonton area. As noted earlier, inter-municipal relations in the Edmonton area had been severely damaged by the annexation dispute of the late 1970s. This extended to the planning process throughout the region. It affected the work of the Regional Planning Commission, a provincially mandated body, which was characterized by ongoing disputes between the centre and the suburban/rural periphery. The City of Edmonton was finally forced to take a hard look at its planning process through a community-based Planning Process Round Table, which began in 1993. As a result of this exercise, combined with the dissolution of the Regional Planning Commission by the province, the city moved to establish a more consensual approach to planning with its neighbours. The Capital Regional Forum came into existence on April 1, 1995. Participation is strictly voluntary for the 19 municipalities in the greater Edmonton area, and funding is provided on a proportional basis by the participants. (One legacy of past urban expansionism was that three of the four rural municipalities in the region initially refused to participate.) With the assistance of a contract staff person, the municipal politicians sitting on the forum work to define and discuss issues, not to come up with hard and fast plans. Decision making is by consensus to reduce the prospect of the emergence of winners and losers in inter-municipal planning.

These and other examples of voluntary inter-municipal collaboration are important. For some, they may be of interest as living examples of public choice prescriptions for councils of government. Their more important contributions are as experiments in dealing with inter-municipal relations in a period when grand designs for institutional co-operation, such as Ontario and Quebec's two-tier regions, are being called into question.

CONCLUSION

This chapter has illuminated the complexity of the intergovernmental relations accompanying urban governance in Canada. We have seen that intergovernmental relations for Canadian cities are shaped significantly by the constitutional context. If one were to think of governmental victims in our federal system, then urban governments might seem to fill the bill. But this is not entirely accurate as several new directions in intergovernmental relations emerge. First, there is a general movement toward municipal autonomy and empowerment, although this is occasionally punctuated by unilateral provincial actions that cut grants or shift policy responsibilities. A second trend has been numerous experiments in creating a neater separation of provincial and municipal responsibilities. In a number of cases, however, the disentanglement initiative has itself become entangled with provincial attempts to download costs onto municipalities. Third, there have been an increasing number of important tri-level, inter-municipal, and cross-border achievements in intergovernmental co-operation. In addition, urban governments are gradually beginning to deal directly with Aboriginal peoples and their governments to address long neglected concerns. Finally, we have seen how urban governments have moved into new intergovernmental arenas and improved their approach to intergovernmental management.

This chapter has paid relatively little attention to a very important aspect of the urban intergovernmental relationship, the financial dimension. The next chapter picks up this thread of the intergovernmental web, before we turn our attention to the challenges of economic development and sustaining livable cities.

SUGGESTED READINGS

Andrew, Caroline. (1995). "Provincial–Municipal Relations: Hyper-fractionalized Quasi-Subordination Revisited." In *Canadian Metroplitics*, edited by James Lightbody. Toronto: Copp Clark Ltd., pp.137–60. This article examines current debates about provincial–municipal relations in Canada and shows how larger cities are developing increasingly dynamic strategies for dealing with intergovernmental relations.

Cameron, Kenneth, ed. (1980). *Canadian Public Administration: Municipal Government in the Intergovernmental Maze* 23(2). A survey of issues in provincial–municipal relations, with particular emphasis on fiscal questions and the arguments for greater municipal autonomy.

Feldman, Lionel D. and Katherine Graham. (1979). *Bargaining for Cities.* Montreal: Institute for Research on Public Policy. A detailed review of the problems experienced by Canadian cities in the intergovernmental arena, derived from case studies of seven urban areas.

Rothblatt, Donald N. and Andrew Sancton, eds. (1993). *Metropolitan Governance: American/Canadian Intergovernmental Perspectives.* Berkeley, CA and Kingston, ON: Institute of Governmental Studies Press and Institute of Intergovernmental Relations. This collection of essays explores whether Canadian and American metropolitan regions have similar or distinctive patterns of intergovernmental relations by comparing the case studies of nine cities.

Royal Commission on Aboriginal Peoples. (1996). *Volume 4: Perspective and Realities.* Ottawa: Canada Communications Group. Chapter Seven in this volume provides a comprehensive overview of issues affecting Aboriginal people in the urban context. Topics covered include cultural identity, urban demographics and socio-economic conditions, and governance for Aboriginal people in urban areas.

BIBLIOGRAPHY

Adam, Mohammed. (1997). "Region Warns of $500 Tax Boost." *Ottawa Citizen,* January 23, p. A1.

Alberta Report. (1994). "Democracy in Your Own Backyard," April 11, p. 16.

———. (1995). "Shifting for Themselves," July 31, p. 12.

Alfred, Gerald. (1995). *Heeding the Voices of Our Ancestors.* Don Mills, ON: Oxford University Press.

Andrew, Caroline. (1995). "Provincial–Municipal Relations: Hyper-fractionalized Quasi-Subordination Revisited." In *Canadian Metropolitics,* edited by James Lightbody. Toronto: Copp Clark Ltd., pp. 137–60.

Andrew, Caroline and Jeff Morrison. (1995). "Canada Infrastructure Works: Between 'Pick and Shovels' and the Information Highway." In *How Ottawa Spends 1995–96: Mid-Life Crises,* edited by Susan D. Phillips. Ottawa: Carleton University Press, pp.107–36.

Artibise, Allan J. (1996). "Redefining BC's Place in Canada: The Emergence of Cascadia as a Strategic Alliance." *Policy Options* 17(1): 27–30.

Association of Municipalities of Ontario (undated). *AMO: How It Works.* Toronto

Bose, Mayor Robert. (1996). Remarks to the International Institute on Social Policy. Kingston: Queen's University, August 29, 1991.

Cameron, David M. (1980). "Provincial Responsibilities for Municipal Government." In *Canadian Public Administration: Municipal Government in the Intergovernmental Maze,* edited by Kenneth Cameron. 23(2): 222–35.

Canada, Minister of Finance. (1997). *Budget Speech,* February 18, Ottawa.

City of Winnipeg. (1991). *Budget Topics* 1,2.

Cohn, T. and P. Smith. (1995). "Developing Global Cities in the Pacific Northwest: The Cases of Vancouver and Seattle." In *North American Cities and Global Economy: Challenges and Opportunities*, edited by Peter Kresl and Gary Oappert. Thousand Oaks: Sage, pp. 251–85.

Crone, Greg. (1997). "Tory Restructuring Plan Puts Cities in Jeopardy, Author of Main Report Says." *The Ottawa Citizen*, January 31, p. A4.

Dupré, J. Stefan. (1968). *Intergovernmental Finance in Ontario: A Provincial–Local Perspective*. A Study for the Ontario Committee on Taxation (Smith Committee). Toronto: Queen's Printer for Ontario.

Elazar, Daniel J. (1981). "The Evolving Federal System." In *The Power to Govern*, edited by Richard Pious. New York: Academy of Political Science.

Federation of Canadian Municipalities. (1985). *Municipal Information in Canada: Physical Condition and Funding Adequacy*. Ottawa.

———. (1996). *Year in Review: 1995–96*. Ottawa.

Feldman, Lionel D. (1973). *Provincial–Municipal Relations: The Ontario Dynasties*. Toronto: Ontario Economic Council.

Feldman, Lionel D. and Katherine A. Graham. (1979). *Bargaining for Cities*. Montreal: Institute for Research on Public Policy.

Golden, Anne. (1997). "Tory Downloading Will Hurt Metro the Most." *The Toronto Star*, January 22, p. A21.

Graham, Katherine A. (1995). "Collective Bargaining in the Municipal Sector." In *Public Sector Collective Bargaining*, edited by Gene Swimmer and Mark Thompson. Kingston, ON: IRC Press, pp. 180–200.

Graham, Katherine A. and Susan D. Phillips. (1996). "Social Diversity and Urban Services: The Twin Myths of Volunteerism and Local Control." August 29. A presentation made to the International Institute on Social Policy. Kingston, ON: Queen's University.

Greater Toronto Area Task Force. (1996). *Report of the Greater Toronto Area Task Force*. Toronto: Queen's Printer for Ontario.

Lakey, Jack. (1997). "Tonks Feels Betrayed by Province's Moves." *The Toronto Star*, January 15, p. A14.

Lapointe, Jean-Louis. (1980). "Reforme de la fiscalité municipal au Québec." In *Canadian Public Administration: Municipal Government in the Intergovernmental Maze*, edited by Kenneth Cameron. 23(2): 269–80.

Lidstone, Donald. (1996). "An Overview of the Changing Provincial–Municipal Relationship Across Canada." A presentation to The Cities of Tomorrow Conference. Toronto: Municipality of Metropolitan Toronto and Federation of Canadian Municipalities.

Lithwick, Harvey. (1970). *Urban Canada: Problems and Prospects*. Ottawa: Central Mortgage and Housing.

Magnusson, Warren. (1983). "Introduction." In *City Politics in Canada*, edited by Warren Magnusson and Andrew Sancton. Toronto: University of Toronto Press, pp. 3–57.

Mittelstaedt, Martin and James Rusk. (1997). "Municipalities Facing Major Changes to Social Spending." *The Globe and Mail*, January 14, p. A7.

Nova Scotia Department of Municipal Affairs. (1993). *Provincial–Municipal Service Exchange: A Discussion Paper*. Halifax: Government of Nova Scotia.

Oberlander, Peter H. and Patrick J. Smith, (1993). "Governing Metropolitan Vancouver." In *Metropolitan Government*, edited by Donald Rothblatt and Andrew Sancton. Berkeley, CA and Kingston, ON: Institute of Governmental Studies Press/Institute of Intergovernmental Relations, pp. 107–36.

O'Brien, Allan. (1975). "Father Knows Best: A Look at the Provincial–Municipal Relationship in Ontario." In *Government and Politics in Ontario*, edited by Donald C. MacDonald. Toronto: Macmillan, pp. 154–71.

Ontario Ministry of Community and Social Services. (1997). News Release: *Ecker Announces New Plan for Social and Community Health Services*, January 14. Toronto.

Ontario Ministry of Municipal Affairs and Housing. (1997). *Consultation Paper: Outline of the Proposed New Municipal Act*. Toronto: Queen's Printer for Ontario.

Ross, Ijeoma. (1997a). "Crombie Criticizes Transfer Method." *The Globe and Mail*, January 28, p. A7.

———. (1997b). "Ontario Overhaul Hits Toronto Taxpayers Hard." *The Globe and Mail*, January 20, p. A7.

Royal Commission on Aboriginal Peoples. (1996). *Final Report, Volume 4: Perspectives and Realities*. Ottawa: Canada Communications Group.

Royal Commission on Metropolitan Toronto. (1977). *Report*. Toronto: Queen's Printer for Ontario.

Sancton, Andrew. (1992). "Provincial–Municipal Entanglement in Ontario: A Dissent." *Municipal World*, July. See also Remarks to the Conference on the Future of Municipal Government, March 5, 1996. Ottawa: Institute of Public Administration of Canada and Federation of Canadian Municipalities.

———. (1996). "Assessing the GTA Task Force's Proposals on Governing." *Policy Options* 17(7): 38–41.

Siegel, David. (1992). "Disentangling Provincial–Municipal Relations in Ontario." *Public Management*, Fall.

Smith, Patrick J. (1992). "The Making of a Global City: Fifty Years of Constituent Diplomacy: The Case of Vancouver." *Canadian Journal of Urban Research* 1(1): 90–112.

———. (1996). "Restructuring Metropolitan Governance: Vancouver and BC Regions." *Policy Options* 17(7): 7–11.

———. (1997, forthcoming). "More than One Way towards Economic Development: Public Participation and Policy-making in the Vancouver Region." In *Citizen Engagement: Lessons from Local Government*, edited by Katherine A. Graham and Susan D. Phillips. Toronto: Institute of Public Administration of Canada.

Task Force on Local Government. (1992). *Report to the Government of Nova Scotia*. Halifax: Government of Nova Scotia.

Tindal, C. Richard and Susan Nobes Tindal. (1995). *Local Government in Canada*, 4th ed. Toronto: McGraw-Hill Ryerson.

Union des municipalités du Québec. (1992). *Notre force collective*. Montreal.

CHAPTER NINE

◆

FINANCING CANADIAN URBAN GOVERNMENT

INTRODUCTION

Canadian urban governments are experiencing financial stresses in the 1990s as severe as any they have encountered since the recovery from the Great Depression of the 1930s. This squeeze on fiscal circumstances is rooted in both the revenue and expenditure sides of municipal budgets. It is forcing urban governments to respond by rethinking their mandates, cutting expenditures and costs, searching for new modes of service delivery, and developing new and more productive sources of revenue. In the midst of all this, many are also attempting to generate additional fiscal capacity to initiate new programming, particularly in the area of economic development.

All this turmoil and restructuring is another factor prompting a fundamental debate about the appropriate range of municipal government activities, and about who should pay for and benefit from these activities. The preoccupation with financial issues provides another context in which we can think about issues of urban structure and local government organization.

In this chapter, we first describe the nature of the financial stresses facing urban governments. We then go on to discuss a number of key elements contributing to this picture and some of the new thinking and responses being developed. We conclude the chapter with an overview of municipal budgeting and its implementation under all these stresses.

OVERVIEW OF URBAN FINANCE

We begin with an overview of urban government finance, centred on the data presented in Tables 9.1 and 9.2. These tables show the major components of revenue and expenditure and provide some indication of trends over the past two decades. The data in these tables refer to all municipal governments in each province. The cities on which we focus are, of course, the major components.

Table 9.1 presents information on the revenue systems in the six provinces in which our eight cities are located. Over the 1975–85 decade, total revenues increased substantially; in all provinces, total local government revenues more than doubled, and in some cases increased three or fourfold. During the following period (1985–94), increases were much more moderate, reflecting in part the general environment of restraint in the 1990s.

Over the period shown, **own-revenues**, that is, the revenues that local governments raise through their own efforts, decreased as a share of total revenue in Manitoba and British Columbia but increased in the other four provinces.

TABLE 9.1

PERCENTAGE DISTRIBUTION OF REVENUE BY SOURCE
1975, 1985, 1994

Revenue Source	Nova Scotia	Quebec	Ontario	Manitoba	Alberta	BC
Total Revenue (%)						
Total Own-Revenue						
1975	39	45	49	56	45	62
1985	36	45	57	49	50	57
1994	41	53	60	51	50	44
Own Source Revenues (%)						
Property Tax						
1975	31	32	38	42	29	49
1985	23	33	41	32	26	37
1994	27	39	45	35	24	23
Fees/Sales						
1975	5	8	6	6	12	10
1985	8	8	12	10	15	14
1994	9	10	11	10	17	15
Transfers						
1975	59	55	50	43	54	37
1985	62	54	41	49	49	41
1994	58	46	39	48	49	55

Source: Adapted from Statistics Canada, *Public Sector Finance*, 1995/96 (68.212) and *Public Finance Historical Data*, 1965/66 – 1991/92 (68.512) pp. 143, 145, 146, 147, 149, and 150. Reproduced by authority of the Minister of Industry, 1997, Statistics Canada.

The other side of this coin is that in Manitoba and British Columbia, grants from the provincial governments increased in relative importance, while in the other provinces, they declined as a share of the total. (Absolute dollar amounts, of course, increased in all provinces.) In all cases, the main source of local government own-revenues continues to be the real property tax, though the share of own-revenue derived from **user fees** is increasing.

Table 9.2 provides information on the major functions on which municipal governments spend money. This is shown for the years 1975, 1985, and 1994. There are some clear differences across provinces. These partly reflect the differences in local government priorities, but we must also keep in mind that they reflect differences in financing arrangements between local governments and provinces. For example, Table 9.2 shows significant differences in the shares of expenditures that local governments devote to social services. In large part, these differences can be explained by differences across provinces in the responsibilities for social spending taken on by the provincial and local governments. The differences shown in the table are not reflective of differences in overall levels of social spending but only of the government level responsible for them.

Table 9.2

Percentage Distribution of Revenue by Main Function
1975, 1985, 1994

Revenue Source	Nova Scotia	Quebec	Ontario	Manitoba	Alberta	B.C.
General Services						
1975	8	11	7	7	5	8
1985	7	13	7	10	6	7
1994	5	11	7	9	7	8
Protection						
1975	12	15	13	12	10	16
1985	14	14	15	14	8	19
1994	10	14	13	14	10	18
Transportation & Communication						
1975	12	24	20	24	23	16
1985	10	18	17	19	18	15
1994	7	19	12	16	18	13
Health						
1975	20	0	8	14	21	2
1985	15	0	10	13	24	4
1994	14	0	8	13	22	5
Social Services						
1975	4	1	10	2	2	7
1985	23	0	13	5	1	0
1994	32	1	26	10	1	0
Conservation & Development						
1975	2	0	2	1	1	1
1985	2	1	2	1	3	1
1995	1	1	2	1	2	1
Environment						
1975	5	16	14	10	14	16
1985	10	14	12	10	9	13
1994	17	17	12	13	11	17
Recreation & Culture						
1975	5	10	11	14	11	16
1985	8	10	11	10	9	15
1994	7	10	9	8	10	16
Planning & Development						
1975	5	2	3	3	3	3
1985	2	2	1	2	1	2
1994	1	2	1	1	2	2
Debt Charges						
1975	8	15	8	11	9	13
1985	8	20	6	13	17	23
1994	3	16	4	11	13	17

Source: Adapted from Statistics Canada, *Public Sector Finance*, 1995/96 (68.212) and *Public Finance Historical Data*, 1965/66 – 1991/92 (68.512) pp. 156, 158, 159, 160, 162 and 163. Reproduced by authority of the Minister of Industry, 1997, Statistics Canada.

Thus, rather than the amounts, the trends over the years are more significant. Generally, the proportion of expenditures devoted to general government services, protection services, conservation and development, environment (including garbage collection and disposal), planning, and recreation and culture have remained fairly stable. Spending on transportation and communication has declined relatively, and social service spending has increased (except in British Columbia and Alberta where the provincial government assumed full responsibility). Debt charges, which tended to rise from 1975 to 1985, declined in relative terms in all provinces by 1994.

THE MAIN FISCAL ISSUES

The pressures that have developed over the 1990s on urban budgets are both severe and wide-ranging. It should come as no surprise, therefore, that the emerging responses raise questions about the role and operation of municipal government. In this section, we review some of the major themes and issues that have emerged as part of the urban response to fiscal stress. While none of these issues are new, they have acquired renewed prominence and are now being reconsidered from a more explicit financial perspective.

Expenditures and Service Delivery

The tightened fiscal circumstances outlined above have brought to the forefront a number of issues relating to the delivery and organization of local government services.

THE BEST LOCUS OF RESPONSIBILITY

The "best locus" of responsibility refers to the proper or appropriate designation of responsibility for some services, education and social welfare being foremost among them. The choice is between responsibility residing at the local level (usually with some, often quite strong, directives imposed by the provincial government) or at the provincial level (with local authorities possibly acting as delivery agents for the province). One direction in which these choices have been pushed by cost pressures is toward disentanglement, that is, the clear delineation between provincial and local responsibilities and authority. Nova Scotia and Ontario have been prominent in this regard.

Traditionally, in education, the balance has been weighted toward the local level, with local authorities responsible for much of the policy and delivery as well as for raising a significant portion of the necessary funding. In the field of social welfare, while a high percentage of the costs have long been paid by provincial governments, there have been considerable variations across regions with respect to the delivery of benefits and the range of non-core services available. In recent years, the trend in both these areas, usually under the pressure of cost containment, has been to assert the provincial role in delivery and financing more strongly.

In Ontario, the plan for disentanglement laid out by the Crombie Panel in late 1996 would have more neatly separated provincial and municipal responsibilities by moving education (which was solely municipal) and social services (which had been jointly funded) to the provincial level. In return, municipalities would have assumed complete funding for hard services (including transit and some provincial roads). While the Ontario government chose to follow Crombie's recommendations on education and hard services, it further entangled funding of social services, although a greater share of it was placed on municipalities.

ACHIEVING LOCAL ECONOMIES OF SCALE

The perceived presence of **economies of scale** that may be gained by providing some services at a regional rather than municipal level is another delivery organization issue pushed onto the agenda by fiscal considerations. In popular debates, this concern is often expressed in terms of eliminating duplication and overlap. In Ottawa-Carleton, for example, it may be the case that functions performed by the lower-tier municipalities could be provided at lower per unit costs if one large-scale regional service were organized. The Ontario government's initiative to eliminate the six lower-tier municipalities that constitute Metro Toronto and to form a new unified Toronto is prompted (at least on the surface) by this logic. It is interesting to note, though, that the proposals of the Golden Report, which drew attention to potentially more significant economies of scale gains through the enhanced role of the Greater Toronto Area (GTA) authority as a service provider while retaining lower-tier municipalities within the boundaries of Metro Toronto, have been largely ignored.

The counter to the economy-of-scale argument is that a larger number of smaller jurisdictions promotes cost **efficiency** through competition. As we discussed in Chapter Two, this is a foundation of public choice theory, although similar arguments are made outside of the public choice framework. In this context, competition is not as direct as in a private market where two suppliers compete for the same buyers. Public sector competition is more often in the form of political pressure applied to high-cost providers to attain the same levels of efficiency as their lower-cost counterparts. In some instances, however, especially within urban areas, competition can be more direct as individuals have the flexibility to move from one jurisdiction to another within the same urban area (see Tiebout, 1956). The motivation for such mobility simply may be the lower costs (and hence lower taxes) achieved by some municipalities or, more fundamentally, a better match between the wishes of individuals and the basket of public services provided by a municipality. Reorganization potentially precludes both these advantages because it eliminates this form of competition.

DEALING WITH URBAN SPILLOVERS

Yet another consideration in urban structure that has been motivated by financial concerns in recent times is the existence of **externalities** or **spillovers** between jurisdictions in an urban region. Interjurisdiction spillovers are the consumption-side counterpart of economies of scale in production. When the benefits of a particular service provided by one municipality flow across the municipal boundary to the citizens of nearby municipalities (in addition to those in the providing municipality), cost concerns suggest that these external beneficiaries be included when determining the optimal level of service to provide.

One way in which this can be accomplished, that is, the externality can be internalized, is to create a level of authority that encompasses all of the people deriving benefits from the service. Part of the rationale for regional tier urban governments or unicity models stems from this reasoning. If all the residents of a metropolitan area benefit from a given service (e.g., environmental programs, cultural programs), a single authority responsible to the entire population is one way to address the issue of optimal quantity. That, in turn, raises issues of governmental structure, such as the selection of regional or unicity councils and the determination of their taxing authority. The unicity approach, when implemented without special arrangements for representation and revenue raising for different parts of the city-region and for different services, masks differences in the nature of externalities across the range of urban services. For example, the externalities associated with the provision of fire services across a large city-region are quite different than those associated with transportation services.

Another way to address the externality problem and the financial concerns it raises is to have a broader level of government, such as the province, provide grants to the municipalities that are structured to induce the recipients to adjust their levels of service provision by taking into account the spillover benefits accruing to other jurisdictions. The discussion of grants later in this chapter will pursue this discussion.

THE ALLURE OF ALTERNATIVE SERVICE DELIVERY

The fiscal circumstances have prompted renewed discussions of the forms of organization of government service provision. Direct provision and production of services by municipal governments, which has become the traditional form, is now just one among several options. Generally, we refer to these options as co-production with the voluntary and/or private sector. Among these options are continued government responsibility for provision, but with production carried out through a more arm's length organization operating according to stricter business practices, and **contracting out** arrangements in which governments contract private market firms to produce the required services. Other arrangements involve government moving away not only from production but also from provision of the service (although continuing a regulatory or monitoring role). This full scale **privatization** removes functions from the municipal budget and relies on prices or user fees to finance them.

The terms "contracting out" and "privatization" are sometimes used imprecisely and interchangeably, and distinctions between them are legitimately indistinct. As the previous paragraph suggests, in this context, contracting out refers to activities that are performed directly for a municipal government by a private sector supplier, with standards determined and monitoring done by the government. Privatization refers to an arrangement in which the government further detaches itself from provision of the service by permitting/inviting private sector suppliers to replace public provision in providing service through market arrangements. The government may continue to subsidize the privatized service, and in such circumstances, the distinction between the two arrangements begins to break down.

CHANGING SERVICE LEVELS

In addition to prompting municipalities to consider the modalities of service organization, the fiscal squeeze has forced them to confront two other basic conundrums:

- Should they reduce levels of service?
- How might they reduce the cost per unit of service?

Canadian urban governments have attempted both strategies.

Reducing Service Levels

Service reductions come in several forms, most of which are identified with less ominous sounding labels. Redefining service standards provides one such route. Municipalities have determined, under the pressure of fiscal stringency, that road maintenance can be reduced, that streets need not be plowed until greater amounts of snow have accumulated, that grass can wait longer between mowings. While not all urban government services can be similarly reduced, in recent years city governments have carefully (and often quietly) looked for areas where they can spend less by doing less. In some cases, for example, the City of Burlington and the Regional Municipality of Hamilton-Wentworth, these discussions have been undertaken after significant efforts to engage the public. In both of these cases, surveys of citizens sought views on the range and level of services desired by local residents (Fenn, 1997).

A similar though distinct response has been to redefine the core business of municipal government. During the relatively flush years of the 1960s and 70s, urban governments found themselves being called upon to provide a broad range of services to their residents that went well beyond the array of traditional municipal services. Urban councils more often than not responded positively to these demands. Among these new programs were support for community associations and arts and culture groups; enhanced social services for disadvantaged populations, including employment and other forms of counselling, and housing and medical services; and enriched recreational programming.

These programs may well have been beneficial in terms of contributing to the quality of urban life. In the 1990s, however, with growth all but disappeared and with strong tax antipathy from constituents, city councils have begun to question the wisdom and necessity of such a broad range of activities. They have instead begun to return to less expensive, less involved visions of local government under the rubric "returning to core business." We discuss these debates at greater length and the implications of restricting the activities of urban governments in Chapter Eleven.

Reducing Unit Costs

Cities have also opted to reduce per unit costs of providing services. Possibilities include reducing labour costs, exploring new forms of service delivery, and employing new operating methods.

Seeking to reduce labour costs is an obvious route to achieving overall cost reductions because many urban services are labour intensive. However, whether through reduced compensation or workforces,[1] this route is obviously a contentious one. Municipal employees are, for the most part, unionized, and several cities have found themselves in the midst of serious disputes with their labour unions as they have understandably sought to protect their memberships against layoffs and downsizing.

New forms of service delivery most often involve contracting out or privatizing a service that heretofore had been provided by the government directly. Examples of contracting out services by city governments include the collection and disposal of garbage, operation of landfill sites, street maintenance, and parking by-law enforcement. Functions that have been privatized or where privatization is under consideration include low-income housing, water and sewage services, and some recreation facilities (e.g., municipal golf courses).

The City of Montreal recently privatized its urban planning function. It now relies on private sector planning firms to undertake the work formerly done by permanent city staff. There may be similar experiments afoot with other corporate functions, such as the provision of legal services. Somewhat ironically, such moves by large urban governments mirror the traditional practice of small and rural municipalities in Canada.

Categorizing changes of this sort is somewhat arbitrary because the forms of privatization and the links to cost reduction are varied. In some instances, an activity is moved from a municipal government's budget to an off-budget activity that is financed through user fees (discussed later in this chapter). In the process, costs of providing the service may or may not decline, and service levels and standards may or may not change. But the call on government's direct budgetary resources is clearly reduced. In other cases, privatization reduces costs by circumventing (sometimes eliminating) union collective agreements so that wage bills are reduced. In still other instances, privatization or contracting out reduces costs because of more efficient management systems that are able to utilize the resources of an organization more effectively.

Finally, service delivery may be altered within the public sector through the adoption of new management techniques or the adaptation of private sector methodologies. The use of business plans to better focus an organization's activities and utilize its resources more effectively is one example. In the City of Calgary, use of business plans is compulsory for all city departments and agencies. The implementation of management innovations, such as Total Quality Management (TQM), is another. A TQM initiative has become a prominent feature of the city administration in Winnipeg.

Revenue

As the data presented in Table 9.1 illustrate, there are three principal sources of revenue for urban governments: the property tax which municipalities levy themselves, user fees, and transfers that they receive from provincial governments. The first two sources constitute the bulk of local government own-revenues. There are interesting and difficult issues associated with each of these revenue sources, and we discuss each of them in turn.

PRINCIPLES FOR GOVERNMENT REVENUE SYSTEMS

In public finance analysis, government own-revenue or tax systems are generally evaluated on several criteria including equity, efficiency, and reliability/stability. The equity criterion relates to the fairness of the tax (or tax system) in terms of the relative amounts paid by people with different characteristics. Among the relevant characteristics that are usually regarded as legitimate distinguishing features for tax purposes are, most prominently, income or wealth and sometimes age and family size. People who are alike in terms of the relevant characteristic (e.g., equal incomes) should pay the same amount of tax. This principle is known as **horizontal equity**. People who are not alike should pay appropriately different amounts of tax. This relationship is called **vertical equity**.

The efficiency criterion, in narrow terms, refers to efficiency in administration, that is, to being able to administer the tax effectively and at low cost relative to the amount of revenue collected. In broader terms, efficiency refers to the impact of the tax on the economic behaviour of the taxpayers and whether this impact is consistent with efficient resource allocation.

The third criterion, reliability, refers to the ability of governments to count on a stable revenue flow from the tax and the ability to predict changes in revenues systematically as circumstances change.

Using these or similar criteria, analysts tend to consider taxes from one of two perspectives. The first of these, the benefit (or benefit received) principle, says that tax payments should be related to the consumption of public services. In equity terms, the relevant characteristic might be the amount of a public service consumed (e.g., litres of water used, kilometres of road travelled), and from this perspective, fairness is achieved if tax payments are correctly related to the benefits of public sector services. Efficiency is achieved, from this perspective, if the benefit tax leads people to consider the resource costs of producing the service when deciding whether to consume more or less of it. Finally, benefit taxes can be reliable if they are linked to a service, the consumption of which is stable and predictable.

Benefit taxes may be closely linked to the related service, ultimately becoming analogous to a price in a private market. User fees are an example of a closely linked benefit tax. Alternatively, benefit taxes may have a looser connection to a service or group of services. Taxes determined using approximate or proxy measures of service consumption may be of this type.

The second perspective for the consideration of taxes is ability to pay. By its very nature, the equity criterion is accorded much stronger weight in the ability-to-pay framework than in the benefit framework. The basis for the principle is some measure of income or wealth that is deemed to be the primary criterion for the determination of relative tax shares. Additional considerations, namely, efficiency and stability, are also important, if less prominent. In the ability-to-pay framework, efficiency is most often meant to refer to a tax that minimally affects (distorts) the economic behaviour of taxpayers compared to what it would be without the tax.

THE ALGEBRA OF THE PROPERTY TAX

The strengths and weaknesses of the property tax as the primary source of municipal government revenues can be better understood when considering its basic characteristics in comparison to other taxes levied by other governments. In simple terms, the revenue (R) that is derived from a tax can be described as $R = \sum t_i B_i$ where t represents the tax rate, B represents the defined tax base, and the subscript i represents the taxpaying unit or "activity."[2] Thus, for example, in the case of the personal income tax, taxable income is B, i represents the individual taxpayer, and t the applicable tax rate.[3] In the case of a sales tax, the price of the taxable commodity is represented by B, the sales tax rate is t, and the taxable transaction is designated by i.

For most taxes, the administrative determination of the base (B) is relatively straightforward and non-contentious, as in the definition of taxable income[4] or the price of a taxable commodity. The magnitude of the base is readily expressed in terms of dollars and is typically established in the economy through a transaction (e.g., a sale) or series of transactions. While taxpayers may not be particularly happy about paying these taxes or may dislike aspects of the tax policy of the government, there is normally little technical dispute about what the tax should be in any specific case.

Property taxation is quite different. A market transaction is not often available to form the basis for determining the tax base. Consequently, this must be done in a less straightforward manner. There are basically two approaches utilized to determine the base (B), which in the terminology of property taxation is known as the assessed value of a particular property (the i).

The first approach relies on physical characteristics of the property which are readily understood and easy to measure. The most common of these is the land area of the property and the number of square metres in the building. These measures, or some combination of them, are then converted by formula to an assessed value. It is in this last step that problems arise.

Along with the size of the lot and buildings, property values depend upon many other factors as well. Attributes such as location and neighbourhood amenities, for example, influence values. Thus assessed values generated by a formula based on physical characteristics alone will frequently neither bear resemblance to property values as perceived by owners nor reflect relativities among properties that correspond to perceptions. The assessed values will therefore reflect neither ability to pay nor perceived ability to pay.

These assessments may be better measures when judged from the benefits principle. For at least some urban government services, measures of size may be reasonable approximations of the cost of providing standardized services to a property. For example, the cost of running water and sewer lines past a property are related to the length of the street frontage. Other services charged to property owners, however, may be quite unrelated to size. Examples of the latter type include cultural and recreational services.

In the final analysis, **assessment (assessed value)** schemes based purely on physical characteristics (unit value assessment) have failed to gain the required political acceptance because they are inconsistent with prevailing norms about fairness. Analyses based on more formal concepts of ability to pay would likely reach similar conclusions. Sometimes popular perceptions about fairness and formal analyses arrive at different conclusions. In the case of the property tax, however, they probably are very close to each other.

The second approach to determining the base, which recognizes the importance of relating assessments and therefore taxes to more accepted ideas about what is fair, is to set the base directly in relation to a property's value. The main difficulty with this approach is that, as already noted, real estate is traded on the open market relatively infrequently. Therefore, the central question for the assessors is to estimate a value of a property that is acceptably close to what the property would have sold for on the open market if it had been sold during the year. Many assessment acts describe this as the price that would be established in an arm's length transaction between a willing seller and a willing buyer.

In practical terms, there are three methods commonly used to estimate these values. The first is to estimate the replacement cost of the property by drawing on information about construction costs. While it may be possible to estimate fairly accurately the value (cost) of structures in this fashion, it still requires some other technique to account for the land component of the property.

A second method is the one that most directly follows the spirit of the willing buyer/willing seller phraseology of the assessment acts. This technique is to directly estimate the market value of a property. There are several ways in which this can be done, each relying on detailed knowledge of a local real estate market. Real estate agents, for example, based on their knowledge of conditions in a local market, routinely provide prospective vendors and purchasers with estimates of what they think a house is worth. Government assessors must be somewhat more formal and systematic, and have developed methods that they can defend, if necessary, in an appeal and that provide reasonable relativities across properties.

The third method, used in the case of properties that generate a flow of income for their owners, is based on the income earning potential of the property. The market value of an asset can be determined if one knows the (risk adjusted) flow of annual income that can be obtained from that asset. The capital or market value of the asset can then be estimated as equal to the present (discounted) value of that earnings stream at some appropriate interest rate. This method of assessment is applicable when assessing the value of commercial property, while the other two are potential methods for both commercial and residential properties.

All these assessment methods rely on the judgement of assessment officers rather than emerging as a by-product of some generally accepted "objective" process such as a market transaction. Consequently, the determination of B in the case of the property tax tends to be contentious, and dissatisfied taxpayers are much more likely to appeal their individual assessments (B_i) than is the case with any other major tax. From time to time, these appeal processes can be very disruptive of urban government financial planning, as happened in Winnipeg in the mid-1990s.

The assessment problem relates not only to getting the value right once. A fair and politically acceptable method must be found to maintain correct assessments over time. If assessments are not kept up to date to reflect changing absolute and relative property values from year to year, they will tend to become unfair and lose their public acceptability as primary instruments of municipal finance.

Frequently, this precise problem occurs. For example, new developments and subdivisions may be assessed to reflect market values at the time they were built, while assessments in older areas, which once may have been correct, tend to lag behind, even though the actual market values of the two areas may be similar. Owners and occupants of the new properties understandably view this as a serious flaw in the tax system; occupants of old units, who are beneficiaries of these lags, understandably resist attempts to correct relative assessments. The political problems awaiting reformers are indeed daunting.

Toronto and the GTA provide an interesting case in point. In central Toronto, where older properties tend to be located, the assessments of some units have not been updated since the 1940s. These properties are thus often seriously under-assessed compared to newer, but comparable, properties elsewhere in the city. With respect to the rest of the GTA, the problem tends to be even more severe. Early in 1997, the government of Ontario, as part of a number of far-reaching changes in local government, announced that all properties in the province would be assessed using a market value methodology. The relative shifts in taxation between the city and the GTA will, in many cases, be extreme.

Finally, in this section, we briefly note a variation across provinces in who does assessments. Some provinces have provincial agencies that undertake property assessments for the whole province. In other cases, municipalities (or regional governments) are left on their own. In Manitoba, the City of Winnipeg operates its own assessment agency while the provincial government performs the function for the rest of the province. On balance, province-wide systems are likely to be preferred because they are able to guard against inequities developing across municipalities. Probably the most successful system is in British Columbia. There, a provincial authority maintains a market value assessment system for the whole province and updates values on a regular basis. Because British Columbia's assessors have developed methods and expertise to estimate actual market values reasonably well, and have established a reputation for accuracy, assessment disputes have been greatly reduced throughout the province.

BOX 9.1 THE TROUBLESOME PROPERTY TAX: THE UNHAPPY
WINNIPEG EXPERIENCE

The potential problems in the administration of a property tax system are
dramatically illustrated by the difficulties encountered by the City of
Winnipeg in 1996. Because market values of properties are estimated for
assessment purposes, appeals procedures must be in place to provide a fair
hearing for taxpayers who believe and can establish that they have been
over-assessed. Winnipeg, which initiated a market-value based assessment
system in 1990, regularly made allowance for successful appeals in its budget. In 1996, $7.5 million was budgeted for this eventuality. (To provide
some context, total property tax collections were about $350 million.)

During the year it was discovered that, due to a flood of successful
appeals, the amount required (to cover less than expected revenues and
reimbursements of taxes paid in previous years based on the original
assessment) would exceed the budgeted amount by about $55 million,
more than 15% of expected property tax revenues. The problem arose
because the assessors utilized a version of the "replacement cost method"
for estimating values while, on appeal, values based on an "income generating potential" method were upheld. The latter tended to be lower than
the former, in part because of the generally poor economy during the first
half of the 1990s. Interestingly, the assessors have no power to compel
property owners to provide information that they can use to estimate values based on the "income" method; yet owners are free to bring this information forward on appeal if it is to their advantage.

The appeals "storm" in Winnipeg seriously disrupted budget plans ("Budget
called sham") and forced the resignation of the head of the city's assessment
division. Further, the overall confidence of the elected officials in their administration was seriously eroded. It also raised questions about tax levels in future
years as the city struggled to find ways to make up the shortfall.

Source: Excerpted from Aldo Santin and Treena Khan, "Budget Called
Sham — Tax Appeals to Hit City Hard," Winnipeg Free Press, February 22,
1996. Reproduced with permission of the Winnipeg Free Press, p. A4.

SETTING THE TAX RATE

Having defined the tax base (B), the revenue (R) generated by the property tax
is then determined by setting the tax rate (t). In the case of the property tax,
this rate is referred to as the **mill rate**. A rate of one mill means a tax of $1 per
$1000 of assessed value. Generally, two sorts of issues arise around the setting of
the mill rate.

The first relates to the relatively high visibility associated with the property
tax. As you will see in the later section on budgeting, much political attention
becomes focussed on property tax increases, and these are typically measured in
terms of percentage increases in the mill rate from year to year. The annual

debate about whether mill rates should be increased, frozen, or reduced thus becomes one of the more high profile activities of municipal councils.

The second issue revolves around the relationships of the mill rates established for different classes of property. In some instances, commercial and industrial property may be taxed at a different rate than residential property, and rental residential may be taxed differently than owner-occupied property. These differences often give rise to heated debates about the overall fairness of the property tax system and its impacts on the economic development of the community.

OTHER ISSUES CONCERNING PROPERTY TAX

In addition to assessment problems, other issues also commonly arise from the use of the property tax. One common source of difficulty is the proportion of total property tax revenue that should be raised from various classes of property (e.g., owner-occupied residential, rental residential, commercial, industrial). Municipalities usually tax different classes at different rates, thus prompting debates about what differentials are appropriate. For example, arguments are often made that commercial and industrial (C&I) property tax rates should be kept as low as possible because high rates would make a city economically uncompetitive compared to other cities that may have lower C&I rates. Of course, the lower the C&I tax, the higher must be the residential tax to raise any given sum of revenue.

Another issue that has received increasing attention in recent years is the exemptions granted to certain classes of property. Churches and other religious institutions are commonly exempted from property tax, as are some charitable and service organizations that own property. The exemption has aroused more interest as the fiscal squeeze facing urban governments has become tighter. Another type of exemption is that received by property owned by other governments and their agencies. This occurs because municipalities have no legal authority to tax provincial and federal governments. These governments voluntarily pay **grants-in-lieu** to the municipal governments in recognition of the municipal services the properties receive. However, in most instances, these grants-in-lieu are notably smaller than the amounts that would be paid if the properties were subject to normal property taxation. In areas with large government installations, such as Ottawa, this differential is a source of complaint by the local governments. Further, in recent years, the federal government and some of the provinces have responded to their own financial difficulties by unilaterally lowering their grants-in-lieu payments.

THE PERSISTENCE OF THE REAL PROPERTY TAX

The real property tax is clearly a problematic revenue source for urban governments. In addition to the difficulties discussed above, there is a general perception that the tax is regressive. This means that relative to income, the tax imposes a larger burden on lower-income taxpayers than on those with higher incomes. While there is some debate about the regressivity of the property tax in academic economics literature (e.g., see Bird and Slack, 1993), this concern acts as a general restraint on the amount of revenue that can be raised from this source and on the range of services that should appropriately be funded in this way. For example, it would not seem to be sensible to fund wholly or partially redistributive programs with revenues generated from a regressive tax.

Given these concerns, what then accounts for the persistence of the property tax? Partly it is due to the fact that no other significant tax source is either suitable to local governments or made available to them by provincial governments. From time to time, the possibility of revenue sharing arises, whereby a provincial government would designate some of its revenue from, say, income taxes to be shared by municipal governments. To date, however, no significant moves in this direction have actually been undertaken.

But the persistence of the property tax is not entirely due to a lack of alternatives. In many ways, the property tax is a good revenue source for municipal governments. It can be easily administered by a relatively small jurisdiction, whereas other taxes, such as the income tax, really only become feasible if one can attain high-level economies of scale. The tax base, while troublesome in the sense discussed above, is easy to access. Real property is fixed; while some development is mobile between jurisdictions, much is not. Finally, at least on an approximate basis, a link can be made between property tax payments and the benefits accruing to property owners and occupants from municipal services, particularly in the case of piped services.

USER FEES

The stresses on urban government budgets, some resulting from problems with their own-revenue systems and some resulting from the downloading of provincial (and indirectly federal) budget problems, have affected decision making in urban governments in important ways.

One route has been to seek out new forms of revenue and new revenue sources. The most politically charged and, in dollar terms, most prominent of these initiatives to date has been the increasing trend to user fees. Specific charges for services that fully or partially cover their costs is not new to urban governments. For example, many cities have long charged for water and sewage services, parking, and some recreation facilities. In the early and mid-1800s, fire fighting services in Ottawa (Bytown) were semi-private and financed, at least in part, through a system of voluntary contributions and user fees. In recent years, the areas to which user fees have been applied and that are being considered have multiplied.

Urban governments have increased the levels of charges for those services where they already existed and have looked to apply them to new areas including the collection of garbage, various licensing and inspection services, and even for police and fire services when attending traffic accidents in which non-residents of the municipality are involved. Preventable costs or "non-necessary" aspects of essential services are also becoming chargeable services, such as when police respond to a home or business security call that turns out to be a false alarm.

The increasing reliance on user fees has three immediate effects. First, it taps into new revenues for urban governments faced with declining provincial transfers and taxpayer resistance to higher property taxes. Table 9.1 shows how the proportion of total revenues coming from user fees has increased in recent years.

Second, because prices are now attached to some services that previously were provided for free to residents, there are often some beneficial effects in terms of consumption of the affected goods and services. For example, higher fees for water and sewer services may prompt conservation efforts. The extent to which this occurs depends on two factors: the structure of the user fee and the responsiveness of demand to higher fees (the elasticity of demand). The structure of the fees is important. If fees are unrelated to actual usage, they have no beneficial effect in terms of prompting conservation of resources. For example, cities that set water and sewer charges as a percentage of property taxes really are doing nothing more than renaming a portion of their property tax, probably in response to taxpayer pressures. Charges keyed to the volume of water used, however, may well prompt conservation. The other factor, the responsiveness of demand, generally varies according to whether the service is regarded as a necessity or an optional commodity. Thus, user fees applied to recreation services are likely to elicit a greater demand response than fees applied to more basic services such as garbage collection or water.

The third effect is related to equity. Services with user fees for which demand is somewhat responsive will likely drive low income individuals out of the market first. This is the case with any price. In cases where individuals have little opportunity to adjust their consumption, the switch from conventional taxation to user fees means that the cost of the service is shifted from individuals as taxpayers to individuals as purchasers. In either case, equity questions arise.

If some citizens are forced out of the market because of the introduction or increase of user fees, are these individuals whose inability to access these services of special concern? For example, there may be strong public policy reasons why we would not want to have such a policy disproportionately affect the poor or the elderly. But that may be the actual effect of user fees.

If, on the other hand, costs are shifted from taxpayers to users of a service, what are the effects? The issue is how user fees and property taxes (paid directly or indirectly) fall on individuals at various levels of income, or on home-owners versus renters. In all likelihood, the answer will vary for different user fees. The point we make here is that while this shift in financing offers immediate budgetary relief to urban governments, there may be other consequences that should be of concern as well.

DEVELOPMENT CHARGES

One particular type of user fee is worthy of special comment. In recent years, development charges or lot levies have become more prominent in the budgets of some cities and in the financial debates of other cities.

When new development occurs, costs are created for the city. Roads must be built and maintained, water and sewer lines need to be extended, sometimes new recreational facilities are built, new schools are constructed, and so forth. A traditional means to finance these costs is to borrow and then to pay off the costs over a long period of time out of current revenues, which includes the additional property tax revenue generated by the new development. Development charges potentially provide another financing method. Developers are assessed a levy per lot at the time of development. This levy often amounts to several thousand dollars per lot. These charges, which most economists agree are passed on to the developers' customers, provide at least part of the financing for public infrastructure.

In the mid-1980s in Ontario, for example, there were expectations that these charges had the potential to be a highly productive cash cow. The provincial government passed legislation enabling municipalities and school boards to levy development charges. However, by the end of the decade and into the early 1990s, in the midst of severe economic recession, the development industry generally entered a deep slump. Few projects were undertaken and, correspondingly, little revenue was generated. Further, questions were raised as to whether the charges themselves discouraged development activity, particularly commercial and industrial development, and many municipalities became reluctant to levy them. In the end, a sluggish construction industry could be detrimental to the overall economic health of the metropolitan area and to the finances of local governments.

Other questions have been raised about the merits of development charges, which are essentially the same as those discussed above with respect to user charges in general. What are the consequences of changing the financing arrangements to the ultimate bearers of the costs? As noted above, costs are shifted, in the first instance, to purchasers of the developed properties. Beyond that, the impacts may be different for residential development on the one hand and commercial and industrial development on the other. In the case of residential development, questions arise about the impact on the prices of existing residences when the prices of new residences are forced up by the development charges. In the case of commercial development, questions arise about the impact of the charges on the competitive position of businesses and their ability, or inability, to pass these costs on to their customers. Thus, debate centres around the allocation and equity consequences of shifting development costs more completely onto new entrants to the community.

PROVINCIAL GRANTS

Historically, the other main source of local government financing has been funding from their respective provincial governments. From the perspective of municipal governments, there were both pluses and minuses attached to this funding. On the positive side, provincial transfers often represented a stable source of revenue (and a significant one at that, as illustrated in Table 9.1) that local governments did not have to raise themselves. Indeed, over much of the last two or three decades before the 1990s, provincial grants were often growing faster than municipal own-revenues.

On the negative side, these monies came with tight strings attached. The grants were generally program-specific (e.g., for policing, urban transit, recreation), requiring municipal services to meet specific criteria. As well, they often were item-specific (e.g., to subsidize the purchase of police cars or buses) and did not allow municipal governments to divert funds from one aspect of a service to another. Thus, for example, a grant for the purchase of new buses may not have been available for the maintenance or retrofitting of old buses.

There were clear reasons for these conditions, at least from the perspective of the donor provinces. First of all, especially in urban areas divided into more than one municipality, many public services are characterized by benefit spillovers from one jurisdiction to another. By attaching appropriate conditions to grants funds, municipal governments could be induced to provide the optimal amount of the service which took into account the benefits accruing to the neighbouring municipalities. As discussed above, the inter-municipal spillover or externality phenomenon is widespread. Residents of one jurisdiction benefit from the road and transportation services provided by another jurisdiction. The central municipality of an urban area provides services to low-income individuals and families by picking up the tab for the other municipalities as well. Even though the recipients tend to be concentrated in the core of the urban area, they are, in a real sense, the responsibility of the larger community.

Provincial governments have traditionally dealt with spillover issues such as these in one of two ways. One method, discussed in Chapter Four, is through urban government structure — the creation of two-tier urban governments with responsibility for the services most affected in this manner, the creation of metropolitan governments, and more recently (in Ontario and Nova Scotia) the creation of unified municipalities (as established in Winnipeg in the 1970s). The second method is to use conditional grants that partially direct the character and influence the quantity of services provided by the municipalities receiving the grants.

A second reason for the conditions attached to grants relates to the fact that municipal governments are ultimately the fiscal responsibility of the province that creates them. Provincial governments have long been concerned with monitoring the fiscal circumstances and borrowing of municipal governments. Conditional grants have been attractive in this context because they are an indirect instrument in controlling municipal spending.

Of course, from the perspective of municipal governments, these conditions have been seen quite differently. The view of the recipients has basically been that these grant programs distort the priorities of the urban government and do not reflect local needs, which have often been very local indeed. The spillovers or externalities, as noted above, have generally been those among municipalities, and, therefore, municipal governments often have seen themselves in a position of having to provide services that mainly benefited non-residents. Central city municipalities having to spend money to build and maintain roads, with a large part of the benefits accruing to suburban resident commuters, is a case in point. Issues such as these were a major focus of the Golden Report.

In recent years, as provincial governments grappled with their own deficit problems, one of the areas in which they have cut spending is grants to local governments. Recognizing the consequences for local government budgets, the provinces have increased the flexibility of local governments to adjust to these cutbacks by easing the conditionality associated with the reduced grants. Ontario, for example, has moved toward its own version of block funding rather than linking specific grant money to any specific municipal service. At the same time, however, the cutbacks in grants in Ontario were more severe and were concentrated over a shorter period than in any other province.

While lessening the conditionality of grants does ease the adjustment difficulties faced by urban governments, the underlying spillover problems that in part motivated the conditional funding in the first place have not gone away. This perhaps explains why the alternative approach to address these issues — changing the structure of urban governance — has become more prominent. Regionalization and municipal consolidation can internalize spillovers by amalgamating jurisdictions or shifting more responsibilities from lower-tier municipalities to upper-tier regional or metropolitan governments.

Such moves may bring to the surface underlying fundamental differences in interests between centre city and suburban residents. For example, suburbanites may regard central city spending on social assistance and cultural and recreational activities as wasteful. Central residents, as already mentioned, may resent the large roadway expenditures to carry suburbanites into the downtown core and back home again. These differences did emerge in the early political dynamic of the unified City of Winnipeg during the 1970s (Kiernan and Walker, 1983, p. 231). Tracking similar political debates will be crucial in the newly unified Halifax municipality and in the aftermath of the GTA reforms.

BUDGETING IN LOCAL GOVERNMENT
The Unique Context of Local Government Budgeting

To understand budgeting in local governments, one must start from a number of basic structural parameters and explore their implications. First of all, local governments are the only governments in Canada that explicitly distinguish between current (operating) and capital (investment) accounts in their budgets. Further, by provincial law, municipal governments cannot plan for deficits on their current operations; this portion of their budget must be balanced or in surplus. While capital investments may be financed by borrowing, in virtually all cases, some form of provincial approval is required. For example, in Ontario, an arm's length authority of the province, the Ontario Municipal Board (OMB), must approve capital financing plans of the municipal governments. The reason for this level of control is that the provinces, which establish municipal entities through legislation, are ultimately responsible for local government debt. It therefore seems only prudent that provincial governments would put in place mechanisms — balanced operating budgets and borrowing approvals for capital projects — to protect their own financial interests.[5]

The balanced budget requirement creates an immediacy between spending and tax decisions that sets municipal governments apart from their federal and provincial counterparts. Because municipal administrations cannot resort deliberately or by default to deficits, the choice to spend on a new or expanded program must simultaneously involve a decision on how to pay for it. The two sides of the budget are intimately linked in the budget decision process, whereas at the federal and provincial levels, they are largely divorced from each other.

Moreover, the revenue component of the budget decision is closely tied to the property tax, despite the growing importance of user fees in recent years. Thus one could almost speak of the direct expenditure–revenue link as being an expenditure–property tax link. Given the difficulties with the property tax identified earlier in this chapter and the high levels of public resistance to this very visible tax, it is, in a political sense, relatively difficult for municipal governments to spend.

This sense of being on the political firing line when setting the budget is one reason for the detailed involvement of elected municipal officials in the budget process, again in contrast to the practice at more senior levels of government. At the federal and provincial levels, the normal process is that the budget is assembled by the executive officers of the government and presented to the legislature for ratification. Local councillors, in contrast, tend to play a very hands-on role in determining the contents of the budget on which they will ultimately vote.

The process will typically involve the members of council and/or the mayor setting an initial total budget guideline in light of what they know or assume will be external funding, most importantly provincial grants. This overall budget guideline is often explicitly characterized in terms of a property tax guideline, reflecting the relationships described above. Thus, for example, council may determine that the permissible property tax increase for the forthcoming fiscal year is to be equal to the rate of inflation, or perhaps some other absolute number.

The municipal staff, given the global budget target that can be accommodated by the prescribed property tax rate increase, will then draw up a preliminary budget for the council and mayor to consider. Often this draft budget will exceed the council's guideline. The council will then set the final budget, sometimes by going through the draft item by item to determine what stays, what is added or eliminated, and what is augmented or reduced.

The Politics of the Local Budgetary Process

The fact that the preliminary budget produced by the city staff is not within guidelines does not necessarily reflect a failure or an inadequacy of the city bureaucracy. The "overage" may, in fact, be deliberate, reflecting several considerations. It may be interpreted as a reflection of democratic politics at the municipal level. Ultimately, choices about what should and should not be funded (i.e., what programs and services should be provided) should be made not by bureaucrats but by elected municipal officials, via agreements between individual members and coalitions of council. In this sense, the first draft budget should be regarded as something of a menu of services from which the council makes its final choices.

In addition, a process that unfolds in this ritualistic fashion serves the interests of the elected politicians. It provides an opportunity for them to be seen acting as tough-minded guardians of the municipal public purse. If their constituents see them being forced to make difficult decisions and to exclude or cancel worthwhile programs, any increases that may remain in the budget are easier to justify and defend. Finally, the process serves the interests of appointed officials who are able to introduce their own priority programs into the budget, potentially for funding in the current budget or perhaps to begin to build a constituency for future funding.

In recent years, a strong consensus has emerged in many cities that the permissible rate of increase in property taxes should be zero, that is, rates should be frozen (and some have argued that they should be rolled back). For example, several mayors and councillors (in Winnipeg, Ottawa, Calgary, and elsewhere) have made property tax freezes central platforms in their election campaigns. Given some unavoidable cost increases, cutbacks in provincial grants, or both, city administrations have been forced to make politically and socially difficult choices to meet this objective. Budget trade-offs have become particularly severe, and members of councils have discovered that their relatively direct involvement in setting their cities' budgets comes at a cost as they grapple with contentious and painful choices.

The environment of restraint has carried over to the capital budget as well. As noted, borrowing is permissible and in past years was the most common form of financing capital projects. The rationale behind borrowing for capital investments by municipal governments is analogous to that in the private sector. Over the life of the facility, the flow of benefits (or income) generates the resources and revenue flows in the current budget needed to pay off the loans used to finance construction.

In recent years, local governments have shifted their approach. They have become much more reluctant to take on debt for a number of reasons. Some of them have become unduly burdened by debt. Some debt-financed investments have had poor payoffs. From the early 1980s until the mid-1990s, very high interest rates increased carrying costs. Finally, voters have become more antagonistic to public sector debts in general. Consequently, many cities are trying to eliminate their debt and move toward pay-as-you-go financing. To do this, they establish capital or sinking funds to save the required money in advance of the investment, as well as take some financing out of current revenues.

While the political motivations for this shift are fairly clear, the economic advisability is less so. Essentially what is being changed is the distribution of costs over time. In the traditional borrowing model, residents of a city paid for the investment during the time they were receiving the benefits. In the pay-as-you-go approach, taxpayers today are paying for investments that will benefit residents in future years. In a static situation where investment programs do not vary much from year to year, the difference between these approaches may not be all that meaningful. However, in growing cities or when the investment program varies considerably over time for other reasons, the distribution consequences may be substantial. Rather than think of current financing of capital investment as pay-as-you-go financing, it would be more appropriate to distinguish the two approaches as pay-as-you-use versus pay-as-you-build. When couched in these terms, the distribution issues are more apparent.

CONCLUSION

This chapter has explored several themes and issues involved in the financing of Canadian urban governments in the 1990s. Some of the more important of these issues are as follows:

- The very tight fiscal circumstances of municipal governments. These circumstances have (in addition to other factors discussed throughout this book) raised debates about the role and extent of municipal government. Questions have arisen about who does what (provincial or municipal government), who pays and how, methods of service delivery, and the organization of government in Canada's large urban centres. These issues, which are also being debated from other perspectives, have origins in the cities' fiscal circumstances as well.
- The sources of finance for municipal governments. The real property tax is the single most important own-revenue source. While it has several characteristics that make it very suitable for municipal governments, and which help to account for its longevity, there are serious difficulties in administering the property tax. The most problematic issues are the establishment of fair assessments and their maintenance over time. There are also issues surrounding the shares of the overall tax load allocated to different classes of property, tax exemptions, and the political difficulty in reforming the property tax.
- User fees as a growing source of local government revenues. Their increased prominence raises issues of the impacts for the efficient allocation of resources and for equity in the financing of local services.
- Diminishing provincial grants. A growing source of funds for local governments for many years, provincial grants have been restrained in the 1990s as provincial governments have addressed their own deficit problems.
- The nature of the municipal budget process. The legal requirement for balanced operating budgets creates an immediacy between the expenditure and revenue sides, which distinguishes local government budgeting from that at the provincial and federal levels. Moreover, the close tie between the expenditure and revenue sides often effectively links spending and the property tax. Elected officials are much more involved in the formulation of municipal budgets than are their elected counterparts in more senior governments.

NOTES

1. Reducing work forces to reduce costs at some point begins to cloud the distinction between seeking reductions in per unit costs and reducing service standards (doing less).
2. The operator "Σ" indicates the sum of the individual terms.
3. In reality, the calculation is somewhat more complicated due to the presence of credits and other adjustments, but this simplified formula accurately represents the basics of the tax calculation.
4. There may be important conceptual debates about what should be counted as income, but once this decision is made, the administrative decisions are relatively straightforward.

5. The 1994 Alberta Municipal Government Act relaxes these restrictions to some degree. Municipalities in the province are now permitted to run short-term deficits within an overall balanced budget financial plan.

SUGGESTED READINGS

Bird, Richard M. and Enid Slack. (1993). *Urban Public Finance in Canada.* 2nd ed. Toronto: John Wiley & Sons. A comprehensive overview of the principles and trends in urban finance in Canada.

Ontario Fair Tax Commission. (1992). *Property Tax Working Group Report.* Toronto: Ontario Fair Tax Commission. An assessment of the Ontario property tax and comprehensive recommendations for reform.

Sproule-Jones, Mark. (1994). "User Fees." In *Taxes as Instruments of Public Policy,* edited by Allan M. Maslove. Toronto: University of Toronto Press for the Ontario Fair Tax Commission, pp. 3–38. A survey of user fees and discussion of appropriate and inappropriate areas for user fee implementation.

Tiebout, Charles M. (1956). "A Pure Theory of Local Government Expenditures." *Journal of Political Economy.* 64: 416–24. A classical piece that lays out a theory of local government finance and structure from a public choice perspective.

BIBLIOGRAPHY

Bird, Richard M. and Enid Slack. (1993). *Urban Public Finance in Canada.* 2nd ed. Toronto: John Wiley & Sons.

Brault, Lucien. (1946). *Ottawa: Old and New.* Ottawa: Institute for Historical Information.

Fenn, Michael. (1997, forthcoming). "Expanding the Frontiers of Public Participation: Public Involvement in Municipal Budgeting and Finance." In *Citizen Engagement: Lessons from Local Government,* edited by Katherine A. Graham and Susan D. Phillips. Toronto: Institute of Public Administration of Canada.

Kiernan, Matthew J. and David C. Walker. (1983). "Winnipeg." In *City Politics in Canada,* edited by Warren Magnusson and Andrew Sancton. Toronto: University of Toronto Press, pp. 222–54.

Kitchen, Harry M. (1992). *Property Taxation in Canada.* Toronto: Canadian Tax Foundation.

Ontario Fair Tax Commission. (1992). *Property Tax Working Group Report.* Toronto: Ontario Fair Tax Commission.

Sproule-Jones, Mark. (1994). "User Fees." In *Taxes as Instruments of Public Policy,* edited by Allan M. Maslove. Toronto: University of Toronto Press for the Ontario Fair Tax Commission, pp. 3–38.

Tiebout, Charles M. (1956). "A Pure Theory of Local Government Expenditures." *Journal of Political Economy,* 64: 416–24.

♦
ECONOMIC DEVELOPMENT

INTRODUCTION

It is not an accident that this book begins with a vignette about local economic development. It should be evident that the attraction and retention of capital investment — both financial and **human capital** — is seen as crucial to cities' survival. Witness the "bombed out" central cities, in places such as Detroit and Buffalo, right on Canada's border. Visit the east end of Montreal or the core area of Winnipeg to see the impact of de-industrialization and other aspects of economic restructuring. Check office vacancies in glass-plated buildings in many Canadian cities to see the effects of corporate restructuring and downsizing on white collar employment.

Economic development has been a preoccupation of city governments for a long time. Some observers have suggested that there has even been a tendency to assume that cities must pursue economic development to the detriment of other objectives (Miranda and Rosdil, 1995, p. 868). As this chapter demonstrates, however, the contemporary period is characterized by an increasingly complex constellation of issues pertaining to urban economic development. This prompts questions concerning whether urban governments, in Canada and elsewhere, have the wherewithal to deal with these issues in terms of their delegated and quasi-constitutional powers and their organization and management capacity (Lambooy and Moulaert, p. 219). The main focus of this chapter is to explore this question in the Canadian context.

The chapter begins with a historical refresher. We briefly examine the traditional manner in which economic development issues were conceived and dealt with by local governments in Canada. We then proceed to examine contemporary issues of urban economic development. The allusion to these issues being arrayed in some form of constellation is apt. We will see the range of economic development issues Canadian cities now face and their interrelationship with one another, as well as and with other issues such as creating livable cities, financing city governments, and stimulating local democratic life. The chapter concludes with an examination of the management of economic development issues by urban governments in the contemporary period and a discussion of possible future trends.

HISTORICAL CONTEXT

In earlier chapters, we discussed the traditional prominence of local business elites in civic affairs. Manifestations of this include:

- restriction of the local franchise to "men of property";
- the vision of local government through a corporate paradigm; and
- preoccupation with the development and well-being of enterprise within the city. Enterprise existed to serve surrounding markets (recall the discussion of the metropolitan thesis in Chapter Three); to boost the city's relative importance in the regional or national urban pecking order; and, in some cases — most particularly Montreal and Halifax in the early period — to feed and prosper from international markets.

After 1867, all of this was occurring in the context of a developing federal system. We see the influence on local economies of nation building. Development of independent fiscal, monetary, and trade policies at the national level are perhaps most important in this context. We also see the influence of province building on the local economic development scene. Provinces developed with somewhat diverse political and social cultures. Provincial governments exhibited different degrees of robustness at different times as well. Nonetheless, emerging province-wide *systems* of education and training, roads, and hydroelectric generation were crucial influences on the economic development and competitive advantage of our cities.

Within this broad context, how might we characterize the local approaches to economic development that prevailed up to the contemporary period? In terms of local government policy, we can see four predominant trends:

- Preoccupation with local taxation levels. Recall the discussion of debates between the "boosters and the cutters" in Chapter Three. Even among the boosters, who embraced the idea of undertaking civic works as a carrot to attract new enterprise, there was concern that local tax levels be at least comparable to those in other cities. The cutters, of course, took the position that comparatively low levels of local taxation were the key to attracting new capital investment, which would then fuel the development of local infrastructure.
- Support for urban "progress." All of our city governments have embraced the technologies and ideas associated with the modern city. In part, this has been seen as essential in the competitive economic development game. Investing in new technologies, such as tramlines and electric railways, and embracing the concept of the planned suburb are two manifestations of this.
- Investment in lands dedicated to economic development. Across Canada, cities have created or otherwise supported industrial land banks. One model has been for city governments to buy, service, and then sell or lease these properties. Another approach has been for local governments to support private landholders who want to create dedicated industrial or business parks. This support has traditionally taken the form of up front provision of roads and water and sewer services.
- Tailor-made enticements. Inter-municipal competition to attract new enterprise has been controlled, to a certain extent, by provincial governments. The most significant limitation is that municipalities have been prohibited

from **bonussing**. This refers to the practice of offering tax breaks to enterprises looking to establish themselves or relocate. In Ontario, for example, bonussing has been prohibited since the 1920s. Nonetheless, municipal governments still have some means of competition. These include a willingness to change or relax municipal zoning, agreement to provide municipal infrastructure or other services on a priority or tailor-made basis, and fast-track approvals for construction.

There have also been some trends in the institutional and management approach which Canadian cities have taken in the economic development field. These include:

- A business-like approach to providing services central to economic development. The rise of arm's length agencies, boards, and commissions was discussed in Chapters Three and Seven. Local special purpose bodies, with responsibility for services such as water, electricity, and public transit have commonly been used to develop and manage services central to local enterprise. Recall the arguments that such institutions are both efficient and safe from the hurly-burly of municipal council politics, characteristics that would make them attractive from a business perspective.
- Close links between the local state and business organizations. The importance of the local business lobby in civic affairs has been noted repeatedly. In Chapter Six, we suggested that boards of trade or chambers of commerce often have an advantage compared to other segments of the local voluntary sector. This advantage may or may not be evident at local election time with the campaigns of pro-business candidates. Regardless, local business organizations can influence local governments' agenda through public and not-so-public advocacy. As we have also noted, there has been increasing entanglement between city governments and the private sector as the practices of contracting out and engaging in public–private partnerships have become more prevalent.
- Establishment of economic development departments in city hall. Many Canadian cities have had an economic development department on their organization chart for some time. Commissioners or directors of economic development assumed increasing importance with the rise of the municipal industrial/business park. Municipal staff responsible for economic development also typically are charged with marketing the municipality as a good place to locate and do business. The links between municipal economic development staff and local business organizations are conventionally very close. Such staff are another voice for existing local enterprises within city hall.
- A pattern of intergovernmental entanglement in urban economic development. From a public policy and management perspective, urban governments' economic development fortunes have been linked to some key provincial and federal initiatives. The contextual importance of nation building and province building was mentioned above. There have been more

specific federal and provincial initiatives as well. These have been particularly important in the post-World War II period. For example, the federal government, through the Canada Mortgage and Housing Corporation, has attempted to prime the national economy at different times by easing the flow of funds for housing construction. Most of this has occurred in urban areas. For their part, provincial governments have supported major urban infrastructure projects. (Sometimes the federal government has been involved as well.) Major water and sewer schemes and expressway developments have enhanced the capacity of cities to function and grow from an economic development perspective.

In summary, the history of local economic development has set the stage for the contemporary period. We see a strong emphasis on enterprise and a tendency for municipal councils and local special purpose bodies to coalesce with the indigenous business community in the pursuit of continued prosperity and additional capital. The pursuit of economic development cleaves to the image of urban regimes, as discussed in Chapter Two.

CONTEMPORARY URBAN ECONOMIC DEVELOPMENT

History may set the stage, but it does not inform us about the full panoply of issues associated with urban economic development in contemporary times. At the most basic level, the logic of public policy associated with urban economic development is becoming murkier. There have always been technological, social, and political influences on urban economic development. Equally important, the pattern of economic development has affected social and political affairs, as well as the diffusion of technology within urban space. However, it is increasingly difficult to diagnose the relationship among these four realms — the economic, the technological, the social, and the political. As the difficulty of linking cause to effect becomes more acute, so too does the difficulty of coming up with policy prescriptions, especially given the constrained circumstances in which Canadian urban governments find themselves.

The second feature of our current world is that the issues themselves are changing. For the purposes of this chapter, we present recent developments in the interrelated economic, technological, social, and political contexts in highlighted form. Indeed, many of them have been the stuff of headlines. Sometimes these speak to a new phenomenon; sometimes to something long-standing. The highlights of the current environment related to urban economic development are as follows:

The Economic Context

- **Financial capital** has become even more mobile than in the past. Human capital, which has traditionally been thought of as relatively stable, has become much more mobile. The increasing mobility of both forms of capital is evident both within nation-states and internationally.
- International trade barriers are falling. One effect has been the decline of Canadian branch plants, which were set up in a more protectionist period.

International firms are closing branch plants or re-aligning them, as part of an international corporate structure.

- Attention is shifting from traditional manufacturing to the service and **knowledge-based sectors**. Manufacturing is becoming more high tech.
- The natural resource sector continues to be important to the Canadian economy. From an urban perspective, the issues related to this sector concern where resource companies will locate their head offices and other major administrative functions, and where activities that add value to extracted resources will be performed. There is an increasing and important cultural gap, however, between urbanites and those who extract Canada's natural resources. Cities are important sites for the clash between the economic interests associated with resource extraction and environmental or social groups who challenge industries such as mining and forestry. Reflecting this, the Mining Association of Canada undertook an urban-based campaign in 1996 to "Keep Mining in Canada."
- Within cities, leisure, cultural, and sports activities are no longer informal pastimes. They are big business in economic terms and in terms of urban marketing. For example the City of Winnipeg's council and staff, not to mention its citizens, were preoccupied with losing the city's NHL franchise in the early 1990s. Our other city governments have also been preoccupied with gaining or retaining regional, national, or world-class leisure, cultural, and sports activities.

The Technological Context

- Virtual communication has arrived, affecting not only the flow of information within and among cities but also the relationship between rural and urban. One rural county in Ontario, Lanark County, used to advertise itself as "quiet, quaint, and beautiful." Its new slogan is "Ten seconds to Tokyo; ten minutes to the cottage."
- New techniques and emphasis on just-in-time production of both goods and services have heightened the interdependence among cities. Transportation links, as well as communications links, are more crucial than ever before. Frequently, the most crucial links are international ones.
- "High tech" has emerged as an important economic sector. With this phenomenon, we see the emergence of **technopoles**, urban centres with a significant cluster of high-tech research and development establishments. High technology enterprises have developed their own priorities for determining where they will locate. In cities where they are clustered, high-tech employment has resulted in new social challenges as well as economic benefits.

The Social Context

- The diversity of participants in the urban labour market is increasing. Perhaps the most dramatic change was the influx of large numbers of women into the labour market beginning in the late 1960s. However, an increasingly diverse and well educated international immigrant population has also entered the labour market in our large cities in recent years. These people tend to be better educated than the general population, but they also suffer higher rates of underemployment and unemployment.

- There is a perceptible gap between participants in the "new" economy and those who lack the skills or other means of access to the world of high-tech, knowledge-based, and highly mobile employment. Observers have suggested that there may be significant social and political costs associated with having these two groups exist as two solitudes within the same urban space (Mayer, 1991). We have also yet to address, in public policy and social terms, the implications of a possible decline in the total labour force requirements of the increasingly global, high technology economy (Rifkin, 1995). A decline may mean that we have a higher percentage of the population in our cities who are excluded from the labour force, as we have traditionally conceived it.
- There is increasing concern about urban quality of life issues. This arises from several sources. The voice of women is heard increasingly on issues related to the need for flexible services to accommodate the twin challenges of child rearing and employment. Local child care, public transit, and recreation services are three important preoccupations in this context. Urban safety issues are also increasingly at the forefront of the urban public agenda, particularly as they affect women and children. Urban quality of life is much more broadly conceived as well. Preserving and fostering a good natural environment within the urban context and having cultural and recreational amenities are seen increasingly as important for the quality of urban life and for attracting new population and investment.

The Political Context

- There is increasing pressure on governments to do something about the economic challenges facing many Canadian cities. This is not directed exclusively to the local level. For example, the Quebec government is very preoccupied with the economic situation of Montreal, as is the government of Nova Scotia with that of Halifax. There is, however, a sense that city governments should also be proactive. Prescriptions for action vary, from suggesting that city governments remove the roadblocks and permit enterprise to flourish to advocating that local political leaders champion a coherent local economic development strategy that addresses social and environmental, as well as economic, concerns.
- The increasingly global economy has made the political arena for urban economic development more international in nature. International relations of city governments and Canadian cities with international businesses are becoming increasingly important.
- The increasing complexity of the economic development field is creating the need for urban governments to be clear about what they really can do to respond to the myriad challenges highlighted above. Regardless of the prevailing ideology within city hall, Canadian urban governments must focus on two questions. First, what policy levers do they have to influence the course

of economic development? Second, what must they negotiate with other governments and other sectors in order to achieve local economic development goals?

THE MANAGEMENT OF CONTEMPORARY URBAN ECONOMIC DEVELOPMENT
The Policy Dimension

> City-regions have come to be recognized as key nodes of the global economy, as places where capital, workers, institutions, and infrastructure (soft and hard) come together to provide the foundations for successful economic activity. However, it is equally clear that the trajectory along which such regions develop is not predetermined, but is a matter of active social choice. (Gertler, 1996, p. 12)

> Far from being a public good, growth appears more often to benefit a coalition of corporate leaders, downtown real estate interests, and local political elites at the expense of neighbourhoods and the city's low income population. (Miranda and Rosdil, 1995, p. 869)

> [W]e can only conclude that the fewer public sector resources committed to intervention in the economy designed to promote local economic activity the better. High visibility but low cost activity may satisfy the political need for demonstrable effort, since the issue is a matter of symbols, not substantive interventions (which have rarely, if ever, produced change efficiently). (Meyer, 1991, p. 177)

These three assessments illustrate the spectrum of views concerning local economic development experience and prospects. They range from arguing the futility of pursuing local economic development policy, except in symbolic terms; to seeing such policy as the preserve of local economic and political elites; to asserting that a dedicated focus on the economic fortunes of major cities is essential as we make basic choices about the nature of urban society. We now proceed to explore where our selected city governments might be placed in this spectrum. This again entails an examination of the relationship of the local state to other sectors of urban society and other governments, as we examine responses to the challenges of economic development.

Local Policy Tools for Urban Economic Development

Summarizing the approaches to urban economic development in selected cities around the world, P.B. Meyer developed a taxonomy of local economic development intervention possibilities which we have built upon and modified (Meyer, 1991, p. 173). In the Canadian context, some of Meyer's original elements would be only in the arsenal of a provincial government or part of a national economic/industrial policy. For example, only provincial and federal levels of government could offer tax subsidies or loans to attract new business. (Think of New Brunswick's courtship of new enterprises, particularly to the Moncton area, by offering tax breaks for each job created.) Similarly, these are the two levels of government that would be involved in making grants to assist in the development of new products by existing businesses. (Witness the federal government's 1996 loan to Bombardier-DeHavilland to modify its executive jet design.) Nonetheless, city governments in Canada are not entirely without policy and program levers for economic development. Some of the most important of these are summarized in Figure 10.1.

FIGURE 10.1 CITY GOVERNMENTS' LOCAL ECONOMIC DEVELOPMENT INTERVENTIONS

I: Efforts Directed Primarily at New Business Attraction
SPENDING INITIATIVES

- infrastructure construction (to attract new businesses to relocate)
- business facilities construction for private sector use (e.g., facilities for major league sports)
- probity regarding the local tax structure and rates

REGULATORY INITIATIVES

- relaxation of zoning
- bonus zoning (e.g., trading height for housing)
- fast-track development approval
- fast-track building permit approval/inspection

II: Local Business Stimulation
SPENDING INITIATIVES

- "buy local" programs
- infrastructure assistance (e.g., municipal parking facilities)
- probity regarding local tax structure and rates

REGULATORY INITIATIVES

- hours of operation for local business
- parking rates, transit, taxi fares/regulation

III: Geographically-Based Initiatives (for New and Local Enterprises)
SPENDING INITIATIVES

- establishment of designated parks — industrial, business, or research
- targeted revitalization zones — urban renewal, business improvement areas, etc.

REGULATORY INITIATIVES

- official plan and zoning designations

IV: Research and Analytical Efforts
SPENDING INITIATIVES

- economic planning in the context of broader local planning exercises
- support for local economic development corporations (with an analytic function)

(continued)

(continued)

V: Marketing Efforts

SPENDING INITIATIVES

- tourism and convention marketing
- marketing to attract new business
- marketing partnerships for designated local business sectors (e.g., the film industry)
- local image management — civic pride/identification

VI: Human Capital Strategies

SPENDING INITIATIVES

- worker training and retraining through local employment programs
- provision of child care, health care, and other human services

VII: Quality of Life Strategies

SPENDING INITIATIVES

- provision of cultural and recreational amenities
- emphasis on the functioning city — transportation, public safety, etc.

REGULATORY INITIATIVES

- local pollution control

It should be evident that most of the policy and program levers available to city governments for economic development are related to land use, local expenditure, and regulation affecting economic life. Within the constraints of provincial legislation, there is also room for individual cities to manoeuvre on the quality of life front. For example, environmental legislation at the provincial level sets the stage for local pollution abatement and control.

It is significant that city governments have no powers related to important underpinnings of the modern economy. Specifically, they have no powers over communication or the regulation of financial markets. Until very recently, city governments in Canada have had no role in inter-city transport. The recent transfer of control over airports from the federal government to **local airport authorities** in our selected cities is therefore very significant. City governments still have no power to determine air routes or schedules, but they now have much greater control over the most important gateway to their metropolitan area.

Perhaps the most significant limits to municipal control over economic development, in public policy terms, relate to strategies aimed at improving the state of human capital in our cities. The list of city government initiatives related to human capital, as shown in Figure 10.1, is relatively brief. Notably absent is a major role for city governments in improving basic education within their borders. Yet study after study has indicated that the presence of a well educated and appropriately trained labour force is a crucial factor in firms' location and relocation decisions (Lithwick, 1988). If city governments have relatively little influence over the development of local human capital through education and training, they have even less influence over the importation of people with appropriate skills. This is in the realm of immigration policy and regulation, a federal (and, in the case of Quebec, a provincial) government responsibility. Even those policy and program tools that are readily available to urban governments for improvement of local human capital are under stress. For example, we are currently seeing cutbacks in public funding for child care, public health, and the other human service programs operated or managed by city governments.

The limitations for direct action, as shown in Figure 10.1, suggest two possible strategies for city governments wishing to undertake a more comprehensive approach to local economic development. First, they can *exhort* other parts of the local state (most particularly school boards) as well as the local private sector and the local volunteer/not-for-profit community to meet the challenges of human capital development. Parallel to this, city governments can lobby other levels of government to play a constructive role, using the additional policy and program levers at their disposal. A second approach is for city governments to *lead*. This implies actively engaging other key actors at the local level and beyond to develop a comprehensive economic development strategy for the urban region and leading its implementation. Here, economic development policy and the management of that policy come together.

For some, this vision of city government leadership in local economic development is misguided or inappropriate. Given the constitutional strictures in place, others might think of it as an impossible dream. Regardless, urban governments continue to be preoccupied with economic development. We now turn to the approaches taken by our selected cities to economic development in order to assess their vision for local economic development and their attempts to manage the achievement of local goals.

Managing Economic Development: Works in Progress

The priorities for and approaches to economic development vary significantly across our selected city-regions. In part, these variations are associated with differences in the prevailing political culture, related to whether or not urban governments should take a lead role in this field. Other differences relate to the diverse economic circumstances, which have characterized our city-regions historically and which influence contemporary strategies and management of local economic development. The following cases highlight current trends in local economic development in each of our selected city-regions. Generally, they emphasize developments at the city-region level — the Halifax Regional Municipality, the Greater Montreal Area, the Greater Toronto Area, and so on. There are also microcosmic developments within the boundaries of each region, such as the establishment of **business improvement areas**. These have been included when they constitute a major element of the local economic development effort in the city-region context.

Each case summarizes the main preoccupations related to economic development; the principal strategies in place; the extent to which city government is leading the effort and how this is being done; the level of intergovernmental involvement; and whether or not co-production, involving the municipal sector with other sectors in the community, is being employed. The chapter will then conclude by summarizing trends and differences in approach.

HALIFAX: RESTRUCTURING FOR ECONOMIC PROSPERITY

Halifax is increasingly focussed on retaining and augmenting its status as the "capital of Atlantic Canada." This is occurring in the face of increasingly imaginative and entrepreneurial efforts by the government of New Brunswick to transform Moncton into the region's dominant centre and recognition that economic activity related to the exploitation of mineral resources in the region might be concentrated in St. John's, Newfoundland. The main element of the current strategy in Halifax is the restructuring of the region's local government arrangements to form the Halifax Regional Municipality. This initiative is seen as improving the region's economic prospects in a number of ways. It brings to an end invidious competition among the former municipalities to attract new enterprises to their industrial and business parks.[1] Establishment of the regional municipality is also seen as providing a sound foundation for local government finance throughout the region and as the key to dealing with some major environmental problems that threaten the region's quality of life and attractiveness.

The Halifax Regional Municipality has vested management responsibility for economic development with the chief administrative officer. In the region's early days, priorities for council and staff have been to connect the new government to the local business community and to market the region competitively as a location for high technology activity. The decision to locate a major blood products facility in Halifax, announced in late 1995, was seen as a crucial victory.

Economic development in Halifax is accompanied by a very high level of intergovernmental involvement. The region's economic health is a major preoccupation for the government of Nova Scotia. The federal government is also involved, for example, in planning a strategy to improve transportation links to Halifax. Co-production with the private sector is another feature of contemporary economic development in the region. The first steps in this direction were embodied in the Greater Halifax Economic Development Partnership Launch Plan of October 1995, which set out an arrangement whereby the new regional government would partner with the Metro Halifax Chamber of Commerce to market the region. Out of this, an economic development board has been created, with equal membership from the municipality and the chamber. The municipality, however, provides the majority of funding for this initiative.

MONTREAL: CHARTING AN INDEPENDENT COURSE

From an economic perspective, Montreal is no longer the premier city in Canada. By the late 1990s, Canada's corporate elite were more likely to be found in Toronto or Calgary than on rue Saint Jacques, once the street on which the Montreal-based business elite directed its Canadian empire. Nonetheless, Montreal's economic fortunes remain important for Canada and are arguably crucial to Quebec (Polese, 1996; Latouche, 1996). The Montreal region's economy is diverse in its character and prospects. On the positive side, the region has a strong knowledge-based economy, particularly in the pharmaceutical and aerospace sectors. Within the region, these are clustered to the west and north. At the same time, the central and eastern parts of the region, particularly on the Island of Montreal, are in very difficult straits. What were formerly good industrial and trades jobs in the city's petroleum refineries and rail yards have vanished.

The fragmentation of local government in the Greater Montreal Area was discussed in Chapters Three and Four. Recall also the rivalry between the City of Montreal and its surrounding municipal governments. This extends to intra-regional competition related to economic development. The political and economic stakes are so high that the government of Quebec has moved in to assume the dominant public sector role. From a political perspective, successive recommendations that the Montreal region become more of a coherent metropolitan entity have proved to be indigestible. Instead, in 1996, the premier of Quebec appointed a high profile *ministère de la métropole*, responsible for overseeing the fortunes of the Montreal region. As discussed in Chapter Four, the minister named to this post initially sought to deal with the challenges facing the region by undertaking structural reform. This was, however, killed in Cabinet. The minister remains preoccupied with economic development as a key to Montreal's future but must now focus on other strategies.

The approach to dealing with Montreal's particular challenges is still emerging. It appears, however, to involve support and promotion of dynamic sectors of the regional economy through the provision of loans and other guarantees. It is likely that the relatively strong connection between the provincial government and Quebec's private and labour sectors will be a feature of the economic development strategy as it continues to unfold. The federal government is also active, undertaking varied economic development initiatives in the Montreal region. These include relocation of the National Space Agency to Montreal from the national capital, in the 1980s, and the 1996 federal loan to Bombardier, mentioned earlier. Federal economic development initiatives in the Montreal region are unique compared to those undertaken in other cities. They are tied to the government's battle for the hearts and minds of Montrealers and Québécois more generally. They are undertaken independent of federal–provincial collaboration and bear the political stamp of unity politics. The role of local governments in the area is unclear. Intra-regional competition remains. Within the City of Montreal, the current mayor's priorities seem to be environmental issues and securing Montreal's place as a cultural Mecca.

REDOING THE CAPITAL

Canada's capital provides another example of a metropolitan economy in transition. Until the late 1970s, the capital region was known as a "government town." This moniker evoked some powerful images and masked some important characteristics of the Ottawa-Carleton-Outaouais region. Canadians viewed their capital as the home of well-paid, tenured public servants, who sat at their walnut-veneered desks and pushed endless paper, isolated physically and psychologically from the ups and downs of economic life in the rest of the country. At the same time, the capital was dull, having little to attract any but political addicts, who could spend their weekends and even their evenings in more vibrant Montreal. This image concealed the fact that the capital region was home to one of the best educated work forces in the country, an increasing proportion of which worked in high technology fields, both within government and in the private sector. The region also had exceptional amenities, ranging from a many thousand hectare federal park to new and revitalized national facilities for the arts and culture. The capital may have been perceived to be "fat cat city," as one member of Parliament alleged, but its true character was little known.

By the mid-1990s, life had changed significantly in the capital. Beginning with the 1984 election, momentum had gathered to reduce the size of the federal public service. Direct federal government employment declined significantly. In some cases, public servants were replaced by "just-in-time" consultants or employees with fixed-term contracts. In other cases, public service jobs just disappeared. Many of these were clerical and administrative positions. At the same time, the high technology sector in the capital took off. Government and pioneering high technology firms, such as Northern Telecom, Mitel, and Cognos, spawned new high technology firms at an increasing rate. On the one hand, then, the region's prospects looked buoyant; on the other, concerns about public sector unemployment and uncertainty about the role of the national capital in a changing federal system shook local investor and consumer confidence.

Within the capital region, it was unclear who might take the lead to deal with the challenges and opportunities at hand. Local government was and remains highly fragmented. The existence of a provincial border through the middle of the region has not helped foster inter-municipal co-operation between the two sides of the Ottawa River. On the Ontario side, the Regional Municipality of Ottawa-Carleton had traditionally played a relatively passive role in economic development, leaving the field open to sometimes strong competition among area municipalities to attract new firms. This changed somewhat in 1992, when the provincial government reassigned responsibility for lands dedicated to economic development from the local to the regional level.

That same year marked the emergence of the Regional Municipality of Ottawa-Carleton (RMOC) as a somewhat more active actor in the economic development field. This occurred, in part, at the urging of a blue ribbon Task Force on Ottawa-Carleton Economic Development, which recommended that the "RMOC exercise leadership in developing and supporting partnerships in business, labour, education, finance, and government to achieve a common vision of a great future" (Regional Municipality of Ottawa-Carleton Economic Development Task Force, 1992, Letter of Transmittal). The task force report also marked the beginning of an explicit strategy to pursue economic development in three areas other than public sector employment: high technology, tourism, and environmental technology.

Within Ottawa-Carleton, two long-standing organizations existed as focal points for marketing the region. One focussed exclusively on tourism and conventions; the other on attracting new enterprises to the region and supporting business incubation locally. Both were publicly funded but private sector dominated. Both were subject to periodic scrutiny and criticism by local politicians and researchers, but little had been done to improve them prior to 1995. This was despite the fact that the head of regional council had designated one of these organizations, the Ottawa-Carleton Economic Development Corporation (OCEDCO), as having the lead role on behalf of the regional government in local economic development. As the vignette at the beginning of Chapter One indicates, OCEDCO was brought into the new world of economic development in 1995. It is now pursuing alliances with other sectors in the community to spread the benefits of growth in the high technology sector. Another regionally-funded collaborator in this respect is the Ottawa-Carleton Research Institute (OCRI), which has the specific mandate to create a strong local network within the high technology sector. Both OCEDCO and OCRI now have extensive links into the local university community for conducting research and analyses.

In contrast with Halifax and Montreal, there is less intergovernmental traffic with regard to economic development in the capital. In the wake of downsizing, the federal government funded an **industrial adjustment initiative** for the entire region. This organization, known as REDO, is headed by another blue ribbon committee, dominated by representatives from the local private sector. One goal of the industrial adjustment process, as conceived by Human Resources Development Canada, is to have organized labour as an active partner. This has not occurred in the capital however. There are at least two possible contributing factors. First, REDO embraced expansion of the region's high technology sector as a key to future prosperity. Many of the vulnerable members of public sector unions had clerical or administrative skills that were not obviously transferable. A second factor was the political difficulty anticipated by the national headquarters of public sector unions if they seemed to acquiesce to a reduction in direct federal employment for its members. Public sector unions withdrew their support for the REDO process early in the initiative, in opposition to what they saw as REDO's acceptance of government downsizing and security reduction of the remaining public sector jobs.

For their part, the Ontario and Quebec governments have taken a somewhat hands-off approach to dealing with the situation. This is a continuing reflection of the tendency of these provinces to treat the national capital with benign neglect (Graham, 1992, p. 140). Ontario's main contribution, in recent times, has been to pledge speedy construction of the first four-lane highway to link the capital to Highway 401. A request for Ontario government support for the REDO initiative was turned down by the Ontario Cabinet's Management Board. The Quebec government created a new economic development commission for the Outaouais region in 1994. Two years later, it had yet to become active. The Quebec government also designated Hull as the site for a casino, which is now in operation.

While there are signs that a basic economic development strategy may be emerging in the capital region, at least two questions remain outstanding. The first concerns how the region will market itself to the world outside. This is a very sensitive issue among the local governments in the region. A major break-through occurred in mid-1996 when all of the municipalities on the Ontario side of the region agreed to market themselves outside of the area under the banner "Ottawa." The identity for the full city-region is, however, still being defined. Focussing on the moniker "capital" is a possibility but masks the competing image of the region as "Silicon Valley North." The second question concerns how a constructive link will be forged between the changing high technology and knowledge-based economy and the capital's urban poor and its rural and small-town hinterland. This is not a unique challenge for the capital region, but it is an acute one.

THE GREATER TORONTO AREA: NEW MEANING TO THE "GOLDEN HORSESHOE"

The Greater Toronto Area is an international city-region by many measures. It is Canada's most important financial centre and the location of more head offices than anywhere else in the country. It is the nation's media and communications hub. Finally, it remains an important manufacturing centre. Traditional manufacturing strengths, for example, in the automotive sector, have kept pace with technological advances and the internationalization of production and sales. The region is also home to many specialized firms that produce goods and services (i.e., the tool-and-die industry, legal services) to support other enterprise (Gertler, 1996, pp. 12–13). On top of all this, the region has a very culturally diverse population, which lives in comparative harmony, and a rich cultural and recreational base. *Fortune* magazine proclaimed Toronto the best city in the world for business people in which to live and work, in November 1996 (Precourt and Faircloth, 1996, pp. 130–49).

It might be tempting to think that local officials simply bask in the glory of past achievements and let the forces of the market push and pull new capital to the region to join existing enterprise. To some extent, this is occurring. There are also, however, some very significant issues on the region's economic development agenda. These include maintaining the economic base and quality of life infrastructure, which have made the region so attractive; finding ways to buffer the impact of the cycles of the global economy on the region; and positioning the GTA in its increasingly entangled economic relationship with the north central United States.

These preoccupations have accompanied debates at the local level about the distribution of public funds and works within the region. Among officials in the core, there is a fear that suburban growth will suck the life out of the central city (which is now represented by the new "super city" of Toronto, following the outer boundaries of Metropolitan Toronto rather than the old City of Toronto). Officials in the outer municipalities of the GTA argue that they should receive their fair share of growth and that they are, in fact, the engine of the local economy.

From a public policy perspective, these debates have boiled down to two issues. First, is reform in the structure of local government in Toronto and the GTA going to achieve balanced growth and enhanced prosperity for all? Second, is some form of property tax reform necessary to level the playing field for intra-regional competition for economic development and to better distribute the benefits from the growth achieved?

Although these have been hot topics of debate at the local level, the future of economic development for the GTA, in terms of these issues, is a work in progress. Politicians in the central city and prominent business leaders are keeping a watchful eye on restructuring throughout the GTA and the effects of realigning provincial and local government responsibilities following "mega-week." Along with community groups in Toronto, they are concerned that these radical changes may be detrimental to the health of the core and, ultimately, the entire GTA. In late 1996, the provincial government announced it was going to implement a system of actual value assessment across the province to eliminate inter-municipal discrepancies in determining the property tax base. These have been acute among municipalities in the GTA. The high stakes involved for the different municipalities in the region and the uncertainty regarding how the property tax issue will be resolved have made property tax reform the dominant issue in economic development of the GTA. The provincial–municipal and inter-municipal dynamic accompanying its resolution will shape the political climate for other economic development initiatives. These include initiatives in the social development field, which Golden suggested were important to support growth in key sectors of the GTA's economy.

Within this turbulent context, other more focussed economic development initiatives have occurred in the contemporary period. Municipalities in the GTA have engaged in major efforts to develop central urban spaces in light of contemporary markets. We see, for example, the rise of "city centres" in North York, Scarborough, and Mississauga. In each case, a new city hall anchored the development of office complexes and cultural and retail amenities. There have been crucial redevelopment schemes. For example, after many years of intergovernmental negotiation and discussions with the railways, the former railway yards in downtown Toronto have been redeveloped. An obsolete auto plant, which once dominated downtown Oshawa, is now gone, with new buildings and green space in its place. These and similar initiatives have been the product of partnerships among local governments, other levels of government, and the private sector.

All municipalities within the GTA are active in marketing themselves. Traditionally, within Metropolitan Toronto, tourism and convention marketing were undertaken by the Metro government rather than individual municipalities. At the lower tier, the City of Toronto placed a priority on marketing the city as a location for shooting and producing movies and television. It had a small staff dedicated to this effort and to easing the path of film producers who decided to shoot on location in Toronto. This effort has been judged to be quite successful and has had spillover effects throughout the region.

Across the GTA, there is at least some discussion of economic development issues, in addition to the inter-municipal competition and debates related to political and property tax reform. The GTA mayors have a subcommittee dedicated to economic development issues. Within Toronto, there is heavy traffic between the Metropolitan Toronto Boards of Trade and local politicians. All of these governments and organizations, as well as private sector firms, await the provincial government's resolution of taxation issues within the GTA. That is seen as the key to the future, although, as the GTA task force and others argue, more explicit social policy choices will also affect the GTA's future economic health (Golden, 1996; Gertler, 1996).

WINNIPEG: IDENTIFYING A CORE STRATEGY

Winnipeg stands out as a city where there has been broad public engagement on economic development issues (Fielding and Couture, 1997). Recall the economic and political history of Winnipeg discussed in Chapters Three, Four, and Seven. The 1919 Winnipeg General Strike, the creation of unicity, and the decline of Winnipeg's importance as a national transportation and distribution centre in the post-World War II period are seminal events. The contemporary period reflects an attempt to mute long-standing cleavages, based on class and culture, while rethinking Winnipeg's economic niche and strategies for enhancing local prosperity.

Winnipeg's city government has played a lead role in this effort. By the end of the 1980s, the merits of continuing council support for the Winnipeg Business Development Corporation, a business development agency similar to those found in Ottawa-Carleton and Halifax, were unclear. The city's economy was in trouble. City council established an economic development task force in 1989 to explore alternative possibilities for economic development strategy and management. The deputy mayor chaired the task force, which included people drawn from business, labour, education, and government. The task force's 1990 report was endorsed by city council. The resulting local economic development strategy has guided economic development in Winnipeg since that time. Its elements include the sustainment of community consensus on economic action, in part through a broadly-based Leaders Committee; targeting key sectors, based on Winnipeg's comparative advantage; emphasis on community improvement, through focussed economic and social initiatives in different parts of the city; and more aggressive and focussed marketing of Winnipeg's assets and "open for business" approach.

There have been three specific outcomes of this strategy since 1990. First, the city and local leaders have focussed on gaining local control of the Winnipeg Airport and on the development of Winnipeg as a major hub for air freight. Local advocates of this move contend that the city is centrally located within Canada and North America, making it ideal as an air freight distribution centre for the continent. It is also well positioned in terms of polar air routes to Europe and Asia. There is ample space around the airport for warehouse and other distribution facilities. This takes the city's historic role in transportation into the contemporary period.

Second, the city government has undertaken a major effort to engage the population of the central and northern parts of the city, areas traditionally prone to social problems and unemployment, in preparing a vision for community economic development. Community resource people from business and the not-for-profit/voluntary sectors have also been involved in this process.

Finally, the city has successfully negotiated expansion of the tri-level Core Area Initiative to include other economic development priorities. The Winnipeg Development Agreement of March 1995 committed the three levels of government to thirteen economic development programs in Winnipeg, including downtown revitalization and airport development.

Within city hall, the mayor and council have been preoccupied with economic development issues and marketing the city. Senior management responsibility for economic development rests with the Chief Commissioner (with responsibility for business liaison and intergovernmental relations) and the Commissioner of Planning and Community Services, supported by city departments working in these areas. Public engagement on economic development issues has been a priority for the city, bringing these departments into close and ongoing contact with diverse local interests.

EDMONTON: CITY IN TRANSITION

Like the national capital, Edmonton has felt the impact of changing public sector employment. Significant cutbacks in public service employment resulted from the Klein government's massive restructuring of the Alberta government, beginning in the early 1990s. These have hit the local economy hard. Edmonton has also experienced the ups and downs of a city-region with heavy reliance on the petrochemical sector. Edmonton's fortunes are somewhat more tied to oil and gas activities occurring within Canada than are Calgary's. Edmonton has traditionally been a supply and distribution centre for oil and gas exploration and development, a role that is tied to action in the field. Calgary, in contrast, is home to more head office and scientific/technical support functions in the oil and gas sector. These knowledge-based activities can be temporarily transported to sites around the world while Calgary remains home base.

This situation has not induced a particularly aggressive approach to economic development by Edmonton's municipal governments however. There are a number of possible reasons for this. One factor may be the lingering inter-municipal suspicion within the region after the Edmonton annexation fight, discussed in Chapter Eight. Another may be the significant political fragmentation on the City of Edmonton Council in the early to mid-1990s and the city's tendency to rail against its declining fortunes, rather than getting on with it. Another possible reason for relatively weak city government involvement is that other actors within the region are carrying the ball. The connection between the University of Alberta and the local business community is particularly strong and is seen as important to securing the region's future (*The Globe and Mail*, Report on Business, August, 1995).

There has been some city government action. For example, the city constructed a major convention centre in the 1980s and reconstructed its city hall in the early 1990s as part of an effort to restore a devastated downtown. As in the case of other city-regions, air links and airports have been a major local issue. A referendum to close Edmonton's municipal airport was hotly contested during the city's 1995 municipal election. Advocates of closure argued that the 25 km-plus distance between the municipal airport, which serviced commuter traffic and the North, and Edmonton International Airport constituted an inconvenience to travellers and made Edmonton less attractive as a place to locate. This argument carried the day. The 1995 election also resulted in some changes in the composition of council and election of a new mayor. In the aftermath, the city's emphasis seems to be on marketing.

CALGARY: NO PROBLEMS, JUST CHALLENGES

Calgary has one of the most dynamic economies among Canada's city-regions. It is a knowledge-based centre in the petrochemical sector. It is increasingly a preferred head office location, now second only to Toronto. It has the easiest domestic and international air access of any city between Toronto and Vancouver. When people arrive to live, do business, or holiday, they find a city that functions efficiently and offers an attractive quality of life. The value of efficiency and the value of the marketplace are embedded in the operation of Calgary's city government.

As in the case of Edmonton, Calgary's government is less overtly involved in economic development than some others. Calgary does, however, have a discernable economic development strategy. There are four main elements to Calgary's approach. First, the city sees its role as making Calgary as attractive as well run. This includes a heavy emphasis on a pay-as-you-go approach and other manifestations of fiscal probity.

The second element is to tailor the shape of the city to include features that will attract relocating firms and their employees. In the past, this has included strong emphasis on developments favouring single family homes and large lot sizes. While Calgary is spread out, its system of expressways and ring roads ties it together. This makes it a functional city in the same mode as places in the U.S. Sunbelt and Rocky Mountain states. While it has a Light Rapid Transit system, Calgary is a city for the automobile.

The third element of Calgary's strategy is to get its name on the international map by hosting major international events. The 1988 Winter Olympics are an obvious case in point. At the time of writing, Calgary was also bidding to be the site of a World Fair shortly after the millennium. This bid has the blessing and financial guarantee of the Alberta government. However, consistent with the prevailing ethos in Calgary and Alberta more generally, no long-term debt is intended to result from this event.

The final element of the City of Calgary's economic development strategy is to engage in co-production with the local business sector to promote the city and attract new capital investment. This is the mandate of the Calgary

Economic Development Authority. The major share of the authority's $1.8 million budget comes from Calgary's city government. However, the authority has been established as a separate entity, with its own Board of Governors and staff. Calgary's Economic Development Department was eliminated when the authority was created. All of these initiatives are intended to support market-driven prosperity for existing Calgary enterprises and to complement the other attributes that might make Calgary a good place for relocation.

VANCOUVER: FROM BASTION OF THE EMPIRE TO INTERNATIONAL CITY

As the discussions in earlier chapters have indicated, the Vancouver region has undergone significant growth in the post-World War II period. Once a railway terminus with a dominant Anglo-Saxon population, it now is an internationally-focussed city-region with a very diverse population, including an important Asian entrepreneurial and professional class. As discussed in Chapter Eight, Vancouver is also increasingly linked to the U.S. Pacific Northwest and California.

From an urban government perspective, there are two interesting, if somewhat contradictory, trends in the management of economic development issues in the Vancouver region. The first is the 1995 decision by Vancouver City Council to eliminate the city's economic development department. The City of Vancouver has been characterized as having an increasingly strategic approach to economic development (Smith, 1997). Cornerstones of its approach were a twinning with other cities and developing international market opportunities through trade missions led by the mayor. Like Toronto, Vancouver also has emphasized its potential as "Hollywood North." While much of Canada was coping with a prolonged recession, Vancouver sustained relatively high investment and economic growth into the mid-1990s. The extent to which this success can be linked to the Vancouver government's efforts is unknown. Regardless, the city council of the day decided that the local economy was performing so well that a dedicated economic development function was no longer needed. This decision accompanied the broader review of the city's corporate structure discussed in Chapter Seven.

The second trend emerges when we look at the city-region as a whole. In the Greater Vancouver Regional District, a somewhat broader perspective concerning economic development issues has evolved. The City of Vancouver, as a member of the GVRD, has been part of this broader process at the same time as it has wound down its own activities. Economic development issues have been very much at the heart of development of the GVRD Regional Strategic Plan. In public and political deliberations, these were linked with basic questions about quality of life in the region. This process was discussed in Chapter Eight. The "hands across the border" collaboration on transportation links and similar initiatives, associated with the Cascadia initiative, are also important from an economic development perspective. From a public policy perspective, the emphasis in both instances is on local governments creating the infrastructure to support economic development and working together to reduce impediments to the creation of a strong regional economy.

In another development, Vancouver provides an important example of local initiative related to the development of airports as a central platform for economic development. The Vancouver Airport Authority was one of the first local airport authorities in Canada to take over responsibility for a major airport from the federal government. It immediately embarked on a major program of capital improvements to the facility. These improvements are being financed by an airport passenger fee paid by individuals prior to flight departure. As these improvements are completed, the Vancouver International Airport will not only become an efficient major air hub, it will also have distinctive aesthetic characteristics, befitting its place as Canada's gateway to the Asian–Pacific region.

CONCLUSION

Our trip across the metropolitan areas of Canada reveals relatively few instances in which the governments of city-regions have emerged as the dominant leader in developing a strategy for local economic development. Perhaps the City of Winnipeg and the Greater Vancouver Regional District come closest to this mark.

There are at least three reasons why urban government's role has tended to be more like that of a cheerleader or a team player than a captain of the economic development team. First, there may be antipathy among other sectors of the community, and the public more generally, toward local government playing this role. The idea of an activist local state is not universally acclaimed. In the eyes of some, the role of municipal government should be limited to the provision of basic urban services.

Second, the public policy stance of other levels of government has a great effect on the scope for activism at the local level. For example, the governments of Quebec and Ontario effectively dominate the public policy agenda for local economic development in Montreal and Toronto. The massive re-alignment of provincial and municipal responsibilities undertaken by the Conservative government in Ontario in early 1997 appeared to have little regard for the economic prospects of the province's major cities. In Quebec, the sovereignist government plays a fine balance and is reluctant to make structural reform in the Montreal region. It balances assisting cosmopolitan Montreal as the economic capital and Quebec City as the political and national capital. The governments of Nova Scotia and Manitoba are particularly preoccupied with the economic fortunes of their capital cities. In both of these cases, structural reforms have been undertaken, in part, to enhance urban governments' capacity to deal with economic challenges.

Finally, there are significant limitations to urban government's role in the crucial realm of improving human capital. Overcoming these limitations is a major concern for local governments concerned with economic development.

In this context, we find urban governments tending to focus their economic development efforts by using the vehicles of co-production and other forms of partnership. The local economic development authorities, found in many of our city-regions, are prominent examples of this approach. Responsibility for marketing and other local economic development interventions is vested in an independent authority, headed by a board with representation from the business sector and local council. City governments, however, generally provide the lion's share of the budget of these authorities.

Authorities such as the Greater Halifax Economic Development Partnership, the Ottawa-Carleton Economic Development Organization, and the Calgary Economic Development Authority may have a useful role. The historical role of organizations such as these in marketing seems to be receiving continuing emphasis, despite the fact that there is no research evidence indicating that the marketing side of local economic development is effective (Ernst and Young, 1993). Local economic development commissions find themselves marketing, in an increasingly sophisticated manner, simply because other cities are doing so. From the perspective of urban policy, however, we have to ask whether this is sufficient. As we now know, the urban economic development issues that Canadian city-regions face are complex. They are also entangled with issues in the social and environmental fields.

It has become customary to think of the economic development initiatives by other levels of government in Canada in terms of a team effort. Think, for example, of the Team Canada trade missions, led by the prime minister. In his speech to open the October 1996 summit of business, labour, and government people on the economic prosperity of Quebec, the premier also invoked this team image. If we think in terms of this image, how might it relate to urban governments' role vis-à-vis economic development within their metropolitan areas? While city governments do not have the power to control the moves of all of the players in the interconnected economic, social, and environmental fields, could they take on a role analogous to that of the trainer for a team? A trainer helps individual players achieve peak competitive condition. This is sometimes done by coaching, sometimes by more direct assistance. Ultimately, however, each player is responsible for his or her own conditioning. A trainer also cheers his or her team on during games. Finally, a trainer takes to the field when required. At these times, the trainer helps any player in distress. Equally important, however, is assuring players that the team will remain a power to be reckoned with. Good coaches do this as well. Sometimes, however, players think that their coaches have become too directive and manipulative. Revolution ensues and either the coach or some team members leave. Trainers, on the other hand, tend to have long and excellent relationships with their teams. Good trainers contribute strongly to winning results.

NOTES

1. Andrew Sancton has been critical of this rationale, arguing that there is nothing wrong with inter-municipal competition related to industrial land prices within the same region. Price competition makes the region more attractive, in his view (Sancton, 1994, pp. 48–52). For their part, local business elites, in Halifax and elsewhere, tend to be particularly opposed to inter-municipal competition. They see it as a symbol of local fragmentation.

SUGGESTED READINGS

Coffey, William. (1994). *The Evolution of Canada's Metropolitan Economies.* Montreal: Institute for Research on Public Policy. An examination of the impact of changes in the global economy on Canada's major urban areas.

Ernst and Young. (1993). "The Impact of Taxes on Business Location." In *Business Taxation in Ontario*, edited by Allan M. Maslove. Toronto: University of Toronto Press, pp. 171–221. An examination of factors influencing business decisions regarding location.

Ohmae, Kenichi. (1995). *The End of the Nation State.* New York: The Free Press. An examination of the use of "region states" — transnational economic zones.

Rifkin, Jeremy. (1995). *The End of Work.* New York: Tarcher Putnam. An analysis and set of proposals for dealing with what the author describes as the permanent decline in traditional employment.

Sancton, Andrew. (1994). *Governing Canada's City-Regions.* Montreal: Institute for Research on Public Policy. An examination of the impact of different structures of urban government in Canada on economic development.

BIBLIOGRAPHY

Ernst and Young. (1993). "The Impact of Taxes on a Business Location." In *Business Taxation in Ontario*, edited by Allan M. Maslove. Toronto: University of Toronto Press, pp. 171–221.

Fielding, Gerry and Jeff Couture. (1997). "Economic Development: The Public's Role in Shaping Winnipeg's Future." In *Citizen Engagement: Lessons from Local Government*, edited by Katherine Graham and Susan Phillips. Toronto: Institute of Public Administration of Canada.

Gertler, Meric S. (1996). "City-Region in the Global Economy: Choices Facing Toronto." *Policy Options* 17(1): 12–15.

Graham, Katherine. (1992). "Capital Planning/Capital Budgeting: The Future of Canada's Capital." In *How Ottawa Spends 1992–93: The Politics of Competitiveness*, edited by Frances Abele. Ottawa: Carleton University Press, pp. 125–50.

Greater Toronto Area Task Force. (1996). *Report of the Greater Toronto Area Task Force.* Toronto: Queen's Printer for Onatrio.

Lambooy, Jan G. and Frank Moulaert. (1996). "The Economic Organization of Cities: An Institutional Perspective." *International Journal of Urban and Regional Research* 20: 217–37.

Latouche, Daniel. (1996). "La ville-region a-t-elle un avenir?" *Policy Options* 17: 34–37.

Lithwick, Harvey. (1988). *Economic Development in Ottawa-Carleton.* Ottawa: Ottawa-Carleton Regional Review.

Mayer, Margit. (1991). "Politics in the Post-Fordist City." *Socialist Review* 21: 105–24.

Meyer, P.B. (1991). "Local Economic Development: What Is Proposed, What Is Done, and What Difference Does It Make?" *Policy Studies Review* 10:172–80.

Miranda, Rowan and Donald Rosdil. (1995). "From Boosterism to Qualitative Growth: Classifying Economic Development Strategies." *Urban Affairs Review* 30: 868–79.

Polese, Mario. (1996). "Montreal: A City in Search of a Country." *Policy Options* 17: 31–34.

Precourt, Geoffrey and Anne Faircloth. (1996). "Best Cities: Where the Living Is Easy." *Fortune*, November 11, pp. 130–49.

Regional Municipality of Ottawa-Carleton Economic Development Task Force. (1992). *Partners for the Future*. Ottawa.

Rifkin, Jeremy. (1995). *The End of Work*. New York: Tarcher Putnam.

Sancton, Andrew. (1994). *Governing Canada's City-Regions*. Montreal: Institute for Research on Public Policy.

Smith, Patrick J. (1997). "More than One Way to Do Economic Development." In *Citizen Engagement: Lessons from Local Government*, edited by Katherine A. Graham and Susan D. Phillips. Toronto: Institute of Public Administration of Canada.

Walmsley, Ann. (1995). "Edmonton: An Itch for Innovation." *The Globe and Mail*. Report on Business Magazine, August. Toronto, pp. 57–59.

CHAPTER ELEVEN

◆

CREATING SUSTAINABLE AND LIVABLE CITIES

INTRODUCTION

In 1996, *Fortune* magazine named Toronto the top city internationally in which to balance work and a high quality, affordable, and safe life (Precourt and Faircloth, 1996). Just a year earlier, a Swiss consulting company had ranked four Canadian cities — Vancouver, Toronto, Montreal, and Calgary — in the world's top twelve as best places to live (*The Globe and Mail*, 1995, p. A9). While these Canadian cities were basking in the international limelight, however, other headlines told different stories about Canadian cities. In the spring of 1996, a group of homeless youth who had been evicted from their squats by police camped out in front of Toronto's city hall to draw attention to the need for housing for street youth (Infantry, Mahoney, and Rankin, 1996, p. A7). Earlier in the year, during a ten-day period in January, three people had frozen to death on the streets of Edmonton, and similar deaths were reported in other Canadian cities (Laghi, 1996, p. A4). Public incidents of racially-motivated gang violence occurred in Halifax and Ottawa. A study prepared for the federal Department of Justice estimated that only one in ten hate crimes against racial, religious, and gay/lesbian minorities is actually reported (Bronskill, 1996, p. A3).

These news stories reinforce the point made in Chapter Ten that a city's greatest asset and tool for economic development is its quality of life. They also remind us that while Canadian cities offer high standards of living, comparatively safe and clean environments, urban infrastructure that works, and relatively good social services, not all residents partake of this quality of life in equal measure. There are underlying and mounting social pressures. These arise from growing cultural diversity, cutbacks in programs resulting from financial restraint by provincial and federal governments, and difficulties in balancing livable environments with urban growth. How can our cities continue to sustain a high quality of life under the pressures of globalization and fiscal restraint that characterize the late 1990s?

If we were writing this chapter ten years ago, the answers — or at least the place to look for the answers — to this question would have seemed relatively straightforward. Quality of life was then seen to be primarily associated with the maintenance of "hard" services (e.g., roads, sewers, transit, and parks), good neighbourhoods, and the appropriate ordering among incompatible land uses. The specific solutions were to be formulated by land-use planning departments which, since the 1960s, have been the hub of activity in urban governments. Obviously, the maintenance of quality infrastructure remains a priority, and land-use planning is still an important function of city governments. However, only four of the eight major cities still operate planning departments in a traditional sense. During its reorganization in 1995, for example, Winnipeg incorporated planning into a more encompassing department called Community Services. In a major rejigging of Montreal's administration in 1996, the planning department was slated to be privatized. These organizational reconfigurations partly reflect the limits of traditional land-use planning for addressing contemporary urban issues. They reveal the shift in discourse from the emphasis on order and technical rationality which underpinned traditional land-use planning to a focus on sustainability and diversity. In attempting to grapple with the issues of sustainable development and social harmony, urban governments are redefining both the nature of their business and how they do it. Questions as to which regional structures are appropriate to implement the principles of sustainability are also being hotly debated, as noted in the discussion in Chapter Four about restructuring the GTA. This new emphasis on managing the natural, built, and social environments of cities also goes to the heart of debates over provincial–municipal disentanglement, as introduced in Chapter Eight. This is because the provinces are heavily involved both in overseeing planning and environmental protection and in the funding and provision of social services.

This chapter focuses on two critical dimensions of maintaining quality of life in metropolitan areas. First, it examines issues surrounding sustainable development and land-use planning as key policy tools for development. Second, it addresses how issues of diversity are critical to creating livable communities and explores some of the responses by major cities to diversity. Both of these lead us to consider the fabric of our cities as reflected in their populations' everyday life, the nature of their built environments, and cultural life. As this chapter proceeds, it provides a road map to the issues and institutions central to the challenges of livability and sustainability. It highlights the implications and challenges of current trends at the local level and in the intergovernmental arena. The chapter also demonstrates the link between the reform and restructuring of urban governments with issues of sustainability, livability, and economic development. In doing so, it provides a conclusion to this volume.

TOWARD SUSTAINABLE CITIES
The Sprawling Problem
The quest for new principles and governing structures for urban development must be understood in the context of the continual, sometimes booming, growth that has occurred in Canada's metropolitan areas in the post-war period. As noted in Chapter One, the eight CMAs increased in population an average of 10 percent between 1986 and 1991. Sheer growth created a number of environmental concerns. These include pressures on the capacity of city regions to maintain an adequate water supply as well as dispose of sewage and toxic and solid waste. The amount of residential, commercial, and industrial garbage produced in metro areas is staggering. In 1995, for instance, the GTA produced

4.5 million tonnes of solid waste (McAndrew, 1995, p. B7). The difficulties of finding large, geologically suitable sites for regional landfills and dealing with the opposition from communities near the proposed sites have made the creation of new landfills a particularly prickly issue for many cities (Price, 1990, p. 131). The dilemma concerning how to dispose of Toronto's garbage illustrates this.

It is not only growth itself but the specific form that growth has taken which has magnified the negative environmental impacts of development. As discussed in Chapter Four, in spite of some examples of nodal development in Toronto, Montreal, and Vancouver, expansion has generally followed a low density spread model. This is exemplified by the fact that in the GTA, over 80 percent of the region's overall growth in recent years (1986–1991) has taken place in the four regions surrounding Metro. Almost all of this has been low density in nature (Filion, 1996, p. 1644). Suburban development has occurred in Canadian cities not merely as a result of market forces. Rather it was actively encouraged by the policies of urban governments from the 1950s through 1970s as a means of reducing densities in the core which were believed to be detrimental to people's well-being (Filion, 1995, p. 17). This suburban development was to be fostered by means of ambitious expressway projects that would alleviate the congestion created by suburbanites increasingly reliant on their cars. Provincial governments tacitly supported urban sprawl. While they occasionally intervened to mediate in conflicts between suburban development and protection of agricultural or environmentally sensitive lands, their policy stance was generally pro-development. They were also more directly and actively involved through subsidizing the costs of new roads, and sewer and water lines (Frisken, 1993, pp. 171–77). The federal government, through the Canada Mortgage and Housing Corporation (CMHC), has also been an active agent in encouraging the construction and purchase of owner-occupied single family detached houses. The CMHC, created after World War II to implement the National Housing Act, offers mortgage insurance money to assist in home ownership as well as assistance to social housing and developers in amassing land banks to ensure adequate supply for housing development (Carroll, 1990).

As time passed, low density development generated a set of negative consequences for the environment. The heavy dependence on the automobile has significantly worsened air quality, producing considerable health consequences, and is a contributing factor in climate change. A study by Pollution Probe suggests that periods of heavy air pollution in Toronto alone cause an additional 200 to 400 deaths a year due to heart and respiratory problems (Cameron, 1996, p. 1). Reliance on the automobile became self-perpetuating because sprawl reduced the economic viability of public transit. Although transit ridership made steady gains from the mid 1960s to the 1980s, it has declined significantly in recent years (Filion, 1996, p. 1645; Frisken, 1996, p. 23). This downward trend has been accelerated by the cuts imposed in the 1990s, which have resulted in higher transit fares and deteriorating service in many cities. In some metropolitan areas, these developments have contributed to stresses on the collective bargaining relationship between the municipality (through its transit

---

BOX 11.1 DEALING WITH METRO'S GARBAGE

In Metropolitan Toronto, the inability to find an environmentally acceptable means of disposal has been very costly and politically explosive. In
the early 1990s, Metro developed a scheme to send its garbage 1000 km
by rail to an abandoned mine site near Kirkland Lake. This scheme was,
however, quashed by the provincial government, at least partly on the
grounds that Metro was exporting its problem, thereby endangering the
ecosystem around Kirkland Lake and points on the transportation route
in between. Ironically, the temporary solution seems to be to truck
Metro's garbage down the Highway 401 corridor, through Windsor, to
Michigan. A substantial part of it will then be incinerated; the resulting
emissions will then drift back north. Technology, economics, and politics
seem to interact to form mutant solutions in the case of urban solid waste
management.

---

commission) and unionized drivers and mechanics. Where service disruption
has resulted, ridership has been further eroded as people become attached to
economical and reliable alternatives to public transit, such as carpools, bicycles,
and rollerblades.[1]

In addition, sprawl has generated major conflicts between agricultural production and urbanization. This has been felt most acutely in the Niagara fruit
belt and the Fraser Valley. The real crisis in cities' ability to sustain the sprawl
came with the fiscal pressures of the 1990s. Low density development in new
areas requires heavy upfront investment in infrastructure — roads and utilities
as well as new schools and parks. The question of how costs should be borne
and distributed within city-regions has produced sharp rifts between the centre
with its established, but often deteriorating, infrastructure and the developing
periphery. Over time, each has become less willing to subsidize the other. This
centre–periphery conflict has been further frustrated in many cases, rather than
ameliorated, by governing structures.

The Traditional Planning Framework

THE INSTITUTIONAL FRAMEWORKS FOR PLANNING

Urban development and its attendant conflicts have been managed by regional
land-use planning. The Canadian system of planning can be characterized as
being: 1) institutionalized, 2) operated within a provincial framework that both
mitigates and magnifies provincial–local tensions, and 3) comprehensive or
regional in scope. Local land-use planning was first initiated in Canada in 1909
by the federal government when it established the Commission of Conservation
of Natural Resources to advise on matters concerning natural and human
resources. The commission's staff imported ideas from both the British conservation movement (which stressed state involvement and legislative frame-

works) and the American reform movement (which emphasized order through zoning and apolitical processes).

These hybrid beginnings have evolved into a process that is seemingly schizophrenic at times. Planning was not conceived to challenge the fundamentals of the economic and property systems. Efficiency was to be the central concern, the means were to be scientific, and urban aesthetics were deemed not to lie within the domain of planning (Kiernan, 1990, pp. 59–60; Perks and Jamieson, 1991, p. 495). At the same time, planning was clearly intended to improve social, economic, and physical living conditions. Moreover, governments were seen to have the right and, indeed, the responsibility to intervene in devising appropriate solutions (Perks and Jamieson, 1991, p. 495). Thus, from its very introduction into Canada, the ideology of planning was premised on a framework that required planning to be both *compulsory*, with plans drawn up by municipalities, and *comprehensive*, covering the whole of the functional city-region.

Despite some planning on a modest scale by various cities, such as Vancouver in the 1930s and Halifax after the explosion, the ideas of the commission were not fully implemented until the post-war boom when pressures for new, affordable housing became intense. CMHC assumed a strategic role in mandating community planning. This was levered by its funding role (Perks and Jamieson, 1991, p. 499). As a condition for mortgage insurance, CMHC required that proposed houses be part of a city plan which propelled cities to undertake the task of preparing comprehensive master plans and developing zoning measures. While this was initially contracted out to private consultants, during the course of the late 1950s, cities developed their own full-time planning units. By the mid-1960s, a system of public planning was fully institutionalized and professionalized (Perks and Jamieson, 1991, pp. 499–500).

While urban planning became a central activity for municipalities, this occurred very much within the framework of provincial–municipal relations. Provincial governments have never devolved complete authority for planning to the local level. Local planning is set within a framework as laid out in provincial planning acts (or in the case of Alberta, in the new MGA), which are administered by departments of municipal affairs. Provincial planning legislation across Canada:

- sets out the nature of the planning powers delegated to regional and municipal governments;
- establishes the responsibility of local governments to produce official plans;
- creates procedures for public consultation;
- sets out the terms and procedures for appeal of planning decisions either to the provincial cabinet or to an administrative tribunal, such as the Ontario Municipal Board (OMB) or the Alberta Municipal Government Board; and
- lays out matters of provincial interests to be protected.

In the case of the last point, "matters of provincial interest" are crucial, even in the case of more laissez-faire legislation as now exists in Alberta and Ontario. They may include, for example, environmental and resource protection and social, economic, and fiscal well-being. They justify the province's intervention in municipal planning through unilateral action to overturn a local planning decision. They also constitute possible bases for appeal of local decisions to the province.

The trend to broader definition of matters of provincial interest, as illustrated by the Alberta Municipal Government Act, has generally been praised by municipalities and other commentators. There are, however, some caveats. Rather than clarifying planning, the definitions of provincial interest are so broad and generally worded that they permit provinces wide latitude for intervention (Frisken, 1993, p. 178). Planning acts are usually accompanied by ad hoc policy statements emanating from various provincial ministries that set out further guidelines on some issues. In Ontario, for instance, guidelines have been developed for flood plain planning, mineral aggregates, wetlands, land-use policy near airports, and heritage conservation (Commission on Planning and Development Reform in Ontario, 1993, pp. 10–13). The result is an ongoing tension, and sometimes overt political conflict, between municipalities' autonomy and the often compelling need for provinces to protect broader interests. But as Kiernan notes, "regardless of the relative merits of the municipal and provincial arguments, at the end of the day the bald legal and political reality remains that the provincial government almost invariably has the final say" (Kiernan, 1990, p. 67).

Provincial action on local planning issues has not always reflected the broader public interest. For example, in 1983, British Columbia's Social Credit government cancelled the existing regional plans and revoked the planning authority of regional districts in a dispute over protection of agricultural land in Surrey. The province wished to see this land developed for housing. This was opposed by the GVRD (Oberlander and Smith, 1993, p. 363). The rationale given by the Minister of Municipal Affairs was that because a number of municipal plans were in place, regional planning had become "an unnecessary level of land-use control" (quoted in Oberlander and Smith, 1993, p. 363). The regional planning function was not restored to the GVRD until 1995, although in the interim the region had managed to develop a regional plan through a more consensual process (Smith, 1996, p. 8).

PLANNING PROCESSES IN MAJOR CITIES

Planning in Canada's major cities is now regionalized to a significant degree. Where they exist, upper-tier governments have a planning responsibility. The single-tier governments of Calgary, Winnipeg, and Halifax carry out planning for their city-region. The first step in the planning process is for the regional government/city to develop an official regional plan that sets out a "development concept" based on forecasts of growth and analyses of issues and policy directions. This is a general physical design for the region, laying out locations for future growth, major new infrastructure, protected green space, transportation systems, and major planned private sector development (Smith, 1995, p. 221). Within this framework, the lower-tier municipalities, where they exist, develop their own official and functional plans that fill in detail and set out local priorities, although the division between regional and local matters is never neatly separated. In both one- and two-tier arrangements, there is generally provision for community and public involvement in the preparation of official plans. In some cases, this is mandatory, as a result of provincial planning legislation; in others, the approach taken to public engagement may be a matter of local policy. As discussed in Chapter Six, the origins of broader public engagement with local governments in Canada often lay in planning.

The primary policy tools used to implement official plans are zoning (or designation), subdivision development controls, and **development permits**. By defining permitted uses for particular parcels of land in fine detail for delimited land-use districts, zoning attempts to separate uses deemed incompatible with each other, such as industrial development in residential areas or high-rise apartment buildings in neighbourhoods of single-family detached houses. The underlying principle derives from the common law concept of nuisance which, while recognizing the rights of private ownership, establishes that such rights are not absolute. Ownership does not allow property to be used in ways that are harmful or create a nuisance for other owners, thereby detracting from their opportunity to enjoy the benefits of their own property (Smith, 1995, p. 222). Zoning by-laws thus set out the ground rules concerning what kind of development can occur where, as well as the height, coverage, and density of such development. Any proposed use that is not congruent with existing zoning must receive approval by council for a rezoning of the site. Generally speaking, this gives potentially affected residents an opportunity to oppose redesignation at a public hearing and allows opportunities for appeal.

Subdivision control is the process by which the legal division of lots into smaller parcels is managed. In general, applicants seeking permission to develop a subdivision must submit a detailed land-use plan and a proposal for servicing arrangements to council.

Applications for development of any new building or land or change in use of existing buildings and land are made to the municipality's planning department via a procedure called a development permit. In routine matters, the planning department can exercise minimal discretion. If the proposed project conforms with the existing zoning by-laws, a permit must be issued and cannot be appealed; if it does not conform, a permit must be refused. If the proposed development requires an amendment to existing zoning, the decision involves greater discretion and is open to challenge. In such cases, the application is posted, reviewed by the planning department, and specifics negotiated with the developer. It is also circulated to community associations and, after a public hearing, must be approved or rejected by municipal and/or regional council. There is then the possibility for appeal by affected parties or the province if the decision trammels on provincial interests. In controversial cases, such as the proposal to build a major sports complex in the rural part of Ottawa-Carleton, this process can become very lengthy and costly for all parties.

THE STRENGTHENING CRITIQUE OF PLANNING

While much of what planning departments do is routine approval, a considerable amount involves negotiation and working out compromises. Professional planners employed by municipalities carry out this diplomatic role with their professional counterparts who work for developers. Their relationship may be quite long term, sometimes extending back to shared experience in planning school. As Perks and Jamieson note, "planning and property development [are] interlocking institutions and professional practices" (Perks and Jamieson, 1991, p. 488). Not surprisingly, this situation has generated enormous criticism of urban planning and, on occasion, the planners in city planning departments. The essence of this criticism is that city planners are too close to and sometimes even co-opted by the interests of development. Critics argue that the ability of planners to control urban development is further eroded by the tendency for their plans to be overruled by the even more development-minded technocrats, mainly engineers, who control the actual design of hard services within the civic administration (Rabinovitz, 1969).

In assessing this critique of planning, however, it is important to remember that politicians, not planners, ultimately make planning and development decisions. In doing so, politicians are often pressured by developers with significant land holdings on the urban fringe, who argue that development is needed to accommodate urban growth and ensure local prosperity. This argument has typically convinced municipal politicians and has been bolstered by their desire for increasing the local tax base. In short, municipal politicians have traditionally thought that the benefits of further development would outweigh the costs. There are also cases in which city planners have tried to counter this inclination. Perhaps the most notable recent case is in the development of the Corel Centre. RMOC planning staff objected to the proposed development. As professional planners, they could not be compelled by their employer to argue the contrary view in a legal forum. As a result, the RMOC council had to hire consulting planners to present their pro-development case to the Ontario Municipal Board.

In addition to concerns of co-optation, both within and external to city hall, two other criticisms of the planning process have been consistently levelled against it. The first challenges the ideology of technical rationality that underpins the profession. Jane Jacobs, one of the most eloquent and sustained critics of urban planning, took aim at the planning profession in her 1961 book, *The Death and Life of Great American Cities*. She argues that the danger of planning is that it attempts to impose order on cities that by their inherent nature are exercises in "organized complexity." In her view, their diversity is to be cultivated rather than contained. The proper role of planners is to work with communities to encourage sites and spaces of mixed use, social interaction, and community control (see also Rybczynski, 1995). Citizen protests beginning in the late 1960s against expressways and other mega-projects that were planned without consultation with affected neighbourhoods further undermined confidence in the ability of planning to use scientific principles to fix urban problems.

In response to both a growing lack of public trust and changing ideologies within the profession, the role of planner has evolved significantly over the past two decades from that of technician and judge to community delegate and even advocate (Davidoff, 1965; Ashton, Rowe, and Simpson, 1994; Healey, 1991). Planning practices have shifted from deciding what is best for communities to working with them in joint exercises of community development. In the 1990s, urban planners increasingly are less preoccupied with urban design than with economic development. This new reality has prompted several cities to absorb their planning departments into broader functions, or to merge the engineering aspect of planning into departments of physical services and the community side into departments of community services.

A second criticism is that the planning process is remarkably slow. Consequently, it may take several years to produce an official plan, if it is produced at all. By 1994, only two of the four fast-growing regional municipalities surrounding Metropolitan Toronto (i.e., Durham and Halton) had developed official plans at all (Frisken, 1993, p. 187). Once plans are in the public view, they often get hung up in lengthy appeals and in negotiations with developers. These frequently end up with compromises that please few people.

There are also problems in linking regional planning efficiently and effectively with the environmental agenda. In most provinces, there are separate legislative regimes and regulatory processes governing planning and **environmental (impact) assessment**. When environmental assessment and protection legislation was introduced by provincial governments in the 1970s, it evolved as a parallel track rather than being integrated and closely linked with the planning regimes enacted 30 years earlier. Environmental assessment remains under direct provincial control (although many cities have also begun to initiate their own assessment processes). The problem is that provincial environmental assessments, generally overseen by provincial departments of the environment, cover much of the same ground and kinds of projects governed by planning acts. On the environmental assessment side, provincial processes are front-line; on the planning side, provincial legislation assigns the front-line role to municipalities.

In Ontario, for example, there has been a seemingly neat separation that the environmental assessment legislation applies to provincial and municipal activities. It does not, however, cover undertakings on private land which is under the purview of the Planning Act. But the distinction is not so simple in practice (Richardson, 1994). For instance, if a new development approved by a municipality involves public works, these public works would still need to pass through the provincial environmental assessment process. The result has been considerable duplication, delay, and expense as projects end up being reviewed by two separate ministries and subjected to two different appeal processes. This compartmentalization of legislative regimes has tended to inhibit serious consideration of environmental protection in municipal planning.

In 1993, the Ontario government of the day established the Commission on Planning and Development Reform (commonly called the Sewell Commission) to make recommendations for improving provincial land-use planning legislation. Simultaneously, an internal provincial review examined the environmental assessment side. The Sewell Commission forged a remarkable consensus among a wide range of stakeholders about the need to streamline the planning process and, at the same time, tighten the connection between land-use and environmental planning. While still in power, the Rae government introduced new planning legislation (Bill 163). It established mechanisms to foster closer consideration by municipalities of provincial interest. It also required municipalities to protect significant natural features and agricultural areas from development. This legislation was rewritten only a year later by the Harris government in the name of enhanced municipal autonomy over planning and development.

By the early 1990s, it was evident that although regional planning in Canada had produced much more ordered growth than had occurred in many American cities (Rothblatt, 1994), it had not adequately contained urban sprawl nor facilitated more environmentally sustainable development. This has been exacerbated by the inadequacies of regional government and provincial legislative frameworks. Growth has rendered the existing boundaries of many regional governments or municipalities obsolete as an effective basis for planning the city region. Political fragmentation within urban areas has created competition for development and its control between the outlying areas and the core. In Edmonton, for example, the development of country residences, which has been promoted by adjacent counties, is seen by the city as a significant impediment to channelling and directing growth and controlling costs in future years. Frisken (1993, p. 187) observes that within Metro Toronto, the reluctance of local municipalities to permit Metro to decide how they were to be developed has been a paramount constraint on effective regional planning. Co-ordination among the five regional governments of the GTA has made the establishment of a coherent vision for the entire city region even more problematic. This desire for more encompassing forms of regional governance formed the basis of the Golden Report's recommendation for a super regional body for planning and co-ordination purposes, albeit not a consolidated government.

Policies for Sustainable Development

AT THE LOCAL LEVEL

If concerns over deteriorating environmental quality did not propel cities to begin to rethink the principles of planning and development in the late 1980s, then the escalating costs of servicing low density urban sprawl did. **Sustainable development** has become the dominant discourse of urban planning in the 1990s. Borrowing from the Bruntland Commission on the Environment and Development, sustainable development can be defined as development that "meets the needs of the present without compromising the ability of future generations to meet their own needs" (World Commission on Environment and Development, 1987, p. 43). As used in the context of urban planning, sustainable development does not refer simply to environmental sustainability but is based on a triangular model, involving three sets of interlocking principles: economic (or fiscal), equity (or social), and environmental sustainability (Campbell, 1996, pp. 297–98). A quick review of the recent official plans of the major cities would reveal a strong congruency in how these principles should be translated into urban planning and development practices. Invariably, as shown in Table 11.1, sustainability implies:

- a more compact urban form achieved through infilling and **reurbanization**;
- reduced reliance on cars and greater use of walking and cycling;
- an adequate supply and mix of housing;
- a broad range of employment activities;
- greater opportunities for cultural expression and social and leisure activities reflecting the interests of both residents and visitors;
- conservation and protection of natural systems; and
- programs to "achieve strong communities where diversity is valued and residents have equitable access to services and opportunities" (Metro Planning, 1995, p 4; see also Rees and Roseland, 1991).

The process of reurbanizing city cores involves more mixed uses than the planned homogeneity that traditional zoning has promoted. Rethinking of the goals of urban design is beginning to occur among planners and city councils (see Berridge Lewinberg Greenberg, Ltd., 1991). For example, in 1996, the City of Toronto liberalized zoning by-laws to spur redevelopment of former industrial sites. The intent was to encourage developers to find new non-polluting uses — such as stores and artists' lofts — for large tracts of obsolete and abandoned factory space in the downtown core. The Regional Municipality of Ottawa-Carleton took the first tentative steps to requiring more infilling in its 1996 official plan. It stipulated that 43 percent of the estimated 150 000 new housing units required over the next 25 years be built inside the green belt, that is, in established areas. In so doing, the RMOC expected to save $2.3 billion of the $4 billion it would otherwise have had to spend on new infrastructure to service the development in a low density form (Adam, 1996, p. A1).

Will Canadian cities be able to move in significant ways over the next generation to more sustainable forms and land use policies as prescribed in their own official plans? So far, their steps have been tentative, and the measures outlined above have been mere tinkering at the edges of real sustainable development. Several factors, as Filion (1996; 1995) notes, significantly reduce the likelihood that the major cities can fulfil their commitments to sustainability. First, the fiscal situation has a double-edged impact. While reduced fiscal capacity means that cities can no longer afford to subsidize sprawl on their periphery, reurbanization also requires considerable investment, particularly in improved transit. But the trends are in the opposite direction. With declining ridership in most cities and reduced provincial subsidies (Ontario has ended provincial subsidies entirely), cities are not making substantial new investments and transit fares are rising. This contributes to further decline in ridership. In addition, "brownlands" — former industrial land being recycled for new residential and commercial use — often require high site preparation, architectural, and building costs, especially related to cleaning contaminated soils. This often makes both urban governments and developers timid about brownland developments. For instance, a planned residential development of 14 000 units on former industrial land near downtown Toronto, called the Ataratiri project, was abandoned after the expenditure of $300 million. This was due, in part, to the rising costs of soil depollution; the site had become a financial, as well as an environmental, sink-hole (Filion, 1996, pp. 1648–49).

TABLE 11.1

SOME CHARACTERISTICS OF A MORE SUSTAINABLE COMMUNITY

	A Less Sustainable Community	A More Sustainable Community
Fiscal	•High development costs •High city infrastructure costs •High city maintenance costs •High city operating costs	Lower costs through: •more compact urban form •better utilization of services •less infrastructure
Social	•Little sense of community belonging or neighbourliness •Housing choice excludes certain household types and lifestyles •Design of public areas discourages walking and socializing •Few goods and services provided within community •Rigid separation of uses •Private vehicle essential	•Strong sense of belonging to a community; vibrant community life •Wide housing choice catering to many household types and lifestyles •Attractive public areas encourage walking and socializing •Most routine shopping needs met within community •Some mix of uses including employment •Need for private vehicle much reduced
Environmental	•Inefficient use of land •High level of air pollution through auto dependency •Community design promotes lifestyles where excessive water, energy, and resource consumption are largely unavoidable •No protection of environmentally sensitive areas	•More efficient use of land •Much reduced air pollution through reduced vehicle trips •Community design promotes lifestyles where consumption and waste can be reduced and conservation encouraged •Significant environmentally sensitive areas identified, protected, and integrated into the regional open-space system

Source: City of Calgary, *Sustainable Suburbs Study*, (Calgary: Planning and Building Department, 1995), p. 17. Reproduced with permission of the City of Calgary.

A second factor inhibiting reurbanization relates to the difficulty of changing consumer preferences. There remains a strong entrenched preference among home buyers for detached single-family homes with private yards, although this may begin to shift as the baby boomers retire (Foote, 1996, pp. 133–34). In addition, existing residents often oppose higher density development in their neighbourhoods.

A third factor is the vested interests of developers, who have an important influence on shaping market preferences and decisions of city councils. In most cities, developers have amassed large land holdings on the urban periphery in anticipation of the next major outward growth splurge and are prepared to take legal action should their plans be thwarted. The reaction of a major residential developer in the Ottawa-Carleton area to the RMOC's plan for infilling instead of continued outward expansion is typical. The director of development for Richcraft Homes, noting that homebuilders would push for their fair share of development outside the green belt, said, "The market will decide. One way or another, we will get what we need" (Adam, 1996, p. A1).

Finally, as already noted, regional governing structures of many metropolitan areas are ill-equipped to deal with the growing conflicts that come from intensification between the periphery and the urban core. The lively debates about restructuring — in Halifax, Toronto, Ottawa, and Montreal — have been focussed primarily on efficiency arguments (reducing the number of politicians and saving costs through economies of scale). What is even more critical to redesign than achieving operating cost savings is, or should be, creating the appropriate geographical basis for decision making.

PROVINCIAL FRAMEWORKS FOR SUSTAINABILITY

For their part, provincial governments are moving toward increasing municipal autonomy on planning and environmental issues, although their approach varies significantly from one province to the next. At the one extreme, British Columbia's provincial government has been quite proactive and has taken some very positive steps in establishing frameworks for growth management and sustainability. In 1996, British Columbia became the first province to introduce tough standards on automobile emissions, requiring cars sold in the province to meet the California vehicle low emission standards by 2001 (with less stringent standards to be met in the interim). This move prompted the federal government to announce its support for equivalent standards shortly thereafter (*Vancouver Sun*, 1996, p. B1). In addition, the 1995 Growth Strategies Act reestablished regional planning. In rapid growth areas (such as the GVRD), the region, in association with municipalities, must develop a regional plan that specifies a growth management strategy covering a minimum of 20 years. In the words of the Minister of Municipal Affairs, "communities cannot do it alone. Most of the problems associated with growth are regional in nature. They require regional solutions" (*Plan Canada*, 1995, p. 34). If local–regional agreement cannot be attained, mechanisms for provincial conflict resolution, including full arbitration, are established by the legislation. The strategy also lays out policy guidelines outlining the provincial goals to which planning must adhere. These include prohibition of development on certain lands, avoidance of urban sprawl, protection of environmentally sensitive areas, and minimization of the use of automobiles (Smith, 1996, p. 11).

Alberta and Ontario have gone quite different routes, introducing more hands-off provincial frameworks. In 1994, the Klein government of Alberta deregulated provincial requirements for regional planning when it repealed the Planning Act and incorporated some of its provisions into the Municipal Government Act. It also withdrew funding from the regional planning commissions. This was much to the approbation of tax-starved rural counties surrounding Calgary and Edmonton, which wanted even greater freedom to undertake commercial development in the urban fringe. The regional planning commissions had long suffered competition for representation between the city and the fringe areas, being structured from the beginning to favour rural over city representation (Thomas, 1993, p. 267).

The demise of the provincially mandated commissions has given rise to some innovative experiments in locally driven, co-operative planning. As discussed in Chapter Eight, the Capital Regional Forum (CRF) was created in the Edmonton region by the city and all but two of its surrounding eighteen municipalities and counties as a forum for discussion of regional issues. The forum is distinctive because it features voluntary participation, local funding by participating municipalities, no pre-specified decision making powers, and consensus decision rules. While it is still in its infancy, the CRF may emerge as a much more effective instrument for co-operation and dispute resolution than the long criticized and ill-fated regional planning commissions.

Since its election in 1995, the Conservative government of Ontario has taken the hands-off approach several steps further. The government's intent is to eliminate red tape, expedite the planning process, empower municipalities, and balance economic with environmental interests (Speech from the Throne, 1995, p. 11). The changes made have weakened the role of the "provincial interest" under the Planning Act, deregulated many controls over environmental protection, and limited citizen participation.

First, changes to the Planning Act give municipalities greater autonomy in planning by:

- removing the province's ability to prescribe the contents of an official plan;
- altering provincial policy guidelines (enacted as a result of the Sewell Commission only a year earlier) to allow municipalities to have "regard to" rather than the requirement to be "consistent with" provincial interests vis-à-vis agriculture, natural resources, etc. (The immediate response in Newmarket, a rapidly developing area north of Toronto, was to eliminate all farmland within its boundaries, converting it to residential or commercial categories.) (Sanders, 1996, p. A6);
- deleting provincial prohibitions on building on lands (such as wetlands and ravines) with significant natural, cultural, or heritage features;

- removing requirements for environmental impact assessment and deleting the need for provincial approval of new suburban communities;
- removing the right of home-owners to create apartments in their homes — a measure originally designed to promote "granny flats" and higher density development on an incremental basis. (Municipal approval is now required.);
- removing the requirement that municipalities consider social needs in planning new developments (as development charges are to be applied to "hard" services only), support social housing, or plan for the disabled; and
- cutting time frames for the development process in half and giving municipalities greater freedom to revise or grant exemptions from official plans.

Second, parallel changes were made to environmental laws. Among other things, the province:

- exempted 30 percent of companies from registering their pollution abatement plans;
- cut half of the provincial environmental regulations;
- repealed a ban on municipal garbage incinerators;
- cut budgets of the ministries of Environment and Natural Resources by 30 percent;
- reduced funding to conservation authorities and allowed municipalities without provincial approval to wind up these special purpose bodies altogether; and
- ended a special preservation program for fruit land on the urban fringe.[2]

Finally, intervener funding to citizen groups to appear before environmental assessment and OMB hearings has been ended. This will undoubtedly curtail the ability of citizens to oppose development initiatives using appeal mechanisms. In the interests of streamlining the development process, the number of persons and public bodies required to receive notice of councils' decisions regarding official plans is limited, and provincial ministries no longer need to publicize environmental regulations in a registry (Mittelstaedt, 1996, p. A3).

While these measures are consistent with the province's stated goal of giving greater autonomy to municipalities to oversee their own development, many critics argue that the real motive is to make development easier, faster, and less expensive. These changes may be aimed particularly at the "905 belt" (the suburban fringe of the GTA named after the telephone area code), from which the Harris government drew strong electoral support. One fear is that the combined effect of this deregulation is to remove rather than enhance municipalities' planning tools and to strip municipalities of the tools to say no (Cooper, 1996, p. 3; cf. Longo and Williams, 1996, p. 18). In the words of John Sewell, former mayor of Toronto and chair of the Commission on Planning and Development, the new Ontario law "allows you to do anything you want. It is very frightening" (Toughill, 1996, p. A8). The Canadian Environmental Law Association lays out what it believes will become a typical development scenario in Ontario:

The system will return to the bad old days of site-specific battles each time a development application comes along. For example, if a municipality wants to disallow development that could degrade environmentally significant natural areas, they will face developer challenges at the OMB. If, on the other hand, a municipality chooses to approve such developments, citizens will very likely object. They will then mount an appeal to the OMB, although hampered by limited resources, a reduced provincial role, and no intervenor funding. The government appears to be under the impression that if it strips out environmental protection tools, then public concern and motivation to protect the environment will also disappear. This impression is sadly mistaken and the inevitable result will be community discord and costly delay. (Cooper, 1996, p. 3)

Certainly, without provincial mechanisms for conflict mediation as contained in British Columbia's legislation, the potential for conflict between the urban periphery (which is likely to continue to seek low density development) and the core (which is increasingly pursuing reurbanization) is exacerbated. Appropriate regional decision making bodies or processes that have authority over an entire city-region will be more critical than ever before. In the absence of these, the fiscal and environmental pressures of current forms of development will soon remove Canadian cities from the world's top ten.

CELEBRATING DIVERSITY AND CREATING LIVABLE COMMUNITIES

So far, we have concentrated on the environmental aspects of sustainable development which, as noted, are inextricably linked to fiscal aspects. We now turn to the social and equity dimensions of sustainability. Addressing issues of social and cultural diversity and promoting social harmony are major concerns of Canada's major cities. They have involved rethinking how civic governments relate to communities and how they deliver services.

The Implications of Diversity

THE MULTICULTURAL CONTEXT

Sometimes it is useful to see ourselves through the eyes of others. Jan Morris, the internationally renowned travel writer, recalls her first impressions of Toronto:

Multiculturalism! I had never heard the word before, but I was certainly to hear it again, for it turned out to be the key word, so to speak, to contemporary Toronto. As *ooh-la-la* is to Paris, and *ciao* to Rome, and *nyet* to Moscow, and *hey you're looking great* to Manhattan, so multiculturalism is to Toronto. Far more than any other of the great migratory cities, Toronto is all things to all ethnicities. The melting-pot conception never was popular here, and sometimes I came to feel that Canadian nationality itself was no more than a minor social prerequisite, like a driving licence or a spare pair of glasses. (1990, pp. 85–86)

Canada defines itself as a multicultural society. The composition of Canada's immigrant population has shifted significantly over the past twenty years from primarily European-based to being predominantly drawn from developing countries in Asia, Africa, Latin America, and the Caribbean. Consequently, Canada's **visible minority** population has grown rapidly in recent years. This multicultural diversity is highly concentrated, however, in the major metropolitan areas. In fact, 93 percent of Canada's visible minority population lives in the largest CMAs with more than two-thirds in the three largest city-regions. (Kelly, 1995, p. 4).[3]

Moreover, the size of Canada's visible minority population is projected to triple between 1996 and 2016 to just over six million people. Metro Toronto's racial minority population, for instance, is projected to constitute 53 percent of the total by 2001, affirming Toronto's place as one of the world's most ethnically diverse cities. A reminder of today's urban diversity is that more people living in Vancouver speak a foreign language at home than speak English (Ouston, 1996, p. A4).

Recent immigrants from abroad are not the only source of diversity in urban Canada. Thirty-one percent of Canada's Aboriginal population live in the eleven largest CMAs. The urban Aboriginal population is relatively young and is expanding quickly by natural means and as a result of further urban migration.

The conventional stereotype of visible minority communities often conjures up images of people who are poorly educated, have high levels of unemployment, and are dependent on social assistance. The statistics, however, do not support this stereotype. While it is true that, overall, the visible minority population has slightly higher rates of unemployment and poverty than the general population (with some very dramatic differences across specific minority groups), the visible minority population is slightly better educated (when standardized for age) than the rest of the population and has similar rates of labour force participation (Kelly, 1995, p. 3). As data from Metro Toronto indicate, the image of dependence on government transfers is also misplaced since the reliance on social assistance among racial minorities is lower than the Metro average. These discrepancies indicate that visible minorities tend to be underemployed for their educational attainment level. This may be explained by a number of factors, including systemic discrimination. What these statistics also suggest is that the critical differences among urban minority communities are overwhelmingly cultural, rather than being based on length of residence or education. Culture is the main source of difference between minorities and the general population as well. This indicates an imperative for cultural sensitivity on the part of urban governments today.

URBAN POVERTY

In spite of the relatively high quality of life in Canadian cities, urban poverty is on the rise. Over the past 20 years, the pattern of poverty in Canada has shifted from predominantly rural to mainly urban (Lithwick and Coulthard, 1993, p. 264). The average poverty rate ranges from a high of 22 percent in Montreal to a low of 14 percent in Ottawa and Halifax (Lochhead and Shillington, 1996). On average, one in five children in Canadian cities lives in poverty. For the urban Aboriginal population, poverty is particularly acute with unemployment rates hovering around 30 percent and poverty rates as high as 47 percent in Winnipeg and 40 percent in Edmonton.

Rising poverty coupled with growing social and cultural diversity have led to an increased demand for cities' social services delivered in ways that are sensitive to the needs of the wide range of communities. The withdrawal of funding and the off-loading to both municipalities and the voluntary sector of many social services by senior governments have put greater pressure on urban governments to fill the service gap. But they, too, have diminishing resources to do so. Urban governments have responded to the challenges of diversity using two broad strategies. First, they have devised new ways of relating to minority communities, as well as the public at large, including such measures as diversity training, partnerships, and integrated service delivery. In addition, city governments have attempted to enhance the representation of minorities within the state by means of **employment equity**.

The bigger issue hanging over the delivery of social services at the municipal level, however, is the ongoing process of deciding which government should do what, or disentanglement as it is commonly called. Our analysis of policies related to human services starts with this bigger, jurisdictional issue.

Disentangling the Delivery of Human Services

CONCEPTUALIZING HUMAN SERVICES

It has been traditional to think about local governments in Canada in terms of their role in the provision of social welfare. It is now timely to take a somewhat broader approach. We need to consider the role of urban governments in the provision of human services (Wharf, 1990, pp.176–78). Human services are those dedicated to the development and protection of human capital. They include education as well as what have traditionally been labelled social services. A useful guide for conceptualizing the provision of such services is to ask three questions: Who sets the policy? Who pays? Who delivers the service? Human services encompass the following:

- *Income Support.* These mainly income-tested programs are provided as cash or tax credits to individuals to raise their basic standard of living. Responsibility for policy, funding, and delivery is overwhelmingly vested with the federal government (e.g., Employment Insurance, Old Age Security, Child Tax Benefit) and with provincial governments through social assistance. In most provinces, welfare and related social services are centralized at the provincial level. The exceptions are Manitoba and Ontario.
- *Personal Social Services.* These include a wide range of programs such as services for children and families, employment and language training, transition houses and emergency shelters, homes for the aged, services for disabled persons, and settlement adjustment. In most provinces, planning and funding for personal

services is done by provincial ministries, although many cites still play a significant role. Increasingly, the actual delivery of personal services is done by the voluntary sector. The debate over the jurisdictional issues surrounding personal social services is a lively one in several provinces, and the alternative evolving models for this category are discussed in more detail below.

- *Preventative Social Services.* These can be thought of as those that enhance social harmony, integration into communities, and/or individual development. They include recreation services, youth programming, and multicultural initiatives. Such services are almost exclusively the responsibility of local governments, with delivery often undertaken as co-production with community associations and other voluntary organizations.
- *Education.* Traditionally thought of as being in a distinct category guarded by independently elected boards and the province, schools are increasingly becoming an integrative base for ancillary services such as childcare, nutrition, and health services. Several provinces are examining a variety of issues related to education: whether funding should remain on the property tax, the development of independent charter schools (following Alberta's lead), and the reduction in the number of school boards. Although big changes are occurring in the education area, the funding and management of schools is likely to remain removed from the control of municipal governments.
- *Social Planning.* This is defined as "systematic and research-based efforts to identify causes of social problems, to develop programs to remedy these problems, and to identify the social consequences of other kinds of planning activities" (Wharf, 1990, p. 173). Generally speaking, city governments have some departmental unit that is assigned responsibility for social planning. In many cities, voluntary, independent social planning councils are full partners in the social planning process, although they are often vocal critics of government policy.

Models of Human Service Delivery

Governance in the field of human services is in a state of turbulent change. The significant changes currently underway relate not only to disentanglement of responsibilities among governments but also to the role of the voluntary sector in this field. Discussions around responsibility for policy, funding, and delivery of income support and personal services have been particularly lively because these responsibilities constitute a significant portion of government spending. Governments are also redefining their role in relation to society. The general pattern of the late 1990s has been that the federal government has abandoned an active role in human service policies, provincial governments have rejigged responsibilities in a number of ways, and municipalities and voluntary organizations have been left to pick up the pieces. The presence of large numbers of Aboriginal peoples in Canadian cities, for whom provincial and federal governments traditionally have avoided assuming full responsibility, adds to the jurisdictional morass.

As a backdrop to the debate over who should do what on income support and personal social services, three distinct models of provincial–municipal responsibilities are currently operative. The first might be called the separate model, with centralization of funding and policy setting at the provincial level. It is best exemplified by British Columbia, although Nova Scotia has also moved in this direction somewhat more tentatively. In British Columbia, the province currently has virtually sole responsibility for social assistance and most personal social services. In spite of provincial dominance, the experience of Vancouver reveals that it is untenable for a large, socially diverse city not to have some involvement in the provision of human services if the civic administration is to connect with and understand the needs of its population. Consequently, almost to compensate for provincial centralization, a very active social planning function has emerged in Vancouver. The city has gradually reasserted itself in the provision of some services such as child care and social housing.

The second model is a regional one in which social policy is determined by provincially established and funded regional authorities. Quebec implemented a system of regional health and social service districts in the early 1970s based on a conceptual model of holistic well-being. Two aspects make the Quebec regional system distinctive. First, health and social services are integrated at both the policy end (with a single ministry for both) and at the delivery end with health-based institutions as the hub of the delivery network of a wide range of related services. Second, the community and health care establishments involved in delivery are represented on the regional boards, providing a link between the community and the governing structure.

In 1994, Alberta also announced the creation of a regional model. Consisting of seventeen Children and Family Services authorities with boundaries matching the existing regional health boards, this model should come into full effect in 1998. Previously, the province was responsible for income support and most, but not all, aspects of social services. The goals of the regional boards are to provide early intervention and improved integration of services. One of the two cochairs of each region must be Aboriginal so as to enhance the involvement of First Nations and Métis communities in child welfare services since 40 percent of the total cases involve Aboriginal children (*Alberta Report*, 1996, p. XX). It remains to be seen, however, whether the boards will in fact be closer to communities or whether they will serve as a means for the province to exert greater central control and to force greater cost cutting on municipal social services.

Ontario and Manitoba currently follow a third model. The entangled model has municipal and provincial involvement in funding, policy, and delivery of some income support and many personal social services. We have already discussed the intergovernmental relations associated with the disentanglement of social services funding in Ontario. It is significant that, even as the post "megaweek" 1997 negotiations were occuring between Ontario and municipal governments, the province was implementing extremely detailed procedures for municipalities' operation of its new Ontario Works (workfare) program. This suggests that entanglement in the field of social services will remain a fact of life.

DISENTANGLING HUMAN SERVICES: A CRITIQUE

The ideas that cities are primarily deliverers of hard services and that there should be a separation of responsibilities for physical and human services into watertight compartments remain strong themes in municipal political discourse. But this mantra of disentanglement is fundamentally flawed. There is no basis to expect local financial savings; instead different obligations will occur. The Vancouver case illustrates how one major city has felt compelled to respond to its distinct social needs in the face of provincial centralization of human services. This hints at the unique and important role local governments play in building citizenship and social harmony.

The particularly strong relationship between city governments and the voluntary sector is also critical to the sustained health of our cities. City governments have a more extensive and long-standing relationship with the voluntary sector than other levels of government in Canada. Urban governments and the voluntary sector understand and respect each other and exist in a symbiotic, if not always harmonious, relationship. Provincial and federal governments have discovered the potential of the voluntary sector more recently. Their efforts to develop a rapport with this sector have been hindered for a number of reasons. First, they have been slow to recognize the critical role sustained government funding plays in maintaining the basic organizational capacity of voluntary organizations. Temporary funding for projects or fee-for-service does not lead to sustainable voluntary organizations. Second, provincial governments, in particular, have tended to announce *ex cathedra* that the voluntary sector will fill in the gaps as government abandons traditionally public programs. Finally, it has sometimes proven politically attractive for provincial and federal politicians to criticize the same voluntary organizations that they are trying to induce to fill the human services void. Charges of special interest pleading have attended criticism of government cuts by voluntary organizations. Volunteers and their organizations have ideas about what should be done to help their clientele and how to do it best. The pressures on the voluntary sector may, however, prompt many potential volunteers to ask, Why bother?

In short, the debates over the rethinking of human services are not following the principles of subsidiarity which were discussed in Chapter Eight. Instead, two trends are evident. In many provinces, we are witnessing a regionalization or centralization of social services by provincial governments in the interests of cost containment and levering new kinds of provincially prescribed behaviour (such as workfare) out of municipalities. In Ontario, we see significant efforts to download responsibilities to municipalities. Both of these trends ignore traditional links between voluntary organizations and government at the community level. The likely result will be a breakdown in the capacity to deliver human services in urban centres in a manner that is sensitive to the needs of their diverse populations.

Enhancing Relationships with Communities

The exercise of citizenship at any level of government rests on two basic principles, equality and participation (Library of Parliament, 1994, p. 7). In the interests of promoting both equality and participation in civic life, municipalities have undertaken a number of innovative measures to learn more about their diverse populations, to implement appropriate management practices to better serve a variety of publics, and to promote self-help by communities.

LEARNING ABOUT COMMUNITY DIVERSITY

First, city governments have attempted to gather better information about citizen needs and preferences using community surveys, focus groups, citizen advisory councils, and test marketing (see City of Winnipeg, 1993). Such information gathering helps governments to understand differences both across cultural communities and within, as they have learned that one of the pitfalls in managing for social diversity is assuming that ethnocultural communities are internally homogeneous.

A second vehicle for promoting understanding and respect for social and religious groups is through ethnocultural and race relations committees. Over 40 cities across Canada have established such committees to advise councils on human rights issues and monitor their effectiveness in dealing with minority concerns. Race relations committees have had mixed success. In some cities, such as Ottawa, a majority of council has viewed the committee as either a threat or as useless. In such cases, councils have sometimes shown their displeasure by wielding the budgetary axe.[4] Concerns about relations with Aboriginal communities have prompted Calgary and Edmonton to create committees to advise specifically on concerns of Aboriginal peoples. Whether they will develop sustained working relationships with city councils is still in question, although the Calgary committee has existed for some time.

Both external pressure from race relations committees and internal recognition of the need for greater sensitivity to cultural differences have resulted in extensive use of cross-cultural (sometimes called diversity) training. The goal is to help staff at all levels appreciate cultural norms and to encourage more appropriate kinds of staff behaviour that better facilitate equitable treatment and access to city services. Diversity training has been particularly important in police services because the police are the most overt embodiment of the dominant group's power (Ungerleider, 1994, p. 91). There is often considerable fear of police by immigrant communities, as well as longstanding concerns regarding unequal treatment and overt racism of minorities by police officers. Diversity training has also been used to enhance community relations in other municipal services. In the fall of 1996, for example, bus drivers in Ottawa reported that they benefited greatly from cross-cultural training organized by the Somali community following a number of confrontations between drivers and Somali youth.

The major cities have also created their own in-house resources for diversity training, of which Vancouver's Hastings Institute is probably best known. Established in 1989, the Hastings Institute is a private, non-profit corporation owned by the City of Vancouver that does research and offers training in equity issues, cross-cultural relations, and workplace language. The institute is governed by a board that includes the mayor, four councillors, and the city manager and is plugged into cultural groups through a citizen advisory committee.

"TAKING IT TO THE STREETS"

Attempts to improve the quality of services by putting the customer first have been part of the mantra of management in the 1990s at all levels of government. While improving service benefits the public at large, it is particularly important for serving minority populations. A customer-focussed management style involves "taking it to the streets" though greater presence and visibility to communities.

Community-based policing is a prime example of the reorientation of police departments. It has seen police officers working out of storefront operations and establishing a visible presence through foot, bicycle, and rollerblade patrols. In many cities, the paramilitary structures and cultures of police forces, often now called police "services," are being shaken to the very core by philosophies of quality management and client service.

Another good illustration of innovation in ongoing community-based problem solving is Vancouver's Integrated Service Teams, which began operation in 1995. Each interdepartmental team is assigned to one of fifteen geographic districts and is composed of members from Planning, Permits and Licensing, Library, Engineering, Health, Fire, Social Planning, Parks, and the school boards. The team's mandate is to work with the community to solve problems in the community, not at city hall (City of Vancouver, 1995). They are also intended to serve as resources to the communities and to build ongoing bridges to them. Although these terms are still in their infancy, initial reports from the communities regarding their effectiveness have been very favourable.

Similar innovation has taken place in Winnipeg, where the civic administration has attempted to find better ways of serving the city's Aboriginal population. In 1991, Winnipeg had about 45 000 people who identified themselves as having Aboriginal ancestry and Aboriginal identity. This constituted 5.4 percent of the total population of the Winnipeg CMA (Royal Commission on Aboriginal Peoples, 1996, pp. 4–607). Generally speaking, Winnipeg's Aboriginal community is facing serious problems of high unemployment, poverty, and increasing suicide and murder rates. The Aboriginal community in Winnipeg is itself very active politically but by no means uniform. It contains many factions, and there is considerable tension between the Aboriginal political establishment and the grassroots organizations that do program delivery and are made up almost completely (99 percent) of women.[5] One of the City's responses has been to establish a Neighbourhood Resource Centre, funded through the Winnipeg Development Agreement, that brings together in one location the police station, social services, and health, parks and recreation, and housing services. The key has been that front-line staff are friendly and practical and have come to know people in the Aboriginal community on an individual basis.

BOX 11.2 MAKING A QUALITY ARREST

The attempt by Chief Christine Silverberg, the first female police chief of a major Canadian city, to transform the Calgary Police Service into a more community responsive organization is a good example of the type of organizational change under the rubric of "quality service" that is occurring in most major cities as a response to growing diversity. While the Calgary Police Service has a long-standing tradition of community policing, Silverberg, who became chief in 1995, set about to make the service even more community focussed, with a particular mission to combat domestic and youth violence. Her approach included reducing the rigidity of the paramilitary structure and delayering the hierarchy, creating quick response issue teams, empowering the front lines, and building more linkages with community organizations. A key element has been to give freedom to the rank-and-file to engage in constructive problem solving. Chief Silverberg argues that this "bolsters their job commitment and makes them more involved to care about serving people." Personally, she has tried to lead by example and to get to know the concerns of the officers by riding around in squad cars to develop shared understanding of the communities they serve. As Silverberg told a conference of administrators, there is "a personal responsibility held by each and every one of us to strive to understand our organizational diversity. We talk, we visit, we have coffee breaks, we live in a time of information exchange. This is not an extremely complicated challenge. It is day-to day learning, day-to-day inquisitiveness."

Source: Personal interview with Chief Silverberg. Information adapted from "The Well Performing Organization," presentation to the Institute of Public Administration of Canada, Calgary, November 8, 1995; "Silverberg Juggles her Forces," *Calgary Herald*, February 21, 1996, p. B12; Darcy Henton, "Calgary's First Female Chief Takes Police in New Direction," *The Toronto Star*, January 20, 1996, p. B4.

PROMOTING SELF-HELP

Minority communities have long recognized their joint responsibility for helping themselves. They have initiated a number of partnerships with city governments to help spawn community self-help programs of their own. An excellent example of a community-based program designed to help minorities make an effective transition into the workforce is SUCCESS, a program run by the United Chinese Community Enrichment Society in Vancouver.[6] Its goal is to provide job support to unemployed Chinese people facing language and cultural barriers by improving English language proficiency, but also by teaching computer, customer service, and life and job search skills. The program has been very successful with 80 percent of its graduates securing employment within eight weeks of completion. Part of the success of this and similar programs is that they address the single greatest barrier to integration experienced by new immigrants — culture shock. They also help to forge realistic expectations about life in Canada and do this by reinforcing the strong sense of family and community integral to most minority communities (Fournier, 1996, p. 18).

Reflecting Diversity Within

It has become generally accepted that the government should reflect the diversity of the society it serves. Representation of minority communities within the administrative state enhances its legitimacy and provides valuable internal resources for understanding and working with a wide range of communities. The front-line nature of so much of the work and the need to connect with minority communities make employment equity even more imperative as a requisite management practice at the municipal level than at provincial and federal levels.

Canadian municipalities have, in many respects, been leaders in equity policies. The issue of representation is particularly critical in police services where positive community relations are vital, and most police services acts contain their own equity provisions. Many police departments have gone beyond meeting minimal requirements of equity laws, however, to undertake aggressive recruitment of minority candidates. This has certainly been the case in Winnipeg, which recently recruited 100 women and 50 Aboriginal candidates without lowering standards in any way. The police department puts potential non-traditional candidates through a ten-month training program, run in conjunction with Red River College, to get them ready to meet departmental standards.

Metro Toronto faced a problem of rising crime in its Asian communities. The problem was exacerbated by limited reporting due to fear of reprisal and cultural barriers to communication. The Metro force went out of its way to recruit actively Asian officers who understand cultural norms and speak Mandarin, Cantonese, or Vietnamese. The improved community relations that resulted from these initiatives had a direct impact on reducing crime and building better relationships between the police and the Asian community (Infantry, 1996, p. A6).

In 1993, the Rae government of Ontario introduced some of the toughest equity legislation in North America. It was to be applied to municipalities by 1996. In 1995, the Harris government dismantled the legislation, denouncing it as a quota law (Nolan, 1995, p. A8). The demise of the provincial legislation had little effect on Toronto municipalities. Metro Toronto, for example, had independently declared itself to be an equal opportunity employer in 1980. Since then, it has implemented policies aimed at removing systemic discrimination both by reviewing job descriptions for subtle forms of discrimination and by practising outreach in its recruiting. Each department set goals for representation of its workforce and reported annually on its achievements in meeting these objectives. Not only the total number but the distribution of designated groups (i.e., Aboriginal people, women, racial minorities, and persons with disabilities) across the departmental hierarchy was considered important. The City of Toronto established a similarly strong equity policy in 1985. But the impact of Toronto's employment equity policy extended beyond the confines of its own staff. Like the federal legislation that covers contractors with and companies regulated by the federal government, Toronto's equity policy applied to "all those firms which provide goods and services to the City and have a direct contractual relationship" (Federation of Canadian Municipalities, 1991b, p. 18). Statistics showing that, collectively, municipal governments buy 25 percent more goods and services than the federal government suggest that the impact of such a policy, if extended across all major cities, could be far-reaching (Federation of Canadian Municipalities, 1991b, p. 18).

Other cities have chosen to work on a less formal basis. In Vancouver, the Assistant City Manager has recruited department heads as champions of employment equity and encouraged them to appreciate that diversity is good for their departments, rather than imposing reporting requirements from above. The city also has a strong emphasis on cultural and language training.

While these and similar initiatives suggest that urban governments are struggling to reflect and respond to the increasing cultural diversity among the population they serve, the achievements of employment equity have been retarded. This has occurred for two major reasons. First, the backlash from white male applicants, particularly for police, fire, and emergency service units, has raised a cry that cities are practising reverse discrimination. Second, hiring freezes have meant that there is little new recruitment into or promotion up the hierarchies in many departments. Consequently, the overall representation of minority groups in municipal corporations has not increased significantly in recent years, in spite of employment equity policies.

FOSTERING VIBRANT COMMUNITIES: CITY GOVERNMENTS AND CULTURE

Defining the Field

A robust culture is essential to sustain and enhance any city. As we first suggested in Chapters One and Three, the attraction of "city lights" is both mythical and real. The eminent urban scholar Lewis Mumford trenchantly argued that cities are "expressions of the human spirit" (Mumford, 1937, p. 179). The vitality and freedom of expression of that spirit, in the unique context of urban density and the urban form, can make or break a city, as it affects the daily lives of residents and visitors. In short, the cultural dimension is a crucial ingredient in healthy cities. It contributes to their livability and, hence, their attractiveness to residents and newcomers, be they new arrivals or temporary visitors. Beyond this human dimension, it can be argued that there is a connection between vibrant cultural life and the attraction and retention of capital in particular cities.

The importance of culture is frequently recognized in urban planning statements. The 1995 Cityplan, passed by the City of Vancouver Council, provides a good illustration. It noted:

> Vancouverites want art and culture to contribute more to their city's identity, their neighbourhoods' character, and their own learning and self-expression.

Vancouver will maintain a strong arts community that encourages local artists and reflects Vancouver's diverse cultural heritage. Art and cultural activity will increase through more co-operation between arts organizations and business, recreation, and education partners. (City of Vancouver, 1995, p. 24)

Embedded in this statement are the important elements of culture in the urban context. In its broadest sense, the orbit of city governments' cultural policy and programming includes the following:

- The arts. Bartlett (1989, p. 101) distinguished among the *fine arts* — "those performing and visual arts created or presented to a professional standard"; the *applied arts* — such as architecture, industrial design, graphics, and fashion, which are essentially market oriented; and *recreational arts* — which are "essentially leisure pursuits carried out for the personal development and pleasure of those involved."
- Recreation. This includes both passive recreation (fostered through the provision of parks and open space) and active recreation (supported through programming and the provision of dedicated facilities).
- Professional sports. Now very much big business, professional sports are a very distinctive part of urban culture. With few exceptions, only cities — particularly big cities — can sustain professional teams.
- Cultural institutions. The most notable examples are libraries, art galleries, museums, theatres, and archives.
- Heritage sites. These include both buildings and natural sites.

Trends and Challenges in Urban Cultural Policy

City governments recognize the importance of the cultural dimension but face some significant challenges as they confront the realpolitik of situating themselves in the increasingly complex world of urban culture. These challenges are exacerbated by contemporary fiscal difficulties and the suggestion that city governments restrict their role to the provision of urban infrastructure. Along with human services, cultural policy and programming present an acid test of the broad-mindedness of politicians and appointed officials at the local level, as they confront the following:

- Local cultural policies and programming must be adapted to reflect the increasing cultural diversity of the population in many of our cities. In addition, the circumstances of the urban population more generally are undergoing significant transformation as a result of aging, immigration, and changing patterns of employment. In some cases, this results in pressure to shift capital spending priorities — to soccer pitches rather than hockey rinks, for example. In other cases, the pressure is for more inclusiveness in access to existing facilities and in programming. For example, libraries are now important sites for job seekers wanting access to employment information via the Internet and other means. Community arts groups, reflecting an increasing diversity of cultures and lifestyles, are now making political claims on urban governments.

- Community-based requests for city governments to support cultural initiatives must compete with other municipal priorities and with the claims of professional arts groups and sports teams. This has contributed to occasionally wrenching political debates. In the City of Ottawa, for example, council had to ponder its support for the now-defunct Ottawa Rough Riders football team while simultaneously cutting grants to local arts organizations and raising user fees for recreational facilities, programs, and municipal cultural institutions. Winnipeg's agony over the NHL Jets team's demand for a new arena facility was discussed in Chapter Ten.
- There is now more widespread co-production with the private and voluntary sectors. This has resulted from sustained and increasingly complex public demand for a vibrant cultural dimension in urban life, coupled with city governments' current financial straits. In the case of recreation, we are now seeing a return to reliance on the voluntary sector to organize and operate activities which, in recent times, had become part of the mandate of municipal government. The private sector is also increasingly involved. City governments are increasingly embracing the idea of corporate sponsorship. This extends to both cultural events and institutions. The main challenge here, which most Canadian city governments have yet to confront, is how to undertake sponsorship arrangements without compromising the municipalities' other relations with sponsoring firms, for example, on issues related to property development. Issues of recognition and taste in sponsor advertising may also be a concern.
- Finally, the complexity and political dilemmas associated with these issues may be contributing to political change. In Ontario, for example, 1997 reforms included elimination of local library boards and a dedicated library grant, in favour of direct municipal council control.

If we assume that these trends will continue, city governments in Canada may have to concentrate on two priorities to maintain a responsive and balanced stance related to urban cultural life. First, they will have to keep the big picture front and centre — namely an understanding of the importance of the cultural dimension and the need to balance the new pattern of interests across this field. Doing so is no small task, given the unequal structure of representation among different cultural interests in our cities. The second priority will be to regularize their relationship with the private and voluntary sectors in this era of co-production. This will necessitate dealing with the issue of how different elements of the cultural envelope will be funded. There may be merit in using different approaches for different elements. Equally important will be development of management and governance arrangements for situations in which co-production occurs. Regardless of the approach adopted, the broader public interest will have to be reconciled with the interests of the voluntary and/or private organizations involved. To the extent that fostering the positive cultural dimension of urban life is central to the task of city governments in Canada, we have to return to the crucial question, Who governs?

CONCLUSION

Sustainable development is about improving the quality of life in urban areas in ways that not only we but our children and grandchildren will be able to enjoy. Quality of life is important not only in its own right but, as we saw in Chapter Ten, as a key tool for economic development. In this chapter, we discussed the interrelated three Es of sustainability — efficiency, environment, and equity — and explored some of the challenges of implementing more financially viable, compact urban forms that are less reliant on the automobile and more accommodating of social diversity. These challenges include market pressures, an undiminished attachment to our cars, and tensions between the core and peripheries within urban areas. In spite of consistently recorded aspirations of official plans toward sustainability, there is not cause for optimism regarding serious sustainable development in the near future. One of the more pressing issues will be to develop or reinforce appropriate governing structures or processes that facilitate planning on a regional basis, over boundaries that have extended well beyond existing regional government boundaries in several cases. The institutions and processes of urban governance must also successfully mediate suburban–core conflicts and withstand the new fiscal pressures and policy responsibilities of downsizing from provincial and federal governments. A related major challenge will be to sort out provincial–municipal relationships and responsibilities on both the planning/environment and human services sides of sustainability.

With regard to disentanglement, particularly in social policy, the principle of watertight compartments, with hard services provided by cities and human services by the provinces, is based on efficiency arguments. We have argued that this principle is both misguided and unsustainable. Every major city that has gotten out of human services due to provincial centralization has begun to reassert itself in these fields due to the need to serve a diverse population. Suggestions that cities should stick to hard services do little to enhance our understanding of the increasingly important role that cities play in citizenship and in promoting social harmony in a new social union within Canada. From our perspective, the dialogue on urban governance must become louder and more far-reaching. This is essential to realizing the broad and important role of urban governments as we approach the next millennium.

NOTES

1. For example, in late 1996, the regional transit system in Ottawa-Carleton was shut down for 24 days as a result of a bitter strike. When the strike ended, the transit commission found it necessary to temporarily reduce fares in an effort to woo back ridership. (Mohamed Adam and Jeremy Mercer, "Worried Transpo Woos Riders," *Ottawa Citizen*, December 18, 1996, p. A1.)
2. Polling data show that the government is out of step with the Ontario public on issues of environmental deregulation as the public overwhelmingly supports a strong environmental regime. (Martin Mittelstaedt, "Voters, Harris Split on Green Issues," *The Globe and Mail*, July 15, 1996, pp. A1, A4.)

3. It should be remembered that not all visible minorities are immigrants. For example, only three-quarters of Metro Toronto's visible minorities had personally immigrated to Canada.
4. Ottawa's Advisory Committee on Visible Minorities and Race Relations had its budget reduced from $60 000 in 1995, including a full-time staff person, to $2900 and no staff in 1996 and to a projected budget of only $1700 in 1997. (See Fournier, 1996.)
5. One of the issues resulting from the diversity of the Aboriginal community in cities like Winnipeg and the "big P" politics of reaffirming Aboriginal nations concerns whether urban services for Aboriginal peoples should be offered on a status-blind or on a more restricted basis. The Royal Commission on Aboriginal Peoples recommended the former approach be considered a viable option, responding in part to the representations of the Aboriginal Women's Unity Coalition, which is based in Winnipeg. (Royal Commission on Aboriginal Peoples, 1996, pp. 3: 559–61.)
6. This example was brought to our attention by one of our graduate students, Cheri Fournier, in her 1996 term paper, "The Development of a Municipal Reform Agenda toward the Integration of Cultural Diversity." A discussion of SUCCESS also appears in Canadian Labour Force Development Board's *Visible Minorities Making Transition* (Ottawa: July 28, 1995, p. 21.)

SUGGESTED READINGS

Campbell, Scott. (1996). "Green Cities, Growing Cities, Just Cities?" *Journal of the American Planning Association*, 62(3): 296–312. This article lays out a conceptual framework for sustainable development in the urban context.
Filion, Pierre. (1996). "Metropolitan Planning Objectives and Implementation Constraints: Planning in a Post-Fordist and Postmodern Age." *Environmental and Planning A* 28: 1637–60.
Jacobs, Jane. (1961). *Death and Life of Great American Cities*. New York: Vintage Books. A classic critique of urban planning and a vision of urban vitality.
Perks, William T. and Walter Jamieson. (1991). "Planning and Development in Canadian Cities." In *Canadian Cities in Transition*, edited by Trudi Bunting and Pierre Filion. Toronto: Oxford University Press, pp. 487–518. A historical overview of the contribution of urban planning to the development of Canadian cities.
Smith, P. J. (1995). "Urban-Planning Systems for Metropolitan Canada." In *Metropolitics: Governing Our Cities*, edited by James Lightbody. Toronto: Copp Clark, pp. 215–39. A contemporary examination of the politics and power of urban planning in Canada.
Wharf, Brian. (1990). "Social Services." In *Urban Policy Issues: Canadian Perspectives*, edited by Richard A. Loreto and Trevor Price. Toronto: McClelland & Stewart, pp.170–88. A critical examination of the role of Canadian municipal governments in social services.

BIBLIOGRAPHY

Adam, Mohamed. (1996). "Regional Puts Brakes on Urban Sprawl." *Ottawa Citizen*. October 1, p. A1.
Alberta Report. (1996). "Devolution Made Difficult." September 30, p. 12.

Ashton, Bill, Jennifer Rowe, and Mary Simpson. (1994). "Lessons for Planners." *Plan Canada*, November, pp. 16–19.

Bartlett, David. (1989). *Ottawa-Carleton Regional Review: Phase Two Report.* Toronto: Queen's Printer for Ontario.

Berridge Lewinberg Greenberg Ltd. (1991). *Guidelines for the Reurbanisation of Metropolitan Toronto.* Toronto. Paper prepared for Metropolitan Toronto.

Bronskill, Jim. (1996). "Racially-Motivated Attacks Common." *Calgary Herald,* February 12, p. A3.

Cameron, Jill. (1996). "Breathless in Toronto." *Canadian Environmental Law Association Newsletter*, May/June, 1.

Campbell, Scott. (1996). "Green Cities, Growing Cities, Just Cities?" *Journal of the American Planning Association*, 62(3): 296–312.

Carroll, Barbara W. (1990). "Housing." In *Urban Policy Issues: Canadian Perspectives*, edited by Richard A. Loreto and Trevor Price. Toronto: McClelland & Stewart, pp. 86–106.

City of Vancouver. (1995a). *CityPlan: Directions for Vancouver.* Vancouver.

City of Vancouver. (1995b). *Administrative Report: Integrated Service Teams.* Vancouver: City Manager's Office.

City of Winnipeg. (1993). *Know Your Customer.* Winnipeg.

Commission on Planning and Development Reform in Ontario. (1993). *Final Report: New Planning for Ontario.* Toronto: Queen's Printer for Ontario.

Cooper, Kathleen. (1996). "Bill 20 — Green Veneer over Political Favouritism." *Canadian Environmental Law Association Newsletter*, January/February, 3(5).

Davidoff, P. (1965). "Advocacy and Pluralism in Planning." *Journal of the American Institute of Planners* 31: 342–62.

Federation of Canadian Municipalities. (1991b). *Breaking the Barriers: Equality in Employment.* Ottawa.

Filion, Pierre. (1995). "Planning Proposals and Urban Development Trends: Can the Gap Be Bridged?" *Plan Canada*, September, pp. 17–19.

———. (1996). "Metropolitan Planning Objectives and Implementation Constraints: Planning in a Post-Fordist and Postmodern Age." *Environmental and Planning A* 28: 1637–60.

Foote, David K. with Daniel Stoffman. (1996). *Boom, Bust & Echo: How to Profit from the Coming Demographic Shift.* Toronto: Macfarlane, Walter and Ross.

Fournier, Cheri. (1996). "The Development of a Municipal Reform Agenda toward the Integration of Cultural Diversity." Unpublished graduate seminar paper, School of Public Administration, Carleton University, Ottawa.

Frisken, Frances. (1993). "Planning and Servicing the Greater Toronto Area: The Interplay of Provincial and Municipal Interests." In *Metropolitan Governance: American/Canadian Intergovernmental Perspectives*, edited by Donald N. Rothblatt and Andrew Sancton. Berkeley, CA: Institute of Governmental Studies Press, pp. 153–204.

———. (1996). "The Importance of Public Transportation." *Policy Options* 17(7): 23–27.

The Globe and Mail. (1995). "Three Canadian Cities among Top 10 in World." January 18, p. A9.

Healey, Patsy. (1991). "Debates in Planning Thought." In *Dilemmas of Planning Practices: Ethics, Legitimacy and the Validation of Knowledge*, edited by Huw Thomas and Patsy Healey. Aldershot, UK: Avebury Technical, pp. 11–33.

Infantry, Ashante. (1996). "Ethnic Crime Squads Praised by Some, Called Racist by Others." *The Toronto Star*. January 28, p. A6.

Infantry, Ashante, Jill Mahoney and Jim Rankin. (1996). "City Hall Squatters Ousted." *The Toronto Star*. May 10, p. A6.

Jacobs, Jane. (1961). *Death and Life of Great American Cities*. New York: Vintage Books.

Kelly, Karen. (1995). "Visible Minorities: A Diverse Group." *Canadian Social Trends*. Summer, pp. 3–8.

Kiernan, Matthew J. (1990). "Land-Use Planning." In *Urban Policy Issues: Canadian Perspectives*, edited by Richard A. Loreto and Trevor Price. Toronto: McClelland & Stewart, pp. 58–85.

Laghi, Brian. (1996). "Shelter Helps Street People Survive City's Harsh Winter." *The Globe and Mail*. January 16, p. A4.

Library of Parliament, Research Branch. (1994). *Canadian Multiculturalism*. Ottawa.

Lithwick, N. Harvey and Rebecca Coulthard. (1993). "Devolution and Development: The Urban Nexus." In *How Ottawa Spends 1993–94: A More Democratic Canada . . .?*, edited by Susan D. Phillips. Ottawa: Carleton University Press, pp. 257–90.

Lochhead, Clarence and Richard Shillington. (1996). *A Statistical Profile of Urban Poverty*. Ottawa: Canadian Council on Social Development.

Longo, Leo F. and Christopher J. Williams. (1996). "The Planning Act Amendments: Major Surgery?" *Municipal World*, January, pp. 16–18.

McAndrew, Brian. (1995). "Whole Heap of Garbage Problems Facing GTA." *The Toronto Star*. January 28, p. B7.

Mendell, Marguerite. (1994). "New Social Partnerships: Crisis Management or a New Social Contract?" In *Urban Lives: Fragmentation and Resistance*, edited by Vered Amit-Talai and Henri Lustiger-Thaler. Toronto: McClelland & Stewart, pp. 71–92.

Metropolitan Toronto Planning Department. (1995). *A Guide to the Metropolitan Planning Department*. Toronto.

Metropolitan Toronto. (1989). *Equal Employment Opportunity: A Strategy for the 1990s*. Toronto.

Mittelstaedt, Martin. (1996). "Environmental Intervenor Funds Cut Off." *The Globe and Mail*. April 1, p. A3.

Morris, Jan. (1990). *City to City*. Toronto: Macfarlane, Walter and Ross.

Mumford, Lewis. (1937). "What Is a City?" *The Architectural Digest*. Reprinted in *The City Reader*, edited by Richard T. LeGates and Frederic Stout. (1996). London: Routledge.

Nolan, Dan. (1995). "Harris Trashes Ontario's Employment Equity Law." *The Toronto Star*. July 20, p. A8.

Oberlander, H. Peter and Patrick J. Smith. (1993). "Governing Metropolitan Vancouver: Regional Intergovernmental Relations in British Columbia." In *Metropolitan Governance: American/Canadian Intergovernmental Perspectives*, edited by Donald N. Rothblatt and Andrew Sancton. Berkeley, CA: Institute of Governmental Studies Press, pp. 329–73.

Ouston, Rick. (1996). "English a Minority Language in Vancouver." *Ottawa Citizen.* November 4, p. A4.

Perks, William T. and Walter Jamieson. (1991). "Planning and Development in Canadian Cities." In *Canadian Cities in Transition,* edited by Trudi Bunting and Pierre Filion. Toronto: Oxford University Press, pp. 487–518.

Plan Canada. (1995). "BC's Growth Strategies Act." July, p. 34.

Price, Trevor. (1990). "The Environment." In *Urban Policy Issues: Canadian Perspectives,* edited by Richard A. Loreto and Trevor Price. Toronto: McClelland & Stewart, pp. 124–44.

Precourt, Geoffrey and Anne Faircloth. (1996). "Best Cities: Where the Living is Easy." *Fortune,* November 11, pp. 130–49.

Rabinovitz, Francine F. (1969). *City Politics and Planning.* New York: Atherton.

Rees, William E. and Mark Roseland. (1991). "Sustainable Communities: Planning for the 21st Century." *Plan Canada* 31(3): 15–24.

Richardson, Nigel. (1994). "Moving toward Planning for Sustainability: Integrating Environmental Assessment and Land Use Planning in Ontario." *Plan Canada,* March, pp. 18–23.

Rothblatt, Donald N. (1994). "North American Metropolitan Planning: Canadian and U.S. Perspectives." *Journal of the American Planning Association* 60(4): 501–20.

Royal Commission on Aboriginal Peoples. (1996). *Final Report.* Ottawa: Minister of Supply and Services.

Rybczynski, Witold. (1995). *City Life.* Toronto: HarperCollins.

Saunders, Doug. (1996). "Urban Sprawl Growing on a Building Spree." *The Globe and Mail.* June 29, p. A6.

Smith, Patrick. J. (1995). "Urban-Planning Systems for Metropolitan Canada." In *Metropolitics: Governing Our Cities,* edited by James Lightbody. Toronto: Copp Clark. pp. 215–39.

———. (1996). "Metropolitan Governance: Vancouver and BC Reforms." *Policy Options* 17(7): 7–11.

Speech from the Throne. (1995). Address of the Honourable Henry N.R. Jackman. Toronto: Queen's Printer for Ontario. September 27.

Thomas, Ted E. (1993). "Edmonton: Planning in the Metropolitan Region." In *Metropolitan Governance: American/Canadian Intergovernmental Perspectives,* edited by Donald N. Rothblatt and Andrew Sancton. Berkeley, CA: Institute of Governmental Studies Press, pp. 245–81.

Toughill, Kelly. (1996). "Tories Accused of 'Gutting' Law." *The Toronto Star.* January 3, p. A8.

Ungerleider, Charles S. (1994). "Police, Race and Community Conflict in Vancouver." *Canadian Ethnic Studies* XXVI: 3.

Vancouver Sun. (1996). "Feds to Follow B.C. Lead in Setting Standards for Exhaust from Vehicles." June 5, p. B1.

Wharf, Brian. (1990). "Social Services." In *Urban Policy Issues: Canadian Perspectives,* edited by Richard A. Loreto and Trevor Price. Toronto: McClelland & Stewart, pp.170–88.

World Commission on Environment and Development. (1987). *Our Common Future.* Oxford: Oxford University Press.

GLOSSARY

ALPHABET PARTY: A slate of candidates (or loose civic party) that usually lasts for only one or two elections then disbands and reforms with different people under a different name. The name "alphabet" reflects the tendency to use acronyms, such as WIN (Winnipeg in the Nineties).

AMALGAMATION: The combination of two or more municipalities to create a new municipality.

ANNEXATION: The transfer of lands from the jurisdiction of one municipality to another.

APOLITICAL IDEAL: The goal of the turn-of-the-century urban reform movement to remove political influence from the operation of local government.

ASSESSMENT (ASSESSED VALUE): The value attached to a property (usually including land and structures) for property tax purposes. Market value assessment attempts to ensure that the value for tax purposes matches the value of the property in the marketplace.

BALDWIN ACT: Passed in 1849, it was the first piece of legislation to create a uniform system of municipal government over an entire province, the province of Ontario.

BOARD OF MANAGEMENT MODEL: A model of administrative organization that assigns responsibility for the management of a city's affairs to a group of senior managers rather than to a single individual.

BOARD OF TRADE: The name given to the chamber of commerce in larger cities.

BONUSSING: The practice of offering tax breaks to enterprises looking to establish themselves or relocate.

BUSINESS IMPROVEMENT AREAS: Designated sections of a municipality that are subject to beautification, infrastructure improvements, and other initiatives by area businesses and the municipality. These are specifically designed to assist commerce. Financing of municipal improvements is generally subject to a special levy on resident businesses, which are represented on a special committee overseeing the entire improvement project.

CENSUS METROPOLITAN AREA (CMA): An urbanized area, defined by Statistics Canada as having a minimum population of 100 000 and a population density of at least 500 persons per square kilometre in its urban core. Municipalities within a 40 km radius of the urban core are included if their population shows significant attachment to the urban labour market.

CENTRAL URBAN GROWTH MODEL: An urban area with intense and dense population and commercial growth in its core and little urban development outside established urban boundaries.

CHIEF ADMINISTRATIVE OFFICER (CAO) MODEL: A model of administrative organization that assigns responsibility for selected departments (usually those carrying out administrative or staff functions) to a chief administrative officer, while other department heads (most commonly those responsible for provision of direct services by the municipality) report directly to council and to designated council committees.

CITY MANAGER MODEL: A model of administrative organization in which all municipal departments report to a single manager, who is responsible to council.

CITY-REGION: A coherent economic, social, and spatial entity whose population shares a common orientation or cohesiveness. The economic, social, and spatial dimensions of the city-region are not necessarily congruent with its political boundaries.

CIVIC PARTY: A party that is unique to a particular municipality and not officially affiliated with any provincial or federal political party. Civic parties run slates of candidates on party platforms, take responsibility for campaign financing, are active to some degree between elections, and have longevity over successive elections.

CIVIL SOCIETY: The sphere of social interaction between the economy and the state, composed of the family, voluntary associations, social movements, and other forms of organization and communication among citizens. It is created through the mobilization and actions of non-governmental actors but may be institutionalized by a variety of state and societal means.

COMMUNITY POWER STUDIES: Studies of urban politics and government that examine the question, Who has influence at city hall?

COMMUTERSHED: The web of commuting patterns that help delineate an economic region.

CONFLICT OF INTEREST: A conflict of interest occurs when a public official is involved directly or indirectly in an activity, a conduct, an interest, or an association (other than a job-related professional association or labour union) that will, or may, influence the official's actions, recommendations, or decisions in carrying out his or her duties as a public official.

CONSTITUENT ASSEMBLY: A representative body of citizens to whom is delegated the power to decide or to make recommendations on a major policy issue(s). The citizen volunteers are normally expected to consult with both experts on the issue and with the public at large and to have the opportunity for deliberation among themselves.

CONSTITUENT DIPLOMACY: The establishment and conduct of international relations by local governments which, although they have no status in international law, display considerable independence in the international sphere.

CONTRACTING OUT: Purchasing the services of private sector firms, which are under contract to the municipal government and for which the municipality assumes responsibility. This is in contrast to direct provision of the service by municipal employees.

CO-PRODUCTION: An arrangement between a government and a voluntary or private sector partner for (some combination of) joint policy-making, funding, production, delivery, and management of a service or goods to a particular constituency or the public at large.

DELEGATED OR EXPRESS POWERS: The assignment of powers and responsibilities in a very restrictive manner. Governments receiving their mandate in this manner are only permitted to undertake responsibilities that they are specifically mandated to perform. In the absence of this specific mandate, they must appeal to a higher government or to the public to obtain approval for any new initiative.

DEPARTMENTAL MODEL: A model of administrative organization in which each municipal function has its own designated organization or department, the head of which reports to council, often through a council committee with particular responsibility for the function in question.

DEVELOPMENT PERMIT: Permission to use or develop property in accordance with a municipality's zoning regulations. Development permits for major developments may require rezoning approvals. A building permit gives permission to actually carry out the development (i.e., to demolish, excavate, renovate, or construct).

DISENTANGLEMENT: The attempt to separate the activities of different levels of government in a clear manner. Efforts to do this are intended to emulate the watertight compartment image of federalism and delegation.

DOWNLOADING (Ch.1): The practice of a government imposing an obligation on another level of government to support or provide a service by mandating that government to do so (without appropriate compensation) or by simply withdrawing from the particular field.

DOWNLOADING (Ch. 4): The transfer of responsibility for a particular function from one government to another without commensurate financial resources.

DOWNLOADING (Ch. 8): The assignment of a new responsibility by one level of government to another without transferring the required financial and other resources. This sometimes takes the form of abandonment of a service or another activity.

DOWNSIZING: The reduction in the number of units and/or staff in an organization.

ECONOMIES OF SCALE: Production processes that attain lower per unit costs as the size (scale) of production increases.

EDGE CITY: A node of settlement containing both residential development and significant employment, located on the periphery of an established city.

EFFICIENCY: As defined by economists, a situation in which resources (e.g., labour, capital, land) are utilized in a manner that maximizes the value of the resulting outputs. No re-allocation of resources can achieve a higher valued combination of outputs.

ELITE THEORY: A branch of community power studies asserting that power in cities is controlled by a small group of notables who are interconnected politically, economically, and socially.

EMPLOYMENT EQUITY: Policies designed to overcome overt and systemic discrimination by promoting equality of opportunity in employment and encouraging the recruitment and advancement of traditionally under-represented social groups. Under Canadian equity policies, the four designated groups are women, visible minorities, Aboriginal peoples, and persons with disabilities.

ENVIRONMENTAL (IMPACT) ASSESSMENT: Evaluation of the positive and negative, intended and unintended consequences on the physical and social environment of a proposed project, regulation, or policy.

EXECUTIVE COMMITTEE OF COUNCIL: The committee of council responsible for overseeing the corporate activities of the municipality, such as human resource management, managing the municipality's property, legal affairs, and, in many cases, the budgeting process.

EXTENDED PARTY: A party running in a municipal election that is officially connected to and bears the same name as a provincial or federal party. These types of parties are not currently active in Canada.

EXTERNALITIES (SPILLOVERS): In this context, situations in which the services provided by one local government benefit the residents of other jurisdictions in addition to the residents of the providing jurisdiction.

FEDERALISM: A system of governance in which the constitutional or legislated responsibilities of governing are formally divided between two or more orders of government.

FEMINIST APPROACHES: Perspectives arguing that urban analysis must take gender into account by considering how public policies and urban design may have differential impacts according to gender and how gender relations are structured and represented by government institutions.

FINANCIAL CAPITAL: The financial resources available for economic activity.

GLOBALIZATION: The breakdown of political and economic borders resulting from reduced barriers to communication, commerce, and mobility.

GRANTS-IN-LIEU: Payments made by another government (or government agency) to municipal governments in recognition of the services provided by the municipalities. Strictly speaking, these grants are voluntary because the municipal governments have no legal authority to levy taxes on other governments.

GROWTH MACHINE THEORY: An approach to urban government and politics that focusses on the role of the property industry and its allies in influencing local governments to endorse urban growth.

HORIZONTAL EQUITY: The criterion often used in tax analysis stipulating that taxpayers in the same position (i.e., equal income and/or wealth) should pay the same amount of tax.

HUMAN CAPITAL: The human resources available for economic activity.

IDENTITY POLITICS: The direct representation and participation in political life by people who personally share in the experiences of the social and cultural groups for whom they claim to speak.

INDUSTRIAL ADJUSTMENT INITIATIVE: An effort by government and a community to respond to major changes in the local economy. Human Resources Development Canada provides core funding to local industrial adjustment committees for this purpose. These committees typically have a broad base of community participation.

ISSUE-ORIENTED CITIZEN GROUPS: Citizen groups whose members act together to influence public policy on specific issues or in policy sectors rather than on a geographical basis. The issues may be quite narrowly defined or very broad, such as the environment. In contrast to NIMBYs, these groups usually have greater longevity and are both proactive and reactive.

KNOWLEDGE-BASED SECTORS: Types of work requiring mental aptitudes and skills rather than physical skills.

LOCAL AIRPORT AUTHORITIES: Special purpose bodies established to oversee the development and management of a local airport. Until the early 1990s, airports in Canada's urban centres were developed and managed by Transport Canada.

LOCAL SPECIAL PURPOSE BODIES: Organizations with a mandate to carry out a limited number of designated government functions. They operate in an area roughly coterminous with a municipality or a small group of municipalities and have some autonomy from the municipal corporation. They receive a significant amount of funding from municipal governments or from the local property tax base.

LOCAL STATE: The local government organizations that interact with the voluntary and private sectors for the purpose of urban governance. The two basic components of the local state are municipal government and special purpose bodies.

MANAGERIAL REFORM MOVEMENT: The effort to professionalize the operation of municipal government by hiring city managers and to have municipalities operate in as business-like a fashion as possible.

METROPOLITAN GOVERNMENT: A governing form associated with recognition of the unity of interest of an urban agglomeration through the development of some area-wide political arrangements.

METROPOLITAN THESIS: A conception of Canada's development focussing on the economic and ecological relationship between urban centres and their hinterland. It is rooted in Harold Innis's staples theory of development.

MILL RATE: The tax rate applied to the assessment value of a property to determine the amount of property tax. The mill rate is expressed in terms of dollars of tax per $1000 of assessed value.

NEIGHBOURHOOD OR COMMUNITY ASSOCIATIONS: Citizen groups oriented toward improving or maintaining the quality of life in a geographically delimited residential area.

NIMBY (not-in-my-backyard): A reactionary protest group of citizens formed to stop or influence the siting of a specific facility or project. The group forms quickly, has minimal organizational infrastructure, and usually disbands once a decision on the project is reached.

NODAL URBAN GROWTH MODEL: A form of urban development emphasizing the development of designated centres for the concentration of population and employment. Typically the nodes consist of a central city and a few designated suburbs. The nodes are connected by transportation and other communication links.

NON-PARTISAN PARTY SYSTEMS: Electoral systems without party politics. Electoral candidates run as independents and, once elected, have no obligation to vote as a block.

OPEN GOVERNMENT: The set of conventions in municipal government that makes its operations accessible to the public and transparent. Basic components of open government include openness of all council and board meetings, the right to make presentations to council and/or its committees, conflict of interest rules, and requirements for public notice and procedural standards for the disposal of real property.

ORIGINS DEBATES: Intellectual debates regarding the relative importance of British colonialism and American revolutionary populism as seminal roots of Canada's local government system. These debates also consider whether the Canadian population sought a system of local governance or whether it was imposed.

OWN-REVENUES: The taxes (e.g., property tax) and other revenues that a government raises itself as opposed to the funds it receives in the form of grants from other governments.

PECUNIARY INTERESTS: Interests consisting of, measured in, or related to money.

PETITION: The opportunity for citizens (as specified in some municipal acts) to force the municipality to hold a plebiscite on an issue by collecting a specified minimum number of signatures of eligible municipal voters in a given time period.

PLEBISCITE: The opportunity for eligible voters to vote on a policy or issue-specific question, although results are not binding on council. Such votes may be held at election time or in-between elections. While often commonly referred to as a "question on the ballot" or referendum, many scholars make the technical distinction that a referendum is binding on the government, whereas a plebiscite is not.

PLURALIST THEORY: A branch of community power studies that argues, from a descriptive basis, that power in cities is fragmented and diffused and, from a normative basis, that such fragmentation is desirable.

POLITICAL ECONOMY PERSPECTIVES: Approaches that focus on the structural conditions of economic relations and the conflicts generated by these forces.

POST-BUREAUCRATIC PARADIGM: A conception of public organization and management emphasizing innovation, risk-taking, empowerment, teamwork, a client orientation, flat bureaucracies, quality, and continuous improvement.

POST-FORDIST ECONOMY: The emerging economic relations stemming from the shift to more flexible forms of production, the shrinking of the welfare state and government economic intervention, and the polarization of the labour market into high-end and low-end workers.

PRIVATIZATION: The shifting of responsibility for a publicly provided service to a private sector organization, which may provide the service on a profit or not-for-profit basis. This is different from contracting out where responsibility remains with the government.

PUBLIC CHOICE THEORY: An examination of local government in terms of competitive markets for the delivery of urban goods and services.

PUBLIC PARTICIPATION (OR ENGAGEMENT): An opportunity between elections for the council and/or administration to reach out to learn from the public by its direct involvement in decision making. At the very minimum, public participation involves two-way communication, deliberation, and learning. Public engagement is seen by many urban governments as an ongoing means of conducting civic business, rather than as limited and fixed occasions of allowing the public to be involved in policy making.

QUASI-AUTONOMOUS MUNICIPAL GOVERNMENT ORGANIZATION: Special purpose body established with the financial support of the municipal government but with significant autonomy in its management and operations.

REGIME THEORY: A theoretical approach seeking to identify how and under what conditions often competing interests join together to achieve urban public policy goals.

REGULATION SCHOOL: A theoretical approach that focusses on changing economies in a global context, attempting to illuminate the social, cultural, and political implications of post-fordist economies. The changing role of cities in this context is an important aspect of this exploration.

RENTIERS: In the context of the growth machine model, the term applies to property owners who try to maximize their rental income by intensifying the use to which their land is put and who are important intermediaries between the corporate elite and local citizenry.

REURBANIZATION: Redevelopment of already urbanized areas through infilling (building on unoccupied lands and subdividing existing parcels of land), higher density developments, and conversion of uses. It is intended to reduce pressures for sprawl and new development on the urban fringe.

SOCIAL MOVEMENT: An informal network of organizations and individuals who, on the basis of a collective identity and shared values, engage in a political and/or cultural struggle and undertake collective action designed to affect the behaviour of both the state and society.

SPECIAL COMMITTEES OF COUNCIL: Temporary or cross-functional committees of council charged with the responsibility for making recommendations on a particular issue or advising on the management of a particular project or initiative.

SPREAD GROWTH MODEL: The outward expansion of a central city, with low density development on the outskirts for residential and commercial purposes.

STANDING COMMITTEES OF COUNCIL: Groups of council members with delegated responsibility for the oversight and policy development related to a particular city service or cluster of services.

SUBDIVISION CONTROL: The process by which the legal division of lots into smaller parcels is controlled.

SUBSIDIARITY: The assignment of responsibility for policy and delivery of particular functions of government to the lowest level possible.

SUSTAINABLE DEVELOPMENT: Development that meets the needs of the present without compromising the ability of future generations to meet their own needs.

TECHNOPOLES: Urban centres with a significant cluster of high technology research and development establishments.

TWINNING: A formal agreement between two municipalities, usually in different countries, for cultural, business, or bilateral aid purposes.

TWO-TIER GOVERNMENT: A form of municipal government with two levels. A region-wide government has designated responsibility for matters thought to be of common interest to all area residents or thought to be more efficiently or effectively delivered on this basis. Two or more area municipalities exist within the geographic boundaries of the upper tier and carry out responsibilities deemed to be more local in nature.

UNICITY: A single municipal government with sole jurisdiction over an urbanized area.

URBAN: An area of dense population whose labour force is not directly engaged in farming or other forms of natural resource harvesting activities on the area's land surface. Urban places are the site of complex social and economic interactions.

URBAN GOVERNANCE: The collective capacity to set and achieve public policy goals in the urban milieu.

URBAN INFRASTRUCTURE: The physical services associated with the development and sustainability of cities. These have typically included a road system, water and sewer systems, and a dedicated arrangement for public transit. Other forms of communications systems, both within and between urban centres, are assuming increasing importance.

URBAN POPULISM: Efforts to engage the public in urban issues through involvement in local politics and political action, both during civic elections and between them.

URBAN REFORM MOVEMENTS: The three streams of urban reform evident at various times. These are the push to inculcate a managerial ethic into urban government, the effort to inject populist energy into urban politics and government practices, and moves to "rationalize" urban government by changing urban political boundaries and servicing responsibilities.

URBAN RESTRUCTURING: Reform of the political boundaries, governing arrangements, and responsibilities in an urban area to reflect changing needs stemming from urban development and changing economic, social, and spatial relations within the city-region.

USER FEES: Fees charged for a public service that in some fashion is directly linked to the usage of the service. In this sense, user fees are akin to prices in private sector transactions.

VERTICAL EQUITY: The criterion often used in tax analysis stipulating that taxpayers with differing abilities to pay (i.e., different levels of income and/or wealth) should pay appropriately different amounts of tax.

VISIBLE MINORITY: Members of a racial/ethnic minority, whether they are native-born or immigrants. Statistics Canada identifies ten visible minority groups: Blacks, Chinese, Filipinos, Japanese, Koreans, Latin Americans, Other Pacific Islanders, South Asians, Southeast Asians and West Asians, and Arabs (Kelly, 1995, p. 3).

WARD: The geographical district (called a "riding" in federal and provincial politics) from which political representatives are elected in municipalities. One or more councillors may be elected from each ward. The alternative to election by wards is an at-large system in which eligible voters in the entire municipality (not just the geographic ward) elect all the councillors. In all Canadian municipalities, the mayor is elected at large.

ZONING: The process that regulates the development of property through a set of by-laws which establish the permitted types of use of specific parcels of land, as well as height, coverage, and density of building on the land.

NAME INDEX

SUBJECT INDEX

READER REPLY CARD

We are interested in your reaction to *Urban Governance in Canada: Representation, Resources, and Restructuring*, by Katherine A. Graham and Susan D. Phillips with Allan M. Maslove. You can help us to improve this book in future editions by completing this questionnaire.

1. What was your reason for using this book?

    _____ university course

    _____ professional development

    _____ college course

    _____ personal interest

    _____ continuing education course

    _____ other (please specify)

2. If you are a student, please identify your school and the course in which you used this book.

    _____

    _____

3. Which chapters or parts of this book did you use? Which did you omit?

    _____

    _____

4. What did you like best about this book? What did you like least?

    _____

    _____

5. Please identify any topics you think should be added to future editions.

    _____

    _____

6. Please add any comments or suggestions.

    _____

    _____

7. May we contact you for further information?

    Name: _____

    Address: _____

    _____

    Phone: _____

(fold here and tape shut)

MAIL ⇒ POSTE

Canada Post Corporation / Société canadienne des postes

Postage paid
If mailed in Canada

Port payé
si posté au Canada

**Business
Reply**

**Réponse
d'affaires**

0116870399   01

0116870399-M8Z4X6-BR01

Larry Gillevet
Director of Product Development
HARCOURT BRACE & COMPANY, CANADA
55 HORNER AVENUE
TORONTO, ONTARIO
M8Z 9Z9